Dr. Charles Joyce

OHIO SCHOOL FINANCE

Ohio School Finance

A Practitioner's Guide
Second Edition

Richard E. Maxwell
Dale Baughman
Donald E. Overly

Anderson Publishing Co. / Cincinnati

ISBN: 0-87084-785-6

Contents

Preface

School finance is, without a doubt, the most widely discussed topic of chief school administrators and boards of education. There is common agreement that the teaching-learning process and the curriculum affecting learning are the most important aspects of schools. Funding of schools, however, is what either makes it possible or limits potential.

Our intent in writing *Ohio School Finance: A Practitioner's Guide* is to provide a resource book for both current and prospective school administrators. School treasurers and boards of education should also benefit from deepened understanding of detailed information concerning how the funding process works currently and how this process may be improved.

The first two chapters provide a perspective of what helped shape educational policy at both the national and state levels. A greater awareness of what has happened in the past can help in creating desirable changes for the economic issues depicted in chapter three.

Current local and state funding processes are examined in chapters four and five. Problems associated with these funding practices are detailed in these chapters. Another problem, the lack of adequate capital funds, is discussed in chapter six. The deteriorating conditions of many school buildings in Ohio must be addressed.

Chapters seven and eight relate to federal funds and specialized school districts and agencies. The following three chapters all detail processes for accounting and managing funds for schools. Improved managing can create stronger community support.

Chapter twelve covers court cases in other states. Some of the very same issues that are being reviewed in Ohio's courts have been debated in other states. A critique of the outcomes of these state supreme court cases and resulting state legislative action may help pave a desirable path for Ohio funding in the future.

The final three chapters address funding in other states, related issues and concluding comments. The challenge is not only to resolve inequity and inadequate funding issues for Ohio's schools, but also to determine the "connecting links" of adequate funding with programs that promote student learning.

The book concludes with sections of the Ohio Administrative Code that are pertinent to the contents of this book. This was done to give the reader an easy background reference.

January, 1996

Richard E. Maxwell
Dale Baughman
Donald E. Overly

Acknowledgments

A book as extensive as this required the assistance of many people. Our appreciation is expressed first to Rod Rice, Executive Director of the Buckeye Association of School Administrators (BASA). In the initial stage of writing, Rod provided insightful comments concerning the need for a school finance book for both practitioners and graduate students in educational administration who are preparing to be superintendents of schools. Rod was also extremely helpful in contacting Anderson Publishing Company and in agreeing to help market the book through the BASA organization.

As authors of this book, we assume full responsibility for its contents. However, there are a number of other people who played vital roles in completing the final document. Ellis Joseph, Dean of the School of Education at the University of Dayton, encouraged the writing since a finance text specifically for Ohio schools has been non-existent.

The initial edition of this book was completed early in 1994. More than two years were involved in assembling the manuscript due in part to legislative enactments that required updating content. The initial edition owes a debt of thanks to the following people: Dr. Roger L. "Skip" Sauer for editing and Mrs. Carolyn Boehmer, Miss Sally Griffin, Mrs. Linda Frennette, Miss Rebecca Mallin, and Mrs. Mary Galion for their expert typing. The authors wish to thank Mrs. Mindy Owens for expert assistance with the second edition.

Revision and updating for this second edition obviously did not require the extensive amount of time as invested earlier. However, this was not the major difference in the authors' coordinated efforts. The most dramatic difference was that Ken Crim, our co-author and loyal friend, was not available as the result of his death in March of 1995. He lost his lengthy battle against cancer but went on to his reward of eternal life. We miss his presence, leadership and companionship. And finally, we are indebted to John Maxwell, who, while a student at the Ohio State University in the College of Law, served as legal reference assistant, researching numerous Ohio Senate and House of Representatives bills and state and federal Supreme Court cases.

About the Authors

The authors bring many collective years of experience as superintendents of schools in Ohio. Their experiences have been varied and have included positions at the local and county levels, the joint vocational school level, and the suburban city school level. All have lived through numerous legislative enactments that have changed the funding structure for schools.

Richard E. Maxwell served as a local superintendent for eleven years followed by twelve years as the Holmes County Superintendent. He is currently working for the Buckeye Association of School Administrators (BASA) where his responsibilities include conducting workshops on school finance. He is also employed as a professor at Ashland, where he teaches administrative classes specializing in the university field of school finance and economics. Maxwell, a past president of BASA, served as an expert witness in the suit filed by the Ohio Coalition of Educational Organizations challenging the equity and adequacy of state funding for Ohio's schools.

C. Dale Baughman is currently Superintendent of Miami Valley Career Technology Center, a position that he has held since 1976. He was involved in the planning and constructing of joint vocational school (JVS) facilities and also in emergency replacement of facilities destroyed by fire. In 1973-74 and again in 1989-90 he served as President of Administrative Division for the Ohio Vocational Association. In 1993-94, he served as president of the Ohio Association of J.V.S. Superintendents. He was also selected as Ohio Superintendent of the Year for 1994-95. Baughman has had considerable experience in funding and constructing vocational facilities.

Donald E. Overly is an Assistant Professor of Educational Administration at the University of Dayton, a position he has held since 1988 when he retired as Superintendent of Centerville City Schools. During his seventeen years as superintendent, he was involved in helping to pass several operating levies, bond issues and permanent improvement programs to construct and renovate facilities. Overly is a past executive committee member of B.A.S.A. and was involved with legislative lobbying efforts regarding funding Ohio's public schools.

Chapter 1:

A National Historical Perspective

1.1 Introduction

The financial structure of schools in this nation, and more specifically in Ohio, did not evolve overnight. The structure has roots in the principles accepted by our nation's founding fathers. Tracking some of the major events involving the funding of schools will serve as a basis for developing an understanding of and an appreciation for how we arrived at today's funding process in this state.

1.2 The United States Constitution

People often question why the federal government does not step in and play a major role in financing schools. After all, some of the major criticisms in recent history have emanated from national policy makers. Nationally recognized reports such as *A Nation at Risk: The Imperative for Education Reform, Tomorrow's Teachers: A Report of the Holmes Group,* and *A Nation Prepared: Teachers for the Twenty-First Century*, have indicated that the education of youth is paramount to a strong nation. We are in competition with our neighbors throughout the world. If the United States is going to remain economically and politically aggressive, our children, the future leaders of this country, must have a firm grasp of the sciences, communication skills, foreign languages as well as our native language, and yes, many other skills universally emphasized as essential for the well-being of children. These demands have been heard by and reacted to at both local and state levels. Many reactions have concluded with observations such as, "It costs money to produce better products so put your money where your mouth is," and "If we agree education is important then why doesn't the federal government pay more of the cost?"

The questions of why the federal government does not pay more for public school education in Ohio and the other states hardly seem out of line since its share of the financial picture is only 4 to 6% of the total Ohio expenditures for K-12 public education programs. In addition to this, a most efficient system for collecting tax revenues is already operative—the federal income tax system. The answer to the questions related to the federal government's minimal role in funding public schools is obvious when specific principles of *The United States Constitution* are understood.

No direct reference was made to education in *The United States Constitution.* Historians have revealed that this absence of reference was due to three primary reasons. First, the original thirteen colonies had already established their own patterns of school organization. These patterns clearly recognized each colony's obligations for educating youth. Second, many needs and changes were occurring in the colonies at the time *The United States Constitution* was adopted. These needs were viewed as more urgent at that time. Third, a lack of reference to education occurred as the result of attempts to compromise and reach agreement on *The United States Constitution.* Many of the leaders of government thought discussion of controversial issues surrounding education might lead to disagreement and impasse for the entire document.[1]

Some shortcomings of *The United States Constitution* were experienced almost as soon as it was adopted. Individual rights were not protected to the extent needed. As the result of these deficiencies, the first ten Amendments were adopted in 1791 as the Bill of Rights. These Amendments formed much of the legal basis for the system of education which is currently operative in Ohio.

The Tenth Amendment has particular significance in that it made education a function of state government. The Tenth Amendment stated that, "The Powers not delegated to the United States by the Constitution, nor prohibited by it to the states, are reserved to the states respectively, or to the people."[2] The *Constitution of the State of Ohio* reflects this delegated-power concept. Many state court decisions have reinforced this responsibility. Therefore, the main responsibility for public school funding rests with the State of Ohio. As such, it appears unlikely that the federal government will play any greater role in providing financial resources to public schools.

1.3 The Law of 1642

Delegation of educational responsibilities was even apparent as a principle prior to the adoption of *The United States Constitution*, as colonies struggled to fulfill identified needs. Delegation to parents was evidenced in *The Law of 1642* when parents in Massachusetts were charged with teaching their children to read and know the major laws at that time in addition to learning a trade. The emphasis upon religion was also obvious with the general education law passed in 1642 since all children had to know the catechisms. It was clear that Massachusetts was very serious about the need to educate children as the

---

[1] The information regarding the relationship between public education and the United States Constitution was reprinted, with permission, from Percy E. Burrup and Vern Brimley, Jr. *Financing Education in a Climate of Change* (Boston, Mass.: Allyn and Bacon, 1982), at 127–28 [hereinafter *Financing Education*].

[2] U.S. CONST. amend X.

law gave town officials the authority to levy fines upon those parents who refused to teach their children these perceived essentials.[3]

1.4 The Law of 1647

Only five short years following *The Law of 1642*, the Massachusetts Legislature passed a law requiring all towns of fifty or more families to appoint a teacher to assist in the educational process. This law, *The Law of 1647*, authorized the payment of these appointed elementary teachers out of public taxes, provided the townspeople voted for such taxation. Thus, the democratic process for acquiring school funds was theoretically already established via this Massachusetts law.

Teachers authorized for employment under *The Law of 1647* were employed to teach primarily reading and writing. Teachers were classified as elementary teachers since many of the children at that time concluded their formal schooling at the elementary level.

Larger towns of one hundred or more families were required, under *The Law of 1647*, to employ secondary teachers. These secondary teachers had a background and training in Latin and grammar, thus helping to foster the Latin grammar school concept.

Secondary education was not considered essential for most young women and men in the early formation of our educational system. Secondary students were young men planning to enter professions of ministry, law, or medicine. Their curriculum consisted mainly of Latin, Greek, and rhetoric.[4]

1.5 The American Academy of 1751

Time revealed deficiencies in the Latin grammar school curriculum. It did not meet the needs of the students being served and was eventually replaced in 1751 by the American Academy. The Academy was actually founded by Benjamin Franklin.

Later, an educational charter granted landowners and businessmen the right to incorporate as boards of trustees. At the time, the American Academy was expanded to form several "corporate" schools. Trustees were given the authority to purchase land, construct buildings, charge tuition, appoint teachers and, essentially, to operate and manage a school.

Academy and corporate concept schools, like their forerunner the Latin grammar school, were not without problems. The major problem was that a high tuition rate limited accessibility to children of fairly wealthy families.[5]

1.6 The Northwest Ordinance of 1787

In 1787 the new *United States Constitution* was being drafted and debated at the Constitutional Convention meeting in Philadelphia. The Convention sought to foster unity among the states and replace the nation's first national constitution which was known as the *Articles of Confederation*. During this same year, the Continental Congress meeting

---

[3] *Financing Education* at 128.
[4] *Id.*
[5] *Id.* at 127–129.

in New York City passed a most significant act, *The Northwest Ordinance of 1787*. This enactment, providing national governance over a vast tract of land known as the Northwest Territory which extended above the Ohio River and between the Appalachian range and the Mississippi River, is generally regarded as one of the most notable actions of the Continental Congress. Embodied in the enactment was the following proclamation: "Schools and the means of education shall forever be encouraged."[6]

The colonists complied with the ordinance's directive to promote schools and granted tracts of land for such purposes. Since land was so plentiful, with thousands and thousands of acres available throughout the country, it was used as a means of providing financial assistance for schools. Land was a most accessible commodity and its use, in addition to helping finance education, stimulated the westward migration of people.

The Northwest Ordinance of 1787 incorporated a land grant provision. The law actually provided for the survey of land and the reservation of what was known as *Section 16* (containing 640 acres) of every township for education.

Schools were permitted to use these given acres with essentially no constraints. Schools could be built on the land, or portions could be rented or sold. The funds, in turn, were used to help finance the costs of educating youth. Since there were essentially no restrictions, the funds from rent or sale were sometimes used unwisely. With more forethought, restrictions could have been applied that could have guaranteed more prudence.

The land grant provision embodied in *The Northwest Ordinance of 1787* became available for Ohio when it was admitted to the Union in 1803. At that time, Ohio received one section of land per township for educational purposes. Some states gave schools additional sections per township. Fourteen states gave two sections of land per township, while three sparsely populated territories, Arizona, New Mexico, and Utah, gave schools four sections for each township.

Interestingly, the original colonies received no federal lands for school purposes. In addition, Kentucky, Maine, Texas, Vermont, and West Virginia also received no federal lands for school purposes. It would appear, from the exclusion of these states from federal land grants, that the primary moving force behind the Continental Congress's action was to stimulate migration to the west. Nevertheless, the land grants involved more than 154 million acres and, indeed, did help considerably in financing and developing public education. Very definitely, the issuing of land grants implied that financing public education was a state responsibility.

1.7 The Morrill Act of 1862

Although the federal government did not, and still does not, play a major role in financing public schools, it did play a major role in providing the impetus for vocational education. *The Morrill Act of 1862* was the first federal program in which Congress tried to influence

---

[6] Congress of the Confederation, *An Ordinance for the Government of the Territory of the United States, Northwest of the River Ohio* (now commonly referred to as *The Northwest Ordinance of 1787*), Third Article, July 13, 1787.

the school curriculum by enticing state land grant universities to offer instruction in vocational agriculture and mechanical arts.[7]

1.8 "The Kalamazoo Case of 1874"

Another historical event that altered the course of education occurred in the latter part of the nineteenth century in Kalamazoo, Michigan. "The Kalamazoo Case of 1874," as it is popularly known, established a legal system of taxation for funding secondary education. As was indicated earlier in this chapter, taxation had been approved over two hundred years before for elementary education. The decision rendered by the Michigan Supreme Court in *Stuart v. School District No. 1 of Village of Kalamazoo*, 30 Mich. 69 (1874), established the same taxing basis for public high school education as had existed for public elementary schools.[8] This now-famous case inaugurated the concept of funding high schools on an equal basis with elementary schools.

1.9 The Smith-Hughes Vocational Education Act of 1917

One of the fears expressed when people voice a desire to have the federal government play a bigger role in financing public schools is the fear of control. History reveals that very little control was exerted in the stipulations of the land grants of 1787, but a significant contrast was evidenced in 1917 when *The Smith-Hughes Vocational Education Act*[9] was signed into law by President Wilson. This act provided funding for vocational education in the fields of agriculture, home economics, and trades and industry.[10] The funds were provided for the salaries of vocational teachers, supervisors, and directors.[11] The law required that local and/or state funding match the amounts of revenue provided by the federal government.[12]

Many other controls and restrictions were required by the law; the Federal Board for Vocational Education was established to monitor and regulate programs. Stipulations also included the following: (a) a statewide vocational plan must be adopted by participating states, (b) ages of vocational students must be recorded by participating institutions, (c) vocational programs must exhibit a controlling purpose of preparing students for useful employment, and (d) participating state and/or local communities must provide necessary buildings and equipment.

1.10 National Defense Education Act of 1958

The amount of federal financing desirable has been an area of continuous debate since the early 1900s. This was, and continues to be, due to the difficulty of acquiring funding to cope with local inflation and in meeting revenue needs for program improvement and

---

[7] Morrill Act, ch. 130, § 1, 12 Stat. 503 (1862) (current version at 7 U.S.C. § 301 (1980)).

[8] *Stuart v. School Dist. No. 1 of Village of Kalamazoo*, 30 Mich. 69 (1874).

[9] Smith-Hughes Vocational Education Act, ch. 114, § 1, 39, Stat. 929 (1917) (current version at 20 U.S.C. § 11, (1979)).

[10] 20 U.S.C § 11 (1979). *See also Financing Education* at 165.

[11] 20 U.S.C. §§ 12, 13 (1960).

[12] 20 U.S.C. § 19 (1979).

initiation of change. Still, the federal government, in keeping with the same laissez-faire philosophy that prevailed at the time *The United States Constitution* was signed, has maintained a distance in providing additional financial support. Only occasionally has the government stepped in to apply more leadership and control. Such was the case in 1958 with the *National Defense Education Act* (*NDEA*).[13]

The *NDEA* of 1958 was considered a "breakthrough" law for public schools. The flight of Sputnik in 1957 created a feeling of uneasiness that the United States was falling behind Russia in science and space exploration. To spur an improvement in mastery of science by young people, the federal government provided funds to aid in improving the teaching of science. Science courses and inservice sessions were offered around the country, and teachers were paid to take advantage of those opportunities.[14]

1.11 Elementary and Secondary Education Act of 1965

Another "breakthrough" law for public schools occurred with the *Elementary and Secondary Education Act of 1965*.[15] This law was spawned in response to the government's desire to improve education in areas adversely affected by poverty.[16] As such, the federal government assumes part of the financial responsibility of financing public education on a compensatory basis.

The federal government also provides financial aid to nonpublic schools through the *Elementary and Secondary Education Act of 1965*.[17]

1.12 Title IX of the Education Amendments of 1972

Several laws have created financial expenditures in school districts without additional revenue to counterbalance such. *Title IX of the Education Amendments of 1972*[18] (*Title IX*) is a prime example of this scenario. Sex discrimination was prohibited by *Title IX*. Specifically, the law states that no one shall be discriminated against on the basis of sex for any educational program or activity receiving federal financial assistance.[19] Employment

---

[13] National Defense Education Act of 1958, Pub. L. No. 85-864, 72 Stat. 1580 (codified as amended at 20 U.S.C. §§ 401–403 (1958)). These provisions have either been repealed or are inactive in that Congress stopped providing funding in the 1970s for the programs originally created by the statute.

[14] 20 U.S.C. §§ 401–403 (1958). *See also Financing Education* at 156-57.

[15] Elementary and Secondary Education Act of 1965, Pub. L. No. 89-10, 79 Stat. 27 (codified as amended in scattered sections of 20 U.S.C.).

[16] The congressional declaration of policy supporting the Elementary and Secondary Education Act of 1965 appears at 20 U.S.C. § 236 and provides, in part:

> In recognition of the responsibility of the United States for the impact which certain Federal activities have on the local educational agencies in the areas in which such activities are carried on, the Congress hereby declares it to be the policy of the United States to provide financial assistance. . . .

20 U.S.C. § 236(a) (1988). *See also Financing Education* at 171–72.

[17] *Id.*

[18] Education Amendments of 1972, Pub. L. No. 92-318, Title IX, 86 Stat. 373 (codified as amended at 20 U.S.C §§ 1681–88 (1972)) [hereinafter Title IX].

[19] Title IX provides:

> No person in the United States shall, on the basis of sex, be excluded from participation in, be denied the benefits of, or be subjected to discrimination under any education program or activity receiving Federal financial assistance. . . .

20 U.S.C. § 1681(a).

and promotion practices, physical education programs, and girls athletic programs have changed dramatically as a result of the 1972 law. Most people recognize that these changes are for the better but also think many of the financial problems resulting from the mandates could have been avoided if federal funds had been available to implement the mandates.[20]

1.13 Education for All Handicapped Children Act of 1975

While many federal laws create mandates without providing additional funding, *Public Law 94-142*, the *Education for All Handicapped Children Act,*[21] did provide funds to the states to assist local districts in modifying programs to assure that all handicapped children had access to a "free appropriate public education."[22] The law provides funding for transportation of handicapped children; for services from specialists such as physical and occupational therapists, audiologists, speech pathologists and psychologists, and for other supportive services.[23] Other expenditures that are covered include medical evaluation and diagnosis, and related items such as early identification and assessment of disabilities, and even parent training and counseling.[24]

1.14 Education Amendments of 1978

The *Education Amendments of 1978*[25] were directed toward elementary and secondary schools. The comprehensive amendments closely reflected the financial relationship between local school districts and state and federal funding. While trying to solidify that financial relationship, the amendments' authors sought efficiency in requirements affecting programs for elementary and secondary schools.[26] The law also required that before any data collection plan is approved, the cost must be justified and a rationale for the use of the data must be provided.[27]

One aspect of the *Education Amendments of 1978* was to direct the Secretary of the Department of Health, Education and Welfare to conduct a three-year nationwide study of public school financing procedures. A wide range of concerns was addressed including

---

[20] *Financing Education* at 171–72.

[21] Education for All Handicapped Children Act of 1975, Pub. L. No. 94-142, 89 Stat. 773 (codified as amended in scattered sections of 20 U.S.C.).

[22] 20 U.S.C. § 1400(c) (1975). The stated congressional purpose of the Education of the Handicapped Act is:

> to assure that all handicapped children have available to them . . . a free appropriate public education which emphasizes special education and related services designed to meet their unique needs, to assure that the rights of handicapped children and their parents or guardians are protected, to assist states and localities to provide for the education of all handicapped children, and to assess and assure the effectiveness of efforts to educate handicapped children.

20 U.S.C. § 1400(c). (1975).

[23] *Financing Education* at 171–72.

[24] *Id.*

[25] Education Amendments of 1978, Pub. L. No. 95-561, 92 Stat. 2143 (codified as amended in scattered sections of 20 U.S.C.).

[26] *Financing Education* at 171–72.

[27] *Id.*

equity of financial distributions and costs, public policy toward private schools, and present and future roles of the federal government in school finance.[28]

1.15 Summary

In summary, there have been numerous actions of the federal government that have impacted upon the present financial picture for public schools. Ohio schools have been affected by state legislation that provides for differences and uniqueness as compared to other states. Ohio's historical perspective is the focus of chapter two while unique aspects of other states' funding methods are included in chapter twelve of this manual.

---

[28] *Id.*

Chapter 2:

Ohio: A Historical Perspective

2.1 Beginnings

Early funding of the first schools in Ohio was accomplished through a system known as subscription schools. Such schools were formed when families, interested in the education of their children, banded together to seek the services of a teacher. However, the first legislation that dealt with funding of public education for Ohio, was likely to have been *The Northwest Ordinance of 1787*. This ordinance provided that, "schools and the means of education shall forever be encouraged."[1]

Shreve, in writing about the history of Ohio's county school districts, pointed out that the *Supplemental Act* creating the State of Ohio in 1803 provided for the following:

> One section of each township had ostensibly been reserved for school purposes. In addition Congress specified that the Northwest Territory set aside one thirty-sixth

[1] Congress of the Confederation, *An Ordinance for the Government of the Territory of the United States, Northwest of the River Ohio* (now commonly referred to as *The Northwest Ordinance of 1787*), July 13, 1787.

of the United States Military Tract and the Virginia Military Lands, fourteen quarter townships from the Military District for the Western Reserve, and one thirty-sixth of all lands subsequently purchased from the Indians for the support of schools.

Unfortunately, the law had no safeguards to protect the interest of the schools in the lands. Ohio achieved statehood in 1803. Since the State served as trustee of the lands, it determined to lease the land. Mismanagement resulted in some of the lands being leased for ninety-nine years at ridiculously low rates. Many lessees simply removed the valuable timber and then abandoned the land. After twenty-five years of turmoil and neglect, the legislature determined to abandon the leasing policy and sell the lands in 1828.[2]

2.2 Early Constitutional Provisions

The Ohio Constitution, as originally submitted to the United States Congress in 1802 contained two sections that related directly to education. Both sections are contained in the Bill of Rights enumerated in Article VIII, which states in part:

> §3. [R]eligion, morality and knowledge, being essentially necessary to good government and the happiness of mankind, schools and the means of instruction shall forever be encouraged by legislative provision, not inconsistent with the rights of conscience.[3]
>
> §25. [N]o law shall be passed to prevent the poor in the several counties and townships within this state, which are endowed, in whole or in part, from the revenue arising from donations made by the United States for the support of schools and colleges; and the doors of the said schools, academies and universities, shall be open for the reception of scholars, students and teachers, of every grade, without any distinction or preference whatever, contrary to the intent for which the said donations were made.[4]

2.3 Early Legislative Actions: 1820-1900

State legislation enacted by the general assembly in 1825 further mandated that each district created by this legislation, must levy taxes for the schools of the district. Interesting is the fact that, "the legislation passed only because the friends of the canals traded votes with friends of the schools. The canals bill passed on February 4, 1825 and the public school bill passed the next day."[5] These constitutional provisions and legislation led to the state mandating, in 1838, that all youth in the state would be provided with a free education.

The state initiated a more definite policy of contributing to local school support and

---

[2] Robert P. Shreve, *History of Ohio's County Boards of Education* (Columbus, Ohio: Ohio Department of Education, 1989), at 7 [hereinafter *History of Ohio's County Boards of Education*].
[3] Ohio Const. of 1802, art. VIII, § 3.
[4] Ohio Const. of 1802, art. VIII, § 25.
[5] *History of Ohio's County Boards of Education* at 8.

pledged $200,000 a year in 1838.[6] The revenue was derived from a half-mill general property tax (increased to one mill in 1873) levied on all taxable property in the state and from special taxes on banks, insurance companies, and bridge companies.[7] The initial payment was made in December, 1838, and was distributed to the schools on the basis of enumerated white youth between the ages of four and twenty.[8] The policy of distributing an appropriated amount of state money on the basis of enumeration was followed until the turn of the century.[9]

2.4 Ohio's Constitutional Provisions

The Ohio Constitution of 1802 as well as the one that is currently in effect enunciates the importance of public education for the youth of the state. Article VI, Section 2, of the current *Ohio Constitution* states the following:

> The general assembly shall make such provisions, by taxation, or otherwise, as, with the income arising from the school trust fund, will secure a thorough and efficient system of common schools throughout the State; but, no religious or other sect, or sects, shall ever have any exclusive right to, or control of, any part of the school funds of this state.[10]

This constitutional provision, the Thorough and Efficient Clause, was at issue in the *Board of Education v. Walter*[11] litigation. The case arose in the Hamilton County Court of Common Pleas in response to a constitutional challenge by the Board of Education of the City School District of the City of Cincinnati and several other plaintiffs. The plaintiffs argued that Ohio's system of financing public elementary and secondary education violated both the Thorough and Efficient Clause[12] and the Equal Protection and Benefit Clause[13] of the Ohio Constitution. Although the trial court found for the plaintiffs and held that Ohio's statutory scheme for financing public education did violate the constitutional provisions in question, the presiding judge failed to articulate a working definition for a thorough and efficient system of schools. On appeal, the Court of Appeals of Hamilton County reversed the trial court's ruling as it applied to the Thorough and Efficient Clause, noting that the finding of unconstitutionality could not stand because the legislature had already addressed the issue of public school financing:

> The insurmountable obstacle confronting the trial court, however, is the terminology of Article VI, § 2 which in simple and straight forward language designates the

---

[6] Hobart H. Bell, "Financing Public Education in Ohio for 150 Years," *Ohio Schools* (Vol. 30, Issue 5, Ohio Education Association) (May 1952), at 104 [hereinafter *Financing Public Education in Ohio for 150 Years*].

[7] *Id.*

[8] *Id.*

[9] *Id.*

[10] Ohio Const. art. VI at § 2.

[11] *Board of Education v. Walter*, No. A 7602725 (C.P. Hamilton County, Ohio, Dec. 5, 1977), *aff'd in part and rev'd in part*, 10 Ohio Op. 3d 26 (Ct. App. 1978), *aff'd in part and rev'd in part*, 58 Ohio St. 2d 368, 390 N.E.2d 813 (1979), *cert. denied*, 444 U.S. 1015 (1980).

[12] Ohio Const. art. VI at § 2.

[13] Ohio Const. art. I at § 2.

General Assembly as the branch of government with the power to determine a system which is "thorough and efficient."[14]

The Ohio Supreme Court ultimately upheld the constitutionality of Ohio's statutory scheme.[15]

2.5 Legislative Actions: 1900-1930

The practice of distributing an appropriated amount of money on the basis of the enumeration of youth was continued until 1900. The amount for each youth was determined by dividing the amount appropriated by the general assembly, by the number of enumerated youths. The legislation, enacted that year, changed the method to one that distributed the state's money on the basis of $1.45 per each enumerated youth between four and twenty years of age.[16] This method of guaranteeing each school district the receipt of a specified, minimal amount for each enumerated youth continued until 1920. During this 20-year period, the amount guaranteed for each enumerated youth had risen to $2.00.[17] The money was raised by the state through an imposed property tax and through appropriations from the state's general revenue fund.[18] In 1920, legislation was enacted that imposed a general property tax of 1.8 mills for the state's common school fund and an additional levy of one mill was authorized to provide funds to be retained in the counties.[19]

Slightly more than 2.7% of the amount collected for the state was used to help poorer districts. This legislation was in effect for only one year.[20] In 1921 legislation was enacted that imposed a 2.65 mill levy on property statewide.[21] The revenue raised by the tax was to be retained and distributed within the county of origination. The state distributed only that money which was appropriated for poor districts.[22]

2.6 Effects of Stock Market Crash—Voters Change Constitution

With the crash of the stock market in 1929 and the chaos that ensued, property owners sought help in meeting the financial needs of the schools of their communities. Two sources of help came as a result of the enactment of legislation that imposed a one cent tax on the sale of each ten cigarettes and a one cent tax on each gallon of gasoline sold. Another source of help that relieved the property owner of property taxes was the change in the *Ohio Constitution* which further limited the right of political subdivisions to tax without the vote of the citizens. In 1933 the voters of Ohio changed the *Ohio Constitution* to read as follows:

---

[14] 10 Ohio Op. 3d at 33.

[15] *Board of Education v. Walter*, 58 Ohio St. 2d 368, 390 N.E.2d 813 (1979), *cert. denied*, 444 U.S. 1015 (1980).

[16] *Financing Public Education in Ohio for 150 Years* at 105.

[17] *Id.*

[18] *Id.*

[19] *Id.*

[20] *Id.* at 105–06.

[21] *Id.*

[22] *Id.*

> No property, taxed according to value shall be so taxed in excess of one per cent of its true value in money for all state and local purposes, but laws may be passed authorizing additional taxes to be levied outside of such limitation, either when approved by at least a majority of the electors of the taxing district voting on such proposition, or when provided for by the charter of a municipal corporation.[23]

Prior to this voter-approved amendment, Section 2 of the *Ohio Constitution* permitted all of the political subdivisions (school districts, townships, villages, towns, cities, and counties) to levy up to 1.5% (15 mills) on the true value of their properties without voter approval. The change effectively reduced the revenue from property taxes by one-third in most of the political subdivisions of Ohio. Figure 2:1 shows how the reductions were made for the school districts in one Ohio county.

2.7 Further Legislative Action Affecting Local Revenue

Since the enactment of the 1933 constitutional provision, legislators have further reduced the provision's effectiveness by enacting laws that require levies to be changed annually so they will yield only the amount specified to be raised initially, and by granting to taxpayers a 10% (12½% for owner-occupied residences) rollback/tax credit on tax bills. These actions have effectively limited growth of local revenue for existing voted millage.

To ease the loss in revenue as a result of the reduction of the inside millage from 15.0 mills to 10.0 mills (the constitutional provision is reflected as a percentage figure), the legislature enacted a 3.0% tax on all sales including foods. This legislation passed in December, 1934. The portion of this law that taxed foods was soon repealed.

2.8 First Foundation Program

After the enactment of the sales tax, and following a study conducted by a school finance specialist of Columbia University, the first foundation program was enacted by the legislature and signed by Governor Martin L. Davey on June 12, 1935. This foundation program provided for payments to be made to school districts on the basis of a specified amount per day for each pupil in grades one through eight in average daily attendance; another specified amount on the same basis for those attending kindergarten; and another amount for those in grades nine through twelve. The length of the school term and size of the district in terms of the average daily attendance were also factors affecting the foundation program. After these payments were calculated, the amount of money that would be raised from applying three mills to the assessed value of the district was added. If such calculations did not yield sufficient funds to meet the "minimum operating costs," the district was entitled to additional aid. Districts also received an allowance for costs of maintaining approved pupil transportation and any tuition payments.[24] These funds, provided through the foundation program, were to be used for school operating expenses.

---

[23] Ohio Const. art. XII at § 2.

[24] H.B. 466, 91st Gen. Ass., 2nd Sess., 1935 Ohio ___, at 589.

Table 2:1

Background Data Used to Determine the Inside Millage Rates for the School Districts in Montgomery County, Ohio

District	1929	1930	1931	1932	1933	5 year Average Annual Levy Rate	2/3 Average Levy Rate
	Year						
Butler	7.197	7.197	7.197	6.649	6.943	9.687	6.457
Clay	4.932	5.020	5.465	5.281	5.200	7.830	5.220
Jackson	3.976	3.969	4.087	3.983	4.206	6.694	4.463
Jefferson	8.128	6.586	6.331	5.617	5.576	9.098	6.065
Madison	7.138	7.437	7.279	5.037	6.214	9.271	6.181
Mad River	7.259	7.247	7.247	6.884	7.459	9.869	6.579
Perry	4.506	1.106	3.732	7.809	8.221	7.725	5.149
Van Buren	4.732	7.285	5.017	5.146	6.981	8.482	5.654
Washington	5.346	4.612	5.706	4.068	4.100	7.416	4.944
Wayne	7.686	7.674	7.616	7.484	5.400	9.822	6.548
Clayton	7.592	7.592	7.592	7.462	7.614	10.220	6.813
Germantown	3.027	4.181	4.181	4.181	4.629	6.690	4.459
N. Lebanon	7.667	7.687	7.687	6.436	7.337	10.013	6.675
Northridge	°	°	6.890	6.173	7.225	6.708	4.471
Prymont	5.306	2.706	5.551	6.836	8.221	8.374	5.582
West Carrollton	5.517	6.145	6.618	5.001	5.670	8.440	5.626
Oakwood	3.987	4.067	3.713	3.721	3.542	6.456	4.303
Dayton	4.152	4.152	4.152	4.006	3.898	6.722	4.481
Miamisburg	2.959	3.540	3.930	3.799	4.033	6.322	4.214
German Twp.	4.136	3.530	4.516	6.974	6.907	7.863	5.241
Brookville	7.592	7.522	7.522	7.146	7.286	10.064	6.709
Phillipsburg	6.374	6.362	7.188	7.306	7.162	9.528	6.352
Randolph	6.592	6.592	6.592	6.262	6.434	9.144	6.096

Note: The source for the information in the above table is from documents on file in the Office of Ohio's Department of Taxation.

° The information for these years for Northridge is not known. Apparently only the three years were used in the calculation.

The first five columns of data are the tax rates used for school purposes for the identified years, the sixth column is the average of those five years of taxes agreed at the county level and the 2.65 mills imposed in 1921 (see Table 2:1), the seventh column represents two thirds of the average annual rate. No political subdivision can demand more of the "inside millage" than this formula generates. The number of the school districts indicated in this table has been reduced to sixteen at the time of this writing.

2.9 Basic Foundation Program Concepts

The foundation program initiated two basic concepts that still exist. These concepts are as follows: (a) the education of pupils in grades K-12 is a shared responsibility between the state and local districts; and (b) in order to receive money through the foundation program, a district must levy a specified minimum number of mills.

From the late 1930s to the early 1950s, this foundation program, with some changes, remained the method of financing the public schools in Ohio. The current foundation

Table 2:2
The Monetary Effect of Using Average Daily Membership as the Basis of Counting Pupils Instead of Average Daily Attendance

Number of Days	Total	Average Attendance	Allocation per Pupil	Total State Guarantee
Enrolled	86,174	473.49	$3,315	$1,569,619.35
Absent	6,463	35.51	3,315	117,715.65
Attendance	79,711	437.98	3,315	$1,415,903.70

Note: Computations made by authors. The allocation per pupil is used in calculating the foundation program line 13 for FY 1996.

program continues to be based on a partnership between the local school district and the state, each producing a portion of the funds.

2.10 Continuing Problems

Even with the passage of the sales tax and the foundation program, the financing of public education remained a problem in Ohio. In 1937 the state had failed to make the February quarterly payment and one commentator predicted, that, by December 31, 1937, the shortage in the state's financing of schools would not be less than $7,000,000.[25]

2.11 Changes in Method of Counting Pupils

Legislation was enacted in 1950 that changed the method by which pupils would be counted for foundation program reimbursement. This legislation called for counting of pupils by the average daily membership (ADM) method rather than by the average daily attendance (ADA) method that was in practice at the time. Opponents of the proposed law argued that using ADA as the basis for the count would help to maintain a higher level of attendance as school officials would try harder to see that pupils were in school. Proponents argued just as determinedly that the cost of maintaining a child in school began with the first day of enrollment in the school since textbooks must be provided, a pupil desk must be available, records had to be kept, and a teacher must be in the classroom whether the enrolled pupil was in attendance or not. The proponents prevailed and the ADM method was adopted. This legislative act resulted in the allocation of more state funds for school districts. This was considered to be a positive act and continues to be the basis for counting pupils for the state's reimbursement through the current foundation program. Table 2:2, using 1990 fiscal year pupil allowances, illustrates what the difference would be, when ADA is used as the basis of counting pupils as opposed to ADM.

From Table 2:2, it can readily be seen that if the calculations for the illustrated,

[25] Walton B. Bliss, "The Financial Picture of Schools," *Ohio Schools* (April 1937), at 149.

hypothetical Ohio school district were based on an ADA pupil count, this "formula" district would lose $117,715.65 based on a 7.5% rate of absence.

2.12 Legislative Initiatives to Reform Ohio School Finance

Numerous studies of the problems facing Ohio's public schools were conducted by Ohio's legislative bodies, the Ohio Department of Education, and other interested agencies and organizations from the early 1940s through the early 1950s. However, the problems were of such a nature that the state legislature believed that it was essential that another statewide study be made. Legislation was, therefore, enacted in 1953 that provided for a comprehensive study. This study, funded by an appropriation of $75,000, was headed by Representative W. L. Manahan.[26] In the first paragraph of the report, Manahan noted:

> The successful individual pauses from time to time to review what he has accomplished and to plan his future course of action. The successful business corporation also engages in such evaluative and planning activities, because the price of inadequate planning is bankruptcy. Public education has the same need for periodic appraisal if it is to serve well its intended purpose.[27]

2.13 The Manahan Report—Methods Used to Make Study

O. Alexander of Southern Illinois University was employed to direct the study of the committee. Alexander served until December 31, 1954, when J. Herrick of The Ohio State University was employed to succeed him. Herrick served until the report was completed.

This study was one of the most comprehensive studies of public education ever completed in Ohio. It involved various segments of Ohio citizenry including the following: members of the general assembly; professional educators including nationally known persons who were recognized for their expertise in particular phases of education; business persons; and ordinary citizens who were interested in the education of Ohio's youth. Committees were organized in each county to help in the vital work of this School Survey Committee. Due to the limitations of time and money, the scope of the study was limited to elementary and secondary education. Components studied in this comprehensive review included the following: instructional program, school personnel, teacher education, the Ohio Department of Education, school district organization, school facilities, transportation, and finance.

2.14 Finance Recommendations in the Manahan Report

This study's importance to the financing of public education in Ohio is demonstrated by the fact that over 25% of the text of the report was devoted to the singular topic of finance. Ten of the 28 major recommendations are interpreted by the authors of this book as dealing directly with school finance issues. These selected recommendations (numbered as they were in the original report) are as follows:

---

[26] William L. Manahan, *Report of the Ohio School Survey Committee* (Columbus, Ohio: Heer Printing Co., 1955), at 1.

[27] *Id.*

15. Permissive legislation should be enacted to permit boards of education to pay dues to school board associations.
16. A plan must be found for assisting school districts in meeting building needs which cannot be financed from legally available local sources. This need might be met by one or more of the following plans: (a) a substantial increase in the biennial state appropriations for buildings; (b) creating a state school building authority; (c) a state bond issue; (d) an increase in the 8.0% debt limitation; or (e) a separate foundation program for capital outlay.
17. State allocations for transportation should include an allowance for depreciation to be applied to the purchase of board owned buses.
18. The formula used for calculating state aid for transportation should be revised.
22. The foundation program should be based on the number of "teacher units" rather than the number of pupils.
23. The state's share of the foundation program should be increased. At the present time Ohio provides 25% of school costs from state funds; the national average is over 40%. Ohio should raise its level of support to around 40%, but at no time should exceed the national average.
24. The survey committee approves the foundation program as recommended by the finance study committee, exclusive of the capital outlay provision.
25. School districts should be permitted to vote extra levies for operating purposes for five years at special elections and ten years at regular elections. Voters should be permitted to approve for an indefinite period the millage required for participation in the foundation program.
26. State payment for tuition should be abolished.
27. Boards of education should consider adopting salary schedules which will reward outstanding achievement as well as college training and experience.[28]

It should be noted that one legislator voted against recommendation number 24 because he thought that the level of support for wealthier districts was too low. Another legislator voted against the same recommendation because he thought the support level was too high for wealthier districts and would be unfair to poorer districts.[29]

2.15 The Legislature Acts

The report was completed in time for the legislature to act on the recommendations in the first session of the 101st Ohio General Assembly (1955). However, the major sections of the bill dealing with improving financing of the schools were not to be implemented until the fall of 1956. Millions of dollars were saved for the state by delaying the revenue increases for school districts.

The foundation program that evolved from this report was known as the "teacher unit" plan. This plan unified the professional members since it provided for regular teachers,

---

[28] *Id.* at 210–11.
[29] *Id.* at 211.

special teachers (such as art, music, and physical education), guidance counselors, supervisors, and administrators.

The total approved teacher units for a school district was based on the number of pupils (divided by a factor of 30 to provide for basic teachers), plus the number of approved special and vocational units and factors for administration, special instruction and supervision.

The following factors were used to determine the dollars that would be available to the school districts: (a) salaries based on the training of all certificated personnel, the number of days worked for these persons, and administrative and supervisory responsibilities; (b) 10% of the salary calculation for retirement and substitute teachers; (c) approved transportation; and (d) an allowance for operational expenditures based on a specified dollar amount for each approved teacher unit. An amount determined by multiplying the district's assessed valuation by 10 mills was then subtracted from the total dollars determined by these four factors. This figure became the total state support for the year for districts receiving money through the formula. Such districts were known as additional aid districts. However, all districts were guaranteed a specified amount per approved teacher unit if that amount would exceed the amount calculated through the formula. Districts receiving such state support were known as non-additional aid districts or guarantee districts.

This plan, with some adjustments in the dollar factors, remained basically intact until the first session of the 107th Ohio General Assembly meeting in 1967.

2.16 The Ohio Education Association Study

A study funded by the Ohio Education Association in 1962 and agreed to by other educational organizations reiterated the basic principles of the 1955 study. This study was directed by W. R. Flesher, Director of Cooperative Educational Enterprises. A special consultant of the study was T. C. Holy, a professor from Indiana University who had been a participant in the Mort study made in 1930. This 1962 study reinforced the recommendations of the Manahan Report and recommended changes that would have improved the basic principles of the earlier study as follows: lowering the pupil divisor for determining basic teacher units; increasing the number of special education and vocational units; decreasing the divisor for determining support teachers, supervisors, and administrative personnel; and reiterating the need for a capital outlay factor in the foundation program. It was also recommended, according to Flesher, "that the salary allowances in the Ohio Foundation Program be based on the average salaries being paid to full-time certificated personnel (nine months)."[30]

The cost to implement the improved program was estimated to be an additional $200,000,000. The organizations supporting the study thought that amount was too extensive for the legislature to accept, and reduced the recommended amount to $130,000,000. Both candidates for governorship agreed to seek this latter figure if elected. However, when James Rhodes took office as Governor of Ohio in January, 1963, he claimed the

---

[30] William R. Flesher et al., *Public Education in Ohio* (Columbus, Ohio: School Service, Inc., 1962), at 291.

state was in a financial crisis and that it should not seek new taxes. In addition, any improvements for education would have to be postponed. The result of this inaction was that the public schools of Ohio received less state money during 1965 and 1966 than they had received from the state during the previous biennium.

From the time the recommendations of the Manahan Report were enacted until the mid 1960s, marked improvements had been made. Teachers were more highly trained, school districts were able to expand their vocational and special education programs, and additional supervisors, administrators and other support personnel were employed as the result of recommendations of the report.

2.17 Period of Decline: 1965-1973

The period between 1965 and 1973 again saw the state's effort waning to provide adequate funding for public schools. Legislative opponents to the teacher unit plan talked about the plans' open-endedness which permitted school districts meeting minimum requirements to secure funds easily for approved programs. Critics also complained of difficulties calculating the formula. Added to these complaints were those of representatives of wealthier school districts who were saying that they were unable to afford approved special education and vocational programs, since these factors were all a part of the inclusive nature of the teacher unit formula. In reality this foundation program was not difficult to calculate and it had logic to it that most educators could understand. Many of the wealthier districts could have received additional funds if they had chosen to ask the state to approve special and vocational units for their schools. In some cases, had such districts asked for such approval they would have become additional-aid districts.

The program was changed, however, despite the fact that the program had been successful in a number of important ways. The new program made two substantial changes that were different from the old formula. One change provided for a specified amount of money to be allowed for each regular ADM pupil when calculating the equalizing portion of the basic aid formula. The second change assured that all districts would receive the same dollar amounts for approved vocational and special education units, municipal overburden, transportation, and extended service. These changes resulted in an incentive whereby each interest group could lobby for that segment of the formula that most benefitted it.

In 1967 John M. Parsons declared the following in one of the biennial publications of the Ohio Department of Education, *The Ohio Law for The State Support of Public Schools*:

> The gradually increasing educational costs have made it almost impossible for the poorer districts to maintain quality programs or to establish salary schedules competitive enough to employ or retain well-qualified personnel. The local school tax burden combined with additional municipal, state, and federal taxes has resulted in general reluctance of the voters to approve additional levies on local property for support of schools. . . . In response to the obvious need and continued requests, the 107th General Assembly has significantly changed the level of state support, the concepts

of distribution, and increased state taxes for support of public schools.[31]

In spite of the changes that had been made by the 107th Ohio General Assembly the state's funding of education fell short of needs. The situation deteriorated further during the remaining years of the 1960s and through the early 1970s to the extent that legislators finally recognized that the state's revenue for the public schools had to be increased. Thus, members of the 109th Ohio General Assembly searched for ways to meet the demands of education. An article in Ohio Schools briefly described the situation as follows:

> Eight school districts, including Dayton, . . . had closed their doors for varying periods of time because they were bankrupt. Local voters defeated school finance issues in wholesale lots in an attempt to stem the rising tide of property taxes. Many school districts cut staff and programs. A state austerity program was instituted, slashing state school aid by three percent.[32]

2.18 Passage of State Income Tax

A state income tax had been discussed by the members of earlier state legislatures but it was not until 1971 that such a tax received serious attention. It was only after bitter and divisive discussions that Ohio's first income tax became law. Although this tax was promoted based on needs of education, it was not earmarked for education. Thus, it must be remembered that other segments of the state's responsibilities also benefitted substantially from the revenue derived from this new tax.

The foundation program resulting from the legislation enacted in 1971 had two major parts, basic and special needs. The basic program allowed $300 for each kindergarten pupil and $600 for each pupil in grades one through twelve. The following categories of pupils were excluded from being counted: (a) all pupils in special education programs; (b) full-time equivalent of pupils in approved vocational classes; and (c) 25% of pupils attending a joint vocational school. The yield of assessed valuation multiplied by 22.5 mills was then subtracted from the sum of the number of ADM pupils multiplied by a specific dollar guarantee for each child. The answer derived from these calculations determined the amount of state money a district would receive through the basic portion of the program.

There were districts that received amounts greater than the formula generated as the result of the 22.5 mills that were applied to their valuations. Again, these districts were guaranteed a specified amount. The initial amounts guaranteed were between $179 per basic pupil in ADM for districts with valuations of $20,000 per pupil valuation to $79 per basic pupil in ADM for districts with $32,000 valuation per pupil.

The special needs portion of the formula (the disequalizing portion of the program) provided the same dollar amounts to all school districts for the following: (a) approved vocational units depending on the training and experience of the teacher; (b) approved

[31] John M. Parsons, *The Ohio Law for the State Support of Public Schools* (Columbus, Ohio: Columbus Blank Book Co., 1968), at 6.

[32] *See* "OEA Achieves Top Legislative Goals With Passage of Education—Tax Bill," *Ohio Schools* (Vol. 49, Issue 17, Ohio Education Association) (Dec. 24, 1971), at 8–11.

special education units; (c) approved transportation; and (d) approved extended service.[33]

Even with the passage of the income tax and changes in the formula, the funding of Ohio's elementary and secondary schools was still not sufficient. The 110th General Assembly, noting the dilemma, authorized another comprehensive study of public education with special emphasis to be placed on the question of the adequate funding of Ohio's schools. Note that this was just twenty years after the Manahan study had been authorized.

2.19 The Syracuse Report and Legislative Action

This study was directed by a group of professors from Syracuse University and was conducted mainly during the latter part of 1973 and throughout 1974 with recommendations being made to the 111th General Assembly meeting in 1975. The study proposed a change in the foundation program that was to equalize the funding of public education for the children of Ohio; it was intended to prevent the wide disparities that existed between the amounts being expended per pupil in poor districts and wealthy districts.

The formula that evolved from this study was called the equal yield formula. The purpose of the formula was described as follows:

> The new funding program—known as an equal yield plan—was designed to provide an equal return to school districts making an equal taxing effort. The primary goal of the new system is to provide a method of distributing state money that would guarantee that every child in Ohio will have available an adequately financed education regardless of the wealth in his or her particular school district.[34]

The equal yield plan eventually would make the value of each mill, up to the first 20 mills levied by a school district, worth $48 per pupil. Each mill levied between 20 mills and 30 mills would be worth $42 per pupil. This latter provision was the state's method to help local districts more adequately fund their schools. The state would make up the difference between what the local district could raise on its tax duplicate and the $48 and $42 per pupil amounts that were being guaranteed.

Again, as was the case with the recommendations of the Manahan study the legislature delayed the full funding of the new plan, this time for three years. For the first year it was stated:

> The cost to bring all districts in the state to the uniform guarantee level is so great, however, that the program will be phased in over a period of years. For the current biennium, the phase in distribution will be 17 per cent [*sic*] of the additional cost for the first year of the biennium and 26 per cent [*sic*] the second year.[35]

This delay also saved the state substantial sums of money. It was not until fiscal year 1979 that the new formula was fully implemented. And even then certain factors were not fully funded due to actions of the legislature and the financial condition of the state.

---

33 *Id.*

34 "A New Plan for Financing Ohio Schools," *Ohio Schools* (Vol. 53, Issue 11, Ohio Education Association) (Sept. 12, 1975), at 7–8.

35 *Id.*

Table 2:3

Ohio's Foundation Program Guaranteed Amounts Per Basic Pupil for the Fiscal Years 1982 Through 1992 Compared to the Average Per Pupil Expenditure

Fiscal Year	Guaranteed Amount°	Expenditure Per Pupil°°	Ratio Guaranteed Amount to Expenditure (1 to . . .)
1982	$ 1,410	$ 2,327	1.65
1983	1,680	2,516	1.49
1984	1,835	2,811	1.53
1985	1,943	3,079	1.58
1986	2,080	3,322	1.60
1987	2,235	3,438	1.54
1988	2,280	3,622	1.59
1989	2,360	4,019	1.70
1990	2,530	4,349	1.72
1991	2,636	4,605	1.75
1992	2,710	4,857	1.79
1993	2,817	5,045	1.79
1994	2,871	5,218	1.82
1995	3,035	---	---
1996	3,315	---	---
1997	3,550	---	---

Note: The data are from the following publications of the Ohio Department of Education:
° *The Ohio Law For State Support of Public Schools,* A biennial publication.
°° *Cost per Pupil,* an annual publication.

By this time the complaints about the new formula were being heard and changes were being demanded. The complaints were heard by legislators and in 1981 the "equal yield" concept in the foundation program was discarded. The funding for the basic portion of the program was again based on a guaranteed amount per pupil. This guaranteed amount was comprised of a combination of state and local funds, the local contribution being that amount raised per pupil from a levy of twenty mills.

Table 2:3 represents the guaranteed per pupil amounts for the fiscal years 1982 through 1991. The guaranteed amounts in the first column do not reflect "cuts" that were made in a number of bienniums. This table also presents the state average expenditure per pupil for the same years. This illustrates one of the continuing problems of the adequate funding of public education in Ohio—the substantial difference between what the state is willing to guarantee and what it costs to educate the youth of the state.

2.20 The Enactment of House Bill 920

In 1975 when recommendations of the Syracuse study were enacted, the legislature enacted *House Bill 920.* This legislation has ever since affected the adequacy of funding Ohio's elementary and secondary schools. This bill has effectively limited the revenue from voted millage to the amount that the initial levy was to yield on all real property

Table 2:4
The Effects of H.B. 920 on the School Tax Rates of an Ohio School District

Levy Description	Voted Rate	Residential and Agriculture Effective Rate
Inside	4.22	4.2200
Bond	1.22	1.2200
1976 General Fund	20.90	10.2687
1977 General Fund	4.92	2.4181
1981 General Fund	5.00	3.0932
1984 Permanent Improvement	1.25	0.8448
1989 Permanent Improvement	0.50	0.3987
1995 Permanent Improvement	1.94	1.9400
Total	39.95	23.4035

Note: Data from the Ohio Department of Taxation. Rates for residential, agricultural properties are for the 1995 tax year payable in 1996.

(residential, agricultural, commercial, industrial, and public utility real property). As assessed values of real and personal property within the boundaries of a political subdivision increase, the rates on the classes of real property are effectively reduced.[36] This law limits the revenues from voted levies for all political subdivisions, but it affects the school districts more since they are so heavily dependent upon the voted levies for their income.[37] Tax reduction factors apply only to real property; they do not apply to inside millage nor are they applied to personal property valuations.[38]

2.21 Effects of House Bill 920 on One Local District

Table 2:4 illustrates the rate reductions for one suburban school district. It should be noted that on the first line of data in this table the inside (unvoted) millage is not affected by this law.

The levy approved by the voters in this district in 1977 for 4.92 mills was effectively reduced to 2.4181 mills on residential and agricultural property for the 1991 tax year. This represents a 49% reduction in the tax rate approved by the voters in 1977 on residential and agricultural property. Thus, there was no growth realized in the revenue raised from this levy on residential and agricultural real property.

The district did realize an increase in the revenue when new construction was added to the duplicate and from increases of personal property taxes paid by businesses. It should be noted that during this fourteen year period the consumer price index increased from

---

[36] Ohio Rev. Code Ann. §§ 319.301, 5713.01, 5713.04.1, 5715.24, 5715.33, 5715.34. For a more detailed discussion of the tax reduction factor, as it relates to reductions in voted tax levies, *see* Robert T. Baker & Kimball H. Carey, OHIO SCHOOL LAW GUIDE (Cincinnati, Ohio: Anderson Publishing Co., 1992), §§ 5.24, 5.25 [hereinafter OHIO SCHOOL LAW GUIDE].

[37] OHIO SCHOOL LAW GUIDE at § 5.24.

[38] *Id.*

60.6 average for calendar year 1977 to a 132.4 average for calendar year 1991, an increase of 118.82%.

2.22 Aid to Non-Public Schools

In the late 1960s the legislature authorized the first provision for aid to non-public schools. This aid was in the form of providing transportation for non-public pupils. The enactment increased the cost for elementary and secondary education in Ohio. No line item for this added expenditure for the transportation of non-public school pupils has ever been included in the State's biennial appropriation measure even though it was generally understood that one hundred per cent of such expenditures were to be borne by the State. As yet there has been no system developed to accurately figure the cost of transporting pupils to non-public schools. However, an internal memo within the Ohio Department of Education estimated this cost to be $31,656,795 for the 1988-89 school year or $234.16 per pupil for the 135,191 non-public pupils being transported. Legislation enacted in 1973 also added to the cost of elementary and secondary education when the General Assembly approved monies for "auxiliary services." This act provided monies for certain items used by non-public schools such as audiovisual equipment and certain curricular materials. However, this act was declared unconstitutional by the U.S. Supreme Court in *Wolman v. Essex.*[39]

Due to the court's action, a more carefully drafted law was enacted in 1975 which was more extensive than the 1973 bill. This law was also tested in the U.S. Supreme Court in the case of *Wolman v. Walter.*[40] The basic components of this bill were upheld by the Court.

Table 2:5 presents data showing the amounts of the appropriations (exclusive of transportation moneys) made for the non-public schools since the enactment of the laws that permit aid to such schools in Ohio.

Considering the $14,905,929 of reimbursement from the State for the transportation of non-public pupils in FY 1991, one can see that the state's expenditure (budgeted and reimbursed) for non-public school pupils exceeded $104,000,000 for that fiscal year. This figure does not take into consideration the cost that exceeds the reimbursed amount for transportation that must be borne by public school districts. The average cost for transportation of pupils in FY 1991 was $256.07 per pupil. Thus the total cost for just transporting the 136,292 non-public pupils exceeds the reimbursement from the state by nearly $20,000,000.[41]

It should be noted that Amended Substitute House Bill 117[42] increased the non-public administrative cost reimbursement from $100.00 to $150.00 per pupil starting in fiscal year 1996. This 50% increase in the authorization expanded the authority to reimburse

---

[39] *Wolman v. Essex*, 421 U.S. 982 (1975). *See infra* chapter 12.

[40] *Wolman v. Walter*, 433 U.S. 229 (1977). *See infra* chapter 12.

[41] Two page document produced by State of Ohio Department of Education, Division of School Finance, Pupil Transportation Analysis, Program: 140386 dated March 3, 1993, at 705. Page 2 of document is titled "Pupil Transportation Statistics."

[42] *See* Ohio Rev. Code Ann. at § 3317.063.

Table 2:5

Line Item Amounts Appropriated by the Ohio General Assembly for Aid to Non-Public Schoools Since 1973

Type of Aid

Fiscal Year	Auxiliary Services	Administrative Costs	Mobile Unit Repair	Total
1974	$ 3,239,150	N.A.	N.A.	$ 3,239,150
1975	3,039,150	N.A.	N.A.	3,039,150
1976	44,400,000	N.A.	N.A.	44,400,000
1977	44,400,000	N.A.	N.A.	44,400,000
1978	44,400,000	N.A.	N.A.	44,400,000
1979	44,400,000	N.A.	N.A.	44,400,000
1980	45,400,000	N.A.	N.A.	45,400,000
1981	45,400,000	N.A.	N.A.	45,400,000
1982	45,400,000	$ 2,250,000	N.A.	47,650,000
1983	41,831,560	9,306,140	N.A.	51,137,700
1984	46,965,140	10,025,525	N.A.	56,990,665
1985	49,949,309	10,667,137	N.A.	60,616,466
1986	55,593,581	11,872,523	$ 5,000,000	72,466,104
1987	60,597,003	12,941,051	5,000,000	78,538,054
1988	61,473,396	13,283,050	1,000,000	75,756,446
1989	63,133,178	13,641,693	1,000,000	77,774,871
1990	68,335,351	14,765,769	1,000,000	84,101,120
1991	72,483,307	15,662,051	1,030,000	89,175,358
1992	72,483,307	15,662,051	1,030,000	89,175,358
1993	76,107,472	16,445,154	1,030,000	93,582,626
1994	78,771,918	17,020,734	1,070,170	96,862,822
1995	81,528,227	17,616,460	1,111,907	100,256,594
1996	85,408,337	34,921,510	1,147,488	121,477,355
1997	91,386,921	35,434,515	1,191,093	128,012,529
Total	$1,326,126,307	$251,515,363	$20,610,658	$1,598,252,328

Note: Figures from annual appropriation measures, passed by the General Assemblies, for the years indicated.

non-public schools significantly. The appropriation reveals more than a 50% increase as revealed in administrative cost column of table 2:5. This is a result of an under appropriation in previous years.

2.23 The Lottery

The legislature enacted legal provisions in 1975 which permitted the state to operate a lottery. Table 2:6 presents data pertaining to the amounts that have been received and distributed to education from ticket sales since the beginning of the lottery in Ohio. Most of the lottery receipts distributed to Ohio schools replaced similar amounts that had originally been appropriated in the state's budget.

2.24 Changes in Foundation Program

No comprehensive statewide study of elementary and secondary education in Ohio has

Table 2:6

Receipts of the Lottery Commission and the Amounts Distributed to Education for the Fiscal Years 1975 Through 1991 (in $1,000,000)

Fiscal Year	Total Sales	Profit
1975	$ 91.9	$ 30.5
1976	120.9	46.8
1977	142.0	60.5
1978	101.0	44.1
1979	68.1	21.7
1980	126.0	36.7
1981	296.7	110.1
1982	364.9	144.0
1983	399.0	145.0
1984	604.3	250.0
1985	855.6	338.4
1986	937.0	370.0
1987	$1,068.2	376.0
1988	$1,375.8	406.0
1989	---	537.3
1990	---	595.3
1991	---	676.2
1992	---	660.5
1993	---	685.2
1994	---	646.0
1995	$2,182.3	645.4

Source: Ohio Lottery Commission, September 12, 1995 communication from Paul Wasilewski, Public Relations, Ohio Lottery Commission.

been made that would be comparable to the studies that led to the major changes formulated by the legislative sessions held in 1955 and 1975. However, numerous changes have taken place since 1975. The equal yield formula has been abandoned for a formula that provides for a guaranteed amount per pupil for basic aid. This portion of the formula provides for basic equalization on the basis of a 22 mill local share deduction. A new variable in basic aid is the school district equalization factor. This factor, also known as the "cost of doing business factor" was added to the formula to provide for the variations in the perceived cost of doing business in the 88 counties.

2.25 The School Income Tax

House Bill 694 was passed in 1981. This law permitted a board of education to place an income tax before the voters of the district. Such a tax could be a rate of .25%, 0.5%, 0.75%, or 1.0% for the residents of the district.[43] Voters in six districts throughout Ohio approved such a tax, but the voters, in one of the districts, later repealed the tax. In 1983,

[43] Ohio Rev. Code Ann. at § 5748.02. *See* OHIO SCHOOL LAW GUIDE at § 5.20.3.

the legislature, through Amended Substitute House Bill 291 repealed the authority to impose school district income taxes and precluded school districts from proposing any new income taxes after August 31, 1983.[44] However, school districts that imposed an income tax prior to that date were permitted to continue levying the tax.[45]

A law was again passed during the 1989 session of the legislature which permitted voters to approve an income tax for the support of schools.[46] Voters were then, and continue to be, enabled to approve rates that are rounded to the nearest one-fourth of one per cent.

2.26 Responsibilities of State Board of Education for Finances

Every two years the staff of the Ohio Department of Education, in consultation with selected members of the education community, prepares a report that is forwarded to the Ohio Board of Education. After reviewing the report, and making any modifications it chooses, the Ohio Board of Education forwards it to the governor and the legislature as is required by *Ohio Revised Code*, Section 3301.07. Parts "F" and "G" of this section of the code define the responsibilities of the Ohio Board of Education, in regard to the above, as follows:

> (F) Prepare and submit annually to the governor and the general assembly a report on the status, needs, and major problems of the public schools of the state, with recommendations for necessary legislative action and a ten-year projection of the state's public and nonpublic school enrollment, by year and by grade level;
>
> (G) Prepare and submit to the director of budget and management the biennial budgetary requests of the state board of education, for its agencies and for the public schools of the state.[47]

2.27 Recent Legislative Involvement

Instead of following the recommendations of the Ohio Board of Education, the legislature frequently forms committees of its own members to study problems. This tends to duplicate the study efforts of the Ohio Board of Education. For example, in 1987 the 117th Ohio General Assembly established four such committees to study elementary and secondary education problems. Again the 118th General Assembly in 1989, established several new committees and commissions to explore a number of continuing problems facing public education and to give legislative oversight.

One commission, the Commission of Education Improvement (comprised of five members of the Senate, five members of the House of Representatives, the Governor or his representative, a member or representative of the Board of Regents, and a member or representative of the Ohio Board of Education) was allocated over $90,000,000 for the biennium to duplicate many of the activities of the Ohio Board of Education and the

---

44 Ohio Rev. Code Ann. at § 5748.01.
45 *Id.*
46 Ohio Rev. Code Ann. at §§ 5748.01–.06. *See* OHIO SCHOOL LAW GUIDE at § 5.20.3.
47 Ohio Rev. Code Ann. at § 3301.07(F), (G).

Board of Regents. Among the items that the Commission was mandated to undertake were the following:

> Select, review and evaluate education programs operated at the elementary and secondary level; assess uses that school districts make of state monies; select and evaluate programs that are under the supervision of the Ohio Department of Education to determine whether the programs meet their intended goals; select and evaluate pilot projects; determine the cost of the various elements of the state's education delivery system; and evaluate vocational education in public schools and technical education in post-secondary schools.[48]

Amended Substitute House Bill 111, passed in 1989, created the Commission of Education Improvement in concert with *Amended Substitute Senate Bill 140.* In addition to general administrative duties, the Ohio Board of Education is required to "perform a wide and ever-changing variety of tasks specifically imposed by statute."[49] In addition, local school districts have additional reports required by these two bills.[50]

Amended Substitute House Bill 117, the biennial budget bill, was signed by Governor George Voinovich on June 30, 1995. While details of financial changes in the foundation program are discussed in Chapter 5, school choice[51] became reality for the first time in Ohio in the form of a voucher program. This bill established a state-funded program under which the Cleveland school district was designated a pilot project district to offer alternative educational choices to its students. Thus, a number of students in the Cleveland school district may receive scholarships either to attend private schools in the district or alternative public schools in adjacent districts. Barney Dunnan, Director of Legislative Services for the Buckeye Association of School Administrators, expressed concerns, shared by the authors, when he said:

> The Cleveland voucher program is questionable public policy and very unlikely (will) provide reliable research evidence.[52]

2.28 Summary

In summary, the following factors appear to have been characteristic of the funding of public education in Ohio since the early 1800s:

1. The people of Ohio have struggled since the inception of the state to provide an adequate education for their children.
2. Numerous studies of public education have been made in Ohio, but there appears to be an unwillingness to give public education the priority status that is needed.

---

[48] From two page undated and unnumbered publication of the Ohio Department of Education, titled "Duties of the Commissions Established by Amended Substitute House Bill 111 and Amended Substitute Senate Bill 140," at 1–2.

[49] OHIO SCHOOL LAW GUIDE at § 4.09.

[50] *See infra* chapter 11.

[51] Ohio Rev. Code Ann. at §§ 3313.974, 3313.975, 3313.976, 3313.977, 3313.978, 3313.979, and 3317.03.

[52] Barney, Dunnan, Legislative Report, Buckeye Association of School Administrators, July 19, 1995.

3. In a significant number of instances the legislature has frequently delayed the implementation of the recommendations dealing with finances.

4. Equalization of the funding of public education, although a desired goal, has not been achieved notwithstanding past and current efforts.

5. The "thorough and efficient system of common schools" clause in the *Ohio Constitution* remains realistically defined.

6. The direct involvement of Legislators in areas of school finance is to be expected and changes can be anticipated annually.

Chapter 3:
Economic Issues of School Finance

3.1 Intent of Chapter

This chapter is intended to provide an overview of selected economic issues related to school finance for the school finance practitioner; it is not intended to provide an in-depth study of education-related economics.[1]

3.2 Introduction

What is meant by the term *economics*? C. Benson is credited with noting that, "the central topic of economics is the allocation of resources and the central concept is scarcity."[2] R. Heilbroner, in a classic distillation of the concept of economics, has noted, "the economic problem is simply the process of providing for the material well-being of society."[3]

R. Johns, E. Morphet and K. Alexander further clarify the concept of economics by summarizing, "one of the simplest definitions is that economics is the study of human wants and their satisfaction."[4] They further note, "the economic system arranges for the production, exchange, and consumption of whatever is needed to satisfy human wants."[5] The above perspective of economics can be applied to the "business" of public education. The economic enterprise of education can therefore be understood as the process of allocating resources to public education for the betterment of mankind. Neither the allocation process nor the conceptual understandings are as simple as the statement above

---

[1] For a more definitive study of economic issues related to schools, the reader is referred to Roe L. Johns, Edgar L. Morphet, and Kern Alexander, THE ECONOMICS AND FINANCING OF EDUCATION, 4th ed. (Englewood Cliffs, NJ: Prentice-Hall, Inc., 1983 [hereinafter THE ECONOMICS AND FINANCING OF EDUCATION] and Tansy H. Jones, "Taxation for Education," in PRINCIPLES OF SCHOOL BUSINESS MANAGEMENT, edited by R. Craig Wood, (Reston, VA: Association of School Business Officials International, 1986).

[2] Charles S. Benson, THE ECONOMICS OF PUBLIC EDUCATION, 3rd ed. (Boston: Houghton Mifflin Company, 1968), at 5, in THE ECONOMICS AND FINANCING OF EDUCATION, at 10.

[3] Robert L. Heilbroner, THE ECONOMIC PROBLEM, 2nd ed. (Englewood Cliffs, NJ: Prentice-Hall, Inc., 1970), at 8.

[4] Johns, Morphet, and Alexander, THE ECONOMICS AND FINANCING OF EDUCATION, at 10.

[5] *Id.*

may imply. An understanding of basic economic concepts, however, will help to put the process into perspective and assist with comprehension of the dynamics involved in the term "economics" as it applies to the grand mission of public education.

3.3 Scarcity

The term *scarcity* refers to the relationship between an available supply of a given item and the consumer's demand for such. Two forms of demand exist. First, goods or services are sought by consumers to meet their personal wishes; thus, there exists a demand for consumer goods. Secondly, goods or services are sought to facilitate the production/delivery of goods or services to consumers; therefore, a demand for producer goods also exists. Regarding these demands or wants, J. Corbally, in his classic text on school finance, noted the following:

> In creating goods or services to meet both kinds of wants, four things—commonly known as factors of production—are necessary: natural resources; labor; tools, machines, assembly lines, etc., all known as capital; and the enterpriser, the agent who brings together the natural resources, the labor, and the capital for production.[6]

It is this scarcity in the factors of production which comprise the heart of basic economics. These economic issues lead very quickly to social questions. It is scarcity which forces state legislators to make tough decisions regarding requests for money from competing agencies. Scarcity can lead to teacher shortages or lower-than-expected salaries for a trained teaching force. The basic economic issue becomes one of allocating limited resources among various unlimited demands.

3.4 Education as an Economic Enterprise

A primary purpose of education is to increase the ability of the recipient to engage in a useful occupation or profession and, in turn, to produce other goods and services. This purpose is at heart an economic one since it provides the means to satisfy both consumer and producer demands. Few would argue that education adds to the richness of life, broadening the choices for consumer goods. Many "products" of literature, art, music, and so forth would not have been possible without enlightened and educated minds. Thus, education is literally a consumer's good as well as a producer's good.[7]

In the main, funds expended for school purposes "find their way back into the economy" in the form of school employees' personal purchases of goods and services, particularly since 75%-85% of schools' operating budgets are encumbered for salaries and benefits. In addition, approximately 30% of the expenditures for school payrolls is returned to federal, state, and local budgets in the form of income and sales taxes.

The total return of funds into the economy from school employee's personal purchases of goods and services as well as derived-taxes is magnified approximately two-and-one-

---

[6] John E. Corbally, Jr., SCHOOL FINANCE, (Boston: Allyn and Bacon, Inc., 1962), at 26–27. [hereinafter SCHOOL FINANCE]

[7] For the concept that education can be thought of as both a consumer's good and a producer's good, indebtedness is owed to THE ECONOMICS AND FINANCING OF EDUCATION, at 12.

half to three times the original amount by what is commonly referred to as the *multiplier effect*.[8] The multiplier effect is the result of the total expenditure for education being cycled through the economy.

Boards of education are frequently forced to make allocation decisions in which a choice must be made between institutional equity and financial efficiency. For example, it may be more efficient from a financial point of view to have music or art taught by the regular classroom teacher as part of the regular teacher's responsibilities; however, it may be more equitable with regard to program offerings or personnel assignments to hire a specialist for the instruction of such. The concept of *marginal utility* helps to explain the public's growing resistance to approve the allocation of funds for education. Marginal utility can be understood as, "the extent of desire for one more unit of [a good]."[9] Does the consumer, for example, receive a unit of satisfaction from the last dollar spent on schooling equal to the satisfaction that would have been gained from spending that dollar for clothing, an automobile or some other economic good? If the answer is "yes," the consumer may be receptive to additional taxes for the support of schools because he/she believes that the cost of good education is more important to society than the spending of the equivalent amount for his/her own, personal satisfaction.[10]

An economy grows only as individuals consume the products produced by the economy and demand more. Education raises the aspirations of a people and leads to consumer wants and "needs" which cause the economy to expand. Education—through the process of raising the level of wants and needs of the citizenry—contributes to a sound and expanding economy. In fact, few expenditures will serve to foster the expansion of an economy better than expenditures for public education.

3.5 Education as a Governmental Enterprise

Education became widely accepted as a governmental enterprise after the much-cited findings of a court case commonly referred to simply as "The Kalamazoo Case of 1874." The findings of *Stuart v. School District No. 1 of Village of Kalamazoo*, 30 Mich. 69 (1874), legitimatized the seeking of tax revenue for the support of a public education system. J. Corbally noted:

> The school district is a unit of state government—that is, it is a creature of the state legislature. Its powers and duties are delegated to it by the state legislature and it has no rights beyond those specifically granted to it by the state legislature.[11]

As a governmental unit, the enterprise of education has the responsibility to ensure qualitative minimums to meet public goals. Minimum standards are promulgated by state legislatures. Programs are prescribed for promotion and graduation. A funding system is

---

[8] Compare with Robert L. Heilbroner and Lester C. Thurow, THE ECONOMIC PROBLEM, 6th ed. (Englewood Cliffs, NJ: Prentice-Hall Inc., 1981), at 202.

[9] THE ECONOMICS AND FINANCING OF EDUCATION, at 16. Bracketed phrase is that of the authors of this manual.

[10] For the concept of marginal utility, the authors are indebted to THE ECONOMICS AND FINANCING OF EDUCATION, at 16–17.

[11] SCHOOL FINANCE, at 43.

established to provide at least a "foundation-level" of funding. A consequential corollary to this understanding holds that since the public school system is a governmental unit, control and regulation must be exercised over what is taught, how much is taught, how much is spent, and so forth.

As a governmental enterprise, education is subject to the collective will of the people through Congress, state legislatures, school boards, and the ballot box to determine the rate of spending for education. That rate of spending as well as how and where it is spent, may well have an impact on the quality of schools and the resultant educational outcomes.

3.6 Taxes and Education

Taxes shift resources from the private sector to the public sector to be used for education and other governmental enterprises. The taxation process is intended to distribute the "real" costs of education "fairly and equitably" among the taxpayers. Obviously, a firmly-held belief in the importance of a quality education as it accrues to the common good of all, will expedite the use of taxes to fund the educational enterprise.

Over 100 years ago, taxing property meant taxing wealth since those with great wealth were usually landowners. Today, however, the property tax is often considered to be a regressive tax; that is, it is not related to the ability to pay.

Ohio legislators have made several modifications in property tax laws to make the taxation of property less regressive. Legislation has granted an exemption from the payment of property taxes when the property is utilized for public or religious purposes; in addition, a 10% credit on all real estate taxes, a 2½% credit on owner-occupied homes, and a homestead exemption for senior citizens proportionate to their annual incomes reflect additional legislative steps to make property taxes less regressive.

The use of property tax abatements to spur economic development is a concept which is becoming more popular in Ohio. The term *abatement* is used here in the generic sense of "forgiveness of some or all taxes for a specified period of time in return for expected economic growth." For example, jobs, value of property, and so forth might be expected to accrue to a community in which a major enterprise is to be established.

An encouraging trend is the generally-held realization of the importance of economic growth and its relationship to education. Many schools in Ohio are entering into discussions and agreements with other political subdivisions to create economic growth and, thereby, increase the base of financial support for quality educational programs.

3.7 Sales Tax

The sales tax is largely a state-collected tax in Ohio; however, a local sales tax is permitted if approved by the voters of the corresponding governmental unit. Sales taxes benefit political subdivisions other than education. In order to make Ohio's sales tax less regressive, certain non-luxury and food items are exempted from the tax. Sales taxes grow with inflation to provide at least a moderate increase in revenue.

3.8 Personal Income Tax

Personal income taxes grow with the economy. They are widely considered to be taxes that are directly related to the "ability to pay" or taxpayer equity (fairness) issues. In Ohio, a local income tax can be approved by voters for school purposes. By late 1995, this type of tax had been approved in 115 school districts.

3.9 Debt

School districts in Ohio seek voter approval to enter into debt. This debt cannot exceed 9% of the total assessed valuation. As an economic issue, debt is a method by which revenue is transferred from savers to spenders. The availability of funds from savers has an impact on the "cost of borrowing" for the borrowing spenders. On the other hand, the bonds and notes used in generating the capital for schools will extend a certain return in investment to the saver or buyer of bonds and notes.

The above summarizes the major economic concepts related to public education on national, state, and local levels. Expenditures for education expressed as a percent of the gross national product (G.N.P.) have grown from 2.4% in 1954[12] to 4.5% in 1993.[13] Education also changes the desires and wants of the consumer. Education as an economic enterprise has a major impact in almost every community.

3.10 Questions from "Main Street"

The economic issues at the center of legislative debates are, indeed, very important; but to the individual on "Main Street," the economic issues may be reduced to some very pertinent questions. The understandings or misunderstandings that led to the surfacing of these questions will have a significant impact on a particular consumer's willingness to support education with his/her vote for additional taxes.

The answers offered by the administrator to the "man on the street" who asks one of these questions may well "spell the difference" between a defeat or victory at the polls. The writers of this text believe that the answers given to the persons asking the questions below may have a great impact on our school systems and the taxpayers on "Main Street, Your Town, Ohio." School administrators in Ohio would be well-advised to be cognizant of and understand the issues behind the questions which follow as well as to have and to offer a ready, polite, and appropriate response. The writers trust that this manual will assist the school administrator to respond appropriately to the following twelve questions:

1. "Didn't legislation ensure that my taxes would not go up when my property value increased?"
2. "Why do we have to vote for levies every so many years?"
3. "My taxes just went up, so why do you need a levy?"
4. "If we eliminated the 'fat' in the budget, couldn't we eliminate this proposed tax increase?"

---

[12] The percentage for 1954 is from the National Citizens Commission for the Public Schools, FINANCING PUBLIC EDUCATION IN THE DECADE AHEAD, (New York: National Citizens Commission for the Public Schools, 1954), at 6, in Corbally, SCHOOL FINANCE, at 146.

[13] The percentage for 1993 is from Thomas D. Snyder, Project Director and Charlene M. Hoffman, Production Manager, *Digest of Education Statistics*, 1994, National Center for Education Statistics (Washington: U.S. Department of Education, Office of Educational Research and Improvement), at 35.

5. "Doesn't an increase in my new construction values reduce my tax rates?"
6. "By having school year round, wouldn't we eliminate the need for additional money?"
7. "If enrollment is going down, why do we still need more money to operate?"
8. "Why should I support additional taxes for schools when my children are out of school?"
9. "Since you have a 'surplus' of money at the end of the fiscal year, why are you asking for a tax increase?"
10. "How can a district have any money to invest if it is 'broke'?"
11. "Couldn't we eliminate a lot of expenditures if we just taught the basics?"
12. "I hear the lottery fund is growing all the time; doesn't the increase in the lottery fund negate the need for any increase in property taxes?"
13. "Why doesn't the state provide more funds for our district, especially since our district lacks the commercial/industrial base to general additional local funds?"
14. "Why do some politicians continue to advocate taking money from wealthy districts to redistribute it to poorer schools? Aren't we already sending much more money to our General Revenue Fund through Ohio income tax than we have returned to our more affluent districts through the foundation program?"
15. "Will additional revenue really produce additional student achievement?"
16. "Won't fewer districts reduce administrative costs and therefore reduce need to additional taxes?"
17. "Additional money was provided in the past and quality of schools declined. What will be different now?"
18. "Why has vocational education funding experienced a loss in parity as compared to basic aid?"

Chapter 4:
Local Funding of Ohio's Schools

4.1 Introduction

The local funding of schools in Ohio has traditionally been linked to the taxation of property; however, in recent years the taxation of income has emerged as a secondary method.[1] Since both forms of taxes are designated for the support of schools and the voting public can choose either or both, it is important to understand how these taxes are collected and how they are distributed to schools. Property taxes in the State of Ohio provide over 7.1 billion dollars in tax revenue[2] of which approximately 70% is allocated for the support of public schools at the local level.[3]

---

[1] As of September 1, 1995 constituents of 115 districts have voted in favor of the local income tax option as a method for supporting their schools.

[2] The tax revenue is from Donald C. Berno, *Tax Facts* (Report 95-3), Ohio Public Expenditure Council, April, 1995, at 1.

[3] Calculated from information provided by Donald C. Berno, "Wide Disparities in Ability to Finance Local Education Programs—Revenue Gap Wide Despite State Aid," *Education Report* (Report 91-1), Ohio Public Expenditure Council, January, 1991, at 1–2.

The practice of funding public education through voter-approved property taxes reflects a tradition established by voters in the nineteenth century. The reasoning employed originally to establish property taxes could be conceptualized as follows: ability and obligation to pay taxes should be in proportion to wealth which is most easily and accurately identifiable by property holdings. The owning of property was viewed as an index of taxing wealth, that is, owned property reflected a proportional ability to pay taxes.

4.2 Background

Generally, property taxes in Ohio do not increase significantly without a vote of the people; there are, however, exceptions that will be discussed later. According to information provided by the Ohio Public Expenditure Council, property taxes have increased *89.9%* during the ten-year period from 1984-1994.[4] *Personal income in Ohio rose an estimated 69.7%* during that same period. It is evident that property taxes increased at a *faster rate than has personal income.*[5] This has not happened automatically. The willingness of taxpayers to approve higher taxes in some school districts than in others has caused an inequitable situation for Ohio's public schools.

4.3 Variations in the Ability to Raise Taxes on Property

The ability to raise taxes varies in the extreme by a ratio of 31.1.[6] This disparity results in the following: it will take 31 mills of tax effort to produce the same amount of money per pupil in the poorest school district as it does with one mill of tax effort in the wealthiest school district.

When the total assessed property value in a school district is divided by the number of students, an index is derived. This index is commonly associated with the ability to generate taxes at the local level and is most commonly referred to as *valuation per pupil* or *per-pupil valuation*. A comparison of two public school districts will serve to illustrate and underscore the intrinsic funding inequity referenced earlier. The per-pupil valuation of the Huntington Local School District located in Ross County, for tax year 1994 (collected in 1995) was $17,569. Each mill of taxation in Huntington Local School District represents, therefore, an income of only $17.57 per-pupil.[7] Whereas, the district with the highest per-pupil valuation in the State of Ohio in 1995 was Cuyahoga Heights City School District located in Cuyahoga County; in this school district, the valuation per pupil was over $549,690.[8] In sharp contrast to Huntington Local School District, each mill in Cuyahoga Heights City School District produced an income for the school of $549.69 per student for 1995.

---

[4] The information regarding the increase in property taxes was extracted from Berno, *Tax Facts* Report (95-3), at 1.

[5] Compare with Don C. Berno, "School Property Taxes up 3.7% in 1994 (up 33.7% since 1989)," *Education Report* (Report 94-9), Ohio Public Expenditure Council, September, 1994, at 1.

[6] Extrapolated from data provided by the Ohio Department of Education Division of Tax Analysis and Local Government Distribution, "School District Taxable Property Values," *TAX DATA SERIES* (Table SD-1), June 8, 1995.

[7] Information regarding Huntington Local School District was taken from *Ibid.*, at 10.

[8] Information regarding Cuyahoga Heights City School District was taken from *Ibid.*, at 3.

In fiscal year 1995, the twenty school districts with the highest valuation had an average of $253,459 while the twenty school districts with the lowest valuation had an average of $24,832.[9] When comparing the lowest 20 district valuations with the highest 20 district valuations in terms of per-pupil valuations, a disparate millage per pupil is noted! This inequality of valuation per pupil exceeds a ratio of ten to one. Simply stated, it takes more than ten mills of effort by the average of the 20 poorest school districts to equal the income of one mill enjoyed by the average of the wealthiest 20 school districts.

4.4 Basic Concepts and Functions in Property Taxation

4.4-1 Property Classification

Before attention is focused on local taxes, certain understandings and definitions are important to have in mind. First, property taxes are divided into two major types as follows: taxes on real estate and taxes on personal property. Too often, people have referred to property taxes as being synonymous with real estate taxes. In reality, real estate is only one part of the property tax base. Real estate taxes include taxes on land and buildings. Personal property taxes are those taxes levied on furniture, fixtures, equipment, machinery and inventory of businesses, industries and public utilities. Real estate is further classified as "agricultural," "residential," "commercial," or "industrial" properties; and in addition, two related categories have been established as "oil and gas," and "real estate of public utilities."

When agricultural and residential valuations are combined, they constitute *49.3%* of all property taxes used for the support of schools. The other *50.7%* is collected from the business and industry real estate and personal tangible tax categories. On an average across the state (but not as a percentage of each district), businesses and industries are paying the majority of the taxes for the support of schools. District-to-district variations are significant, with as little as 4% of the total taxes collected from agricultural and residential taxpayers in a particular school district to 80-85% of the total taxes from these same two categories in another district.[10]

4.4-2 Exempt Real Estate Property

There are several definitions that are important to keep in mind in order to understand property taxes in general. "Exempt property" is property that is exempt from taxation. This exemption is granted by the Ohio Department of Taxation based upon the approval of a completed application for such. Tax exempt status is normally granted to property owners such as governmental agencies, charitable organizations, churches, and cemeteries.[11]

In order to receive exempt status, the property must not only be owned by a tax exempt

---

[9] Extrapolated from data provided by the *Cupp Printout, April 21, 1995 Ohio Department of Education.*

[10] Extrapolated from information provided by Donald C. Berno, *Education Report* (Report 94-9) September, 1994-2.

[11] *See* Ohio Rev. Code Ann. §§ 5709.07, 5709.08, 5709.10, 5709.111, 5709.12, 5709.121, and 5709.14. *See also* Ohio Const. art. XII at § 2.

agency or organization, it must be used for non-profit purposes. Tax exemptions must be applied for by the appropriate organizations in order to have the corresponding values removed from the tax duplicate by the Ohio Department of Taxation. A school district can request the Ohio Department of Taxation to notify it when an agency is requesting an exemption from property taxes.[12]

4.4-3 Tax Abatement

Tax abatement has become a generic term applied to various types of "tax forgiveness" granted by a governmental agency in return for expected economic expansion and development in the future. This includes foreign trade zones, rural and urban enterprise zones, increment tax financing, and other types of abatements. Local school officials should become involved with governmental agencies when such agencies are considering tax abatement policies. Decisions related to tax abatement options should be made only when all the facts are known and all agencies affected have had input at public hearings to determine what is in the best interest of the public.[13]

Abatement occurs as the result of either trying to entice a business to locate in a community or to encourage a business to expand. There is always the hope that new or enlarged plants will eventually increase the tax base and also create new jobs for community members. However, according to a Dayton Daily News editorial,[14] only two-thirds of expected jobs were actually produced by Ohio companies that had received incentive abatements. Legislative changes occurred in 1994 regarding abatements, reducing the percentage of incentive abatements. The article stated:

> Under the new law, localities alone no longer can abate 100 percent of taxes on new investments. The new maximum is 75 percent in incorporated areas and 60 percent in unincorporated areas. Because public school districts would receive the majority of the money abated, the cap can only be waived with school-board approval.
>
> Under the new law, school districts also will now get to negotiate with local governments for a share of income taxes from companies that gross $1 million annually.
>
> The tightening of conditions is a good way to keep companies honest, while still granting cities and states some leverage in competing with other communities.[15]

The negotiation process provided by the 1994 legislative enactment is now being applied by some Ohio school districts. One example of a city and school district reaching an agreement in which the city will rebate income tax dollars to the school district for economic development projects, occurred with Kettering City and the Kettering City Schools. In an article in the Dayton Daily News regarding the agreement to rebate, it was stated:

> The agreement allows the city to rebate to the school district a portion of income-tax dollars generated by job-creation projects in conjunction with the Ohio Enterprise Zone

---

[12] *See* Ohio Rev. Code Ann. at § 5709.83.
[13] *See infra* chapter 16.
[14] Editorial, "Tighter tax abatement fairer to the school," Dayton Daily News, July 16, 1994.
[15] *Id.*

law. The agreement applies to income-tax revenues from all new jobs created from any tax-abatement projects.

"We just took that legislation one better by saying we would share for all projects in which the school district forgoes property taxes and the abatement project creates new jobs," Kettering City Manager Steve Husemann said. "We feel it's only fair. The agreement lets us both share in the benefit of economic growth while enhancing the overall economic development climate in the community."[16]

Legislation that reduced abatement maximums was certainly a move in the right direction as it will reduce property tax losses to school districts. Actions witnessed between the cooperative agreement between the city and school district in Kettering is commendable. Cooperation and compromise are desirable attributes.

School personnel must be diligent to see that the school's interests are represented.

1. A school district representative is required to sit on tax incentive review councils to monitor compliance and make recommendations.
2. School districts must receive advance notice of at least 14 days before formal action.
3. School districts have authority to disapprove abatements when the request exceeds certain limits, either in percent abated or time of abatement.
4. School districts may negotiate for compensation. Municipalities *must* negotiate when the new payroll created by abatement exceeds one million dollars. School district personnel are advised to make abatement work for school districts, too, when the abatements are a certainty.[17]

4.4-4 Function of the County Auditor

The county auditor has statutory authority for setting the market value of real property within the county for tax assessment purposes.[18] Prevailing prices paid for similar properties in similar locations are utilized by the auditor to assist in the establishment of a market value to be used for taxing purposes. The statute provides:

> In determining the true value of any tract, lot, or parcel of real estate under this section [of the statute], if such tract, lot, or parcel has been the subject of an arm's length sale between a willing seller and a willing buyer within a reasonable length of time, . . . the auditor shall consider the sale price of such tract, lot, or parcel to be the true value for taxation purposes. . . .[19]

A true sale will ultimately establish market value, provided that there have not been any significant losses or improvements to the property subsequent to the sale.[20] The

---

[16] Katherine Ullmer, "City to share with Kettering Schools," Dayton Daily News, June 28, 1995.

[17] For a complete review of abatement see Baker's 1995-1996 *Handbook of Ohio School Law*, section 5.20.2, at 206–208.

[18] Ohio Rev. Code Ann. at § 5713.01.

[19] Ohio Rev. Code Ann. at § 5713.03.

[20] *Id.*

assessed value or taxed value is 35% of the market value. The auditor is also responsible for the distribution of money received from property taxes, both real and personal property.

4.4-5 Function of the County Treasurer

The county treasurer is the tax collector and banker for the county. The treasurer ensures that taxes have been collected and deposited before they have been certified for distribution to the various political subdivisions by the county auditor.

4.4-6 Sexennial Reappraisal

Ohio law requires that an actual visual appraisal of each parcel of property be completed at least once every six years.[21] This is called a "sexennial reappraisal." Once the market value (inclusive of land and improvements/buildings) has been determined, it is multiplied by the rate of assessment to determine the assessed value of property. The assessed valuation is that portion of the total market value which is to be taxed by the appropriate voted millage. Since Ohio's rate of assessment is 35%, taxes are paid on only 35% of a property's value, not the full, true market value. Not only does the specified rate of assessment decrease the total possible funds which could be generated by property taxes, but, in many cases property is simply undervalued even before the assessed rate is applied.

4.4-7 Triennial Update

In addition to the sexennial reappraisal required every six years, a triennial update is required three years after the sexennial reappraisal.[22] The triennial update is intended to adjust previously adjusted market values to reflect current prices paid; this update, however, is accomplished without a visual inspection of real estate parcels. It is accomplished, rather, by comparing the price paid for previously sold property with the tax values of similar property in that particular governmental subdivision and/or county area.

In addition to completing the triennial update, the county auditor is responsible for annually adjusting property valuations to reflect current market values; therefore, it is within the auditor's purview to initiate annual updates with only the reappraisal being completed by physical inspection of property parcels.

4.4-8 Budget Commission and Taxes

In addition to the aforementioned responsibilities of the county auditor and county treasurer, the auditor and treasurer of the county serve with the county prosecutor to comprise the county budget commission.[23] The county budget commission receives budget requests in order to approve the use of inside millage provided for in a manner consistent with the provisions of the *Constitution of the State of Ohio* and in order to approve the

---

[21] *See* Ohio Rev. Code Ann. at § 5713.01. *See also* Ohio Rev. Code Ann. at §§ 5715.33, 5715.34.
[22] Ohio Rev. Code Ann. at §§ 5715.24, 5715.33.
[23] Ohio Rev. Code Ann. at § 5705.27.

use of outside millage consistent with voter approval. The budget commission can be expanded to include citizen-at-large members.[24]

4.4-9 Millage

A *mill* is a description of a property taxation rate with a value of one-tenth of one cent. It is commonly referred to as one dollar in tax for every one thousand dollars of property value. Another common way of expressing millage is as a decimal. As an example, 1 mill is expressed as .001. Ten mills is expressed as .01, and further, a 10-mill rate is equal to a 1% rate (0.01).

In Ohio, millage is referred to as "inside" and "outside" millage. *Inside millage* is the millage provided by the *Constitution of the State of Ohio* and is levied without the vote of the people to support governmental purposes. The "inside" portion in Ohio is limited to ten mills being available for all political subdivisions and charter cities. The average millage allocated to public schools in the State of Ohio is 4.6 mills out of the 10, with the balance being distributed to city, county and other local governments. *Outside millage* is synonymous with voted millage. These terms are derived from the section of the *Constitution of the State of Ohio* which permits the power of unvoted taxation up to 10 mills while providing for the possibility of additional voted (outside) millage.[25]

In practice, Ohioans tax the *assessed value* of property; the Constitution of the State of Ohio, however, permits taxes to be based on *true value.*[26]

4.4-10 Carryover Property

A very important term for the understanding of how millage is affected by increases in the value of real estate is *carryover property*. Carryover property is used to describe the value of the same property existing in the same classification of real estate in two different years. By definition, carryover property excludes any addition to the property value in the second year. Once the *same* properties are compared, a true inflationary rate can be determined which will be used to adjust real estate millage.

4.4-11 Current Agricultural Use Valuation

Current agricultural use valuation (C.A.U.V.) is a term used to refer to an amendment to the *Constitution of the State of Ohio* which allows agricultural real estate to be valued at its actual use value rather than its highest and best use or market value. This is an attempt to allow agricultural land to be taxed on its potentiality as a tool of crop production and not on its market value potential. This is accomplished through an application process to the county auditor and is based on such conditions as soil type, interest rates, price per bushel of certain commodities, and so forth. If the land is sold and used for something other than agricultural use, there will be a recoupment for the past three years for taxes

---

[24] *Id.*
[25] *See* Ohio Const. art. XII at § 2.
[26] *Id.*

not paid on the highest and best use or market value. In Ohio, the vast majority of agricultural land is classified as current agricultural use valuation property.

4.4-12 Tax Formula

The last, basic concept is a simple equation that determines tax when the value and rate are known. The equation can be stated as follows: *rate of taxation* (rate) times *valuation of property* (value) equals *taxes due* (tax). Figure 4:1 may help the reader to understand the functional aspects of the process.

Figure 4:1

Property Tax Equations

1. *Tax* equals *value* times *rate*
   or
2. *Rate* equals *tax* divided by *value*
   or
3. *Value* equals *tax* divided by *rate*

4.5 Recent History of Legislative Actions Affecting Property Taxes

The "*rate* times *value* equals *tax*" equation could be further expanded by explaining how the value is determined. The assessed rate of real estate is multiplied by the actual market value of real estate, the product of which is known as the *assessed value*. It is this assessed value that is taxed. Figure 4:2 may help the reader to visualize the concepts of determining assessed values and computing the amount of tax due on the assessed value.

A problem emerged with this process when different assessed rates were used on different classes of property. For example, typically in the 1960s, agricultural and residential properties were assessed at approximately 25% and sometimes as low as 15% of their market values, while commercial and industrial properties were assessed at 50% of their market values. This multi-tiered assessment practice was held to be in conflict with the constitutional provision mandating that "land and improvements thereon shall be taxed by uniform rule according to value."[27] The Ohio Supreme Court interpreted this constitutional provision as requiring "that real property, whether commercial, industrial, residential or agricultural, must be assessed on the basis of the same percentage of actual value."[28] Therefore, the court directed the Board of Tax Appeals "to see that all real property within the state of Ohio is assessed at a uniform percentage of its true value in money. . . ."[29]

---

[27] Ohio Const. art. XII at § 2.

[28] *State, ex rel. Park Investment Co. v. Board of Tax Appeals,* 32 Ohio St. 2d 28, 29 (1972). *See State, ex rel. Park Investment Co. v. Board of Tax Appeals,* 26 Ohio St. 2d 161, 164 (1971); *State, ex rel. Park Investment Co. v. Board of Tax Appeals,* 16 Ohio St. 2d 85 (1968); *State, ex rel. Park Investment Co. v. Board of Tax Appeals,* 175 Ohio St. 410, 413 (1964).

[29] *Park Investment Co.*, 32 Ohio St. 2d at 28; *Park Investment Co.*, 26 Ohio St. 2d at 162; *Park Investment Co.*, 16 Ohio St. 2d at 87. *See Park Investment Co.*, 175 Ohio St. at 413.

Figure 4:2

Figuring Property Tax

1.	$100,000	market value
	x .35	assessed rate (35%)
	$ 35,000	assessed value
2.	$ 35,000	assessed value
	x .030	millage rate (30 mills)
	$ 1,050	tax due

The rate chosen was 35% of the market value. It was obvious that the tax structure was going to be altered in a major way when property which had been previously assessed at 25% of the market value for residential and agricultural taxpayers was being raised to 35% of the market value, while commercial and industrial property which had been assessed at 50% of the market value was being reduced to 35%. The procedure which was ordered to implement this uniform assessing practice was proposed in *Senate Bill 455*, and was passed by the Ohio General Assembly in 1972.[30] *Senate Bill 455* directed that as inflationary increases occurred in real estate property values, the voted millage rate should be reduced to produce the same amount of money on the voted millage after reappraisal as the political subdivisions had received prior to the reappraisal.[31]

This was a simple mathematical issue. For example, at the next reappraisal, if all real estate increased by 10% on carryover value, the 10% figure was used to drive the millage down in order to produce the same amount of revenue for the school districts from their voted millage.

Senate Bill 455 worked from the school districts' point of view. School districts received no additional revenue from voted millage as a result of this adjustment. However, the individual taxpayer may have paid more taxes as a result of the adjustment in outside (voted) millage. In order to understand this, one needs to be cognizant of the fact that the millage rate was reduced on both real estate and personal property together. Personal property is classified separately from real estate; thus, it was not part of the appraisal (sexennial and triennial) process. Personal property had not been considered subject to the inflationary increase in values for this taxing purpose, yet the personal property millage rate was also reduced. To produce the same amount of tax revenue, real estate taxpayers paid more, and personal property taxpayers paid less. This was further complicated by the fact that an individual homeowner's real estate value may have increased more than the average of all real estate including agricultural, residential, commercial, business and industrial property. Such a taxpayer would then pay even more taxes, as a result of the higher-than-average property value increase on his property.

Senate Bill 455 was to be implemented over a six year period at the time of reappraisal.

---

[30] Ohio Rev. Code Ann. at §§ 5715.01, 5715.24.
[31] *Id.*

After four years of implementation statewide, the legislature passed *House Bill 920.*[32] One of the purposes of House Bill 920 was to stop the shift of taxes from personal tangible holdings to real estate properties. This legislation granted a tax credit to all real estate taxpayers in proportion to the increase of the appraised value of carryover property. This resulted in an *effective millage rate.* The effective millage rate became the actual millage rate payable for property tax liabilities.

The inside millage authorized by the *Constitution of the State of Ohio*, and the outside millage authorized by the taxpayers remained the same for the taxpayers of personal tangible property. The credit extended to real estate taxpayers was in direct proportion to the increase of the *average* increase in all real estate within a political subdivision. As long as the taxpayer's property increased at exactly the average rate of increase of all real estate, *House Bill 920* worked. However, the school district did not receive any additional revenue from its voted millage.

New problems began to emerge in the late 1970s when it was realized that the different classes of property were inflating at different rates. As an example in one county, in 1977 agricultural values increased at 30%, residential values at 25%, commercial property value at 13%, and industrial property value at 11%. The average increase in all real estate value was about 18%. The millage rate was reduced based on the 18% average increase. It is evident that agricultural and residential real estate taxpayers were going to pay more, whereas commercial and industrial taxpayers were going to pay less. There was a new shift within the real estate category. This shift was from commercial and industrial taxpayers to residential and agricultural taxpayers who paid more taxes. However, the net effect on school districts was that no additional revenues from the voted millage were received.

This led to a statewide constitutional amendment which passed in November, 1980, which re-classified the four major classes of real estate into two classes. Agricultural and residential property were grouped together and reclassified as *class 1.* Commercial and industrial property were placed in *class 2.* In the example cited above, this would reduce millage in proportion to a 27% increase in agriculture and residential property values resulting in a new effective millage rate for *class 1* property based upon that increase; whereas *class 2* property would have a new effective millage rate as a result of a 12% increase in commercial and industrial real property which results in a different reduction factor. Since 1981, two different millage rates have been applied to real estate property as a result of the allowance of a *tax credit* based on inflationary increases in real estate in each class; in addition, a third millage rate has been applied to personal property (both general tangible and public utility) that consists of both inside and outside millage.

Does this work now? This could be answered affirmatively as long as the taxpayer realizes that there is no guarantee that he will not pay more taxes when the inflationary rate of his property exceeds the inflationary rate of the average of all property in his group or class in the political subdivision. In the example cited above, as long as a homeowner's property increased at exactly 27%, the same as all agricultural and residential property,

---

[32] *See* Ohio Rev. Code Ann. at §§ 319.301, 5713.01, 5713.041, 5715.24, 5715.33, 5715.34. *See also* OHIO SCHOOL LAW GUIDE at § 5.24.

the homeowner would pay no more taxes on the voted millage. But, if a homeowner's property increases 35% in value, the effective millage rate is going to be reduced based upon a 27% increase in real estate value; thus the taxpayer will pay more taxes. Note that none of these bills provided a guarantee to individual taxpayers; namely, that as the inflationary rate changes on their properties, they would not pay more taxes. These bills were designed to result in a new effective voted millage rate based on the *average* increase in real estate property value.

As a result, Ohioans have three millage rates as follows: (a) the *personal tangible rate* (for business and industry and public utility property) which includes the sum of both the inside millage and the outside millage; (b) the *class 1 real estate rate* which includes both agricultural and residential millage as a result of this new, effective rate based on inflationary increases in these categories; and (c) the *class 2 real estate rate* which is assessed on all the other real property categories at a rate based on the average inflationary increase within the category.

4.5-1 Reappraisal's Impact Upon Schools

For schools, the reappraisal of real estate property means a reduction in the effective millage rate on real estate as long as property values are increasing. That effective millage rate, however, will not be reduced below 20 effective mills including the inside millage. Once a school district's effective millage rate is reduced to 20 mills, it can be reduced no further. Any further increases in property values for districts at this 20-mill level will produce additional revenue to the school district.

In addition, the reappraisal procedure means that the real estate taxpayers *as a group* will not pay any more taxes on their voted millage. However, the individual taxpayer may pay additional taxes on voted millage if the inflationary rate on that particular property increased more than the average real estate property in its class.

Another impact of the reappraisal procedure for school districts is that districts will not receive additional revenue except from the inside millage as property value increases. Inside millage is not reduced as a result of inflation or deflation.

If real estate deflates as a result of a reappraisal or a triennial update, the effective voted millage rate of each levy will be adjusted upward to produce the same amount of revenue per levy provisions. This occurs as long as the millage rate is not adjusted higher than that originally authorized by the voters. For example, a school district that voted a 9.0 mill levy (0.9%) the year before reappraisal during which deflation in real estate occurred, will not receive as much money from the 9.0 mill levy after reappraisal as it would have before the deflation. The 9.0 mill levy cannot be adjusted higher than it was originally authorized by the voters.

What increases *will* a school district receive? School districts can receive additional revenues from the following:

1. Inflationary increases in real estate for those properties where the effective millage rate is 20 mills.
2. Inside millage multiplied by the additional value of property.

3. Additional taxes as a result of an increase in the personal tangible value of property.
4. Additions to the duplicate or new construction in any of these categories multiplied by the effective millage rate for that class of property.
5. Previously approved phased-in (incremental) levy rate, dollar or percentage increase.

If these increases are not enough, and in most cases they will not be enough to keep up with inflation, the school district has no choice but to ask the voters for additional taxes to be levied on real estate and personal property. Of course, this assumes that no increases from the state or other sources make up the short fall.

School district personnel can estimate what could happen as a result of reappraisal by simply taking the values of the two classes of property in both years and working out a proportional calculation. For example, if the agricultural and residential value was $100 million before reappraisal, and now the carryover portion of that existing property is worth $120 million, a proportion of $100 million divided by $120 million is noted (100 divided by 120 equals .833). By multiplying that decimalized quotient times the previous year's effective voted millage rate, the result would be an estimate of what this year's effective voted millage rate would be (.833 times the previous year's effective voted rate of 30 mills equals 24.99 mills).

4.5-2 Special Considerations

Some school districts may continue to have some portion of their joint vocational school's operating millage calculated as a part of their 20 mills. This practice has been phased out for all but a very few districts in the state.

A second consideration to remember is that an emergency levy voted for a specific period of time will bring the stated dollar amount requested from the voters each year. The millage rate is simply reduced or increased to produce the same amount of revenue, depending on the property value. No reduction factor exists for emergency millage. It is either reduced or increased based upon what happens to the total property value in a given school district. Emergency levy millage is not inlcuded in the twenty mill floor.

A third consideration is the reduction factor that appears on the tax bill. This is a composite reduction factor based on all the levies from all the political subdivisions. The reduction factor for a particular levy would have to be known in order to calculate what those taxes would actually produce.

Another potential increase in fund revenues may be worth exploring if a school district is at or close to the 20 mill floor. This possibility involves moving a portion of a district's inside mills from its general fund to its permanent improvement fund. The Wapakoneta City School District requested and received approval from the Auglaize County Budget Commission in 1995 to activate such a change for their non-voted millage. In an article in the Lima News, it was stated:

The Auglaize County Budget Commission on Monday approved the school board's

> plan to shift 2 or its 4.5 inside mills from the schools' general fund to permanent improvements.
>
> The funding shift would generate an additional $317,000 a year for the school district. . . .the money can only be used for buildings, school buses, textbooks and technology.
>
> By state law, the budget commission could only consider the merits of the school's budget and if the school had a need for the additional money generated from shifting its millage.
>
> "Their need is in excess of the millage." said Auglaize County Auditor Karyn Schumann. "The need was shown."
>
> Under the plan, the district would move 2 of its inside mills from its general fund to its permanent improvement fund. Property taxes would probably go up because the county auditor would be required to assess 2 more outside mills to maintain the 20-mill state minimum for the district's general fund.[33]

A distinct advantage of shifting inside millage from its general fund to the permanent improvement fund, when a school district is at the 20 mill floor, is additional dollars with which to operate. As a district considers such a move, potential disadvantages should also be considered. One disadvantage could be that a budget commission could turn down a request if the need is not clearly evidenced. The biggest disadvantage, though, could be the negative reaction by property owners due to increased taxes without the vote of the people. Much care would need to be exerted to explain the rationale to the public and to gain their support.

The Wapakoneta Board of Education and Superintendent demonstrated care and wisdom in their bold move to shift millage by also placing an income tax issue for permanent improvements on the ballot, stating if the income tax issue passed that they would then rescind the transfer of millage. A one-fourth of one percent income tax issue passed by a 64 percent majority on August 8, 1995. At their next board meeting, the board followed through with their promise to voters and rescinded the shift of general fund millage to the permanent improvement fund.

4.5-3 Personal Tangible Value

One means by which districts previously received additional revenue, without asking the voters, was an increase in the tax receipts resulting from increases in personal tangible property values. However, in recent years that increase has been reduced considerably and in several situations the taxes declined sharply. Several reasons account for this. In 1983 the legislature passed *House Bill 260* which lowered the assessment rate on personal tangible value.[34] The rate in 1993 was set at 25% of value. Personal tangible property taxpayers were, therefore, to pay taxes on 25% of their personal tangible property values. Some years ago this rate was as high as 75%-80% which was later reduced to 50% and

---

[33] Russ Smith, "Commission Oks Wapak School Plan to Shift Millage," The Lima News, February 7, 1995.
[34] See Ohio Rev. Code Ann. at § 5711.22.

still later to 35%; and as a result of *House Bill 210*, the rate is decreasing from 35% to 25% over a 10-year period. This has dramatically slowed the increase in personal tangible taxes. As personal property values decrease, there is no rate adjustment upward to produce the same amount of revenue. A district that experiences a decline in personal tangible property valuation should anticipate losing actual tax dollars. This loss may result in a dramatic impact on the district's income and expenditures.

Personal tangible taxes have received a great deal of attention from the legislators in the last 20 years. First, legislation exempted agricultural equipment from being taxed as personal tangible property. Later, legislation excluded agricultural equipment owned by dealers. In addition, an exemption of $10,000 of tangible value was granted to all personal tangible property taxpayers. The loss of revenue from this latter exemption is reimbursed to school districts by the State of Ohio.

Businesses and industries have also impacted on the personal tangible value by modifications in the management of production. "Just in time" inventory systems are now the norm, and very few industries retain a significant inventory (materials or products) on which they would be required to pay personal tangible property taxes.

4.5-4 Reduction in Assessed Value for Telecommunications

In 1995, a reduction was made on the personal tangible value of the telecommunication industry. The value of long distance carriers and value of all new equipment for telephone and telegraph companies subject to taxation first in tax year 1995 was reduced to the same percentage as the personal tangible rate (25% in TY 1995).[35] This reduced valuations from 88% to 25% on much of the personal property of the telecommunication industry.

4.5-5 Minimum Millage (Floor) and Options for Revenue

School districts whose effective operating millage has been reduced to the "floor" or twenty mills have some items to consider when deciding what options to use for additional revenue.

Some revenue producers are not calculated as part of the minimum millage. Therefore, when reappraisal or triennial update occurs, the school district will receive 20 mills of taxes on the increased property values.

The following is a list of revenue options that will not be included in the twenty mill floor calculation:

1. income tax levy
2. emergency levy
3. incremental *amount* levy
4. permanent improvement levy

---

[35] See Ohio Rev. Code Ann. at § 5727.111.

4.6 Other Issues in Local Property Taxes for the Support of Schools

There are a few other issues dealing with local taxes that have been impacted by state legislation. First, a 10% tax credit was extended to every real estate taxpayer. The equivalent amount is paid to the political subdivision by the State of Ohio. This tax credit was enacted as part of the state personal income tax bill that passed in 1971. In order to "soften the blow" of an income tax, a tax credit on real estate was offered to taxpayers. The amount paid by the state on behalf of the real estate taxpayers represents a sizable portion of the state revenue to school districts.

Second, in 1979 a homesite exemption was allocated to those real estate taxpayers who lived in their own homes. This exemption remains in effect and amounts to an additional 2½% credit. The lost revenue from this exemption also continues to be reimbursed to the school district by the state.

Third, a homestead exemption is allocated to those taxpayers who are 65 years of age or over with an income ceiling of $20,800. Those individuals who are permanently disabled are also eligible. The ceiling was increased from $16,500 for fiscal year 1995 when the 121st General Assembly adopted the biennium budget for fiscal years 1996-1997. Homestead exemption credit is based on a graduated scale whereby the lower the income, the greater the forgiveness of taxes. Real property tax on a homestead owned and occupied by a person entitled to homestead exemption is reduced as follows: (a) If total income is $10,800 or less the taxable value is reduced by the lesser of $5,000 or 75 percent; (b) if income is more than $10,800 but not more than $15,800 taxable value is reduced by the lesser of $3,000 or 60 percent; or (c) if income is more than $15,800 but not more than $20,800, the taxable value is reduced by the lesser of $1,000 or 25 percent.

Fourth, as mentioned earlier, every taxpayer responsible for payment of personal property taxes receives an exemption of $10,000 value of personal property. The money not paid on this $10,000 exemption is reimbursed to the local political subdivision by the state.

Many other factors have resulted in the reduction of the tax revenue received by school districts from local real estate and personal property taxes, but these reductions have not been reimbursed by any governmental agency to the local political subdivision. These factors include the following: tax abatement, exemptions, enterprise zones, foreign trade zones, tax increment financing districts, current agricultural use valuation, credit on *House Bill 920* and the decline in the personal tangible assessment rate.

A very recent trend in the tax abatement issue reflects the potential for an agreement between the political subdivision granting an abatement and the school district which would or currently does receive income from the property. An agreement may be entered into which would authorize the political subdivision to make payments directly to the school district for amounts remaining after the abatement becomes effective.

4.7 The Local Income Tax for the Support of Schools

In 1989, the Ohio General Assembly again authorized a local income tax for the support of schools. In the November election of 1989, 82 school districts placed this local income tax option before the voters. Seventeen of those school districts were successful in their request for additional operating revenue from the local income tax. An additional six income tax options passed in February, 1990. As of September 1, 1995, 115 districts had an income tax approved.

A few comments are noteworthy regarding the local income tax option. First, this is a tax on the income of residents and not a tax on business and industrial income. The tax has no ceiling and it can only be levied in increments of one quarter percent. Once it is authorized by voters' approval, the income tax continues to be in effect for an unspecified time period; however, it is subject to repeal in five-year increments. A second option allows for an income tax to be voter approved for a limited period. A third option allows for a property tax reduction to be included in a ballot for income tax approval.

What income is subject to the income tax? An individual's adjusted gross income, minus a deduction for each exemption, is subject to the tax. Senior citizens are granted a $50.00 tax credit per return. From the school district's point of view, the local income tax authorizes a rate and will produce a growth in tax revenue parallel with the income growth of the school district's residents. It relies less on taxes from the agricultural constituency and, therefore, many farm citizens and agricultural agencies are supportive of the local income tax as an option.[36]

4.8 Permanent Improvement Levies

It is important to understand that permanent improvement levies will be factored by the same method as operating levies when real estate values change as a result of reappraisal.[37] Thus, the permanent levy will have three different millage rates applied after a district has experienced a reappraisal or triennial update. Permanent improvement levies can be approved for a maximum of five years or for a continuous period of time if used for ongoing maintenance and can be used only for costs related to the construction and equipping of buildings.

4.9 Types of Operating Levies

For the operation of schools, there are several types of levies available for a school district. These are:

1. Limited levy

The statutes[38] provide that an operating levy, approved by the majority of voters, may be for a limited period of time up to five years. When such a limited term levy is ready to expire, a board of education may choose to place it on the ballot as a renewal levy.

2. Continuing levy

This levy is for a continuing (or indefinite) time period. It would continue to yield the

---

[36] For a concise but detailed discussion of the advantages and disadvantages of the local income tax option for schools, the reader is referred to: Donald C. Berno, "School Income Tax Issues on Ballot in Forty-eight Districts—(Voters in Four Districts to Decide Repeal of Tax)," *Education Report* (Report 90-9), Ohio Public Expenditure Council, October, 1990, at 1–3.

[37] Permanent improvement levies will be more fully discussed in a later chapter on capital construction and capital outlay.

[38] See Ohio Rev. Code Ann. at § 5705.21.

same revenue regardless of how much the tax valuation of a district increased due to inflation. While it may seem that, once passed, by the electorate, a continuing levy would be guaranteed to be forever, it could in fact be voted out or reduced. One way this could happen would be via petition filed by not less than ten percent of qualified electors of a district voting at the last general election, to place the issue on the general ballot in November. This could only happen every five years.

Disgruntled voters in the Northmont School District (Montgomery County) had a tax-repeal vote in November, 1995 for a six mill continuing levy which had been approved in 1987, some eight years prior. A few other school districts over the state have experienced similar attempts to reduce taxes in a like manner.

3. Renewal levy

When a limited levy or emergency levy is ready to expire, it may be submitted to electors as a renewal levy. If approved by the voters, a renewal levy would continue to generate the same annual tax receipts, as the same tax reduction factor is applied. Voters usually approve a renewal levy as the advertising term "no additional taxes" seems to have appeal.

4. Replacement levy

Legislation passed in 1990 permits boards of education to propose to the electorate a replacement levy for an existing levy, including a limited levy ready to expire.[39] However, an emergency levy may not be resubmitted as a replacement levy.

The advantage of a replacement levy is that it generates additional income over the levy it replaces. It is considered a new tax for purposes of applying the tax reduction factor and therefore, has the net effect of negating earlier reductions on a levy. The nominal millage rate, if passed by the electorate, remains unchanged but the effective rate increases. As a result, voters must be advised that, if passed, a replacement levy will increase their property taxes.

5. Emergency levy

An emergency levy may be proposed to the electorate to provide the emergency requirements of a school district or to avoid an operating deficit. Such a levy may be proposed for[40] a maximum of five years. A request for an emergency levy is stated by proposing a specific number of dollars, rather than mills. A reduction factor does not apply, resulting in the same yearly yield for the duration of the levy. Upon expiration of an emergency levy, it may be resubmitted as a renewal levy.

School districts that are at the 20-mill floor, and can show evidence of need such as a forthcoming operating deficit, may want to consider placing an emergency levy on the ballot. If passed, an emergency levy would result in more revenue than a limited or continuing levy since the reduction factor would not be effected on a previously voted mills. Therefore, a district would have the yield from twenty effective mills plus the yield from the emergency levy.

---

[39] See Ohio Rev. Code Ann. at § 5705.192.
[40] See Ohio Rev. Code Ann. at §§ 5705.194, 5705.195.

6. Phase-in levy

Legislation in 1990 also created phased-in or "incremental" levies to help school districts cope with the limiting effects of reduction factors necessitating a need to continually ask the electorate to pass levies every few years. A phase-in levy can be submitted with a maximum of five separate levies for ten years. The duration of the levies would then be either a maximum of ten years, or for a continuing period of time. Each of the phased-in levies is considered a new tax for purposes of applying the tax reduction factor. Non-continuing incremental levies may be submitted to the electorate as renewable levies. Phased-in levies can also be phased-in by a specified dollar or percentage amount.

7. School income tax levy

School district officials must first determine an amount of additional money needed. The rate of tax is then determined by the Tax Commissioner and rounded to the nearest one-fourth of one percent. (See Text 2.25.) This tax levy can be submitted to the voters either as a continuing levy or as a levy for a specific number of years up to five years.

The income tax, when approved by the electorate, is paid by residents of the district. Residents sixty-five years of age or older get a $50.00 credit against the school income tax. However, state retirement benefits, unlike a city or municipality income tax, are subject to the school income tax.

School income taxes for current operating expenses are applied toward the 20-mill floor to qualify for the state foundation program. Also, under 1992 legislation,[42] boards of education may submit and advertise a school income tax issue with an accompanying reduction in school property taxes. It would appear this marketing technique may have merit.

4.10 Summary

A series of property tax policies has essentially neutralized increases in local revenue. These policies include the real property tax reduction factor, abatement policies, and the reduction of personal property tax assessment rates.

When real property values increase due to reappraisal or update cycles, the tax rates are reduced so that the district continues to collect the same amount of revenue from voted levies applied to the same property. Under the current method of real property taxation, a school district would have to pass an additional levy in order to generate more revenue, unless that district is at the minimum of 20 effective mills and/or receives substantial increases from new construction.

Beginning in the late 1960s, the tangible property assessment rates were reduced three times. By 1993, these rates were reduced to 25%. Since tangible property is taxed on the full, voted tax rate, rather than the reduced rate, school districts should continue to be able to experience increases from this source of property tax revenue if the value of personal tangible property continues to increase. However, since companies are now limiting their inventories and since the economy is shifting from manufacturing to service

---

[42] See Ohio Rev. Code Ann. at § 5748.02(B)(2).

industries, this property base has grown at a slower rate than anticipated. Many school districts dependent upon tangible personal property have had to pass additional levies to compensate for anticipated but unrealized revenue increases. The result is that more of the tax burden is shifting from the industrial tax base to the property owner tax base.

Thus, to generate additional tax revenue for increased costs and inflation, a district must pass an additional levy. An increase in real property assessed valuation provides an increase in tax revenue from inside millage but does not provide growth in revenue from voted levies. Additional revenue from personal tangible taxes can occur only when personal tangible valuation increases at a rate greater than the assessment rate declines.

The local side of funding schools is no longer easily explained. Generally, a school district will not receive additional local revenue without the taxpayers approving an additional tax rate. Individual taxpayers are not assured of experiencing a zero change in taxes unless their properties increase in value at the same rate as the average of all property in that class. Ohio's schools are sometimes faced with the dilemma of explaining that the schools are receiving no additional funds from the *voted* levies despite the fact that real estate taxpayers may be paying more. In an accountability model, this leaves the school with an "uphill task" to convince the voter that additional revenue is necessary.

The next chapter will include information related to the affect upon the state funding of schools by changes in property valuation.

Chapter 5:

State Funding of Ohio's Schools

5.1 A Historical Perspective

In an earlier chapter, references were made to the states' responsibilities for the funding of public education. In Ohio, that responsibility is made quite clear. In several instances in the *Constitution of the State of Ohio* references are made to the legislative imperative for the provision of public education by the recurring statement, "the general assembly shall" which prefaces various legislative responsibilities for the provision of education.[1]

Local responsibility for the establishment of and funding for elementary and secondary public schools is derived from the powers granted to local authorities by the state either through constitutional provision or legislative process.

---

[1] Ohio Const. art. I at § 7.

5.1-1 Foundation Formula—General Considerations

In Ohio, as in many other states, funds distributed to the local schools from the state are distributed through a foundation formula. The foundation formula was initiated in Ohio in 1935. The establishment of the foundation formula for the funding of public education marked a drastic change from earlier methods. In essence, the earlier methods of public school funding were characterized by the distribution of money to the public schools on a per-pupil basis regardless of any monies raised locally.

In contrast to the former method, the foundation formula provides a base or "foundation" of financial underwriting upon which school districts can increase revenue through various taxing means. Simply stated, the premise of the foundation program is that the state will assure that each school district has a foundation of adequate revenue to fund a "thorough and efficient" educational program.[2] With the foundation established, the local district through additional taxes, and the state through program funding, may add to the basic foundation program. The four basic assumptions inherent in the concept of funding by means of a foundation formula are as follows:

1. The school program can be "translated into dollars."
2. Program costs are the same from district to district, statewide.
3. Costs will be borne by a combination of tax dollars from both state and local sources.
4. Costs incurred which are beyond the minimum foundation program will be funded locally.

These assumptions reflect the principles of the foundation formula. Most foundation funding formulas begin by incorporating these assumptions and modifying them as necessary. Ohio's modifications will be explained later.

5.2 Various Mechanics of Distribution

State funds are distributed in a variety of ways to public schools across the nation. Most methods represent one of five main categories. Other methods of distribution are combinations of these five versions.

5.2-1 Flat Grant

The flat grant distribution of state money reflects the distribution of dollars on a per-pupil basis. It is simple, understandable, and easy to calculate. Through this method, monies are distributed to schools regardless of the need of the children (programmatic concerns) or the ability of the local school districts to raise taxes (equity concerns).

5.2-2 Weighted Pupil

The weighted pupil method of distribution reflects an extension of the flat grant program. In the weighted pupil approach, funds are distributed to school districts based upon the

---

[2] Ohio Const. art. VI at § 2.

number of "student units." Units are determined by the various program concerns. For example, students in grades four through six might be considered as 1.0 unit each; students in grades nine through twelve might be weighted as 1.2 each; students in the vocational program might be weighted as 1.7 each; and those with hearing handicaps might be weighted as 4.2 each. Once the sum of a school's units is determined, funds are distributed on a per-unit basis. This method represents a fairly simple calculation and distribution system. It takes into consideration the needs of students (programmatic needs) but does not address the local ability to raise taxes to support programs. One drawback in a weighted pupil approach is that it divides educational groups into various constituencies. Representatives of each group lobby toward increasing their own unit's assigned weight.

5.2-3 Power Equalization

Power equalization reflects an attempt to address the equity concern, that is, the concern that equal resources be provided for each student. Power equalization equalizes the dollars per mill of tax effort.

For example, if the state has established that every child should receive $120.00 in revenue for every mill voted by the local taxpayers, various scenarios could develop. A district with an assessed property valuation of $80,000 per pupil would receive $80.00 per mill ($1.00 of tax revenue for every $1,000 of taxable property value it is levied against) in local taxes and $40.00 per mill in state taxes for every mill of effort voted; however, the school district with $30,000 of assessed property valuation per student would receive $30.00 per mill from local taxes and $90.00 per mill from state taxes.

A variation of the power equalization system was established in Ohio in the mid-1970s and was termed *equal yield*. Equal yield was somewhat more complicated in that it required considerable calculation efforts to keep property values current. This program addresses the ability to raise revenue at the local school district level for every student as well as for every mill of effort voted while at the same time allowing a great deal of local control; however, in and of itself, it does not address program concerns.

Yet another variation of the power equalization system is known as *guaranteed tax base*. The guaranteed tax base strategy "guarantees" funding consistent with a predetermined minimum property valuation per pupil. For example, a guarantee of $150,000 property valuation per student will generate $3,000 in revenue per student for 20 mills of effort.

5.2-4 Foundation Formula

The funding of public schools through the means of a foundation formula combines both state and local revenue to provide a "thorough and efficient" program. Conceptually, foundation formula funding can be reduced to two simple equations as follows: (a) A (the amount per student determined by the state for foundation funding) times E (the district's student enrollment) equals T (the total foundation amount for the district); and (b) T (the total foundation amount for the district) minus L (the local share of the foundation program), equals S (the state's share of the foundation program, commonly referred to as "state basic aid").

Simplified, the two equations are as follows: (a) $A \times E = T$, and (b) $T - L = S$.

The foundation formula method of funding schools takes into account the ability of school districts to raise tax revenues as well as the state-determined minimum amount necessary per student to provide an adequate education.

5.2-5 Percentage Equalization

The percentage equalizing formula equalizes the amount realized by the local effort of poorer districts with that realized by corresponding effort of wealthier districts.[3] The percentage equalizing formula neutralizes differences in fiscal potential while giving incentives for local effort. Under this approach, the dollar level of the local educational program is a function of local tax effort but not of fiscal capability. A low valuation school district with a high millage rate or effort will be able to maintain the same quality of educational program as a higher valuation school district with similar millage rates.

Philosophically, the percentage equalizing formula is different from the foundation program in that it utilizes a variable unit formula. The foundation formula assures a uniform level of funding established by the state. The percentage equalizing formula provides funding for a school which does not have the ability to fund education at the predetermined 100% statewide average rate. This method is based on both funding capability (taxing base) and funding effort (actual school district expenditures).

The local capability to raise funds based on per-pupil property valuation can be expressed as a percentage of a statewide criterion. Given the assumption that the statewide capacity to raise funds (based on the average per-pupil property valuation) is equivalent to 100% per pupil, a local district's capacity could be expressed as a comparative percentage. In other words, a capability ratio or comparative percentage can be computed to reflect a local district's potential for generating funds versus the state-wide standard. Such a ratio or percentage would compare the statewide standard with the local capability to generate tax dollars on a per-pupil basis. The derived ratio or percentage could, in turn, be utilized to equalize funding on a per-pupil basis.

For illustration purposes, assume that District *A* has a per-pupil valuation of $40,000 and that the predetermined statewide standard or "touchstone" for appropriately funding public education is a per-pupil valuation of $70,000. The percentage of the local ability to fund education compared to the statewide ability could be expressed as, "40 divided by 70" or a resultant percentage factor of 57.14%. In this example, the state aid ratio (S.A.R.) would be 42.86% which is the difference between the 57.14% ability-to-fund-education factor of the district and the 100% statewide figure. This state aid ratio figured on a per-pupil basis would be applied to the previous year's expenditure level (funding effort) multiplied by the total number of district students. If the district has 2,500 students and a $3,500 per-student expenditure factor, the state aid would be determined by multiplying the factor as follows: 42.86% (state aid ratio) times $3,500 (effort factor) times

---

[3] Roe L. Johns, Edgar L. Morphet, and Kern Alexander, *The Economics and Financing of Education*, 4th ed. (Englewood Cliffs, N.J.: Prentice Hall, 1983), at 253–56.

Figure 5:1
Illustrations Depicting Application of Ohio's Percentage Equalization Formula

	District A	District B	District C
Per-Pupil Valuation (Capability)	$40,000	$40,000	$30,000
Per-pupil Expenditure (Effort)	$3500.00	$4000.00	$3500.00
Enrollment	2500	2500	2500
Average Statewide Per-pupil Valuation (State Standard)	$70,000	$70,000	$70,000
State Aid Ratio (Percent of funding from State Sources)	42.86%	42.86%	57.14%
Total Amount of State Aid	$3,750,250	$4,286,000	$4,999,750
State Aid Per Pupil	$1500.00	$1714.00	$1999.90

2,500 (students). These factors multiplied together result in a product of $1500.10 per pupil of state aid for District *A*.

Assume a second district (District *B*) with the same funding capability as District *A*; however, despite the similar capability level, District *B* actually expends a greater amount. In this case, state aid to the district would increase in proportion to the district's increased expenditure effort.

A third example might be a district (District *C*) with less funding capacity but similar effort than District *A*; however, District *C* demonstrates an expenditure level equivalent to District *A*. Both the percentage and amount of state aid would increase in this case due to the fact that despite District *C*'s greater limitations, its actual expenditures are equivalent to that of District *A*.

The situations described above for districts *A*, *B*, and *C*, can be most easily noted by reviewing Figure 5:1.

Advantages of the percentage equalization concept include the following:

1. State aid is proportionately related to the real expenditure level (effort) of a district.
2. The equalization methodology can be fairly automatic.
3. Once the factors from the previous year are known, the calculation for the following year's state aid level can be accurately determined.
4. Waiting for the finalization and approval of an annual or biennial state budget would no longer be necessary in order to determine formula factors.
5. The concept and factors can be easily amended to include the income figures of a school district's residents in order to utilize such to determine a district's fiscal capacity.

The disadvantages of the percentage equalization concept include the following:

1. Since state appropriations are to reflect local capacity and effort in this funding

Figure 5:2

Comparison of Selected State Funding Models

	Program Needs Considered	Equity Concerns Considered	Simple
Flat Grant	No	No	Yes
Weighted Pupil	Yes	No	Yes
Power Equalization	No	Yes	No
Foundation Formula	No	Yes	No
Percentage Equalization	No	Yes	No

model, the Ohio General Assembly would be placed in a reactive as opposed to a proactive mode.

2. The percentage equalization concept prescribes no state educational plan.
3. The concept does not allow for state response to local need unless rather significant expenditures (efforts) have been made by an already "needy" district which is not in a position to expend significant sums of money.
4. The percentage equalization model would require vast sums of state revenue to equalize the buying power of the poorer/poorest school districts with that of the wealthier/wealthiest districts which share corresponding patterns of effort.
5. The plan does not mandate a required minimum level of local effort.

5.2-6 Synopsis of Distribution Mechanics

In Ohio, as in many other states, the state's distribution of funds to public schools is based on a combination of the elements from the above-referenced models. In some cases, a more sophisticated version is employed.

Figure 5:2 represents an overview of the five different mechanics of the distribution of state funds.

5.3 Equalization and Equity

Two terms which are often cited but frequently misunderstood are *equalization* and *equity*. An understanding of the concepts embodied by these terms is imperative for a solid grasp of both the historical perspective of Ohio's school funding pattern as well as the state's future funding directions.

5.3-1 Equalization

Equalization is not only accepted to include the concept of consistent district-to-district state and local revenue but has also been linked with the concept of educational opportunity for students or program needs. Historically, various attempts have been made to take into account concerns of equality of funding or "equivalent opportunity for students." The first attempt at parity funding sought to equalize resources or minimize the differences of the resources available for each child. Traditionally, power equalization and foundation formula funding approaches have been employed to provide equality funding opportunities for students in various school systems statewide. Both approaches have been used to assure that the combination of state and local revenues produce a pre-determined, per-student, minimum level of support. Parity concerns for program offerings related to student needs have resulted in "categorical programs." In these instances, funds are distributed to schools based upon a particular category identified as a program need for students; this distribution occurs regardless of local district wealth.

Other attempts to assure equivalent programs among schools have resulted in state minimum standards prescribed by state boards of education representing the citizenry. Some attempts have been prescribed by court rulings. Where it has been adjudicated that certain issues of a constitution or law have been abrogated, some courts have suggested or mandated remedies which include specific funding levels and processes as well as specific programs for certain needs, issues and concerns.

5.3-2 Equity

The issue related to *equity* requires additional commentary. The key equity issue that has emerged as a guiding legal principle is that of "fiscal neutrality." This concept holds that the quality of public education should not be a function of local wealth. This principle is violated when wide disparities in funding exist among districts. For example, when high-wealth districts can pay teachers higher salaries, purchase better equipment, provide more programs and build better facilities than low-wealth districts, the principle of equity for students is understood to be violated.

A possible "working definition" of equity that addresses equitable revenue and program needs may be expressed by the following axiomatic definition. Equity is "providing similar revenue for children with similar educational needs and different revenues for children with different educational needs regardless of district wealth."

Equity is a major issue to address as state funds and local resources attempt to reflect educational needs and local preferences rather than differences in local wealth.

5.4 Ohio's Formula for Distribution of Funds to Schools

5.4-1 General Issues

According to Mathew C. Cohen, Ohio's policies regarding school funding can be divided into two types—*explicit* and *implicit*. Explicit funding policies are those which are clearly promulgated by force of law; implicit, are those which are derived from implications of explicit law.[4]

---

[4] Mathew C. Cohen, "State Policy Toward Education Finance," *Ohio School Boards Association Journal* Vol. 28, No. 4 (April 1984), at 14–16.

5.4-2 Explicit School Funding Policies

The explicit policies of Ohio's funding formula include: (a) a local funding responsibility; (b) some equalization; (c) various systems of schools to deliver, educational services; for example, local, city, exempted village, county and joint vocational schools; (d) unit funding or categorical programs for certain programmatic needs; and (e) state aid to non-public schools.

5.4-3 Implicit School Funding Policies

Implicit policies emanating from Ohio's formula for distribution of funds to schools include the following: (a) a constrained local control of expenditures (the taxpayers' willingness to tax themselves is a major factor of funding in Ohio); (b) no limit on expenditures or revenues to be spent on education (Ohio's program establishes a minimum but does not establish a maximum amount that can be received or expended); taxpayers willing to do so in Ohio can accomplish the receiving and allocation of more than the minimal amount by approving taxes which are above and beyond the foundation level); (c) no funding incentive accrues for taxing above the minimum level required by the state (school districts which tax above the foundation level do so entirely with local support and revenue); and (d) a limited level of reimbursement is inherent in every program. (Many programs are referred to as "100% funded" which may mean that they are 100% funded according to prescribed formulas. In almost every case, the funding is limited to a certain level of actual expenditures shared with local school districts, for example, transportation, special education, testing, and so forth.)[5]

5.4-4 Earmarked State Funds

Amended Substitute House Bill 117,[6] passed June 30, 1995, requires that at least 75 percent of personal income tax receipts deposited into the General Revenue Fund be expended on primary and secondary education. Primary and secondary education includes vocational and special education, School for the Deaf, School for the Blind, and for reimbursing school districts for property tax relief. The Senate provision, which was not supported by the Conference Committee, did require that beginning in fiscal year 1996, the percentage of total state appropriations for primary and secondary education each year must not be less than the percentage in the preceding fiscal year. The Senate version also would have required an increase for primary and secondary schools of at least one-half of one percent each year until the per public basic aid formula amount reached an inflation-adjusted equivalent of $4,000 in 1995 dollars. Although the Senate version was not accepted, both of these proposals are worthy and hopefully will be addressed in fiscal year 1998.

---

[5] *Id.* at 16.
[6] *See* Ohio Rev. Code Ann. at §§ 113.091 and 5747.03.

5.5 Ohio's Program for Funding Schools

5.5-1 General Considerations

Ohio's program of funding schools combines the foundation program strategy with line-item "categoricals" for funding specific programs. This system reflects an attempt not only to provide equitable resources for children but also equitable programs. *Almost all aspects of Ohio's school funding program are related to these two basic concepts, either as an expansion of or exception to such.* Figure 5.3 graphically illustrates the effort needed *above* the foundation level for three different districts with varying valuations to produce the same dollar amount per pupil.

5.5-2 Adequacy Concerns

An obvious concern is the issue of *adequacy*. Does $3,315.00 per pupil in Ohio represent adequate resources for an *adequate* or minimum level of education for Ohio's students? Readers should note that as this foundation level "moves up" and the dollar amount becomes higher, not only does the "foundation" provide greater resources for Ohio's children, but it also provides funding in harmony with the concept of equity among Ohio's school districts. With the question of adequacy in mind and with the realization of the potential impact of greater resources focused equitably on Ohio's children, the writers urge support for raising the level of funding.

5.5-3 Varying Abilities to Raise Tax Revenue

A second major concern with the funding mechanism in Ohio relates to the ability to raise money above the prescribed minimum. Again, one of the assumptions behind Ohio's funding system for schools is that any funding above the foundation level is the local district's responsibility. As can be noted in Figure 5.3, if each of the school districts' decision makers decided they needed to have $700.00 more per student than what the foundation level provides, the varying abilities to secure this could be anywhere from 3.09 mills to 38.89 mills to provide the same $700.00 per student above the minimum foundation level.

5.5-4 Reduction in Size of Education's "Piece of the Pie"

A third concern to educators has been the reduction of elementary and secondary education's share of Ohio's economic resources. Over the last 20 years there has been a significant increase in the actual dollars allocated to education; however, there has also been a reduction in the percentage of Ohio's funds allocated for elementary and secondary education. This is evidenced by the decline from over 40% of the general revenue in the late 1960s, to 26.5% of the state's general fund revenue allocated to elementary and secondary education in fiscal year 1995.[7] The funding of education is apparently being viewed as a lower priority than it once was.

---

[7] Donald C. Berno, "Personal Income Increase Greater than State Spending for Four Consecutive Years", *State Budget Update* (Report 95-6), Ohio Public Expenditure Council (August, 1995), at 3.

Figure 5:3

Relative Share of State and Local Money for $4,015 Using $3,315 as Foundation Level

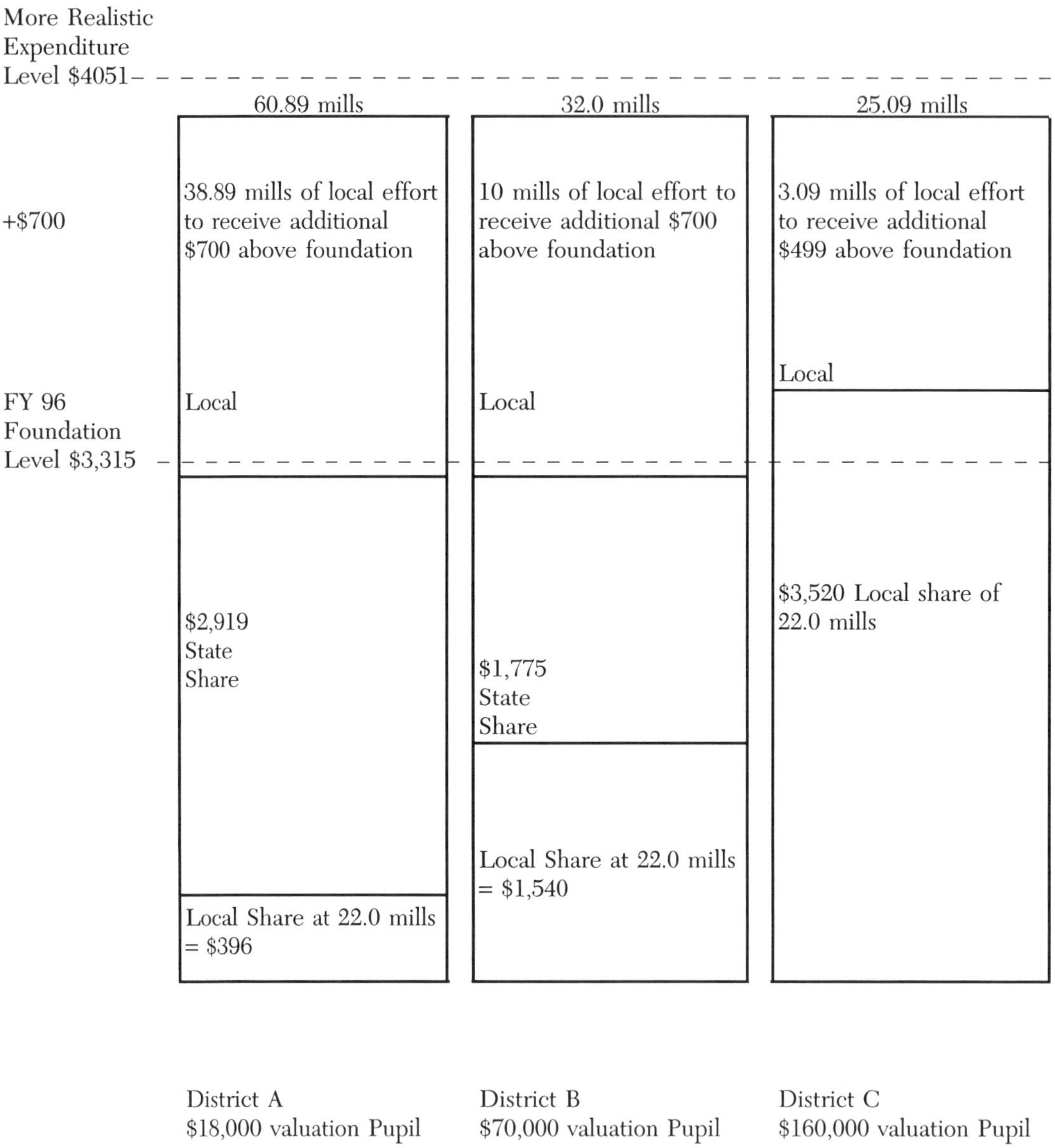

5.5-5 Guarantees

The use of guarantees for Ohio's schools has a lengthy history. When a school district, through the utilization of the formula, appears to be receiving a reduced amount of state revenue, it very often has been "placed" on what is called a hold-harmless guarantee. A *hold-harmless guarantee* assures a district of an allocation of 100% of the previous year's revenue regardless of the formula factors. This guarantee is widely considered to be disequalizing. Historically, there has been at least one hold-harmless guarantee district in almost every foundation-level program.

Impetus for the provision of guarantees has also been politically motivated. No legislator wants to vote for a new budget that will reduce revenues to his/her own school district. Through guarantees he/she is assured of voting for a budget that produces at least the same amount of revenue, and maybe slightly more than the previous year for his/her school district of residence.

Guarantees provide financial stability for schools from year to year. The implications of a decline in student enrollment, change in programmatic needs, and changes in property valuation are sometimes "softened" dramatically through the use of guarantees from year to year. These provide at least a minimum level of predictability for public schools regarding annual state revenue.

Even though there has been a reluctance in the past to change guarantee provisions, Amended Substitute House Bill 117[8] did provide some alteration.

The basic aid guarantee for FY 96 and FY 97 for districts below $200,000 valuation per pupil is 100% of FY 91 or FY 92 basic aid amount. A second tier of schools began phasing out guarantees in fiscal year 1994. School district with valuation above $200,000 per student but less than $285,000 valuation per student will receive a 5% reduction for every year from FY 94 that the district is in this category.

In fiscal year 1996, a district with valuation above $285,000/student will receive a 15% reduction for every year since FY 93 they are above that amount. These last two guarantees have a cumulative effect. They will receive 25% of that amount in FY 97.

Two enrollment subsidy guarantees are also effective for fiscal years 1996-1997. The first is a low enrollment subsidy[9] which increases the amount paid to a small, low-property value school district from $10 to $50 multiplied by the difference between 1,000 and the district's ADM.

The second subsidy guarantee applies to school districts with major enrollment losses.[10] A subsidy is provided in each year of the biennium to each school district with an average daily enrollment over 8,500 which experiences a loss of students to open enrollment programs in adjacent school districts of at least 100 students in the fiscal year. The subsidy works as follows: (a) In fiscal year 1996, a subsidy of one-fourth of the adjusted formula amount for each student enrolled in an adjacent district for the year. (b) In fiscal year 1997, a subsidy of one-eighth of the adjusted formula amount for each student enrolled in an adjacent district for fiscal year 1996 plus one-fourth of the adjusted formula for any increase from fiscal year 1996 to fiscal year 1997.

5.6 Ohio's Foundation Formula and the SF-12

The SF-12 is a form received annually by every city, exempted village and local school

---

[8] Ohio Rev. Code Ann. at § 3317.0212 and section 45.09.

[9] Ohio Rev. Code Ann. at § 3317.0214.

[10] Ohio Rev. Code Ann. at § 45.28.

district in the state. The forms depict the distribution of state dollars to all districts for the year. The composite of the forms statewide, results in the determination of how approximately 80% of the state's aid to education is distributed.

A sample, completed SF-12 appears in Figure 5:4; it can be noted that the line items represent both basic and categorical aid. Section "A" (lines 1 through 13) provided a summary of the components for the illustrated district's basic aid; section "B", categorical aid. The calculations embodied by the two sections reflect the earlier-stated premise that Ohio's funding program is the result of a combination of a foundation formula strategy in tandem with line item categorical program support. The interrelatedness of basic and categorical funding is evident.

As indicated earlier in this chapter, basic aid or foundation funding can be depicted by simple equations as follows: (a) *A* (the amount per student determined by the state for foundation funding) times *E* (the district's student enrollment) equals *T* (the total foundation for the district); (b) *T* (the total foundation amount for the district) minus *L* (the local share of the foundation program) equals *S* (the state's share of the foundation program); and, in addition, (c) *M* (the millage rate of taxation required at the local level) times *V* (the district's assessed property value) equals *L* (the local share of the foundation programs).

The primary determinants for the above equations are the following: (a) *E* (the student enrollment), (b) *A* (the amount per student for foundation funding as determined by the state), (c) *M* (the millage rate of taxation required at the local level), and (d) *V* (the district's assessed property value).

In fiscal year 1996, the millage rate of taxation expected of school districts is 22.0 mills. Assessed property value is multiplied by the 22.0 mills to determine a district's local deduction from the foundation program.

This formula is represented in the SF-12 on lines 5 and 6. In essence, everything else on the SF-12 indicates how factors are either added or adjusted as related directly or indirectly to the equations on lines 5 and 6. Figure 5:5 depicts the composition of each of the four key state funding factors and the role that each has in Ohio's foundation formula strategy.

From the equations illustrated in Figure 5:5 some of the assumptions stated earlier can be noted. A change in enrollment will result in a change in the foundation amount. As *E* increases or decreases, changes will be reflected by *T* which is the product of *E* multiplied by *A*. As the level of foundation support (*A*) increases, the state basic aid will also increase. The foundation level per pupil for fiscal year 1996 is $3,315 and will increase to $3,500 in FY 1997. The contribution rate of the local share of funding is 22 mills in FY 1996 and will increase to 23 mills in FY 1997.

As property values increase, the state basic aid will decrease if the student population remains stable. Stated another way, the greater the level of the ability to raise taxes locally through higher valuation of property, the lower the state basic aid will be. This formula assumes school districts will receive 22.0 mills of local tax receipts multiplied times the increase in property value. In chapter four it was pointed out that this does not necessarily occur during the reappraisal or triennial update processes. In addition, the minimum millage for tax reduction purposes is 20 mills (20 mill floor), not 22.0 mills.

Figure 5:4
Sample SF-12
Ohio Department of Education – Division of School Finance
Form SF-12 Fiscal Year (1995-96 August No. 2 Estimate) (AM. SUB. H.B. 117)

	West Holmes Local S.D.				HOLMES COUNTY
A.	Basic Program Support:				
1.	241 Kindergarten ADM				
2.	2,179 Grades 1-12 (Excludes FTE on Line 14, ADM on Line 16 and 75% of Joint Vocational and Contract ADM)				
3.	2,300 Basic ADM (one-half Line 1 Plus Line 2; SEC 3317.02)				
4.	172,285,124 Assessed Valuation; Valuation Per Pupil = 74,907				
5.	Basic State Aid (Section 3317.022)				
	(A) ($3,315 x 1.026239) x Line 3				7,824,554.00
	(B) Adjusted Valuation	170,757,566.00			
	(C) Adjusted Valuation x .022				3,756,666.45
6.	Line 5A Minus Line 5C				4,067,887.55
7.	Adj Val Per Pup (Line 5B / Line 3)			74,242	
8.	Adjustments (Section 3317.023)				
	(A) Number of Classroom Teachers				
	(B) Training and Exp of Classroom Teachers (50% of Total)				
	(C) Educational Services Personnel				
	(D) County Board Deduction (See Line 23)			118,704.21	
9.	Current Basic State Aid (Line 6 Plus or Minus Line 8)				4,067,887.55
10.	Fiscal Year 1996 Guarantee-Larger of FY 91 or FY 92 Basic Aid (Line 11 Amount, Form SF-12) Times 1.000				3,398,008.76
11.	Larger of Line 9 or Line 10				4,067,887.55
12.	Disadvantaged Pupil Impact Aid x 1.000				
13.	FY 96 Basic Program (Line 11 Plus Line 12)				4,067,887.55
B.	Categorical Program Funding:				
14.	Approved Vocational Units: 7.00; FTE			79.02	
	(A) Salary Allowance + 15% + $9510 (Includes Proprietary ADM of x $4,001.40)				275,967.55
	(OR)				
	(B) (Line 11 / Line 3) x 105% x FTE			146,746.39	
	(C) Larger of Line 14A or 14B x 1.000				275,967.55
15.	Approved Child Study, Occupational or Physical Therapy, Speech and Hearing, Supervisors and Coordinators				
	(A) Special Education Units:		.00	.00	
	(B) Early Childhood Units:		.00	.00	.00
	(C) Line 15(A) + Line 15(B) x 1.000				
16.	Approved Special ED and DH Units:				
	(A) Salary Allowance + 15% + $8,023 376,297.26				
	SPC ED Units 5.00 SPC ED ADM			75	
	PRESCH Units .00 PRESCH ADM			17	
	DH Units 5.00 DH ADM			76	
	(B) (Line 11 / Line 3) x 105% x SPEC. ADM			243,277.36	
	(C) Larger of Line 16a or 16b x 1.000				376,297.26
17.	Gifted Units: Salary Allowance + 15% + $2,678 x 1.000				
18.	Approved Extended Service				7,597.68
19.	Approved Transportation				418,296.60
20.	Total Categorical Program Funding (Sum of Lines 14C, 15, 16C, 17, 18 and 19)				1,078,159.09
21.	Line 13 Plus Line 20				5,146,046.64
22.	Other Guarantees (Specify)				
	(A) Reappraisal (Section 3317.04)				
	(B) Consolidation (Section 3317.04)				
23.	Total State Support (Larger of Line 21 minus Line 8D or Line 22 minus Line 8D)				$5,027,342.43
	West Holmes Local School District		Holmes County		
	JVS ADM Excluded from Calculation			40.50	
	Total ADM as Reported thru EMIS		2,708		
	3 Year Average ADM	2,677			
	Formula District				
	° $4,135,994.67 General Revenue Fund + Profits/Education Fund = $5,027,342.43				$891,347.76 Lottery

Figure 5:5

Factor Formula

This figure depicts the composition of each of the four key state funding factors and the role that each plays in Ohio's foundation formula strategy.

	Factor #1		Factor #2		
(a)	**E** (student enrollment)	x	**A** (foundation level per student in $)	=	**T** (total foundation amount for district)
	Factor #3		Factor #4		
(b)	**M** (millage rate of taxation at local)	x	**V** (district assessed property value)	=	**L** (local share of foundation program)
(c)	**T** (total foundation level)	=	**L** (local share of foundation program)	=	**S** (share of foundation program for district)

In cases where the state basic aid would be calculated to be less than the previous year, those school districts will be placed on a guarantee. That guarantee is evidenced by line 10. Line 10 is used by the state to guarantee that the school district receives at least 100% of a previous year's amount. In fiscal year 1996 the guarantee provides a certain percent of fiscal year 1991 or fiscal year 1992.

The charge-off has increased each year for the last three years from 20 mills in fiscal year 1993 to 20.5 mills in fiscal year 1994; to 21 mills in fiscal year 1995; and then to 22 mills in fiscal year 1996. It will increase to 23 mills in fiscal year 1997. Increasing the charge-off surely has impacted state funding that is provided to local school districts. Couple this millage charge-off increase with an increase in assessed valuation and it is easily seen that if the local district's enrollment happens to decline, even more impact is experienced resulting in less state aid. (See enrollment subsidies exceptions at 5.5-5.)

Some interesting concepts inherent in the SF-12 include the method by which students are counted. Students counted in lines 1, 2, and 3 on the formula do not include students who are in special education programs, vocational education programs or 75% of the number attending a joint vocational school. Because funding for these programs is listed in the categorical program section, the concept behind the process is to prevent the counting and funding of those students twice. The net effect, however, means that the amount that a school district receives for that specific program is the difference between whether the student is calculated as part of the basic state aid or as part of the program aid in the categorical section.

One of the issues assumed in most of the foundation programs is that the costs per pupil are the same statewide. In Ohio, that assumption has been changed by law. A cost-of-doing-business factor is now a part of the foundation program. That factor is approved biennially by the legislature and currently produces a rate of up to 8.2% greater funds for foundation support purposes in FY 96. School districts with the highest cost-of-doing-business factor as measured by average weekly wages for each county as certified by the Ohio Bureau of Employment receive the 8.2% increases.

The state legislature[11] provided in uncodified (temporary) law the first two years the first two steps of a 15-year increase for cost-of-doing-business factors. The factors will range up to 8.2% in fiscal year 1996 and 8.9% in fiscal year 1997. After 15 years, the factors will range up to 18%. Thus, this factor will become more significant in the future for some school districts depending on the factor designated for their county. The cost-of-doing-business factor only applies to the basic aid support and not the guarantees, Disadvantaged Pupil Impact Aid or categorical funding. This factor can be found on line 5-A of the SF12.

During the history of the state foundation program, an income factor had never been included in the basic aid formula. While assessed property tax valuation continues its major thrust in the formula, an income factor was added to the basic aid formula to be phased in over fifteen years through fiscal year 2010. The income factor is applied against the first $60,000 in per pupil valuation. In 1996, the valuation used to calculate the district's share of state foundation level was income adjusted. This factor will be phased in over 15 years. In the year 2010, the first $60,000 valuation/pupil will be adjusted for income. It will be adjusted by multiplying it by the ratio of district median income divided by the state median income. For districts with below median income, the valuation is adjusted lower and thus when calculating the charge-off, the lower amount results in more state aid. The opposite occurs for districts with above median income.

Historically, another assumption made by some in the funding of schools is that the actual program costs are the same from program to program. In Ohio, this assumption is altered by the way programs are funded for vocational education, special education, gifted education, psychological services and so forth, versus basic aid and support for students. Funding for these programs is basically a flat grant for support of certain categoricals.

Another indication that costs are not the same statewide is the inclusion of a factor in Ohio's funding formula to give more state aid to those school districts which have the highest incidence of poverty. This is measured by the number of students receiving assistance through the Aid to Dependent Children (A.D.C.) program. The greater the concentration of those students in the school district, the more state dollars per pupil that flow to that district in state basic aid as indicated on line 12 of the SF-12.

The line items on the SF-12 represent provisions and mandates of Ohio's law; therefore, they reflect state policy for the distributions of funds to school districts.

Policies regarding the funding of programs can be readily noted by observing the way they are funded on the SF-12.

There are adjustments listed on the SF-12 for county boards of education services in local school districts, and in cities and exempted villages electing to be a part of those county service districts. Also, there are financial penalties for school districts not having the minimum number of classroom teachers and/or educational service personnel.

The categorical line items listed in section "B" (lines 14 through 19 of the SF-12) are distributed with little regard to local district wealth. They are distributed based on approved programs that represent student needs. It is interesting to note that categorical programs

---

[11] *See* Ohio Rev. Code Ann. at § 3317.02(E).

are not affected at the present time by the cost-of-doing-business factor reflecting costs statewide.[12]

5.7 "Equity" Distribution

In 1992, Substitute House Bill 671[13] was passed to provide a higher degree of financial equity for Ohio's schools. This bill established precedent for 1996-1997 funding.

The budget bill, Amended Substitute House Bill 117 maintained some aspects of equity funding and made some changes to enhance the concept.

This fund established a higher level of equalization for poor school districts than previously thought possible and did so with a limited amount of money.

In fiscal year 1996, the budget bill established the following principles:

1. Defining district wealth by property valuation adjusted by personal income
2. Distributing a subsidy for small, low-wealth districts
3. Distributing funds for technology use, with low-wealth districts receiving priority
4. Creating a second tier of equalization that effectively brings poor districts up to the purchasing power of 13 additional mills for districts of $65,275 valuation per pupil
5. Equalization is now effectively $4,163 per student as follows:
   $3,315 in basic aid on 22.0-mill effort, plus $848 in low-wealth aid on an additional 13-mill effort basis—the sum of which totals $4,163 (which is the equivalent total of a 35.0-mill effort).

State law assumes 22.0 mills of local effort to receive the first level of money ($3,315) but 35.0 mills of local effort to realize at least $4,163 per pupil equalization level.

Equity funding was increased. Aid for equity is $90 million in FY 1996 and $100 million in FY 1997. This aid will be distributed to the poorest school districts. A total of 279 districts will receive aid in FY 1996 and 286 will receive aid in FY 1997.[14]

5.8 Other State Aid

Additional ways of funding schools in Ohio are reflected in line items in the state's budget that correspond to categorical programs such as bus purchases, reimbursement for testing costs, urban demonstration grants, venture capital, local professional development grants, and so forth.

The largest single portion of the state's budget that is allocated to schools other than the dollars included in the SF-12 program is the amount of state money that is paid to local school districts to reimburse the districts for the various taxpayer subsidies. These include the 10% reduction in taxes that every real estate taxpayer receives, the 2½% reduction that every homesite owner receives, the $10,000 valuation exemption that every personal tangible taxpayer receives, and the reimbursement for homestead exemption for

---

[12] See Ohio Department of Education, Overview: From SF12 (Columbus: Ohio Department of Education, n.d. (for use with the SF12, 1996 and 1997)) a copy of which is included in the appendix.

[13] *See* Ohio Rev. Code Ann. at §§ 3317.0213, 3317.0214.

[14] Ohio Rev. Code Ann. at §§ 3313.98, 3317.02, 3317.022, 3317.0212, 3317.0214, 3365.01: Section 45.09.

Figure 5:6

Second Tier of Equalization

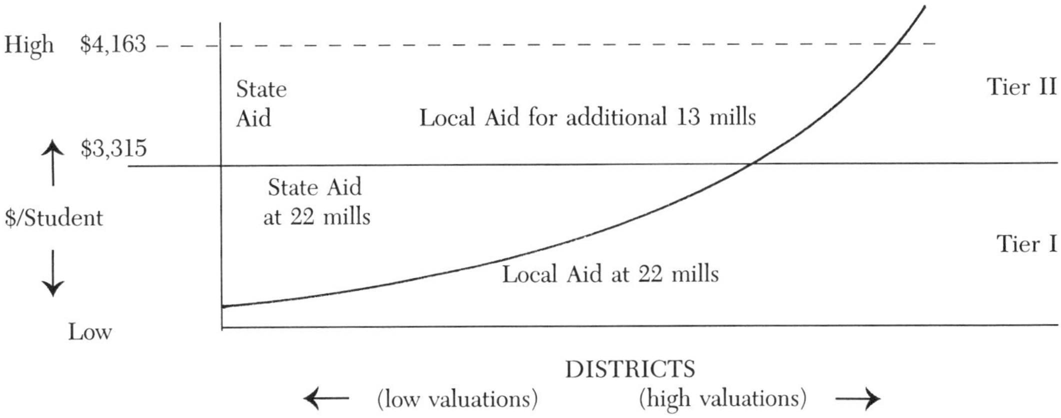

senior citizens whose income is $20,800 or less annually. In Ohio, this reimbursement for property relief in fiscal year 1994 was over $529,800,000.00.[15]

5.9 Lottery Profits/Education Fund

Lottery profits have been "earmarked" constitutionally to support education in Ohio. Previously, lottery profits were allocated to schools but only through the legislative process.

In fiscal year 1996, lottery profits were funding approximately 7% of Ohio's school expenditures. Lottery profits for a given fiscal year that exceed the amount originally estimated by the legislature's budget analysts are called *excess lottery profits*. After satisfying some "set-asides" provided by the legislature (including a certain percentage for a "rainy day fund," some school building assistance funding, and other particulars), the excess lottery profits were distributed to schools on a per-pupil basis.

5.10 Provisions for Adjusting State Aid

Potential adjustments in state aid include the following:

1. Several provisions allow for state aid to be adjusted based upon factors at the local level. These include the following: changes in the personal tangible value, an increase or decrease in the value of Current Agricultural Use Value (C.A.U.V.), exemptions of property taxes and/or revisions in property value. These will change the valuation portion of the funding formula and therefore affect state aid. These changes, originating with the county auditors, are certified to the Ohio Department of Education by the Ohio Department of Taxation; the changes

[15] Donald C. Berno, "Rate of Growth in Ohio Poverty Taxes slowed in 1994; percentage increase lowest since 1985; smallest dollar increase since 1988," *Tax Facts* (Report 95-3), Ohio Public Expenditure Council (April, 1995), at 2.

ultimately result in an adjustment to the foundation level of support for the school districts.

2. There will be a recalculation if the February count of students has changed by more than 3% up or down.
3. At the beginning of the fiscal year (July 1), the SF-12 figures are based on estimates. On or after January 1, actual, calculated SF-12 figures are used which incorporate actual student count and program information. A school district will receive a revised SF-12 if any of the factors change, such as valuation resulting from appeals, late filing of Current Agricultural Use Value (C.A.U.V.) or personal property valuation changes. The official SF-12 for a given fiscal year will usually be a revision received in June.

5.11 Telecommunications Valuation Losses

In fiscal years 1996 and 1997, districts were partially reimbursed for their losses when the assessed valuations of the telecommunications industry were reduced. This partial reimbursement was to provide a temporary "bridge" for the loss of funds. No reimbursement is expected in FY 98 and beyond.

5.12 Summary

The issues of funding schools at the state level can be quite complicated despite the fact that the legislature intended to simplify the process. State aid should account for differences in students, programs and capabilities of raising tax revenue.

Will Ohio support an adequate education funded by adequate resources and still provide equitable resources across the State of Ohio? Thorough and efficient school systems are possibly only through a formula that provides the funds so that each boy and girl will receive a quality, not a minimum, education.

Chapter 6: Capital Funding

6.1 Determining Facility and Equipment Needs

Statewide shifts in expenditures for buildings and equipment closely parallel the patterns reflected on the national level. Expressed as a percentage of the total budget and inclusive of related interest expenses, educational expenditures nationally for buildings and equipment have been reported to be as follows: 19.1% for 1949-1950; 20.1% for 1959-1960; 14.4% for 1969-1970; and 9.1% for 1979-1980.[1]

The 20.1% figure for 1959-1960 is a clear reflection of, and reaction to, the "baby boom" which followed World War II. Following this crest, Ohio's elementary and secondary public school enrollment began a marked decline. Less than three decades later, however, the echo of the baby boom could be heard, or at least counted, and the "die was cast"

[1] Roe L. Johns, Edgar J. Morphet, and Kern Alexander, *The Economics and Financing of Education*, 4th ed. (Englewood Cliffs, N.J.: Prentice-Hall, 1983), at 274 [hereinafter *The Ecomomics and Financing of Education*].

for a modest resurgence of school enrollment at the primary level.

Although school administrators and board of education members who had the unpleasant task of managing the decline now warmly embrace this enrollment turn-around, the following formidable challenges remain:

1. Whereas many districts disposed of previously unneeded buildings, others secured such facilities for possible future use. The re-occupation of "mothballed" facilities frequently requires a substantial investment for neglected repairs and general clean-up prior to re-occupancy.
2. Major facility expenditures may also be required for remodeling, energy retrofitting, the accomodation of current and new educational programs, and bringing facilities in compliance with applicable codes.
3. The replacement of outdated facilities and equipment must be addressed.

The magnitude of Ohio's school facilities problem is demonstrated by the fact that Amended Substitute Senate Bill 140,[2] adopted in 1989, provided $2,000,000 annually for a survey and inventory of school facilities. The 1990 report showed that $10.2 billion would be required to address the total need for construction and renovation of school facilities. Even prior to the legislatively directed study, it could have been predicted that improvement of many Ohio facilities and/or additions to school facilities would be needed during the decade of the 1990s.

6.2 Facility Costs

All too frequently the capital aspect of the school operation receives "low billing." This unfortunate situation is attributable, in part, to the following:

1. Capital projects, unlike the administration of general fund expenditures, are not everyday occurrences.
2. Some school administrators have had little experience, and even less formal instruction, in the many nuances of managing capital projects.
3. Boards of education often take comfort in the fact that the capital dimensions of the school operation are being handled by experts, that is, bonding attorneys and architects.

Nevertheless, any school district would be well-served by having its appropriate school administrator(s) informed and actively involved in all capital programs. Administrative involvement is essential for good planning, financing, and construction aspects of capital projects. Such involvement should result in the saving of thousands of dollars on small projects and up to hundreds of thousands on larger ones. Many experts recommend that districts employ a construction management service as a means of saving both construction time and money.

6.3 Construction Costs Versus Operational Costs

Notwithstanding a district's interest in saving on construction costs, it is imperative that

---

[2] Ohio Rev. Code Ann. at § 3301.07.

the "big picture" be kept in view. An important component of this picture is avoiding the temptation to reduce construction costs to the extent that such "savings" may be more than offset by a myriad of problems, inconveniences, and future operational and/or repair expenses emanating from initial cost-reduction efforts. The following represents types of "penny wise and pound foolish" decisions: inadequate planning, insufficient storage space, low "R-factor" rating (poor insulating), and flat roofs. Some experienced administrators and board members have argued that flat roofs on public buildings should even be prohibited by law.

Regarding the latter issue of flat roofs, the long-term disadvantages of maintenance expenses and inconvenience more than offset the modest savings in construction costs. If a roof is engineered with even a one to three percent pitch (slope) the probability of chronic leaking problems is greatly reduced. If the flat appearance is desired the modest additional cost of a vision screen (facade) will address that preference at a minimal cost.

Another major expenditure which merits long-term consideration is site selection. Expensive as good sites usually are, a school building's useful life of 50 years and beyond, will normally warrant even a premium price for a site which is appropriate to the needs as opposed to settling for a "bargain" site that possesses inherent drawbacks. Attention must be given to infrastructure items including the availability or probable cost of utilities such as gas, electric, water, and sanitary services. Nevertheless, some districts are fortunate enough to have an appropriate parcel donated as a school construction site.

It is worth noting that as soon as a school site is acquired, it qualifies for exemption from property tax obligation; however, such exemption is not automatic so official application must be made.

6.4 Capital Funding Alternatives

Funding of facilities, except in a few states, has been a low priority item in public school finance.

> Sophisticated formulas have been devised for cooperative state and local financing of current operation, of special programs, and of some specific services, but equal diligence has not been exerted in many states in devising feasible programs for state and local support for capital outlay and debt service.[3]

Seldom has the Ohio legislature addressed this problem and even then only cursory treatment has been given.

Throughout the 19th century and into the early 20th century, the local real estate tax proved to be an adequate, even appropriate, source of school construction funds. The facts that a low percentage of youth attended school and school construction costs were comparatively inexpensive, allowed most states, including Ohio, to assume a very passive role in the funding of capital construction.

Changes in these and other factors have caused most scholars, and many practitioners

[3] Monte W. Barr and William R. Wilkerson, *Innovative Financing of Public Schools Facilities* (Danville, IL: The Interstate Printers and Publishers, Inc., 1973), Forward.

of school finance, to espouse a capital funding approach similar to that utilized for operational costs. Nevertheless, we currently experience disparity to the extent that during the 1960s and 1970s and into the early 1980s, approximately 85% of the states' school budgets were spent for operational expenses and only 15% for capital outlay. The following statements support changes in school finance philosophy in reference to such expenditures:

1. Since responsibility for education is legally a state function, responsibility for its financing rests firmly upon each state.
2. There is no justification for financing capital outlays on a different basis from that of financing current expenditures. If state financing of current operations is defensible and fair, so also is state financing of capital outlays.
3. There is no defense for the traditional method of financing school facilities by relying completely on a regressive and unfair local property tax when more equitable tax sources are available at the state level.
4. It is false economy for school districts to be indebted for long periods of time with excessive interest costs.
5. It is paradoxical to provide adequate funds for current expenditures for all districts and then deny some of them good educational programs because low assessed valuations and state-imposed limitations on debt service maximums deny them the fiscal ability to provide satisfactory facilities.
6. Just as no district, regardless of its wealth, should enjoy pecuniary advantages over another in the obtaining of current operation funds, neither should any district enjoy resource advantages over another in the provision for school facilities.[4]

Prior to addressing the more traditional approaches to acquiring school facilities, school administrators should be aware of the lease-purchase option authorized under 3313.375 which permits a board of education to enter into certain lease-purchase agreements for the acquisition of buildings for any district purpose, and provides that such agreements do not constitute school district debt.

6.5 The Bond Issue

The most frequently used means of paying for capital outlay and for the financing of debt service expenditures locally is through general revenue bonds, with approximately two thirds of the nation's public schools using this method. This approach requires taxpayer support in order for the district board of education to issue long-term bonds to obtain funds for the acquisition of property and the construction of facilities.

In effect, the passage of a bond issue authorizes debt up to the amount requested on the ballot. In submitting a bond issue to the electorate, the board of education is actually requesting permission to tax at whatever rate is required to pay back the annual principal payment, plus interest. Through this process the bonds are paid off or "retired."

---

[4] Percy E. Burrup and Vern Brimley, Jr., *Financing Education in a Climate of Change* (Boston, Mass.: Allyn and Bacon, Inc., 1982), at 290 [hereinafter *Financing Education*].

When calculating the "average rate," the county auditor first assumes a constant valuation of property, and then estimates the interest rate. The average rate is determined by the following four factors:

1. Principal of bonds
2. Length of repayment period
3. Estimated annual interest rate
4. Assessed valuation of the district

A seldom used but potentially beneficial option is the "stay at home" bond issue. When a district which has already entered into a contract with the state for school building assistance drops below 4 mills of bonded indebtedness, the district is required to increase the millage paid to the state back to the 4 mill level. However, there is a provision in the law (ORC 3318.051) which permits a local board of education to submit to the voters a bond issue which would increase the local indebtedness to 4 mills. The receipts from the bond issue can then be used for permanent improvement projects.

6.6 Calculating Millage Rate

Figure 6:1 reflects hypothetical data and a formula for estimating the millage necessary for the repayment of a school bond issue on a single annual payment basis.

Following voter approval, the board of education issues and sells bonds to the bonding company which makes the lowest bid in terms of interest charged to the district. Frequently, competing bonding firms will also include a "premium" as a part of their bid. The premium is in the form of a check made payable to the school district. Any premium must also be considered in the determination of the "best" bid.

6.7 The Conversion Option

Although "packaging" of bond issues will be covered later in the chapter, it is worth noting at this point that Ohio school districts have, and may want to exercise, the option of selling notes on a temporary basis and later converting them for a long-term bond sale. This approach has the potential for helping the district realize substantial savings by capitalizing on favorable note and bond markets. Table 6:1 demonstrates the impact of the interest rate on the dollar amount of interest to be paid.

6.8 Permanent Improvement Levy

The financial base of many Ohio school districts allows a "pay-as-you-go" approach to financing all, or at least a portion of, the capital projects. Two common characteristics of districts which utilize this approach are as follows: a high assessed valuation per pupil and a relatively stable student population. This combination of district wealth, stable enrollment, and resultant modest facility needs, allows districts to pay for facilities while such are being constructed or renovated.

A permanent improvement fund can be established in two ways. One way, that applies more to the wealthier school district with large unencumbered general fund balances, is

Figure 6:1

A Sample Millage Rate Calculation

I. School district factors to be considered

Estimated amount of money needed is	$6,000,000
Length of repayment is	20 years
Estimated annual interest is	6%
Assessed valuation of the district is	$200,000,000

II. Formula for calculating millage rate
   A. Amount of bond issue divided by years for repayment equals annual principal payment
   B. Balance due times interest rate equals annual interest payment
   C. Annual principal payment plus annual interest payment equals amount for debt retirement
   D. Amount for debt retirement divided by valuation of the school district equals the average tax rate necessary for debt retirement

III. Calculations
   A. First year principal and interest payment
      1. $6,000,000 divided by 20 equals $300,000 principal payment
      2. $6,000,000 times .06 equals $360,000 interest payment
      3. $300,000 plus $360,000 equals $660,000 total payment
   B. Last year principal and interest payment
      1. $300,000 equals principal payment
      2. $300,000 times .06 equals $18,000 interest payment
      3. $300,000 plus $18,000 equals $318,000 total payment
      4. $318,000 divided by $200,000,000 equals .00159 or 1.6 mills
   C. Calculation to determine average annual millage needed (first year payment plus last year payment divided by 2 equals average annual payment)
      1. $660,000 plus $318,000 divided by 2 equals $489,000 average annual payment
      2. $489,000 divided by $200,000,000 (assessed valuation) equals .002445 or 2.4 mills

Table 6:1

Interest Costs Associated with a 1% Change in Interest Rates Over a 20-Year Period

Amount of Bond Issue, $	Cost per 1% Change in Interest Rate, $
1,000,000	128,000
2,000,000	256,000
4,000,000	512,000
8,000,000	1,024,000
16,000,000	2,048,000

Information for Table 6:1 is taken from D. H. Stollar, *Managing School Indebtedness: The Complete Guide to School Bonding* (Danville, IL: Interstate Publishers and Printers, 1967), p. 3; the table expanded by permission of Interstate Publishers and Printers.

to transfer funds from the general fund to the permanent improvement fund. Boards of education and superintendents need to keep in mind that, while permanent improvement fund, reverse transfers from the permanent improvement fund back into the general fund

Table 6:2

Costs Associated with Principal Repayment as Compared to Interest Charges

Payment	Period	Principal	Interest	Total
1. 12/2/84	12/1/85	$	$593,750.00	$593,750.00
2. 12/2/85	12/1/86	$115,000.00	$475,000.00	$590,000.00
3. 12/2/86	12/1/87	$125,000.00	$464,075.00	$589,000.00
4. 12/2/87	12/1/88	$140,000.00	$452,200.00	$592,200.00
5. 12/2/88	12/1/89	$150,000.00	$438,900.00	$588,000.00
6. 12/2/89	12/1/90	$165,000.00	$424,650.00	$589,650.00
7. 12/2/90	12/1/91	$180,000.00	$408,975.00	$588,975.00
8. 12/2/91	12/1/92	$200,000.00	$391,875.00	$591,875.00
9. 12/2/92	12/1/93	$215,000.00	$372,875.00	$587,875.00
10. 12/2/93	12/1/94	$240,000.00	$352,450.00	$592,450.00
11. 12/2/94	12/1/95	$260,000.00	$329,650.00	$589,650.00
12. 12/2/95	12/1/96	$285,000.00	$304,950.00	$589,950.00
13. 12/2/96	12/1/97	$315,000.00	$277,875.00	$592,875.00
14. 12/2/97	12/1/98	$345,000.00	$247,950.00	$592,950.00
15. 12/2/98	12/1/99	$375,000.00	$215,175.00	$590,155.00
16. 12/2/99	12/1/00	$410,000.00	$179,550.00	$589,550.00
17. 12/2/00	12/1/01	$450,000.00	$140,600.00	$590,600.00
18. 12/2/01	12/1/02	$490,000.00	$97,850.00	$587,850.00
19. 12/2/02	12/1/03	$540,000.00	$51,300.00	$591,300.00
TOTAL		$5,000,000.	$6,219,650.	$11,219,650.

Information for Table 6:2 is taken from *Principles of School Business Management*, (Reston, VA: Association of School Business Officials International, 1986), p. 571.

The previous data are for a twenty-year general obligation bond at 9.5 percent over the life of the issue. Note the delay of the payment of the principal. This example reflects an even payment period over the life of the issue. In many states this even payment schedule is required by statute.

can only be made if certain conditions are met and then only with court approval.[5]

A second way to establish a permanent improvement fund is to obtain approval of the electorate for a new issue. If an issue is passed to provide specific permanent improvements, then expenditures are limited for these specifics. But, if an issue is passed with a broad (non-specific) purpose, then expenditures can occur to satisfy any permanent improvement that will last five years or more.

A district can often save up to 50% of the total cost of school construction when interest charges are not incurred as indicated in Table 6:2. This reality tends to help with the promotion of the necessary tax levy since most voters are usually able to appreciate the long-term benefit to the district as a result of eliminating interest payments.

It should be understood that there are also disadvantages, philosophical and otherwise, to the pay-as-you-go approach.

> In opposition, there are those who argue that the use of current revenue for financing capital facilities results in: (1) creation of tax friction among both taxpayers and governmental agencies because of increased school taxes, (2) failure to distribute

[5] *See* Ohio Rev. Code Ann. at §§ 5705.14(B), 5705.12.

capital costs among the generations who benefit from the school facilities, and (3) failure to realize the economic advantages of borrowing in periods of inflation.[6]

One additional disadvantage is the maximum (five years) duration of such levies. Nevertheless, permanent improvement levies remain a popular and productive source of funding capital projects.

6.9 State-Assisted Capital Projects

Earlier in this chapter it was noted that, in the main, states have not played the same major role in the funding of capital projects that they have with operational needs. More specifically, during the late 1970s less than 20% of all capital expenditures of the nation's public schools were paid from state funds; this is contrasted to the 47% of all operational expenses of public schools that were funded by state resources in the same period of time. It should be noted that these percentages represent the national average only and provide little comfort to states which receive only token assistance from state sources or, as in the cases of Arizona and West Virginia, no support at all for capital expenditures. At the same time, however, Florida, Hawaii, and Maryland were assuming the full burden of school construction and debt service.[7]

Most states, Ohio being no exception, receive more requests for capital funds than they are able to provide. As a result standards are established and guidelines are developed which tend to direct the state's limited resources toward target school districts and/or programs. In a manner similar to the distribution of state funds for operating revenue, most capital participating states use such dollars to add a measure of equity to the generally poorer districts (in terms of local revenue generating capacity per pupil) and/or to address specific needs within such states. The provision of matching funds for the constructing and equipping of vocational education facilities is an example of Ohio's addressing such a need.

6.10 Levels of State Assistance

Generally speaking, the fifty states can be grouped into five categories in terms of their posture on capital financing.

6.10-1 Full State Support

An earlier reference indicated that three states pay the entire cost of funding capital and debt service expenditures. Nevertheless, neither Florida nor Maryland has seen fit to "fully" fund their capital outlay needs.[8]

6.10-2 Equalization

This grant-in-aid approach is designed to provide a high degree of tax equity within

---

[6] *The Economics and Financing of Education* at 277.

[7] *Id.* at 282.

[8] *Id.*

the affected states. Without such assistance taxpayers from districts of low wealth would be required to make a far greater effort to provide school facilities than would their counterparts in wealthier districts.

6.10-3 Percentage Matching

This method of grant approval provides a fixed percentage of support to each local school's capital program. The funding capacity of the district is not considered; rather, state assistance varies only with the cost of the various projects.

6.10-4 Flat Grant

This concept is used to ensure that the state allocates a fixed amount per unit to local school districts. The amount can be "fixed" based upon either average daily attendance or average daily membership.

6.10-5 Loans

Some states provide capital assistance in the form of direct loans to school districts. Usually such states establish a permanent fund, or funds, often through the use of dedicated revenues, for the purpose of providing low-interest loans. Unlike previous state assistance plans, loans made by the state contain the provision that the funds be repaid at some future date. Most loans of this type do not take into consideration the relative fiscal capacity of the local school district and as a result provide little in the way of equalization.[9]

6.11 The Ohio Picture

Ohio's system of capital assistance, which provides a limited measure of equalization, is basically a grant-in-aid approach even though a partial payback is required. This approach gives special consideration to districts which have a high amount of bonded indebtedness as compared to their present tax wealth. The allocation of funds is based upon an Ohio State Board of Education adopted formula. Priority for the actual distribution of funds is based upon the results of an on-site visit and the value assigned to the district's application.

6.12 History

Between 1957 and January, 1993, the state legislature appropriated $184,000,000 and reappropriated more than $70,000,000 to the school building assistance program. During this time period 109 school districts received such funds pursuant to Chapter 3318 of the *Ohio Revised Code.*

Earlier in this chapter reference was made to the fact that *Senate Bill 140* provided for a survey and inventory of school facilities. Also included, contingent on excess lottery profits, was $50,000,000 for school building construction. This figure pales when contrasted to the almost $200,000,000 being requested by more than 40 school districts.

---

[9] *Id.* at 286.

This issue is of particular interest to districts which have a low, assessed valuation but need to construct additional facilities. Many educators believe that notwithstanding the "equity" debate of the late 1980s and early 1990s, equity in capital funding merited even greater concern.

Notwithstanding the results of the 1990 report referenced under 6.1, which demonstrated a tremendous need for construction dollars, Amended Substitute House Bill 117 included only 441 million in a "set-aside" for construction projects. This very modest amount will only fund the projects which were identified as eligible in 1989. In fairness to state lawmakers, it should be pointed out that between the time of the 1990 report and Am. Sub. H.B. 117 in 1993, H.B. 152 contained $68.6 million and H.B. 790, which was passed in 1994, contained $70 million for construction projects.

6.13 How to Qualify for State Aid

School administrators who are not fully apprised of Ohio's school assistance program for the funding of capital projects (including, for example, procedures, requirements, limitations, and so forth) would be well-advised to seek such information as appropriate from the Ohio Department of Education, Division of School Finance, School Building Assistance Section. Asking questions about available funds as well as investing time in reading the program guidelines should provide an indication as to the probability of a given district's ability or inability to qualify for such funds.

The following may help to raise the priority assignment of a given school district's application.

6.13-1 Do Your Homework

This involves not only understanding the guidelines but also having a clear grasp of the district's characteristics and needs. Such understanding should be reflected in the written application and demonstrated during the on-site visit.

6.13-2 Know the Rules

In order to qualify for state building assistance under the amendments to *Ohio Revised Code* Sections 3318.01 to 3318.21, a district must declare by resolution that the district has a net bonded indebtedness of within $5000 of 5% to 7% of the total value of all property in the school district as listed and assessed for taxation on the tax duplicate. A district may also qualify based on a variable percentage of project cost. The board of education must also declare that the district is unable to provide adequate classroom facilities without assistance from the state.

6.13-3 Combine Construction Projects

A district which meets the qualifications, as referenced above, may elect to combine two or more projects. This approach would demonstrate the need for capital expenditures beyond the 9% limitation, in terms of qualifying for participation in the school building assistance program. For most school district's, however, the 9% debt limitation of a school district's tax valuation shall not be exceeded. Special conditions such as a need to make emergency repairs or to install certain energy conservation devices are the only exceptions for school districts to insure indebtedness in excess of the 9% debt limitations.

In order to qualify for such funds, a school district must also have an actual or projected enrollment of at least 275 students in grades seven through twelve. Exceptions are likely to be granted only in those districts where topography, sparsity of population, and other factors make consolidation impractical.

6.14 Determination of Priority Rating

A school district's priority rating is determined by the following three-step method. First, determine the state funding needed, expressed as a percentage of the total project cost. Second, multiply this percentage by the total number of improperly-housed (inadequate classroom facilities) children to determine the number of children to be housed by state funds. Third, divide this number by the total projected enrollment in the school district as of September 1, following the application date. This equation yields the percent of improperly-housed students to be served by state funds and provides the priority rating of the school district.

6.15 Steps in the Application Process

When funds become available in the School Building Assistance program, the Ohio Department of Education will contact districts remaining on the list to determine their status as to plans for the project. The following process is implemented after the surveys are completed:

1. Determination of priority by State Department of Education.
2. Conditional approval by the State Board of Education.
3. Acceptance of conditional approval by the school district board of education and submission of a local bond issue.
4. Approval by the State Controlling Board.
5. Contract between the State Board of Education and the school district board of education.
6. Issuance of bonds for project funding.
7. Submittal of education specifications and architectural plans. Advertising and awarding of construction and loose equipment bids.

It should be kept in mind that, as attractive as the state assistance program is for qualifying districts, it does not provide "free" facilities. Rather, the district must make repayment to the state in accordance with the following procedure.

> Such resolution shall specify that the rate which it is necessary to levy shall be at the rate of one-half mill for each one dollar of valuation except that in those years in which the tax rate for debt service outside the ten-mill limitation is less than three and one-half mills, the rate shall be increased to that rate which is the difference between four mills and the tax rate for debt service outside the ten-mill limitation,

and that such tax shall be levied until the purchase price is paid but in no case longer than twenty-three years.[10]

6.16 Passing Capital Tax Issues

Obtaining voter approval for school construction issues has always been a difficult task. The current situation, however, presents an even more formidable challenge. Whereas in the 1950s approximately 50% of all households included school-age children, the decade of the 1990s shows a vastly different picture with less than 30% of the households including school age children. This demographic reality has had a drastic impact on the public's willingness to support any type of school tax levy, especially those submitted for capital purposes. Although many observers view this voter resistance as Ohio's version of California's "Proposition 13," Ohio's problem began prior to the enactment of California's tax ceiling law.

The capital funding problems of Ohio school districts are similar in magnitude to those of the nation as a whole. Whereas over 70% of school bond issues throughout the United States received voter approval during the early 1960s, the figure dropped to approximately 55% by the mid-1970s. According to the Ohio Department of Education, during the period 1983 through August, 1995, only 42% of Ohio's tax issues for capital improvements received voter approval. The problem facing school districts in the 1970s and 1980s was compounded by increases in per-square-foot building costs and by the resultant high interest costs when bonds were issued. Although the cost per square foot continued to increase through the early and mid-1900s, interest rates did prove more favorable to districts desiring to sell bonds.

The difficulty encountered in passing local property tax issues is evidenced by the plethora of organizations sponsoring, "How to pass your next tax levy" workshops and institutes. No single campaign strategy is the best in all situations, however, the following imperatives should find universal application.

1. Begin strategy planning early.
2. Strive for the active involvement of the citizenry.
3. Ask the community leaders who were actively and visibly involved with the determination of facility needs to continue with promotion of the tax issue(s).
4. Secure adequate funding, that is, consistent with campaign strategy.
5. Develop a positive but simple slogan or theme for the campaign.
6. Ensure that additional information is readily available to those who request more detail.
7. Conduct a balanced campaign that reaches the various sub-groups of the public.
8. Concentrate on the "yes" and "probably yes" voters by making sure that they are registered and have transportation to the polls.
9. Remember the positive absentee voters.
10. Be sure all information is accurate.

---

[10] Ohio Rev. Code Ann. at § 3318.06(C). *See also* OHIO SCHOOL LAW GUIDE at § 6.34.

Table 6:3

Bond Ratings (Moody's) and Yield, 1940-1990 (end of year)

Year	Aaa	Aa	A	Baa
1990	6.63	6.82	6.96	7.10
1985	7.98	8.31	8.64	9.05
1980	9.44	9.64	9.80	10.64
1975	6.50	6.94	7.78	7.96
1970	5.21	5.33	5.60	5.80
1965	3.39	3.47	3.60	3.78
1960	3.12	3.35	3.60	4.03
1955	2.29	2.46	2.81	3.25
1950	1.42	1.60	1.92	2.17
1945	1.11	1.27	1.62	1.91
1940	1.56	1.78	2.11	2.60

Information for Table 6:3 is taken from *Moody's Bond Record*, Volume 58, No. 1 (New York: Moody's Investors Service, January 1991), p. 312.

11. Give special emphasis to heavy voter turn out areas.

Conversely, certain approaches should be avoided in the conduct of a tax issue campaign.

1. Do not spend time and resources trying to "win over" confirmed "no" voters.
2. Avoid trying to tell too much (educators tend to over-estimate the average voter's interest in financial details).
3. Resist the temptation to use acronyms and educational jargon.

6.17 School Bonds and Bond Rating

A high percentage of all funds for capital outlay are raised via general obligation bonds. School districts issue a bond which is, in effect, a debt (obligation) of such district. Generally, there is an inverse relationship between bond quality and yield to investors, that is, "the higher the quality, the lower the yield," as can be seen in Table 6:3.

Although municipal bonds receive federal tax exempt status on interest earned they are not exempt from federal inheritance taxes.

6.18 Importance of Bond Rating

The investment community requires a uniform standard by which to judge the attractiveness of investments; a rating system reflects this need for uniform, standard information. Bond rating firms or agencies are very important in protecting the investor's money and in providing measures for comparability of issues. General obligation issues of any major size are usually rated by a private agency.

The primary national bond rating agencies are Moody's Investors, Standard and Poor's and Fitche, Investors. While each agency is different with respect to rating structure, the ratings are based on the soundness of investment to the lender. The following are explanations provided by Moody for its municipal bond rating system:

Aaa

Bonds which are rated *Aaa* are judged to be of the best quality. They carry the smallest degree of investment risk and are generally referred to as "gilt edge." Interest payments are protected by a large or by an exceptionally stable margin and principal is secure. While the various protective elements are likely to change, such changes as can be visualized are most unlikely to impair the fundamentally strong position of such issues.

Aa

Bonds which are rated *Aa* are judged to be of high quality by all standards. Together with the *Aaa* group they comprise what are generally known as high grade bonds. They are rated lower than the best bonds because margins of protection may not be as large as in *Aaa* securities or fluctuation of protective elements may be of greater amplitude or there may be other elements present which make the long-term risks appear somewhat larger than in *Aaa* securities.

A

Bonds which are rated *A* possess many favorable investment attributes and are to be considered as upper medium grade obligations. Factors giving security to principal and interest are considered adequate, but elements may be present which suggest a susceptibility to impairment sometime in the future.

Baa

Bonds which are rated *Baa* are considered as medium grade obligation; i.e., they are neither highly protected nor poorly secured. Interest payments and principal security appear adequate for the present but certain protective elements may be lacking or may be characteristically unreliable over any great length of time. Such bonds lack outstanding investment characteristics and, in fact, have speculative characteristics as well.[11]

Additional lower ratings are *Ba, B, Caa, Ca,* and *C*. The latter represents the lowest rated class of bonds and can be regarded as having poor prospects of ever attaining any real investment standing.

Those bonds in the *A* and *Baa* group which Moody's believes possess the strongest investment attributes are designated by the symbols of *A1* and *Baa1*. Standard and Poor's system of ratings have different symbols which reflect the soundness of investments. Briefly, Standard and Poor's ratings are as follows: *AAA*, prime; *AA* high grade; *A*, upper medium; *BBB*, medium grade; *BB*, lower medium grade; *B, CCC, CC,* with lowest broad grouping of *C, DDD,* and *DD* indicating various degrees of default.

It should be noted that small issues (below $1.5 million) are generally not rated. Many such issues are sold, pursuant to state statutes, in public sales without a rating. Small school districts often find it advantageous to sell the notes directly to a local bank which re-sells the issue to local investors.[12]

---

[11] *Moody's Bond Record*, Vol. 58, No. 1 (New York: Moody's Investors Service, Inc., Jan. 1991), at 3.

[12] R. Craig Wood, ed., *Principles of School Business Managment* (Reston, VA: Association of School Business Officials International, 1986), at 571 [hereinafter *Principles of School Business Management*].

6.19 Legal Services

Although school administrators and boards of education from less wealthy districts may wish to save money by doing their own bond work, the increasing complexity of statutory requirements for bonding and the complicated legal and financial issues facing the school districts, strongly suggest otherwise. It is almost mandatory for school districts to employ a bond attorney when a bond issue is contemplated.[13]

It is important to realize that the bond attorney functions as legal advisor to the board of education and ultimately to the investor. The attorney is concerned with the mechanics of the issue as well as the overall aspect of the issue in relationship to the legal thinking of the courts regarding the issue's appropriateness.[14]

Fees for bond attorneys vary based on the complexity of the state's statutes and the time and costs involved in researching and examining all the necessary information. As a result, a small privately-sold issue may require very modest legal fees; whereas, a large, complex issue, such as the formation of a holding corporation for an educational cooperative involving many school districts, might result in a fee of $200,000 to $300,000.

Moody's has offered the following advice regarding the selection of a legal advisor:

> The importance of competent legal guidance from the very start of your issue's preparation cannot be overemphasized. Once you decide on an improvement program, and choose to issue bonds instead of paying as you go, your first step should be the selection of an attorney skilled in handling municipal bonds. In general, the more experienced the attorney, the more money he will save you as a bond issuer and the less trouble you will have in bringing your bond issue to market. Your attorney drafts or approves the original bond resolutions and ordinances, the notice of the bond election, and the form of the ballot if an election is required under local law. Once voters have approved the issue, he reviews the preparation of a possible prospectus, financial advertisements, and the entire "package" presented to underwriters for bidding. After the bonds have been sold, printed, paid for and delivered, he renders a final legal opinion. Bond buyers today rarely accept delivery of bonds if such an opinion is not furnished. Perhaps your public unit's own counsel or another local attorney may be able to do as fine a job as a specialist, but it is better not to take the chance. Just a tiny technical error may require that you re-advertise the offering. Also, a bond accompanied by what underwriters call a "local" opinion generally sells at a lower rate (i.e. higher interest cost) than a bond of the same public unit which carries a "marketable opinion." A marketable opinion is simply an opinion by a legal specialist whom underwriters and investors recognize as of proven competence. Dealers want to know before they bid that a final legal opinion will be furnished with the bonds when delivered.
>
> If, for some reason, your community decides not to secure a legal opinion, it must allow the bidders to name their own attorneys. This, quite naturally, will be at the

---

[13] *Financing Education* at 298.

[14] *Principles of School Business Management* at 566.

community's expense. Bidders will subtract it from the price they offer for the issue.[15]

The wisdom of hiring a professional to handle the "packaging" of the bond issue is evident when one considers the potential jeopardy to a school district. The worst nightmare of a school administrator or member of a board of education could become a reality as the result of a single "slip-up" in the entire process, from determination of financial need to the actual sale of bonds and scheduling payments for such bonds. Beyond purely legal considerations, the financial advice available from professionals can result in substantial savings to the school district. Bonding attorneys are also important in drafting ballot language and other legal documents for pay-as-you-go plans.

6.20 Summary

Although several definitive studies have indicated the need for a massive infusion of dollars to adequately address the need for improved school facilities, it appears that most of these funds will have to be raised by way of local taxes. This reality underscores the need for school districts to be even more diligent in planning, designing, and promoting such projects at the district level.

---

[15] *Pitfalls in Issuing Municipal Bonds* (New York: Moody's Investors Service, Inc., 1977), at 24.

Chapter 7: Federal Funds

7.1 Introduction

Federal money for funding elementary and secondary education will presumably continue to be categorical in nature. The money is specified for certain educational problems which Congress, and in some cases the administration, perceive to exist in the schools. *Public Law 94-142*, the *Education for All Handicapped Children Act*, which has provided substantial sums of federal dollars for education, is an example of such categorical funding. But the amount of federal money coming to schools nationwide is relatively small when compared to the total that is annually expended for schools. Also the portion of the revenues of the elementary and secondary schools coming from the federal government has been reduced substantially. Underwood and Verstegen point out that the percentage of total revenues they derived from federal sources dropped from 9.8% in 1980 to 6.2% in 1987, a decline of more than one third in a seven year period.[1] It should be noted that the largest decrease occurred in 1981-82 which was the result of President Reagan's initial effort to reduce federal spending.

The experience in Ohio, using sources of revenue as a base, indicates that the federal funds coming into Ohio accounted for approximately 3.5% of the total funds available to the public schools. Although federal funds for the operation of the elementary and secondary schools in Ohio remain relatively small when one considers the total expenditures, such funds do play an important function for targeted areas of education in the state.

This chapter will: (1) review briefly some ideas concerning the shift in the focus of the federal government's financial commitment to elementary and secondary education since 1960; (2) present in tabular form, using two sets of information, the amounts of federal money that have been coming to Ohio's schools in recent years; (3) list programs that were in place for the fiscal year 1991; and (4) list what may be expected in terms of the federal government's funding of education in the future.

7.2 Federal Funds from 1960 to 1990

Underwood and Verstegen point out the following:

[1] Julie K. Underwood and Deborah A. Verstegen, eds., *The Impacts of Litigation and Legislation on Public School Finance*, Tenth Annual Yearbook of the American Education Finance Association (New York: Ballinger, 1990), 21 [hereinafter *The Impacts of Litigation and Legislation on Public School Finance*].

During the period from 1960 to 1980 federal programs burgeoned. Although the calls for general aid were not heeded, a large number of federal programs of categorical aid (designed to reach particular groups of students or to promote particular activities) were enacted.[2]

During that 1960 to 1990 time period the *Elementary and Secondary Education Act* (ESEA) and the *Education for All Handicapped Children Act* (EHA) were passed. In regards to ESEA's categorical nature, Underwood and Verstegen stated:

Some critics of ESEA said that it was really a disguise for general aid to education; indeed, 95% of the nation's counties and 100% of its congressional districts were eligible to receive aid and were permitted some discretion in its use.[3]

On the other hand EHA was distinctly categorical in nature, targeting a specific problem and limiting the use of the funds, to a specific group of children.

Also during this period, a substantial amount of money was provided by the federal government for the expansion of vocational education programs. This was especially true in Ohio for it was during this period that the majority of the buildings of the 49 joint vocational school districts were constructed. Many such facilities were not only built but equipped with 50% of the cost being paid with federal monies.

During the eighties, increases in support by the federal government, in terms of real dollars (when actual dollars are adjusted in accordance with the Consumer Price Index) were negligible. Underwood and Verstegen point this out when they state the following:

> Congressional appropriations increased from $14.5 billion in fiscal year 1980 to $20.3 billion for fiscal year 1988. However, when appropriations are adjusted to reflect sequesters and deflated to reflect real dollars, they changed only from $13.9 billion in fiscal year 1980 to $13.5 billion in fiscal year 1988. Thus, the Reagan administration succeeded in holding the line on federal expenditures, but it was unsuccessful in reducing overall federal spending for education.[4]

Therefore, local school systems across the nation could no longer rely as heavily on the federal government to supply funds to meet the demands for additional programs and to expand promising programs that had proven to be successful. There appeared to be a shift from an emphasis on all districts receiving some money to targeting certain programs. These targeted programs included programs to decrease the number of dropouts, serve as exemplary programs, and/or identify exemplary schools for additional federal funds.

7.3 Ohio Department of Education Grants

Numerous grants were provided by Ohio during fiscal year 1995. The following are the grants funded and the purposes of the grants which were available by application for Ohio's schools.[5]

---

[2] *Id.* at 8.
[3] *Id.* at 10.
[4] *Id.* at 20.
[5] Information concerning Ohio Grants was supplied through the courtesy of Jack Hansher, Ohio Department of Education, September, 1995.

1. Teen Sexuality and Pregnancy Prevention

This grant has three primary purposes. First, the program is to support the development and implementation of programs and/or services that encourage postponement of teenage sexual activity to prevent teenage pregnancy. Second, the intent is to support services that meet the health care, employment, educational, and/or social service needs of parenting teens. The last purpose is to fill geographical voids in health care services as well as to serve under served populations, such as teenage males. The amount of the grant awards vary depending on proposed activities.

2. Reading Recovery

Reading Recovery grants provide funds for an early intervention program. Funds are used to subsidize regional sites for training teachers and leaders in a year-long program. Grants awards for school districts vary depending on the number of teachers accepted into the program per site.

3. Parents as Teachers

This state grant is for the development of home/school partnerships designed to give children the best possible start in life and to support parents in their role as their child's first teacher. Through Parents as Teachers grants, parent educators help parents of children from birth through age three recognize everyday learning opportunities in their children's lives. Parent educators also provide parents with practical information and guidance in helping their children develop skills that are essential to later learning. The program includes home visits, group meetings, screening to check a child's development and parent centers with toys and materials. Grant awards vary depending on proposed activities.

4. Early Identification

Funds for the development, improvement, and expansion of an early childhood identification process are available through this grant. The process is designed to identify early learning needs of young children. The process includes screening, follow-up, and parent information and referral. Grant awards are for a maximum of $10,000 per school district.

5. Public Preschool Grants

State funds offered through these grants are for the continuation of public preschool programs for three and four year old children. Funds must be used to provide comprehensive child development programs that include components of education, health, parent involvement, and social services. Grant recipients must participate in the development of county "Unified Service Provider Plans" so that existing programs and services will be coordinated for children from low-income families. The grant awards vary depending on the number and poverty levels of children served.

6. Head Start

Head Start funds are for the expansion of the primarily federally funded Head Start programs for disadvantaged preschoolers. All programs must operate in accordance with federal Head Start performance standards. Grant recipients must participate in the development of county "Unified Service Provider Plans" so that existing programs and services will be coordinated for children from low-income families. While grant awards vary based on the number of children served, the minimum award is $3,200 per child served.

7. Community Education Planning Grant

This implementation grant is available to local education agencies, governmental units, and nonprofit tax-exempt public or private agencies. Funds are used to initiate the community education process as a means of addressing local education reform efforts consistent with the goals of Ohio 2000. Emphasis is placed on interagency collaboration. Individual grants are limited to $2,500 for activities related to training, needs assessment, goal setting, and inter-agency involvement.

8. Community Education Implementation Grant

This implementation grant is to assist currently funded planning grantees in the initial implementation of community education and the development of a three-year plan for community education at the local level. Grant awards are for a maximum of $7,500.

9. Entry-Year Program

The purpose of the Entry-Year Program Grant is to provide support for meeting needs of individuals in the first year of employment under a classroom teaching certificate or an educational personnel certificate. The program includes five components. These components are: a) criteria and procedures for selecting mentors; b) orientation to mentoring responsibilities; c) criteria and procedures for evaluating mentors; d) allocation of time for the mentoring process; and e) ongoing professional support for mentors and first-year employees. Grant awards vary based on proposed activities.

10. Venture Capital

Venture Capital Grants are designed to support the creation of a state-wide network of school improvement sites. Funds are to be used to adopt or create school improvement models for transforming the teaching and learning process. These grants are awarded at the building level and the awards are for $25,000 per site.

11. Technology Equity

These grants provide funds to assist poorer school districts to acquire the technological tools and skills they will need to help their students prepare for the 21st century. The financial assistance is designed to held integrate current technologies into present instruction and prepare for future technologies. The awards vary depending on proposed activities.

12. Disadvantaged Pupil Program Fund

This grant, which existed in fiscal year 1995, is not available to school districts now. It has been incorporated with Disadvantaged Pupil Impact Aid (DPIA) funds under the Foundation Program. The purpose of the grant in the past was to assist in designing and operating programs to improve the educational status of disadvantaged pupils. Past grants were awarded based on the number of ADC recipients.

13. Career Development Grant

The intent of this grant is to promote a K-12 program of adult awareness, exploration, and assessment emphasizing the Individual Adult Plan (ICP) document and Career Passport process. Experiences are provided leading to ICP completion, review, and validation.

Grant awards are a minimum of $10,000 and are based on average daily membership (ADM).

14. Economic Education Program Grant

The purpose of this grant is to further understanding of consumer and economic education by both youth and adults. A comprehensive economic education program includes cooperative agreements with community agencies, business and industry linkages, student experiences, curriculum development, and vertification of student competencies. Grant awards are for a maximum of $10,500 per vocational education planning district (VEPD).

15. Educational Mobility Assistance Program (EMAP)

EMAP is Ohio's legislated desegregation assistance to support local school boards that voluntarily adopt and implement plans to desegregate schools within their districts through student transfers. Grant awards are based on the number of student transfers.

16. Training Ohio's Parents for Success (TOPS)

TOPS is a parent education program provided by Ohio school districts. It is designed to increase parental involvement in the education of their children and to address parenting skills. The program is for parents of children from birth through high school. Grant awards vary based on proposed activities.

17. American Sign Language

This grant provides funds for integrating sign language and deaf culture throughout the K-8 curriculum and for offering an American sign language course in grades 9-12. Three pilot site school districts are awarded these grants every two years. Grant awards range from $70,000 to $100,000.

18. Model Projects for Services for Gifted Children

Funds are provided through these grants for the improvement of services to gifted students in the regular classroom through principal-led building teams. Each project will provide baseline and follow-up data regarding the effectiveness of the services provided. Awards vary depending on proposed activities.

19. Governor's Summer Institutes for Gifted and Talented Students

This project provides funds for thirteen state supported universities and three private universities to implement summer institutes for gifted and talented students. Each project enrolls approximately 250 sophomore and junior students. Project awards are based on a set-aside of state funds and vary according to activities.

20. Urban Bicycle/Pedestrian Safety Program

This grant provides urban school districts funds to teach elementary students bicycle and pedestrian safety skills. Grant awards are $4,500 per school district.

21. Applied Academics Grants

These grants are for purchasing equipment needed in vocational education applied academics laboratories and classrooms. The grant awards vary depending on proposed activities—$1,500 for Applied Math and Communications; $10,000 for Applied Biology and Chemistry; and $15,000 for Principles of Technology.

22. School-to-Work Demonstration Project

Funds are provided through these grants for experimental school-to-work transition pilot projects. Grant awards are $70,000 per site.

23. Jobs for Ohio's Graduates

Grant funds are for the purpose of addressing the needs of at-risk 12th grade students. The funds are provided to develop model programs for addressing: a) reducing the dropout rate; b) increasing the graduation rate; and c) increasing the rate of successful transition into the private sector labor force. Grant awards are for $20,000 per teacher.

24. Adult Vocational Education Full Service Center

The purpose of full service centers is to provide business and industry a cost efficient, educationally sound way to train and upgrade personnel skills. The centers provide a foundation of basic course offerings and student services, as well as specialized courses designed to meet local training needs. Grant awards are $20,000 for the first year of operation and $15,000 thereafter.

7.4 Federal Grants Administered by the Ohio Department of Education

A large number of federal grants were offered to Ohio schools in 1995. These grants were administered by the Ohio Department of Education. The following grants were offered to school districts.[6]

1. Foreign Language Assistance Act Grant

This grant provides funds for schools to begin programs in the less-commonly offered foreign languages including Japanese, Chinese, Russian, Arabic, and Korean. Grant awards vary based on proposed activities.

2. Reading Recovery

This grant provides funds for an early intervention program. Funds are used to subsidize regional sites for training teachers and leaders in a year-long program. The awards vary depending on the number of teachers accepted into the program per site.

3. National School Lunch Program

The purpose of this program is to provide a nutritionally balanced meal for children attending public or private nonprofit schools. Schools are reimbursed based on the number of lunches served.

4. School Breakfast Program

This program is designed to provide reimbursement of a nutritionally balanced breakfast for schools eligible to participate in the National School Lunch Program. Schools are reimbursed based on the number of breakfasts served.

5. Special Milk Program

The special milk program reimburses schools for part or full cost of milk providing the schools are not part of the National School Lunch Program. Split-day kindergarten and

[6] Information concerning Federal Grants was supplied through the courtesy of Jack Hansher, Ohio Department of Education, September, 1995.

preschools can participate in this program whenever there is no access to lunch or breakfast programs. Reimbursement is based on the number of 1/2 pints of milk served.

6. Preschool Special Education Program

This grant provides funds for school districts to provide special education programs for children with disabilities ages three through five. Grant awards are based on the December 1 child count.

7. Education of Homeless Children and Youth

The purpose of this grant is to ensure that homeless children have access to a free and appropriate public education. The McKinney Act calls on states to review their laws and policies to eliminate barriers to the enrollment, attendance, and success in schooling of homeless children and to include homeless students in the mainstream school environment. In 1995, $1,100,757 was allocated to this program.

8. Title 6

Prior to fiscal year 1996, Title 6 was identified as Chapter 2. The general purpose of this grant is to provide for the improvement of elementary and secondary education programs, with a focus on those five to seventeen year old students who: a) live in areas with a high concentration of low income families; b) come from low income families; or c) live in sparsely populated areas. Basically, the grant is to meet the special needs of at-risk students. In 1995, $370,000,000 was allocated nationally for this grant with $14,313,188 coming to Ohio schools.

9. Migrant Education

Migrant Education grants are for the purpose of expanding, improving, and coordinating educational programs for the children of migratory farm workers and fishers. Financial assistance is provided to schools serving these students for supplementary educational services and costs. In 1995, $1,470,057 was provided to Ohio schools that served migrant workers' children in order to help provide these children with the same opportunities as other children to meet state performance standards.

10. Impact Aid Program—Public Law 81-874

Impact Aid is a categorical program for which funds are provided by the federal government to local schools in which a government installation or agency results in a significant increase in the number of federally connected children becoming members of a school district during a specified period of time. The funds are provided as the result of the financial strain on school districts due to the tax-exempt status of federal property. The federal government pays a dollar amount per federally-connected child enrolled in the public school.

11. Program Improvement—Chapter 1

Program Improvement funds must only be used for direct educational services. Funds may be allocated by the state education agency to local educational agencies for use in buildings that have been identified, based on Chapter 1 evaluation results, for program improvement activities. Program improvement plans are required, and parents, school staff, and the administration must agree on the best use of the funds. In fiscal year 1995, $1,003,136 was allocated to this program.

12. Capital Expenses of Private Schools

Capital Expense funds are provided for the purchase, lease, and renovation of real and personal property, including mobile or modular education units and leasing of rental sites or space in which to provide Chapter 1 instruction to eligible children off the private school grounds. Funds may only be used for non-instructional goods and services that are incurred as a result of the implementation of alternative delivery systems to comply with the requirements of Aguilar v. Felton. In addition to mobile or modular units, expenditures may include insurance and maintenance costs, transportation, and other comparable goods and services. Instructional equipment may not be included. In fiscal year 1995, $1,330,373 was spent from this fund.

13. Grants to Local Educational Agencies (LEAs) Title 1

Title 1 is a federally funded compensatory program for educationally disadvantaged children in LEAs. Until fiscal year 1996, Title 1 was known as Chapter 1. Funds are allocated based on a formula prescribed in law. Priority educational needs of eligible children must be identified, and supplemental programs must be designed to provide adequate instruction in the areas of early childhood, reading, math, or language arts. In fiscal year 1995 federal allocated funds totaled $274,267,585.

14. Even Start Family Literacy Program

The purpose of this grant is to improve the educational opportunities of children and adults by integrating early childhood education and adult education for parents in a unified program. The program shall be implemented through cooperative projects that build on existing community resources to create a new range of services. Grants awarded to school districts vary depending on proposed activities. The minimum single award amount is $75,000.

15. Title 2

In fiscal year 1995, Title 2 was known as Dwight D. Eisenhower Mathematics and Science Education Grant. Title 2 provides funds for research, development, and dissemination of programs and materials for training, retraining, and in-service training for elementary and secondary teachers in the math and science fields. Grant awards vary to districts based on formula allocation.

16. National and Community Service

Funds are provided through this grant for technical assistance and training to local education agencies for collaborative efforts with nonprofit organizations in order to initiate, improve, or expand community service learning activities for students in grades kindergarten through twelve. Grant awards are for a maximum of $15,000.

17. Nutrition Education and Training (NET) Program Child Care Grants

The NET program is designed to improve dietary habits of children through educational school programs. Emphasis is placed on improving children's decision-making skills, and eating practices, resulting in an increase in children's consumption of vegetables, fruits, and grains. Grant awards vary based on enrollment.

18. Nutrition Education and Training (NET) Program School Grants

The same emphasis is applied to this grant as for NET Child Care Grants. However, this grant provides funds for schools to purchase food, small cooking equipment, and nutrition education materials. Grant awards vary from $500 for a classroom grant up to $5,000 for a school district grant.

19. Comprehensive Arts Education

Grants are awarded to regional partnerships to plan and conduct two-week summer institutes on comprehensive arts education. In 1996 eight regional partnerships have been approved. The grant awards are for $20,000 per regional partnership.

20. Learn and Serve America

Elementary and secondary schools are assisted through this grant to develop high quality community service learning programs. The maximum award for planning school-based programs is $4,500. The maximum for implementing, operating, or expanding school-based programs is $20,000. The maximum for implementing, operating, or expanding adult volunteer programs is $15,000.

21. Title 4

This grant was known as Safe Drug Free Schools and Communities prior to fiscal year 1996. It supports local education agencies in helping prevent violence in and around schools and by strengthening programs that prevent the illegal use of alcohol, tobacco, and other drugs. Grant awards vary depending on enrollment and need.

22. Emergency Immigrant Education Program

Grants from this program are used to provide high quality instruction to immigrant youth. The intention is to assist youth with their transition into the U.S. society and with meeting state performance standards. The awards are based on the number of immigrant children in school districts.

23. Title VII: Bilingual Education, Language Enhancement, and Language Acquisition Program

This grant is used to educate limited English proficient children to meet state performance standards. Grant awards vary depending on proposed activities.

24. Ohio State Educational Agency (SEA)

Fiscal year 1996 represents the third year of a three year grant. The purpose of the grant is to strengthen efforts in promoting equal educational opportunities through race, sex, and national origin desegregation. During fiscal year 1995, $421,000 was appropriated for SEA.

25. Emergency Immigrant Education Program (EIEP)

The EIEP program provides financial assistance for supplementary educational services and costs for eligible immigrant children enrolled in both public and nonpublic schools. Grants are formula funded according to the immigrant student count conducted in April of each year. The funding for fiscal year 1995 was $99,927.

26. HIV Prevention

This grant is also known by the name of Comprehensive School Health Program. The purpose is to expand and strengthen new and existing HIV prevention education and to integrate such education into existing health education programs. Over $300,000 was appropriated by the federal government for Ohio programs in fiscal year 1996.

27. IDEA, Title VI-B Flow-through Funds

Title VI-B Flow-through funds are intended to supplement state and local funds used to educate students with disabilities. School districts receive these funds based on the December 1 child count.

28. Title 1

Title 1 Funds, prior to fiscal year 1996, were known as Chapter 1, 89-313 Funds. These are supplementary funds to be used in meeting the educational needs of students with disabilities. County MRDD Boards receive these funds based on the December 1 child count.

29. Ohio's Javits Project

The federal government supplies funds for Ohio schools to improve methods for identifying and providing services for gifted students who are in kindergarten through grade three. However, the children must be economically disadvantaged. Ohio's project targets only five sites.

30. Project Life

This grant is designed to assist disadvantaged youth in making the transition from youth to adulthood. Proposed activities determine the amount of grant awards.

31. School-Year Training on Delivering Services in Inclusive Settings

This is a state-wide staff development program designed to provide assistance and support in the effective integration of students with disabilities into regular education environments. This staff development program is administered directly by the Division of Special Education.

32. Parent Mentor Project

The federal government supplies funds for experienced parents of children with disabilities to work in public school districts to facilitate positive parent-professional partnerships and to assist other parents of children with disabilities. Grant awards are $25,000 per year.

33. Ohio Classroom Management Project

This federally funded project is a systems change project focused on building-level needs assessment, goal setting, strategic planning, and evaluation relative to critical components that impact discipline. The project is administered by the Division of Special Education.

34. Community-Based Organization (CBO) Grants

CBO Grants are designed to promote collaboration between local education agencies and community organizations. The proposed purpose is to provide specified vocational support services for economically and academically disadvantaged youth. Grant funds are used to facilitate the entrance of youth into a program of transitional services and subsequent entrance into vocational education, employment, or other education and training. Grant awards range from $10,000 to $35,000.

35. Appalachian Regional Commission (ARC) Grants

These grants are used for projects promoting education excellence, workforce training, or youth leadership and community service. ARC projects are conducted with a combination of local and federal funds.

36. Job Opportunities and Basic Skills (JOBS)

These funds are to help participants in making appropriate decisions about their future training and adult choices. Comprehensive vocational assessment/evaluation measures skills, interests, aptitudes and abilities for various jobs, and evaluation of potential for new skill training. Reimbursement through this grant is $40,000 for start-up expenses; $300 per assessment for the first 300 people; and then 60/40 percent state/local match per assessment.

37. Ohio Family Life Program

This program is a community-based service that promotes and builds parenting, family literacy, and life management skills. Grant awards are based on the number of people served and the history of performance.

38. Adult Basic and Literacy Education

This grant supports direct instructional programs for educationally disadvantaged adults. These instructional programs include activities to increase an adult's ability to read, write, speak, compute, and solve problems at levels of proficiency necessary to function on the job and in society.

39. Tech Prep

Tech Prep grants provide planning and demonstration funds to consortia for the development and operation of programs designed to provide education programs leading to a two-year associate degree or a two-year certificate. The federal government funds this program with $525,000 over three years.

40. Comprehensive Support Services (CSS) Grants

CSS Grants provide support services for single parents, displaced homemakers, and single pregnant women. It is designed to enable them to obtain marketable skills to become economically self sufficient. Grant awards are a minimum of $10,000 with allocations based on the economic need of the vocational education planning district and the programs in place which serve the targeted audience.

41. Displaced Homemaker Grant

This program is designed to assist displaced homemakers and single parents to make the transition from homemaking to wage earning. Participants are provided with supportive instruction and services to help them cope with new life situations, to help them become independent, and to assist in acquiring marketable skills. Grants range from $24,000 to $31,500 depending on the timeline of the grant.

42. Graduation, Occupation and Living Skills (GOALS)

The GOALS program is a vocational job-readiness program that helps single parents and homemakers who have dropped out of school to complete their education, train for a job, and be a better parent. The program includes personal development, adult exploration, employability skills, and resource management. Grant awards range from $24,000 to $31,500.

43. Ventures in Business Ownership

This program provides single parents and displaced homemakers opportunities to explore entrepreneurship. Included in the program is an orientation to small-business ownership, interest and aptitude assessment, development of a business plan, and resource management. Grant awards are $39,000 per site.

44. Nontraditional Education for Teens for Work (NETWORK)

NETWORK is a one-year vocational education program for high at-risk female high school students who are interested in exploring training opportunities nontraditional for the female gender. Grant awards range from $50,000 to $65,000 depending on the economic need of the vocational education planning district.

45. Orientation to Nontraditional Occupations for Women

This is an eight week program that assists adult women to explore opportunities in nontraditional areas including construction, manufacturing service, or technical occupations. Grant awards are for $50,444 per site.

46. Promoting Access in Technical Education (PATE)

The purpose of the PATE Grant is to enroll and retain students in technical education programs nontraditional for their gender, as well as job placement within the occupation for which they are trained. Grant awards are for a maximum of $12,000 per year.

7.5 The Future of Federal Funds for Education

Predicting the future is difficult in any field. The same is true in predicting what can be expected from the federal government in helping education. Various people have suggested that a new strategy for education should encourage increased funding to help improve elementary and secondary schools but it should be aimed primarily to help urban schools improve the recruitment, training and pay of teachers as well as to promote research and development for improved instruction in urban secondary schools. These are good concepts as they are focused on the greatest needs of today's public schools. However, such concepts should be extended to all segments of public schools and not limited to urban districts.

Underwood and Verstegen suggested the following ideas about their expectations concerning federal policies and federal funds for the future for elementary and secondary education:

(1) The federal budget deficit and the cost of servicing the federal debt will severely constrain new initiatives particularly any that involve a large expenditure of funds.

(2) Existing categorical federal programs are likely to continue but expansion of their scope of funding is unlikely.

(3) The issue of local control (emphasized during the Reagan years) has been reenergized through the concept of educational choice.

(4) Education will continue to be viewed as playing a key role in keeping the United States competitive economically.[7]

There are some indications that the political leadership of the federal government may be willing to give more attention to education. *The Chronicle of Hiqher Education* reported that President Bush, early in his administration, had indicated four basic ideas about his approach to education as follows:

> First, the administration will reward excellence and success in education: federal incentives, in the form of public recognition and financial awards, will provide new catalysts for educational achievement. Second, the Administration will target federal dollars to help those most in need—where support can make a difference.
>
> Next, the Administration will promote choice and flexibility—for families, students, teachers, principals—to encourage competition and help provide the means and the incentives to achieve educational excellence. Finally, the Administration will work to assure that students are actually receiving the highest quality education, by promoting greater accountability at all levels of the educational system. This Administration is committed to objective measurement and reward of progress toward quality education.[8]

Note that the emphasis in the above statement is on rewards for excellence, family choice, competition and accountability. Nothing was mentioned in President Bush's ideas about equalizing the funding of education that would guarantee that all pupils in the elementary and secondary schools of the United States would have access to quality education programs. It also is to be noted that the administrations from 1980 through 1992 promoted the concept that parents should be permitted to choose the school which their children attend and, if they were to choose to attend non-public schools, they should be supported with public funds.

7.6 Summary

From the material in this chapter it appears that the following statements can be made:

1. Federal funds coming to Ohio are important, but in relation to the total expenditures, they represent a small percentage of that total.
2. Most federal funds are directed toward categorical programs.
3. Vocational education and special education have benefitted greatly from federal funds.
4. A number of programs being funded by the federal government and administered by the Ohio Department of Education have little relationship to elementary education.
5. The likelihood of the federal government becoming a major contributor to the education of elementary and secondary pupils in Ohio is rather remote.
6. Data concerning the total dollars coming from the federal government for the education of pupils in Ohio are confusing.

---

[7] *The Impacts of Litigation and Legislation on Public School Finance*, at 23–24.
[8] *The Chronicle of Higher Education*, Feb. 15, 1989, at 25.

Chapter 8:
Specialized School Districts and Agencies

8.1 Education Service Centers

The primary financial base of support for educational service centers (formerly county boards of education) from direct state subsidy. This subsidy was increased from $29 per pupil in fiscal years 1995 and 1996 to $32 per pupil commencing in fiscal year 1997. Beginning with FY 98, the direct subsidy will be 1% of the basic foundation level for Education Service Centers that represent at least three former County Boards of Education. This is intended as an incentive for merging of Education Service Centers. The per pupil subsidy enables education service centers to be operated. In counties with larger average daily membership (ADM) local districts, the per pupil subsidy will also defer excess costs to such local districts and/or provide for the operational expenses of additional programs.

Legislators of the 121st General Assembly made several significant changes in what were formerly called county offices when they adopted the 1996-1997 biennium budget. They first changed the term "county school district" to "educational service center." In keeping with this change, they changed the term "county school board" and "county superintendent" to "governing board" and "superintendent of educational service centers."

After June 30, 1999, all educational service centers must serve at least 8,000 ADM. This number includes students in local school districts as well as students in city and exempted village school districts that choose to contract with the centers for educational services. If education service centers do not have the required base of 8,000 ADM by June 1, 1999, the center must merge with another educational service center. Failure to merge voluntarily will result in the Superintendent of Public Instruction designating a suitable merger.

Such educational service centers are allowed to receive per pupil funding for service agreements with city and exempted village districts (with ADMs of less than 13,000) that did not have county service agreements during FY 1995, if funding is sufficient and if the agreement had been entered into by June 1, 1995.

In discussing the financial aspects of education service centers, it should be understood that there are vast differences in the scope of programs and services offered among Ohio's various counties. Generally, the larger metropolitan-based offices provide a broader range of services. However, many of the small, more rural counties have become very resourceful, both financially and programmatically, in addressing the need for comprehensive services to local districts within their respective centers. Some center offices also contract to provide services to city and exempted village districts at a mutually-agreed upon cost.

8.1-1 Provision of Instructional Leadership

Supervisory leadership provided by education service centers is funded by a local subsidy. This subsidy consists of a per-pupil "charge back" to the appropriate local districts. For the last decade this figure has remained at $6.50 per student. In addition, a supervisory allowance, excluding special education, is charged back to local districts. The supervisory allowance is based upon the state minimum salary schedule which reflects the training and experience of the supervisor(s) actually hired.

In accordance with the *Ohio Revised Code*[1], education service centers must provide local districts with supervisory services as approved by the Ohio Board of Education. The number of supervisors that can be charged back to local districts is one for the first 50 teachers and one for each additional 100 teachers thereafter, based upon the minimum number of teachers required (40 per 1000 students in average daily membership). A local district is charged based upon its share of the ADM of the local districts in that county.

The local subsidy and supervisory charge is used primarily to pay for such leadership activities as helping to prepare/revise courses of study and to provide supervision of curriculum-related activities. Both the per-pupil subsidy and the supervisory allowance are deducted from the local district's foundation program allocation and are paid directly to the education service center.

8.1-2 Provision for Other Programs

Essentially, all other programs are financed by one or more of the following: (1) state unit reimbursement, an example of which would be costs associated with the provision of special education instructors and supervisors, (2) excess costs for special education, and

[1] Ohio Rev. Code Ann. at § 3317.11.

(3) charges to other school districts or entities for special services provided by the education service center.

An earlier reference was made to the provision of services to non-local districts. For many years several county offices of education, as a means of providing services to additional districts, operated programs and services on a contract basis. Such services were often provided under the auspices of supplemental agreements or contracts with non-local school districts. Recently, however, education service centers have been given statutory authority to serve exempted villages and city districts which have individual enrollments of 13,000 or less. In counties which have obtained agreement among the various boards of education, the state subsidy per pupil is granted to the education service centers and the local subsidy is charged to the exempted village and/or city school districts which are a part of the agreement.

8.1-3 Provision for Education Service Center Office Facilities

The *Ohio Revised Code*[2] stipulates that the provision of facilities and utilities for offices of the education service center is the obligation of the county commission of the respective county. Statutory provisions notwithstanding, there are vast differences among the various boards of county commissioners in terms of the adequacy of office facilities provided. This reality should be expected since "adequacy" has not been legally defined as related to such facilities.

In some counties commissioners exercise the option of providing funds for the rental of facilities in lieu of actual construction, depending upon the availability of suitable rental property and the financial condition of the commission. The trend has been for education service centers to move away from the traditional county courthouse location to other sites which more adequately address space requirements and service dimensions of education service centers.

8.1-4 County School Financing Districts

In 1989 legislation was enacted which authorized the formation of county school financing districts[3]. This legislation stated that such districts may be created solely for the following: (1) the provision of special education, (2) the provision of specified educational programs and services, and (3) permanent improvements of school districts. This section also clarifies that a county school financing district shall not employ any staff. Rather, the governing board of the education service center is to serve as the governing board and use its employees to administer the financing district. Local districts served by such governing boards of education would be automatically included unless they vote to be excluded. City and exempted village districts may join if approved by the county financing district.

---

[2] Ohio Rev. Code Ann. at § 3319.29.
[3] Ohio Rev. Code Ann. at § 3311.05.

8.2 Joint Vocational School Districts

Although included under the classification of specialized school districts, joint vocational school districts (JVSDs) are similar to traditional city, exempted village, or local school districts. Although a relatively new concept, joint vocational school districts experience the same fiscal challenges and frustrations as traditional districts. Although some JVSDs are financially solvent, there are others which are experiencing difficult times, some to the extent of active participation in the state's school loan fund.

8.2-1 Local Property Tax

As with traditional school districts, JVSDs are funded primarily by millage voted on local property taxes and by state foundation funds. The various tax levy options for JVSDs are covered under Section 3311.21 of the *Ohio Revised Code.* This Section states that in addition to the local tax options authorized by Sections 5705.194, 5705.21, 5705.212, and 5705.213, the board of education of a JVSD may adopt a resolution declaring the necessity to levy a tax in excess of the ten-mill limitation for a period not to exceed ten years to provide funds for any one or more of several purposes.[4]

An optional method of financing joint vocational school districts became available in 1969. This option, known as the multi-purpose levy, was authorized as a part of *House Bill 1005*[5] and offered a means of providing funds for the purchase or enlargement of a site, for erecting, equipping, enlarging, or improving buildings, and for current operational expenses of the district. It should be noted that the ten-year maximum period applies only if the multi-purpose option (operation and capital improvements) is chosen. This same section of the code allows tax collections for a continuing period of time if the proceeds of the levy are restricted to current operating expenses.

A very important event in terms of JVSD funding was the enactment of section 319.301 of the *Ohio Revised Code.* This section, in effect, negated the provisions of the reduction factor (created by *Amended Substitute House Bill 920*) on levies totaling two mills or less. The net effect on JVSDs was as follows--the voted millage, up to a maximum of two mills, produces additional revenues as property values increase. However, when the millage exceeds two mills, the reduction factor is applied to the "total" millage until it is lowered to the two mill floor.

8.2-2 State Foundation Funds

Whereas, the more traditional school districts receive a major portion of state funding on a per-pupil basis, calculated on their ADM, state funding for vocational education is provided on an approved-unit basis as a line item in the state education budget. The four major components of unit reimbursement are as follows: (1) a salary allowance which is based upon the state minimum salary schedule currently in effect, (2) an amount for retirement and sick leave which is equal to 15% of the total salary allowance, (3) a unit

---

[4] Ohio Rev. Code Ann. at § 3311.21. *See also* OHIO SCHOOL LAW GUIDE at § 5.20.
[5] Ohio Rev. Code Ann. at § 3311.21.

operating allowance for each approved vocational and special education unit, and (4) an amount for approved extended service since fiscal year 1993, the state minimum salary allowance for a teacher with a bachelor's degree and with no experience has remained at $17,000. The unit operating allowance for each vocational unit was set at $9,510 for fiscal year 1989 and has remained constant through fiscal year 1995. Very modest adjustments increased this allowance to $10,388 for fiscal year 1996 and $10,967 in fiscal year 1997. The average unit increase in unit funding, therefore, is only 2.25% for FY 96 and 1.45% for FY 97. The amount received for extended service is determined on the basis of individual class unit criteria, however, such reimbursement usually represents only approximately 12% of the actual cost to the local school district.

8.2-3 District Equalization

An equalization amount is provided for joint vocational school districts (JVSDs) based upon the following formula: (number of vocational approved units x $20,000) - (.001 x total taxable value).[6] For example, if a JVSD district had 60 approved vocational units, this number times $20,000 per unit would equal $1,200,000. Assuming the district had a $900,000,000 tax base, this figure when multiplied by 1 mill (.001) would equal $900,000. In this example, an additional $300,000 (the difference between the two calculations) in state funds would be received as "equalization." If, however, such district had a taxable valuation of $1,200,000,000, instead of $900,000,000, it would "break even" and thus the equalization calculation would be zero.

8.2-4 Supplemental Funding

Until recently, the state also provided modest reimbursement for the administration and supervision of approved vocational programs. Prior to fiscal year 1991, JVSDs received $10,000 to be applied toward the salary of the district superintendent, $9,000 for the vocational director and $8,000 for each approved local supervisor. It should be noted that the reauthorization of the Carl D. Perkins Vocational Education and Applied Technology Act eliminates the "local administration" category.

8.2-5 Graduation Requirement Funds

With the exception of special projects and programs, the last category which receives foundation funds is comprised of courses other than vocational education which are necessary to meet high school graduation requirements. Such funds comprise only a small percentage of the total state foundation monies received.

8.2-6 Importance of Adult Vocational Education

Changing demographics have resulted in a smaller and smaller percentage of voters with school age children. Most studies show this figure to be approximately 30% for traditional school districts. In the case of joint vocational school districts, it is obviously a

---

[6] Ohio Rev. Code Ann. at § 3317.16(B)(6).

far lower percentage. It is estimated that within Ohio's JVSDs only 2% to 4% of voters have a child enrolled in a joint vocational school at the high school level. This reality points rather emphatically to the importance of the adult education dimension of joint vocational schools especially in terms of voter support. By enrolling from five to ten times as many adults as high school students (even though for a much shorter time period) JVSDs have the opportunity to develop a strong support base among the district's adult learners. Without this larger pool of individuals who receive direct benefit from the programs of the JVSD, the probability of passing local tax issues would be lowered considerably.

Although given little attention in the statutes, adult education reimbursement provides a significant portion of the state monies received by JVSDs. Even so, most such districts are forced to provide a 10% to 25% subsidy to the adult education program with general fund monies. It is important to note that only vocational skill development courses qualify for general fund subsidy. Avocational offerings must be self-supporting.

8.3 Boards of Mental Retardation/Developmental Disabilities

County boards of Mental Retardation and Developmental Disabilities (MR/DD) in Ohio were first created by law in 1967. The primary mission of such MR/DD boards is to ensure the availability of programs and support services which will assist eligible individuals who experience mental retardation and/or other developmental disabilities. Such assistance is designed to help these individuals to achieve a life marked by increasing capability in order that they can live and work in the community in an appropriate manner. County boards also assist and support the families of these individuals in achieving these objectives.

County boards of MR/DD are similar to other districts in that they are labor intensive. Because of this reality such county boards must have adequate financial resources if they are to provide necessary programs and services. Historically, such county boards have relied heavily upon local property taxes. Such taxes are based on real and personal property values and the willingness of the electorate to approve property tax issues. It is noteworthy that the majority of the counties have supported MR/DD issues overwhelmingly. However, some poorer counties have experienced great difficulty in obtaining adequate resources locally. Since variances in the quality of programs and services among county boards are directly related to local wealth, tax-poor counties often rely on state and federal revenues to meet the major portion of their expenses.[7]

8.3-1 Federal Revenues

Several federal revenue sources exist for county boards of MR/DD. One such source is Chapter I funds which come directly from the United States Department of Education under the auspices of the Elementary and Secondary Education Act. Specifically, Chapter I provides for supplemental educational funding for children with handicapping conditions. This supplemental funding is determined by the number of children ages 5-21 who are

---

[7] Charles H. Arndt,"Understanding Ohio's System of County Boards of Mental Retardation and Developmental Disabilities," *MRDD Journal* Vol. 3, No. 2 (Worthington, Ohio: Ohio Association of County Boards of Mental Retardation and Developmental Disabilities, Nov., 1990), at 17–18.

enrolled in school-age programs. County MR/DD boards are also eligible for federal medicaid reimbursement for certain medically-related services. Reimbursements can be for services such as occupational therapy, physical therapy, psychological assistance, and nursing services; reimbursements are also available for persons who reside in intensive care facilities for the mentally retarded.

8.3-2 State Revenues

In fiscal 1983, Ohio MR/DD boards received one program subsidy and one transportation subsidy totalling $23 million. Since that time, the following have been added: unit funding, vehicle purchases, family resources, impact grants, and case management services resources. Transportation and adult subsidies have also been expanded. The major applicable state reimbursement programs are as follows: (1) Ohio Department of Education's line item #552 (vehicle purchases) to assist county boards in replacing buses for pre-school age and school-age children, and (2) Ohio Department of Education's #549/577 (school-age/pre-school unit funding) provides a unit allocation for ancillary personnel and teachers of pre-school and school-age children.

Based on enrollment, one teacher is allowed for every six to eight children with reimbursement based upon the state minimum salary schedule. In addition to the 15% for retirement and sick leave, an allowance of $8,023 was provided in fiscal years (FYs) 1992 and 1993 to pay for classroom and other expenses. Ancillary personnel (specialists) also qualify for reimbursement based upon the number of children served under each speciality. Funding for such personnel follows the same general format as for special education classroom teachers with the exception that they receive only $2,678 (FY 1993) to cover additional costs. Other categories of state MR/DD funds include impact grants, supported living, purchase of service, family resources, case management, and rehabilitation services which are funded by the Ohio Department of Education.

8.3-3 Local Revenues

Local funding from property taxes has several drawbacks. One is that all taxes levied by county boards of MR/DD are beyond the ten mill limitation and as a result are collected at their original voted value. As is the case with traditional districts, levies get "rolled back" to the original dollar amounts collected, with the exception of new construction and improvements.

A second problem, again similar to traditional districts, is the amount of tax revenue actually raised due to the wide variance in local property wealth. On a one mill effective rate, the poorest counties in Ohio collect about $1,000 per enrollee and the wealthiest collect nearly $6,000 per enrollee. One can anticipate the problems encountered by a very low wealth county having to levy six mills for every one mill levied in another county. Proposed remedies for this problem include increased state and federal funding and/or an equalization formula which gives poor counties increased aid while not penalizing the tax-wealthy counties.

8.3-4 Other Income

Sources of additional income may include taxes, interest, donations, excess costs, and miscellaneous reimbursement. Prior to fiscal year 1986, tuition was received from the local public schools at a total annual rate of $12,000,000.

8.3-5 Summary of Funding Sources

Table 8:1 presents an overview of the federal, state, and local funding sources for fiscal years 1983, 1987, and 1991 projections including the percentages of support from each source.

A review of the improvements in state funding may cause one to ask, "Where did all the increased funding go?" Of the various factors which come into play, a major one is the fact that over the past eight years approximately 3,000 individuals have been returned to county programs from developmental centers (with most of these persons possessing severe difficulties compared to those persons previously served). As a result, staff enrollee ratios and the need for more specialized services have caused the cost of care for these persons to almost double. For example, the average cost just for support services for each new enrollee was estimated at $14,000 in 1992. This amounts to a total estimated annual increase of $42 million for these individuals. Although the cost is admittedly high, few individuals who have observed an MR/DD program firsthand would question the need for these services.

8.4 Special Education Regional Resource Centers

Throughout Ohio, there are 16 special education regional resource centers (SERRCs), each of which has several components woven together as a means of providing a continuum of special education services for the children and parents of school districts within each region.

The Miami Valley Regional Center for Handicapped Children (MVRCHC), located near Dayton is rather typical of the state's larger SERRCs in terms of the comprehensiveness of services provided to its six member counties. The services included within the core (basic) program are as follows:

1. The Identification and Program Development component which includes assistance with the identification of youngsters who need special education services, assistance with the development of appropriate programs and services to meet the needs of identified students, and assistance to parents with the interpretation of state and federal laws related to the education of people with disabilities.
2. The Educational Assessment Project component which provides multi-factored assessments of low incidence and hard-to-assess children, a school district's sounding board for and parents' suggestions concerning Individual Education Plan development, and a list of program options available throughout the region.
3. The Instructional Resource Center which provides inservice training for professionals and parents working with children with disabilities, a library of instructional materials for use by teachers and parents of students who have identified disabilities, handicap awareness programs and support services.

Table 8:1

Primary Sources of Funding for County MR/DD Boards

	1983 Actual	% of Total	1987 Actual	% of Total	1991 Projected	% of Total
Federal						
Chapter 1	$ 6,200,000		$ 4,403,000		$ 6,200,000	
Title XX	12,400,000		16,000,000		12,000,000	
Rehabilitation Services	0		793,310		4,000,000	
OBRA						
Targeted Case Management						
Habilitation Center						
Medical Waiver						
Total Federal	$18,600,000	11.6%	$21,196,310	7.4%	$26,200,000	6.5%
State of Ohio						
ED 552 Vehicle Purchase	0		$ 1,022,131		$ 1,128,747	
ED 577 Unit Funding Project	0		12,040,371		11,805,207	
ED 549 Unit Funding School Age	0		32,995,770		37,741,800	
ED 553 Children's Transportation	0		4,165,257		5,838,733	
MR/DD 501 Program Subsidies	$18,200,000		23,013,100		27,930,218	
MR/DD 505 Adult Transportation	4,800,000		5,233,462		5,749,564	
MR/DD 507 Impact Grants	0		2,225,805		1,844,096	
MR/DD 452 Case Management	0		5,562,333		4,914,029	
Total State	$23,000,000	14.4%	$86,258,229	30.1%	$98,952,394	24.6%
Local						
Property Taxation	$100,400,000		$171,000,000		$269,047,606	
Public School Tuition	12,000,000		0		0	
Miscellaneous	6,000,000		8,000,000		10,000,000	
Total Local	$118,400,000	74.0%	$179,000,000	62.5%	$279,047,606	69.0%
Total Revenues	$160,000,000	100.0%	$286,454,539	100.0%	$404,200,000	100.0%

Information for Table 8:1 is taken from Charles H. Arndt, "An Overview of the State Budgetary Needs for Implementation of H.B. 569, the Change in Definition of Developmental Disabilities," Volume 3, No. 2 of *MRDD Journal*, (Worthington: Ohio, Ohio Association of County Boards of Mental Retardation and Developmental Disabilities, November, 1990), p. 24.

8.4-1 Core Funding

Core funding for the various SERRCs comes from Title VI-B federal funds distributed through the Ohio Department of Education. Ohio's SERRCs received $256 per pupil for FY 1991 and $263 per pupil in FY 1992.

8.4-2 Supplemental Funding

Although many SERRCs do not have additional funding sources, others have developed special programs and/or assessments which generate additional revenue. For example, one SERRC recently generated approximately $550,000 through its involvement in related personnel/education services (units), a curriculum development project, the Ohio Inter-Agency Training Network, and a per-child charge back to participating school districts.

8.4-3 Transportation

Due to the vast territory covered by most of the state's 16 SERRCs, transportation costs consume a large percentage of the individual SERRC budget. Specifically, most SERRCs spend considerably more on transportation than all other aspects of the program combined. State subsidies from the Ohio Department of Education assist MR/DD boards in paying transportation costs at the rate of $3 per child per day plus 50% of excess costs.

As is the case with other components of the educational program, there appears to be a high correlation between the degree of involvement on the part of educators throughout the service area and the fiscal stability and programmatic success achieved by the individual centers.

8.5 Summary

Although the types of school districts addressed in this chapter individually comprise only a small portion of Ohio's total investment in education, each is very important for the constituency it services. In order for specialized districts and agencies to be treated equitably in terms of state funding, it is essential that educational leaders realize their responsibility to be advocates for all of Ohio's students.

Chapter 9:
Budget Planning and Development

9.1 Introduction

Budgeting and appropriating funds are two separate and different processes. Different legal requirements exist and different time-lines occur. Both processes should incorporate the opportunity to be an extension of educational planning. Unfortunately, some key administrators and boards of education look at the budget as only a legal requirement and see appropriating funds as the only real process of allocating funds in the various accounts and identifying probable expenses. This is faulty thinking and must be remedied if educational planning is to be properly brought into the financial picture.

9.2 Budget Administration

The preparation and administration of a budget, six months in advance of the appropriation process, presents a written record of how much money is expected to be collected from local, state and federal sources combined with interest from investments and unexpended funds from the current fiscal year. The budget also identifies how much money is desired to carry out specific functions for the next fiscal year. Essentially it classifies financial data that will enable decision makers to make prudent decisions while maintaining control and planning for the future.

While the budget forces planning at least six months prior to appropriations, the justification of financial needs to account for possible increases in revenue, forces deficit budgets to be portrayed. This creates suspicion and doubt by some community residents.

Many different accounts make up school budgets. An account is simply a financial record that relates information about income expenditures, fund balances, and encumbrances and liabilities.

The state of Ohio has mandated that all school districts move from a cash basis of accounting to a system called Generally Accepted Accounting Principles (GAAP) accounting by 1996 in accordance with the following schedule: districts with a total budget in excess of $100 million must have completed the conversion to the new reporting method by fiscal year (FY) 1988; districts with budgets over $20 million by FY 91; budgets over $10 million by FY 92; over $7 million by FY 93; over $5 million by FY 94; over $3 million by FY 95; and all districts below $3 million by FY 96.

The revised system has demonstrated accountability, provided for more reliable information, and provided for valid information to assist management in making decisions. The system essentially breaks down the accounting process into a numbering system identifying fund, function, object, special cost centers, subject areas, and cost centers. Basically it is an accrual system of accounting, listing assets and debits similar to business accounting, and gives new levels of information to schools. A more detailed breakdown of the budgeting/accounting system is listed later in this chapter.

The advantages to the GAAP system are many. First, the Ohio Department of Education can compile data and compare costs for schools within the state. A district can use the data to make program decisions on adding, deleting, modifying, or maintaining. Costs can be compared within the district (i.e., comparing elementary school costs within the district) in terms of the amount and proportion of funds used for instruction, administration, and pupil services. Another advantage is that the classification system is much more clearly understood by the staff and the board of education.

9.3 An Extension of Educational Planning

Long-range planning must become a part of every district's mode of operation. Planning ahead for at least five years can help a district reach established and stated goals that are in keeping with its written philosophy. With proper planning, long-range goals will more likely be realized. Priorities are established in order to maximize the use of available financial resources.

It is suggested that long-range planning be preceded by a district mission statement, belief statements, and strategic plans for accomplishing goals. The mission statement should be broad in nature and clearly convey the overall mission of the district.

Belief statements must be more specific attending to the procedures whereby individuals make decisions affecting finances and the allocations of funds. The how and why of decision making can be boldly stated with belief statements.

Finally, strategic plans can be specific enough to identify major areas of concern which in turn can enable full attention to be directed appropriately. Certainly curriculum and instruction, staff development, school climate, student life, and parental and community involvement are factors that need to be incorporated into the strategic planning process and outcomes.

9.4 Who Should Be Involved in the Process?

The literature speaks loudly and clearly about the need to involve many members of the school public, especially those who are directly affected by decisions on where and how much money is allocated to various accounts. Actually, pre-United States history had bearing on the evaluation of the budgetary concept, and the rights of the people to be associated with the determination of services to be offered and the levying of taxes to pay for such services. According to Johns, Morphet, and Alexander, rights of the Parliament of England and/or the King of England to determine the purposes for which tax monies were to be spent and the right to levy taxes, provided the foundation for the democratic budgetary process incorporated in the United States.[1] They indicated, according to their source, that as early as 1314, Parliament required the King to spend tax monies for the purposes for which the taxes were levied. However, it wasn't until the seventeenth century that Parliament acquired from the King the power to levy taxes. Then, in 1742 the people gained a constitutional right to control their finances through a properly elected legislative body when it became the Cabinet's responsibility to prepare the budget and present it to the House of Commons.

This concept of the people "having a say" in how finances are to be spent through elected officials, is now used by the United States (budget developed by the executive branch of government and presented to the legislative branch) and other modern democratic nations. The same concept is incorporated by Ohio's public schools where the budget is prepared by the administration, with the right of the public to submit input, and is presented to the board of education for consideration and adoption.

As was mentioned previously, current literature espouses the involvement of those that are affected by the allocation of funds to be directly involved in the allocation/funding process. What individuals and/or groups are directly affected? Without question school employees, administrators, and classified employees would be affected. Students are also going to be affected according to how many teachers are assigned to work with them, how much transportation will be provided to them, how many textbooks and supplies are provided, and so forth. Ultimately the public is involved when local tax issues are submitted to the electorate.

---

[1] Roe L. Johns, Edgar L. Morphet, and Kern Alexander, *The Economics and Financing of Education*, 4th ed. (Englewood Cliffs, N.J.: Prentice-Hall, 1983), at 349–351 [hereinafter *The Economics and Financing of Education.*]

The board of education and superintendent should determine who will be involved and how the input shall be provided in the process for preparing the budget and appropriations measure. It would behoove all boards of education to formally state their policy of active participation by all parties concerned. The alternative is to wait and let state legislators mandate this policy, as for example, Kentucky legislators did in 1990 when their reform package included required site based management in each Kentucky school district.

The determination of who should be involved also raises the question of centralized vs. decentralized accounting. Centralized accounting is evidenced when the superintendent coordinates the budget from its formation through the expenditure process after funds are appropriated into various accounts. The Ohio Department of Education requires that a district treasurer and another central controller (normally a business manager, assistant superintendent, or superintendent) account for funds as expenditures occur. Treasurers then account for funds on a quarterly and year-end reporting system to the Ohio Department of Education. This approach is readily adapted to a centralized system.

9.5 School-Based Management

The merits of a decentralized system might be best seen when examining a decision-making arrangement classified as school-based or site-based management. School-based management suggests that budgets can be more effectively developed when those who are more directly affected by the decisions have some say in the allocation of funds.

Natchez and Bupp[2] analyzed the Atomic Energy Commission's budgets for a 15-year time frame. They found that there were significant changes in program priorities during this period, and the priorities were set by program directors actually working on the projects and not by national administrators. This study suggests that effective decisions can occur if operating personnel have adequate discretion over decisions of program.[3] Of course, key to this process is the provision of sufficient funds to accommodate identified program changes.

School-based management is a new decision-making process in public school administration in Ohio. There are a few districts that are moving in this direction. Dayton City Schools, for example, determined that five of their school buildings were to be involved in school-based management for the 1990-91 school year.

School-based management, simply stated, is a way of permitting building-level administrators, teachers, parents, and non-parent adults to help determine how monies should be allocated to support identified program needs. It provides those educational professionals who are most familiar with program and student needs, the opportunity to make decisions about where and how much money should be spent.

Another advantage of school-based management is that the citizenry has more opportunity for involvement. School districts have been encouraged at both national and state

---

[2] Peter B. Natchez and Irvin C. Bupp, "Policy and Priority in the Budgetary Process," *American Political Science Review* (Vol. 67, No. 3) (Sept. 1973), at 963.

[3] R. Craig Wood ed., *Principles of School Business Management* (Reston, VA: Association of School Business Officials International, 1986), at 165.

levels to get parents and business leaders involved in school programs. The premise behind this encouragement is that public schooling will improve if consumers are given more responsibility for determining what programs are offered and how they are packaged for consumption by students.

9.6 Teacher Empowerment

Teacher empowerment is a term that has been discussed in recent years. Empowerment has different meanings to many people. If it can be accepted that empowerment has reference to permitting teachers to become actively involved in the decisions that affect their professional interaction with students, then school-based management holds promise for meeting that expressed need. It permits building-level teachers, administrators, and selected citizens to focus on student needs by properly identifying texts, materials and staff development programs to meet those needs. It also assists in allocating financial resources for the improvement of education. This process should reduce the possibility of teacher militancy.

9.7 The Utilization of Networking in School-Based Management

A district that is considering school-based management needs to do so with a clearly thought-out plan, complete with detailed, written policies. The organizational plan for networking could include the following: teacher representatives, student representatives, and parent representatives.

9.7-1 Teacher Representation

Teacher representatives could be selected according to a unit teacher or team leader plan if a building is organized with identified unit or team leaders. Grade level and/or subject matter specialists could also be identified to meet regularly with the building principal to ponder the budgeting process. Regardless of the organizational framework, it is strongly suggested that all teachers have representation on the decision-making council. This will provide some assurance that everyone has input into the process and will enable all grade levels and disciplines to be represented.

9.7-2 Student Representation

Some districts will consider involving students directly by having student body representatives serve on a council reviewing budgetary concerns. Whether direct representation exists or not, it is recommended that students be invited to offer recommendations through some formalized and consistent process. Such participation should foster active future involvement in the democratic process.

9.7-3 Parent Representation

Some districts have already established advisory councils that meet regularly to wrestle with both immediate and longer range building needs. Some also have district level curriculum advisory councils that involve both parents and teachers. It is important that only the parents who have expressed an interest in serving on an advisory council be selected.

Site-based management can result in greater autonomy at the building level while also achieving quality control at the district level. Healthy competition can exist for achieving excellence provided a management philosophy exists to empower people properly.

9.8 Legal Essentials for Preparing a Budget in Ohio

The preparation of a school district budget and subsequent adoption by the local board of education or educational service center is the first step in a school district's fiscal planning. A budget is the financial plan for a district's operation for the next fiscal year. It is not only a legal mandate that a budget be approved, but it also is the basis for the levying of taxes. A district must show evidence of financial need in order to collect all millage voted for school purposes. Also, the spending reserve should be included in the budget or it cannot be appropriated later. However, it should not be perceived as a continuing source of available funds.

Factors of possible state revenue increases, passing of new millage or income taxes, or new construction that may be applied to existing millage, thereby raising district revenue, all necessitate adopting a deficit budget. Adopting a deficit budget, in itself, makes the budget one of the most misunderstood processes by the general public. Simply stated, the budget explains to the public that "these are the amounts required to fund the educational program as described in the narrative portion of the budget."

All school districts are required to adopt a budget by January 15 for the next fiscal year, which runs from July 1 of the current year through June 30 of the next year. Boards of education are required to have two copies of the proposed budget available in the district treasurer's office for at least ten days prior to board adoption. A board is also required to have at least one public hearing on the budget before adoption. The budget must be certified to the county auditor no later than January 20 although a time extension may be obtained if authorization is granted by the tax commissioner.

Estimates of income and expenditures are required for the approaching fiscal year. It is also required that each district show comparisons of actual expenditures for the last three fiscal years. Other requirements are specified by statutes.

A contingent expense may be included in a school district's budget. It may not, however, be for an amount greater than 13% of current expenses. An exception to the permissible 13% contingency can occur if a school district has recently passed a tax levy. This situation creates the possibility of having a voluntary contingency reserve balance not exceeding 25% of the total amount of the levy that will be available for appropriation in that fiscal year. That percentage decreases to a maximum of 20% of the estimated levy amount for the following fiscal year.

Following the submission of the tax budget to the county auditor by January 20, the budget commission reviews the estimated income and expenditures for each district. No later than March 1, the budget commission certifies resources from each fund that are available for appropriations; the resultant certificate is known as the "official certificate of estimated resources." After receiving the certificate, the board of education must take official action to authorize the levying of taxes and certify its resolution to the county auditor. Board of education action must be taken by April 1. (Note that levies submitted to the board for approval are for voted rates, not effective rates.)

9.9 Rationale for Determining Specific Amounts

As is the case with other aspects of the educational program, there is a variety of options which can be applied to the important task of resource allocation. The option of centralized vs. decentralized budget decision making was addressed earlier in this chapter. It is noteworthy that the move away from centralized budgets, with the resultant involvement of many more individuals and groups, almost guarantees more challenges to the board of education and central administration as to how financial resources are being allocated.

This broader base of involvement resulted in more of an interdisciplinary approach to the budget process. It is no longer just the educational family, more specifically the inner circle, which provides budget input. Not only have business, industry, and labor begun to assume an active role, but a variety of special interest sub-groups have also gotten into the act.

9.10 Program Planning and Budgeting System

In 1965, the federal government also became involved, perhaps inadvertently, when then President Lyndon B. Johnson announced that a program planning and budgeting system would be used throughout the federal government.[4] Soon thereafter, school districts began to apply some of the basic components of this system to their budgeting procedures. A number of school budget experts from the Association of School Business Officials International (ASBO) studied potential benefits of program budgeting and developed materials designed to enhance implementation. They defined program budgeting as follows:

> A structured procedure for determining policy in the allocation of resources for the accomplishment of priority programs; emphasizes long-range planning, analytic evaluative tools, economic rationality in the determination of programs and in the setting of goals and objectives.[5]

A few years later the ASBO developed *PPBES - Show and Tell Handbook* which was designed to provide timely information concerning ways in which planning, programming, budgeting, and evaluation systems had been implemented in a variety of school districts.

As a general rule, in order to implement a planning, programming, budgeting evaluation system (PPBES), school districts should first determine what constitutes a program structure. For example, budget planners must identify the specific units to which resources will be allocated as well as when and where results will be evaluated. This decision should be based upon a careful consideration of the district's various goals and objectives as well

---

[4] William H. Curtis, *Educational Resources Management System* (Association of School Business Officials, International), at 340.

[5] Walter I. Garms, James W. Guthrie, and Lawrence C. Pierce, *School Finance: The Economics and Politics of Public Education* (Englewood Cliffs, N.J.: Prentice-Hall, 1978), at 267.

as the rationale for the grouping of program activities which are designed to accomplish goals and objectives. Generally, program structure is based on organizational structure.

This approach works well where common goals exist among organizational components. However, many organizations retain structures which no longer address, much less serve, current needs. A classification of expenditures by program recommended by the National Center for Educational Statistics appears in Figure 9:1.

Once enrollment and revenue projections are made, department heads and principals are usually asked to submit budget requests according to their particular needs. Generally, however, this "bottom-up" approach is inconsequential. Since a large share of a school district's budget is allocated for salaries, which are usually negotiated at the district level, there is not enough money left to respond to the particular needs of individual schools.[6] When this process is used, the small amount of money that is left is usually controlled by the central office in order to meet the mandates of state law and local board policy.

It would seem prudent to allow department heads and principals more latitude in determining specific needs. This approach might well result in such individuals agreeing that one or two positions are not needed, especially when they see what the dollars saved will buy in terms of other department or building needs.

The programs listed above, and expanded services in general, have major implications relative to the kinds and amount of financial resources required. Other dimensions of the need for added revenues resulting from inflation and other factors include the following: increased salaries, and greater operating costs and building costs. In addition, increased student enrollment in some areas must be considered.

9.11 Planning, Programming, Budgeting Evaluation System

The planning, programming, budgeting evaluation system (PPBES) involved at least the following steps:

1. A determination of the purposes and goals of the education program, including a re-examination of existing purposes and goals.
2. An assessment of the educational needs suggested by both the redefined purposes and the existing goals.
3. The establishment of a set of reasonable long- and short-range priorities.
4. A tentative determination of major programs.
5. The formulation of educational plans designed to achieve the purposes, goals, and program definitions agreed upon in light of priorities established.
6. A consequential analysis of various alternatives.
7. The selection of preferred and defensible alternatives.
8. The recommendation of an educational program and a financial plan that would support it.
9. The development of a comprehensive plan for evaluation.[7]

---

[6] *The Economics and Financing of Education* at 349–351.

[7] John L. Mikesell, *Fiscal Administration-Analysis and Application for the Public Sector* (Belmont CA: Wadsworth Publishing Company, 1992), at 94 [hereinafter *Fiscal Administration—Analysis and Application for the Public Sector*].

Figure 9:1

"Classification of Expenditures by Program as Recommended by the National Center for Educational Statistics"

Regular Programs—Elementary/Secondary
Special Programs
  Mentally retarded
    Educable mentally retarded
    Trainable mentally retarded
  Physically handicapped
    Hard of hearing
    Deaf
    Deaf-blind
    Visually handicapped
    Speech impaired
    Crippled
    Other health impaired
  Emotionally disturbed
  Learning disabled
  Culturally deprived
  Bilingual
  Gifted and talented
  Vocational programs
    Agriculture
    Distributive education
    Health occupations
  Home economics
    Occupational
    Consumer homemaking
    Industrial arts
    Office occupations
    Technical education
    Trades and industrial occupations
  Other vocational programs
    Other instructional programs—elementary/secondary
    School-sponsored cocurricular activities
    School-sponsored athletics
    Other
  Nonpublic school programs
  Adult/continuing education programs
  Community/junior college educational programs
  Community services programs
    Community recreation
    Civic services
    Public library services
    Custody and child care services
    Welfare activities
    Other community services
  Enterprise programs
    Food services
    Other enterprise programs
    Undistributed expenditures

9.12 Zero-Based Budgeting

In the book *Fiscal Administration—Analysis and Application for the Public Sector*, author Mikesell states,

> "In a good control system basic decisions are made during the programming process, which precedes the budget process. And the annual budget process is essentially one of fine tuning the financial plan required to implement these decisions during the budget year."[8]

This quote reaffirms the earlier statement in this chapter that the budget development process is, essentially, an extension of the educational planning process. However, there is usually considerable distance between the desired and the possible. One of the realities is that budgeting, like appropriating and spending, is a process of strategy and role playing.

Aaron Wilavsky, according to Mikesell, diagnoses the process as follows:

> Budgeting is incremental. The largest determining factor of the size and content of this year's budget is last year's budget. Most of the budget is a product of previous decision. . . . The budget may be conceived of as an iceberg with by far the largest part below the surface, outside the control of anyone. Many items in the budget are standard and are simply re-enacted every year unless there is a special reason to challenge them.[9]

Zero-based budgeting (ZBB) provides such a challenge and dictates that each division or department must justify its requests. Notwithstanding the above referenced incrementalist view, ZBB does not anticipate that this year's budget is a reflection of last year's and that next year's budget will closely resemble this year's.

ZBB requires that the budget be defended in its entirety, just as would be the case for a new program. In other words, ZBB practitioners tend to assume a position 180 degrees from the "business as usual" approach. At the very least, this approach to budgeting should prevent the all-too-common practice of focusing on the justification of program increases.

The U.S. Government Office of Management and Budget reported the following objectives of zero-based budgeting:

- Involve all managers at all levels in the budget process.
- Justify the resource requirements for existing activities as well as for new activities.
- Focus the justification on the evaluation of discrete programs or activities of each decision unit.
- Establish, for all managerial levels in an agency, objectives against which accomplishments can be identified and measured.
- Assess alternative methods of accomplishing objectives.
- Analyze the probable effects of different budget amounts of performance levels on the achievement of objectives.
- Provide a credible rationale for reallocating resources, especially from old activi-

[8] *Id.* at 41.
[9] *Id.* at 89–90.

ties to new activities.[10]

Although systems used by different governmental agencies have individual peculiarities, most include elements of the system adopted by the federal government during the Carter administration, which Mikesell describes as follows:

> In the first stage, unit managers prepare decision packages, which are alternatives for performing a particular function with different amounts of money. The package includes funding levels and increments, a description of the activity, compilation of resource requirements, description of the short term objective of the package, and a statement of major objectives of the agency. It also describes the implications for not providing funds for the package. Because of the requirements for preparing the package, the unit manager must be engaged in analysis of objectives, operational planning, consideration of alternatives, and cost estimation.[11]

After unit managers submit their ranked decisions the receiving agency heads consolidate the packages, rank them, and transmit them on through the successive layers of consolidation and ranking to the departmental level. This procedure ultimately produces the budget request which is transmitted to the Office of Management and Budget for inclusion in the presidential budget.

Although the official reference to ZBB ended during the Reagan administration, several of its components remained, including the requirement that formal consideration be given to priorities throughout the bureau or agency.

Some authors and researchers insist that the claims made by supporters of ZBB are vastly overstated. The central concern is that very few organizations or agencies actually start at zero and require the justification of each item and each increment of expenditure. This process, they claim, would be far too time consuming, especially if done on an annual basis. R.N. Anthony, a member of the Harvard Business School faculty, viewed ZBB as a fraud, saying it was time consuming and traumatic.[12] Clearly, ZBB is not a panacea nor is it a fraud if used within the context of determining and reordering priorities.

Obviously a school system must use a historical basis, at least to some extent, when determining budget amounts; that is, there is no use in starting at zero when estimating utility or insurance costs. At the same time, however, the "consideration of alternatives" step involved in ZBB may identify new approaches such as alternative fuel sources or a restructuring of the insurance program to include policy consolidation or self insurance. ZBB proponents claim that it allows those with expertise at the operational level to have input into the budget development process, thus providing them with a feeling of "ownership." Supporters also claim the following:

> School officials are encouraged to make decisions based on program priorities, rather than maintaining programs regardless of current need or merit. . . . ZBB may have important political ramifications. It may help to "sell a budget" to a board or

---

[10] Office of Management and Budget, Congress of the United States. Zero Based Budgeting, Bulletin No. 77-9, April 19, 1977.

[11] Fiscal Administration—Analysis and Application for the Public Sector at 92–95.

[12] *Id.* at 169.

a community concerned with accountability. As an example, one high school principal has stated that the implementation of ZBB in his district resulted in decreasing the time spent at board meetings justifying the budget because the justifications were already documented.[13]

Regardless of the budget development method(s) used, the reality of limited resources and seemingly unlimited needs dictates that the concept of "maximum return on investment" be kept in focus.

9.13 The Official Budget Document

Prior to 1980, school district budgets and appropriation measures were developed on the "object" basis; that is, the service or commodity obtained as the result of a specific expenditure. School administrators and treasurers who were involved in the process during earlier years will recall an accounting system using letters. The "A" accounts were for all salary and wage categories, "B" accounts for supplies, "C" for materials or maintenance, "D" for equipment replacement, and so forth. Even a decade later, veteran budget developers may slip and refer to educational supplies as "B-6" rather than "511."

The pre-1980 method provided for a quick overall "object" picture as to total amount for salaries, supplies, and so forth, as well as a partial delineation as to function within each broad "object" area. Missing was a clear picture as to the cost of the various "functions" schools were supplying.

This is not to say that a reasonably astute school official could not ascertain the cost of the various "functions" in his/her district. However, the "post 1980" fund, function, object approach has made it easier for all school personnel and interested district citizens to obtain a quick, and relatively clear, reading of the cost (proposed and actual) of such functions. We have essentially moved from a budget system that explained "what" to a budget system that now explains "why" and "where".

9.14 Ohio's Uniform School Accounting System

A detailed description of Ohio's official school accounting system is provided in a state auditor supplied notebook entitled *Uniform School Accounting User Manual*. For purposes of this manual, primary reference will be made to the fund, function, and object aspects of the accounting system as defined below.[14]

9.14-1 Uniform School Accounting System Fund

Fund can be defined as a set of accounts which reflect financial activity within the following broad categories as follows:

9.14-2 Governmental Fund Type—General Fund

All revenue and other assets not required by law or contractual agreement to be placed

[13] Auditor of State, *Uniform School Accounting System Users Manual* (1991), B205–B406.
[14] *See* Ohio Rev. Code Ann. at § 5705.35.

in another fund, go into the general fund. The general fund is the fund which receives all monies dedicated to payment of current operating expenses of the district. All revenue from general tax levies for current expenses must be credited to the general fund. In addition, foundation program receipts and any interest from investments of general fund money must be credited to the general fund. The purpose of the general fund is to carry on the current general operations of the school system. Refer to Figure 9:2.

Figure 9:2

"Current General Operations"

Fund Number	*Title*
001	General Fund

9.14-3 Special Revenue Fund

These funds include all of those which are created to be used for designated educational purposes from special sources of revenue. Each of these funds may receive revenue from either public or private sources but expenditures are restricted to specific educational purposes which are not currently a part of the school system's educational program. Refer to Figure 9:3.

Figure 9:3

"Special Revenue Fund Categories"

Fund Number	*Title*
015	Mental Health
016	Emergency Levy
018	Public School Support
300	Athletic Fund
401-410	State Funds
412-414	
416-418	
501-510	Federal Funds
512	
514-522	
524-555	
557-569	
571-575	

9.14-4 Debt Service Fund

These funds are created for the purpose of accumulating large amounts of money which is used to retire outstanding debt, usually in the form of bonds. A debt service fund can be created not only to retire principal of debt, but it can also be created to receive sufficient revenue to permit periodic payment of interest on long term indebtedness. Refer to Figure 9:4.

Figure 9:4

"Debt Service Retirement"

Fund Number	*Title*
002	Bond Retirement

9.14-5 Capital Projects Fund

These funds are created to acquire general fixed assets such as buildings, equipment, machinery and land. Revenue may be realized from either public or private sources as well as from proceeds of bond issues. Refer to Figure 9:5.

Figure 9:5

"Capital Projects"

Fund Number	*Title*
003	Permanent Improvement
004	Building Fund
005	Replacement Fund
010	Classroom Facilities
415	Vocational Ed/Equipment Assistance
511	Local Public Works
513	Major Disaster Area Assistance
523	Appalachia Vocational & Other Education Facilities
556	Energy Conversation
570	Non-Food Assistance for School Food Service

9.14-6 Enterprise Fund

This fund accounts for operations that are financed and operated in a manner similar to private business enterprises where the intent of the governing body is that the costs (expenses, including depreciation) of providing goods or services to the general public be financed or recovered primarily through the users' charges. Refer to Figure 9:6.

Figure 9:6

"Enterprise Fund"

Fund Number	*Title*
006	Food Services
009	Uniform School Services
011	Consumer Services Rotary
012	Adult Education
013	Recreation
411	Uniform School Accounting Network

9.14-7 Proprietary Fund—Internal Service Fund

This fund was created to render services on a cost reimbursement basis to other organizational units that come within the jurisdiction of the school system. The fund is generally intended to be self-supporting. Refer to Figure 9:7.

Figure 9:7

"Internal Service Funds"

Fund Number	*Title*
014	Special Rotary

9.14-8 Fiduciary Fund Types—Trust Funds

Trust funds are created when a board of education accepts the responsibility to serve as trustee for property which may come to it by gift. Trusts are generally specific on how and what funds may be used for. Refer to Figure 9:8.

Figure 9:8

"Trust Funds"

Fund Number	*Title*
007	Special Trust
008	Endowment
200	Student Activity Program Fund

9.14-9 Agency Fund

An agency fund holds property (money) for others and performs duties as directed. Refer to Figure 9:9.

Figure 9:9

"Agency Fund"

Fund Number	*Title*
017	Library Construction Transfer Fund

9.14-10 Function

Function means the action a person takes or the purpose for which something exists or is used. Function includes the activities which are performed to accomplish the objectives of an enterprise. The activities of a school district are classified into seven broad areas or functions as follows: instruction, supporting services, operation of non-instructional services, extracurricular activities, facilities acquisition and construction services, debt service, and other uses of funds. Functions are further divided into sub-functions and service areas which are subsequently subdivided into areas of responsibility.

Each of these program levels consists of activities which have somewhat the same general operational objectives. Furthermore, categories of activities comprising each of these divisions and subdivisions are grouped according to the principle that the activities can be combined, compared, related and be mutually exclusive. For example, subfunctions under instruction include regular instruction, special instruction, vocational, and adult/continuing. Service areas, under the subfunction regular instruction, include elementary programs, middle/junior high programs, and high school programs.

The function dimension consists of four digits. The minimum reporting requirements for the State Auditor's Office is the first two digits. Other agencies may have additional requirements. Each district is to use those codes which are necessary or applicable. Functions are listed in Figure 9:10.

Figure 9:10

"Function Dimension Coding"

Function

1000 Instruction
- 1100 Regular Instruction
- 1200 Special Instruction
- 1300 Vocational Instruction
- 1400 Adult/Continuing Instruction
- 1900 Other Instruction

2000 Supporting Services
- 2100 Support Services - Pupils
- 2200 Support Services - Instructional Staff
- 2300 Support Services - Board of Education
- 2400 Support Services - Administration
- 2500 Support Services - Fiscal
- 2600 Support Services - Business
- 2700 Operation of Maintenance - Plant Services
- 2800 Operation of Maintenance - Pupil Transportation
- 2900 Operation of Maintenance - Central

3000 Operation of Non-Instructional Services
- 3100 Food Services Operations
- 3200 Community Services
- 3300 Enterprise Operations
- 3900 Other Operation of Non-Instructional Services

4000 Extracurricular Activities

5000 Facilities Acquisition and Construction Services

7000 Other Uses of Funds

9.14-11 Object

"Object" represents a further breakdown of the accounting system. This system is represented in Figure 9:11.

Figure 9:11
"Object Coding"

Object	
100	Personnel Services - Salaries
200	Employee Retirement and Insurance Benefits
400	Purchased Services
500	Supplies and Materials
600	Capital Outlay
700	Capital Outlay - Replacement
800	Miscellaneous Objects

For example, using the above accounting system, a code of 001-1300-200 would identify costs for vocational teachers' retirement and insurance benefits, listed under the general fund. The system is also set up to accommodate a further delineation of costs for special cost centers (elementary, middle/junior high, and high school), subject areas (that is, mathematics and/or science), and cost centers (that is, general math, algebra, geometry, etc.). Thus, district personnel could identify the costs for the past year for high school mathematics and even identify what it cost for Algebra I teacher instruction, and/or textbooks costs if desired.

9.15 Budget Time Table

Prior to 1986 when the fiscal year was January 1 through December 31, the district budget had to be adopted by July 15 and filed with the county auditor by July 20. The enactment of *Substitute House Bill 747* changed the fiscal year of school districts from January 1 through December 31 to the period July 1 through June 30.[15]

Each school district is required to adopt a budget for the next fiscal year by January 15th. Prior to its adoption, two copies of the proposed budget must have been on file and available for public inspection in the office of the district's treasurer for at least ten days. In addition, the board of education is required to conduct at least one public hearing on its proposed budget prior to adoption, and notice of the hearing must be given at least ten days in advance, either by publication in the district's official publication or by publication in a newspaper of general circulation in the district. After its adoption, the budget must then be certified to the county auditor no later than January 20. Extensions of time for filing, however, may be authorized by the tax commissioner.[16]

Although the law is silent as to specifically when a budget hearing should be held, it may be scheduled immediately prior to the January meeting. It is also appropriate at this time, to have dialogue between board of education members and district administrators.

9.16 Form of Tax Budget

A school district's tax budget must include not only the information enumerated in

[15] Ohio Rev. Code Ann. at § 9.34.
[16] Ohio Rev. Code Ann. at §§ 5705.28, 5705.30.

Ohio Revised Code § 5705.29, but must also include any information required by the Auditor of State.[17]

* * *

> In general the required information includes estimates of both receipts and expenditures for the coming fiscal year, by category. A three-year comparison of expenditures is also required. The estimated receipts must include anticipated income from all sources including property tax, school foundation funds and federal government funds. Estimated expenditures include both personal service expenditures and those for permanent improvement.[18]

9.17 County Budget Commission

Section 5705.27 of the Revised Code provides for the creation of a county budget commission in each county. The county budget commission shall consist of the county auditor, the county treasurer, the prosecuting attorney, and, should the electors of the county so determine, two additional members to be elected to serve four-year terms.[19]

As noted in section 9.15 herein, the school district's adopted budget must be certified to the county auditor no later than January 20 unless an extension of time for filing has been authorized by the tax commissioner.[20]

* * *

> The [county] auditor, in turn, must present the budget to the county budget commission. Although the county budget commission has no authority to either increase or reduce the rate of any voter approved tax levy, it does have the authority, and duty, to adjust the amounts required from general property tax to conform to the needs demonstrated by the budget.
>
> The budget commission is required to review each school district's budget and certify to the district, no later than the first day of March, a summary of estimated resources from each fund that are available for appropriation, other than funds created by transfer. * * * The summary should indicate, for each fund, the estimated unencumbered balances and receipts. If a tax is to be levied for that fund, the summary should indicate the estimated revenue to be derived from the tax, the rate of the tax, and what portion of the tax is within, and in excess of, the ten-mill limitation.
>
> The budget commission is also required to provide a summary stating the total estimated resources of each fund of the district (other than funds created by transfer) and a statement of the amount of the total tax duplicate of the school district to be used in the collection of taxes for the following calendar year.[21]

* * *

---

17 Ohio Rev. Code Ann. at §§ 5705.29, 5705.30; OHIO SCHOOL LAW GUIDE at § 5.03.

18 OHIO SCHOOL LAW GUIDE at § 5.03.

19 Ohio Rev. Code Ann. at § 5705.27.

20 Ohio Rev. Code Ann. at § 5705.30; OHIO SCHOOL LAW GUIDE at § 5.02.

21 OHIO SCHOOL LAW GUIDE at § 5.04 (footnotes omitted). *See also* Ohio Rev. Code Ann. at §§ 5705.30, 5705.31, 5705.32, 5705.34, 5705.35.

9.18 Appeal of Budget Commission Decision

The Revised Code provides the vehicle for an appeal of decisions of the county budget commission. Such appeal must be brought by the school district within thirty days of receipt of notice of the county budget commission's action.[22] The appeal is made to the board of tax appeals and is initiated by filing a notice of appeal with the county budget commission and the board of tax appeals.[23] Although the finding of the board of tax appeals is substituted for the findings of the county budget commission, this statutory provision:

> does not give the board of tax appeals any authority to place any tax levy authorized by law within the ten-mill limitation outside of that limitation, or to reduce any levy below any minimum fixed by law.[24]

---

[22] Ohio Rev. Code Ann. at § 5705.37. *See also* OHIO SCHOOL LAW GUIDE at § 5.04.
[23] Ohio Rev. Code Ann. at § 5705.37.
[24] *Id.*

Chapter 10: Appropriation and Accounting Procedures

10.1 Transition From Budget to Appropriation Measure

In the preceding chapter it was noted that the budget should clearly reflect the goals and objectives of the school district. This approach not only helps to "fine tune" the educational program but also to quantify the program in terms of dollars. The appropriation measure takes that process one step further by providing financial information which is not only more detailed, but more current. Whereas the budget is adopted to cover a time period of up to eighteen months in the future, the fiscal year addressed in the appropriation is usually already underway by the time such permanent appropriation is adopted. This process of adopting both a budget and an appropriation measure is, essentially, unique to Ohio.

The planning and development of the appropriation measure could well be viewed as the third part of a continuum. The first part is planning of the educational program and the intermediate portion involves the development of the official district budget.

Individuals who have had considerable experience with the development of budgets and appropriation measures will testify to the fact that there is an inverse correlation between the time and energy invested in the development of the district budget and the effort required to accomplish the tasks associated with the development of the appropriation measure. In any event, an appropriation measure is only as good as the advance planning and ongoing review that accompany it.

In the absence of clear board policy related to a district's fiscal procedures, the emphasis placed upon the budget versus appropriation is usually left to personal preference. Some fiscal administrators prefer to devote the major portion of personnel time and energy in developing a detailed budget document. The payback from such an approach is that a correspondingly lower investment of such resources will be required at appropriation time. Readers are cautioned that in addition to the personal preference of those developing the budget and appropriation measures, the district's philosophy and past practice must be taken into consideration.

Some boards of education have traditionally viewed the budget process as basically a "necessary evil," claiming that what really matters is the appropriation of funds. As was noted in the previous chapter relative to the district budget, those responsible for developing the appropriation measure should have an early and clear understanding as to the preference of the board of education.

Since board members and the public at large are frequently interested in comparisons, it is suggested that the proposed appropriation amounts be compared, perhaps in a side by side columnar fashion with the previously adopted budget amounts. Depending upon the evolving financial pattern of the district, it may be prudent also to include the current fiscal year's appropriation figures as a second frame of reference.

10.1-1 Wants versus Needs

Of the many definitions which could be applied to the terms budget and appropriation, the operational vernacular frequently refers to the budget as "what the district would like to have" and the appropriation as "what it can afford," that is, what the school personnel want versus what they will probably get. Experienced administrators know that it is a common practice for school districts to adopt and file a budget which contemplates expenditures in excess of anticipated funds. Such practice is not only legal, it is also a safeguard to collect all available local taxes in case the income available to the district may be larger than could have realistically been predicted at the time the budget was adopted.

10.1-2 Factors Influencing Change

During the six-month period between the budget and the appropriation, it is important to keep a rather complete record of issues, events, and other considerations which will have an impact upon the permanent appropriation measure. In some districts the administrative and fiscal officers may recommend the adoption of a temporary three month appropriation measure due to financial uncertainty. It would appear that in a number of cases a temporary adoption represents an unnecessary step in the fiscal process since, for the most part, the procedure must be repeated for the permanent appropriation. The decision to utilize a permanent versus a temporary appropriation should not be based solely upon past practice but should also consider the extent to which the circumstances listed in figure 10:1 are likely to change:

10.2 Adoption of Appropriation Measure

With the change in the fiscal year as referenced in the previous chapter, it is necessary that either a temporary or permanent appropriation measure be adopted on or about July 1, before any expenditure can legally be made. If the temporary appropriation option is exercised, the permanent measure must be adopted by the first day of October and filed in accordance with Section 5705.38 of the Ohio Revised Code. The official form to be

Figure 10:1
Variables to Consider Prior to Adopting the Appropriation Measure

A. Resources available
   1. Balance carried forward (beginning balance)
   2. Passage of an additional tax issue(s)
   3. Significant increase or decrease in the dollars certified by the county auditor
   4. Increase or decrease in state and/or federal funds
B. Expenditure changes
   1. Increase or decrease in enrollment
   2. Anticipated addition or deletion of programs
   3. Change relative to the anticipated expenditure for items such as roof repairs or asbestos removal
   4. Additional construction
   5. State and/or federal mandates

used for filing the annual appropriation resolution closely resembles that used for the previously-adopted budget.

10.2-1 Amendment of the Appropriation Measure

In most districts, even with the best of planning, it becomes necessary throughout the year to make at least modest changes in the official appropriation. An exception to this general rule would apply for those districts which are in such a positive financial position that a substantial financial cushion could be included within each category. Certainly, in the clear majority of Ohio's school districts, it becomes necessary to amend the appropriation from time to time by official board action. It also stands to reason that a district which is in difficult financial straits, that is, one which has had to pare each area as much as possible, will have to make more adjustments throughout the year than will its more solvent counterparts.

10.3 Accounting Practices—A Process in Transition

Many school districts handle the accounting function on a current "cash" basis, that is, by highlighting balances in the various accounts and funds. When using this method it is extremely important that encumbrances be clearly listed and that the net balance figures include all encumbrances. Such encumbrances (obligations) assume a variety of forms and classifications. Examples would include the following: payroll, specific purchases which have been authorized but not received, and open purchase orders. Although open purchase orders can create a distorted picture of encumbrances, especially if a large number of total dollars are involved therein, the encumbrances must be shown nevertheless. This approach is necessary since the full amount certified on each such open order could conceivably be expended.

Ohio's school districts are currently well on their way in making the transition from the cash to accrual method of accounting. The accrual approach takes into consideration all assets including inventory and all debits, including encumbrances. Some argue that this process is more difficult. However, like many other aspects of school fiscal operations, once the transition process has been completed, it will probably be embraced more warmly.

10.4 Safeguarding the School Expenditure Process

An official system of checks and balances must be adopted and practiced judiciously in all activities involving the fiscal integrity of a school district. Failure to do so increases the likelihood of potentially devastating personal, professional, and institutional loss.

To begin with, ususally any purchase of goods or services should require two signatures in addition to the treasurer's certification as to the availability of resources for such purchase. Exceptions to the above might include organizational structures which endorse school site-based management or self-directed employee teams. Although not required by law, most purchases are initiated by the completion of a "requisition for purchase" form.

Specifications for the acquisition of equipment, services, supplies and so forth should include the name and address of the vendor, the name and department or division of the requesting party, an entry as to the number, specification, and unit price as well as a concise description of the goods or services being ordered.

Once completed, the requisition is usually forwarded to the treasurer's office where the above information is transferred to a purchase order. Since the purchase order number is extremely important throughout each phase of the purchasing process, it should be recorded on the requisition and also be used in conjunction with all records of the actual purchase. All purchase orders must carry the treasurer's signature, certifying the availability of resources, prior to the ordering of the goods or services.

10.4-1 Payment of Warrants

The payment process begins with official verification that the ordered item has been supplied and received consistent with the information on the purchase order as related to bid specifications, price quotes, and so forth. In most instances the appropriate school official involved in the receiving process must verify that the items or articles received are of the proper specification and number. It is also necessary to ensure that such articles were received in good condition. Following the initial inspection and delivery to the appropriate office or department, one of the individuals who originally signed the requisition should physically inspect and ensure that such goods are in appropriate condition for use or storage prior to signing the "approval for payment" form. In instances where the purchased item is to be stored for future use, it is necessary that such action be reflected as a part of inventory as soon as practical. School-owned equipment and furniture items should have an identifying number permanently affixed thereto. This practice not only helps to ensure the integrity of the purchasing and receiving process but also provides more realistic data for purchasing property insurance and, if necessary, provides justification for insurance claims.

10.5 Procedure for Bidding and Letting of Contracts

Effective July 1, 1990, the following procedures must be adhered to in the bidding and letting of contracts:

> When the board of education of any school district determines to build, repair, enlarge, demolish or furnish a schoolhouse, or make any improvements or repairs, the cost of which will exceed fifteen thousand dollars, except in cases of urgent necessity, or for the security and protection of school property, * * * it shall proceed as follows:
>
> (A) The board shall cause to be prepared the plans, specifications, and related information as required in divisions (A), (B), and (D) of Section 153.01 of the Ohio Revised Code.
>
> (B) For the period of four weeks, the board shall advertise for bids in some newspaper of general circulation in the district and two such papers, if there are two. If no newspaper has a general circulation in the district, then the board shall post such advertisement in three public places in the district. Such advertisement shall be entered in full by the treasurer of the board of education, on the record of proceedings of the board.
>
> (C) The sealed bids shall be filed with the treasurer by twelve noon on the last day stated in the advertisement.
>
> (D) Unless the board extends the time for the opening of bids pursuant to Section 153.12 of the Ohio Revised Code, the bids shall be opened at the next meeting of the board, be publicly read by the treasurer, and entered in full on the records of the board; provided that the board may by resolution provide for the public opening and reading of such bids by the treasurer immediately after the time for filing such bids has expired, at the usual place of meeting of the board, and for the tabulation of such bids and a report thereof to the board at its next meeting.[1]

Paragraphs *E* through *J* of Section 3313.46 of the Ohio Revised Code address legal requirements related to the specificity of bids, bidding procedures, and the awarding of bids.

10.6 Disposal of School Property

In circumstances where board-owned facilities, vehicles, equipment or other items are no longer needed to carry out the functions of the school district, they may be disposed of in accordance with provisions as established in Section 3313.41 of the Ohio Revised Code.

10.6-1 Value of Items

A major component of Section 3313.41 is that items valued at more than $2,000 shall be disposed of by public auction. "When a board of education has twice offered real or

---

[1] Ohio Rev. Code Ann. at § 3313.46(A)–(D).

personal property for sale at public auction pursuant to division (A) of this section, and the property has not been sold, the board may sell it at a private sale. * * *"[2]

10.6-2 Inventory Adjustment

It is important that any disposed items be removed from the appropriate inventory list. Such adjustment will provide a more accurate inventory picture which is especially important as districts move to accrual accounting. In addition, it will assist in risk management.

10.7 Receiving and Depositing Funds

Beyond the basic requirements of law as specified in Section 3313.29 of the Ohio Revised Code, the school district treasurer should establish additional procedures/guidelines to ensure that deposit slips accurately reflect the amount and source of monies being deposited. As was stated in reference to the expenditure of funds, at least two individuals should certify in writing both the source and amount of the funds being deposited.

Extreme caution should also be exercised to prevent unnecessary visibility of monies enroute to deposit. Common sense would dictate that funds be placed in the school safe or actually deposited with a financial institution as soon as possible. In no case should large sums of money be handled or stored in such a way as to tempt theft or embezzlement. Further, all district employees who are authorized to handle school funds should be bonded. The amount of the bond should at least equal the maximum amount of cash such employees would likely have access to at any one time.

10.8 Summary

As each year passes, it appears to become more important that boards of education, educational service center governing boards and administrators reassess their roll as stewards of the public's trust. The challenge continues to stretch limited fiscal resources to accomplish education objectives. By using appropriate accounting procedures, the public's trust and financial management objective can be realized.

---

[2] Ohio Rev. Code Ann. at § 3313.41(B).

Chapter 11: The Effective Management of School Funds

11.1 Introduction

The management of school funds is one of the most important functions in the administration of a school district. The immediate deposits of receipts and careful investment of funds can lead to additional funds for a district. Adherence to laws, rules, and regulations will help districts avoid fiscal problems. In addition, the conscientious preparation and review of reports required of school districts also help avert financial crises. Such reports may signal potential problems in time for necessary corrections to avoid serious difficulties.

Many of the procedures for accounting of school funds are prescribed in the Ohio Revised Code. Among these are the ways of raising revenue, methods of handling receipts, methods for the payment for expenses, and procedures for the approval of budgets and appropriations. The Ohio Revised Code also mandates methods to be used in making expenditures and procedures for periodic reporting.

The responsibilities for carrying out the provisions of these laws are assigned to the treasurer, the superintendent, and the board of education. In some cases this responsibility is assigned to an agency such as the County Budget Commission, or to the State Superintendent of Public Instruction. The details of these mandated responsibilities are addressed in Chapters 117, 3313, 3319, and 5705 of the Ohio Revised Code.

11.2 The School Treasurer and Superintendent

Experienced school administrators should have no difficulty in appreciating the valuable services of the treasurer of the school district. It is incumbent upon the treasurer to work with the superintendent and other central office personnel, furnishing data that aid them in making their day to day decisions which pertain to the finances of the district. Section 3313.29 of the Ohio Revised Code goes into considerable detail to underscore the importance of fund accounting.

> The treasurer of each board of education shall keep an account of all school funds of the district. The treasurer shall receive all vouchers for payments and disbursements made to and by the board and preserve such vouchers for a period of ten years unless copied or reproduced according to the procedure prescribed in section 9.01 of the Revised Code. . . . The treasurer shall render a statement to the board and to the superintendent of the school district, monthly, or more often if required, showing the revenues and receipts from whatever sources derived, the various appropriations made by the board, the expenditures and disbursements therefrom, the purposes thereof, the balances remaining in each appropriation, and the assets and liabilities of the school district. At the end of the fiscal year such statement shall be a complete exhibit of the financial affairs of the school district which may be published and distributed with the approval of the board. All monthly and yearly statements as required in this section shall be available for examination by the public.[1]

Section 3313.51 also emphasizes an important role in fund accounting for the treasurer:

> In every school district the treasurer of the board of education shall be the treasurer of the school funds. No moneys of a school district shall be paid out except on a check signed by the treasurer . . . Payroll disbursements constitute an exception to this requirement if otherwise provided by law. All moneys received by a treasurer of a school district from any source whatsoever shall be immediately placed by him in a depository designated by the board of education of such school district, as provided by sections 135.01 to 135.21 of the Revised Code.[2]

An Ohio school superintendent has a unique function in the area of school finance. The superintendent does not physically control the receipts and expenditures of the district but is ultimately responsible for the expenditure of funds. The superintendent authorizes the purchase of equipment, materials, and services as long as such expenditures are legal and are within the approved appropriations of the board of education. However, a board of education may adopt rules that limit the amount of a single purchase which can be made without its prior approval.

The superintendent and the treasurer of a school district are the key figures in the management of its funds. They must work together, recognizing each other's distinct roles which must be discharged. They have the responsibility to develop systems to (1) handle the receipts and the timely deposits of all funds, (2) determine procedures for the handling of purchases, (3) promptly pay bills, (4) timely file legal documents pertaining to budgets, appropriations, and taxes, and (5) timely file mandated reports. This list does not include all the financial responsibilities that fall upon these two persons but it does provide some indication of the diverse nature of the two positions.

11.3 The Local Board of Education

The legal responsibility for the raising of local tax monies falls to the board of education

---

[1] Ohio Rev. Code Ann. at § 3313.29.
[2] Ohio Rev. Code Ann. at § 3313.51.

of the local education agency. This includes the obligation to ask voters for new taxes when needed and the acceptance and approval of the tax rates which have been determined by the County Budget Commission. The superintendent, treasurer, and usually other staff members have a responsibility to participate in discussions pertaining to local taxes. The superintendent then presents the data and recommendations to help the board make intelligent decisions. However, it falls on the members of the board to take the final action to initiate a tax issue. No local school tax measure can move without the positive votes of of the required percentage of the members of an Ohio board of education.

Extreme care must be taken to ensure that a tax proposal is properly processed. In practice it is advisable to have an Ohio law firm that specializes in drafting tax issues, draft the required resolutions.

In other financial matters boards of education are required to approve the budget and the appropriation measure. These documents should be understood by the members in order for them to respond to the financial concerns of the citizens of their district and also to help interpret the continuing need for adequate financial support for the schools. It is critical that members of a board of education take an active role in reviewing the many financial reports of the district, for in so doing they may be able to help avoid financial conditions that would prove detrimental to the district. A number of these reports are discussed later in this chapter.

11.4 The County Budget Commission

The County Budget Commission, comprised of the county's auditor, treasurer and prosecutor, must approve the budget of the school district and:

> shall ascertain that the following levies have been properly authorized and, if so authorized, shall approve them without modification.[3]

It may be advisable for the treasurer and superintendent to attend the meeting of this commission at the time it is considering these legal documents of the school district. This is important since the superintendent and the treasurer could respond to any concerns raised by commission members. By attending and responding properly, school officials can assure that the district will secure all of the local taxes to which it is entitled.

11.5 The State Superintendent of Public Instruction

The State Superintendent becomes involved with a local district's finances when the district and/or the State Department perceives the district may be heading for a serious money problem. In that case:

> The superintendent of public instruction shall analyze the district's financial condition and ascertain what elements of the district's educational program exceed or fail to meet the minimum standards of the state board of education and requirements set forth in the Revised Code, and what, if any, additional revenues or revenue

[3] Ohio Rev. Code Ann. at § 5705.31.

> sources may be available to the district that are not included in its official certificate or amended certificate of estimated resources. The superintendent shall make a written report of his findings to the school district's board of education, the auditor of the state, and the state board of education. The report shall include any recommendations, including reductions in programs which exceed minimum standards of the state board of education or requirements set forth in the Revised Code that, if followed, would enable the district to reduce its expenses while operating an educational program that is responsive to the educational needs of the school district in accordance with its adopted school calendar. . . .[4]

When such difficulties arise the Superintendent of Public Instruction channels the work to the Office of School Management Assistance for its staff members to collect and analyze data on which the recommendations will be made.

11.6 Reports—Introduction

Many of the serious financial problems that develop in school districts could be avoided if reports required by the Revised Code were made on a timely basis and analyzed by all persons responsible for maintaining a healthy financial base for the school district. Such reports must be viewed as not just requirements, but as valuable tools for determining the financial health of a school district.

11.6-1 Budget and Appropriation Reports

The budget and appropriation documents should be viewed as reports. The budget presents an estimate of anticipated income and the programs for which such funds would be expended.

In the appropriations document the expenditures must not exceed the certified resources of the district. It must be emphasized that this document, along with the budget, is essential in maintaining a stable and financially sound school system.

11.6-2 The SM-1 Report

The appropriations measure forms the basis of three very important reports. The first report, School Management Form 1 (SM-1), is an annual spending plan covering the fiscal year and must be filed with the Office of School Management and Assistance by October 30. The Ohio Revised Code mandates:

> A board of education shall adopt as part of its annual appropriation measure a spending plan or in the case of an amendment or supplement to an appropriation measure, an amended spending plan, setting forth the schedule of expenses and expenditures of all appropriate funds by the school district for the fiscal year. A copy of the annual appropriation measure . . . shall be submitted to the superintendent of public instruction and shall set forth all revenue available for appropriation by the

[4] Ohio Rev. Code Ann. at § 3313.487.

> district during the fiscal year and their sources; the nature and amount of expenses to be incurred by the district during such year, the outstanding and unpaid expenses on the date the appropriation measure, amendment, or supplement is adopted; the date by which such expenses must be paid; and such other information as the superintendent requires to enable him to determine whether during such year the district will incur any expenses that will impair its ability to operate its schools with the revenue available to it from existing revenue sources. The plan or amended plan shall be presented in such detail and form as the superintendent prescribes.[5]

This spending plan compiled on the SM-1 form begins with the cash balance of the general fund as of July 1 and shows an estimate of all anticipated receipts from local, state and federal sources as well as all incoming transfers. The second portion of the report deals with anticipated general fund expenditures and an estimate of the cash balance at the end of the fiscal year. This report further requires a month-by-month breakdown of anticipated receipts and expenditures within the required categories, as well as an estimated balance for each month. Table 11:1 is a copy of an SM-1 report compiled by an Ohio school district for the 1996 fiscal year.

The annual estimate (the first column of data) of this report is very important to persons interested in this district's finances. It should be noted that the balance at the beginning of the fiscal year is substantially greater than that expected at the end of the year. Also the expenditures for the year are greater than the receipts for the year. This district should consider ways of enhancing receipts or reducing expenditures to retain a solid financial base in the future.

11.6-3 The SM-2 Report

A second report, School Management Form (SM-2), is a quarterly report required by State Board of Education regulations. This report indicates the current status of a district's finances as compared to the SM-1 report. It is due in the Office of School Management and Assistance by the end of the month which follows the end of the quarter.

Table 11:2 is a copy of the SM-2 report for the first quarter of the 1996 fiscal year. By reviewing this report one should be able to perceive the status of a district's financial condition at the end of each quarter, and note any indication of potential problems.

The Office of School Management and Assistance has developed a Profile Manual that uses data from these two reports to help the financial stability of a school district. Superintendents should become aware of this Manual and learn to use it to analyze their district's financial condition.

11.6-4 Monthly Financial Reports

The last report directly related to the appropriations measure is the monthly financial report. This report is required of the treasurer and is mandated by Section 3313.29.[6]

---

[5] Ohio Rev. Code Ann. at § 5705.391.
[6] Ohio Rev. Code Ann. at § 3319.29.

Table 11:1

A Completed SM-1 Form for an Ohio School District Annual Spending Plan

	School District (1) Annual Estimate	(2) July	(3) August	Countys (4) Sept.	(5) Oct.	(6) Nov.	(7) Dec.	(8) Jan.	Fiscal Year 1996 (9) Feb.	(10) March	(11) April	(12) May	(13) June
Beginning Balance	1578301	1528301	1022730	3117358	2757309	2806113	2490863	1939363	1330863	1500863	1022363	2422363	1783363
Receipts													
For Local Sources													
1. Real Estate Tax	5235298		2500556	70802	14782	14208			800000		150000	10000	
2. Personal Property Tax	1379262		62302	199584	706876					70000	220000		120000
3. Investment Earnings	112378	6778	11058	7193	9209	14120	12000	10000	5000	10000	5000	15000	7000
4. Proceeds from Borrowing													
5. Other	60564	471	3747	6748	13535	9063	1500	1500		1500	20000	1000	1500
From State Sources													
6. Educational	5019003	461741	369076	397208	397208	628650	395000	395000	395000	395000	395000	395000	395000
7. Rollback & Homestead Exemption	734273		59227	31396	243650		50000			100000	250000		
8. Other													
From Federal Sources													
9. Public Law 874													
10. Other													
From All Transfers													
11. Transfers In													
Total Receipts (Lines 1 Thru 11)	12540708	468990	3006466	566367	1385270	637665	408500	40600	1200000	576500	2840000	421000	523500
Total Receipts Plus Cash Balance	14069059	1997291	4029197	3683725	4142629	3492278	2949363	2340863	2000863	2082363	3862363	2843363	2306863
Expenditures													
14. Salaries & Wages	8084304	587070	626987	594433	954801	631011	628000	628000	628000	628000	940000	625000	625000
15. Fringe Benefits	2055517	260392	120530	88952	142295	197848	120000	120000	120000	120000	120000	120000	120000
16. Purchased Services	1149475	92369	78709	104105	94516	104776	100000	100000	100000	100000	100000	100000	75000
17. Materials, Supplies, Textbooks	804010	31105	54373	86500	53177	58555	70000	70000	70000	70000	75000	75000	90000
18. Capital Outlay (Inc. Replacement)	540206	1446	15705	41789	12098	9169	20000	20000	100000	80000	80000	80000	80000
19. Repayment of Borrowing (Prin+int)													
20. Transfer and Advances Out	345000				25000								320000
21. Other	158684	2178	15533	10588	5129	256	28000	25000	15000	15000	15000	15000	15000
22. Total Expenses (Lines 14-21)	13137196	974560	911839	926366	1287516	1001915	1010000	1010000	1080000	1060000	1435000	1065000	1375000
Ending Cash Balance	931863	1022731	3117358	2577359	2855113	2490863	1939363	1335863	1505863	1022363	2427363	1783363	931863

County Superintendent Signature Date

Treasurer Signature Date

City, Ex. Village, Local, J.V. Superintendent Signature Date

Coordinator Area Date

Table 11:2

A Completed SM-2 Form for an Ohio School District
Ohio Department of Education–Office of School Management Assistance
"Spending Plan" Status Report Form SM-2

School: District: County: Fiscal Year: 1996 IRN#: 051284 Quarter: First

	(1) Quarter Estimate	(2) Quarter Actual	(3) Quarter Difference	(4) Year-to-date Estimate	(5) Year-to-date Actual	(6) Year-to-date Difference
Beginning Balance	1,770,545	1,528,301	(242,244)	1,770,545	1,528,301	(242,244)
Receipts						
From Local Sources						
1. Real Estate Tax	2,350,691	2,424,754	74,063	2,350,691	2,424,754	74,063
2. Personal Property Tax	214,622	262,386	47,764	214,622	262,386	47,764
3. Investment Earnings	43,777	25,029	(18,743)	43,777	25,029	(18,743)
4. Proceeds from Borrowing	0	0	0	0	0	0
5. Other	12,053	10,966	(1,087)	12,053	10,966	(1,087)
From Federal Sources						
6. Foundation Program	1,077,535	1,228,064	150,529	1,077,535	1,228,064	150,529
7. Rollback and Homestead Exemption	325,183	90,622	(234,561)	325,183	90,622	(234,561)
8. Other	107,385	0	(107,385)	107,385	0	(107,385)
From Federal Sources						
9. Public Law 874	0	0	0	0	0	0
10. Other	34,499	0	(34,449)	34,499	0	(34,449)
From all Transfers						
11. Transfers In	0	0	0	0	0	0
Total Receipts (Lines 1 Thru 11)	4,165,748	4,041,821	(123,927)	4,165,748	4,041,821	(123,927)
Total Receipts Plus Cash Balance	5,936,293	5,570,122	(366,171)	5,936,293	5,570,122	(366,171)
Expenditures						
14. Salaries & Wages	1,760,648	1,808,492	47,844	1,760,648	1,808,492	47,844
15. Fringe Benefits	438,947	469,873	30,926	438,947	469,873	30,926
16. Purchased Services	315,448	275,183	(40,265)	315,448	275,183	(40,265)
17. Materials, Supplies & Textbooks	180,740	171,973	(8,762)	180,740	171,973	(8,762)
18. Capital Outlay Incl Replacement	130,899	58,940	(71,959)	130,899	58,940	(71,959)
19. Repayment of Borrowing Prin+Int	0	0	0	0	0	0
20. Transfers & Advances Out	0	0	0	0	0	0
21. Other	37,632	28,299	(9,333)	37,632	28,299	(9,333)
22. Total Expenditures (Lines 14-21)	2,864,314	2,812,765	(51,549)	2,864,314	2,812,765	(51,549)
Ending Cash Balance	3,071,979	2,757,357	(314,622)	3,071,979	2,757,357	(314,622)
23. Outstanding Encumbrances		421,093			421,093	
24. Unencumbered or Deficit Balance		2,336,264			2,336,264	

Many financial problems should be avoided by carefully reviewing these monthly statements. The board of education should ask for clarification if needed. Table 11:3 is an example of the instructional portion of this required report.

Even a casual observation of the data in Table 11:3 displaying expenditures for instruction should indicate to any person studying this report that this district has overspent its appropriations for instruction. Five months divided by twelve equals 41.2%. Thus, only 41.2% should have been spent or encumbered. Recognizing that there is a difference of only 2.6 percentage points between the appropriated amounts and what has actually been spent appears to be relatively small. However, the expenditures for instruction have exceeded the appropriated amount by over $200,000. There may be reasonable explanations for this overexpenditure. If so, these explanations should be made to all concerned with the health of the finances of this district.

Table 11:4 is another example of a monthly financial report that is helpful to members of a board of education as they endeavor to stay abreast of their board's financial status. This report gives the total amount of money that the district has and does not present the same balances as indicated in Table 11:3.

11.6-5 Annual Financial Reports

The last report, strictly financial, is mandated by the Ohio Revised Code. Incidentally, this law mandates comparable reports from all political subdivisions of the State. A portion of Section 117.38 states:

> A financial report of each public office, other than a state agency, for each fiscal year shall be made in accordance with rules prescribed by the auditor of State.
>
> The report shall be certified by the proper officer or board and filed with the auditor of state within ninety days after the close of the fiscal year, except that public offices filing pursuant to generally accepted accounting principles shall file their reports within one hundred eighty days after the close of the fiscal year. At the time of the filing of the report with the auditor of state, the chief fiscal officer shall publish in a newspaper published in the political subdivision or taxing district such portions of the report as prescribed by the auditor of state, and if there is no such newspaper, then in a newspaper of general circulation in the political subdivision or taxing district. . . .[7]

A careful review of this report reveals several items that should be of interest to not only members of the district's board of education but also to the citizens and taxpayers of the district.

The first column of data in Table 11:5 represents the financial activity of this district's general fund. Following are a few facts that can be easily determined from the data in column one of this report. Similar facts could be gleaned from the same reports by all school districts.

---

[7] Ohio Rev. Code Ann. at § 117.38.

Table 11:3

Instruction Portion of Monthly Report
Appropriation And Expenditure Comparison
For Period Ending: NOVEMBER 30, 1995

Account Description		Appropriation	Expenditure	Encumbrance	Balance	Spent
001 GENERAL FUND						
1000 INSTRUCTION						
1100 REGULAR INSTRUCTION						
1130 REG INSTRUCTION - H.S.						
100 SALARIES	$	1,120,000.00	565,476.75	.00	554,523.25	50.5%
200 BENEFITS	$	291,000.00	136,201.74	372.78	154,425.48	46.9%
400 PURCHASED SERVICES	$	8,216.70	1,092.45	4,048.55	3,075.70	62.6%
500 SUPPLIES & MATERIALS	$	30,750.00	24,406.37	1,481.81	4,861.82	84.2%
600 CAPITAL OUTLAY	$	1,000	.00	.00	1,000	.0%
700 REPLACEMENT-CAPITAL EXPND	$	1,000	.00	74.00	926.00	7.4%
TOTAL REG INSTRUCTION - H.S.	$	1,451,966.70	727,177.31	5,977.14	718,812.25	50.5%
TOTAL REGULAR INSTRUCTION	$	1,451,966.70	727,177.31	5,977.14	718,812.25	50.5%
1200 SPECIAL INSTRUCTION						
1220						
100 SALARIES	$	190,000.00	84,461.52	.00	105,538.48	44.5%
200 BENEFITS	$	49,000.00	19,762.92	.00	29,237.08	40.3%
400 PURCHASED SERVICES	$	5,000.75	775.88	1,091.50	3,133.37	37.3%
500 SUPPLIES & MATERIALS	$	5,161.91	2,560.91	405.58	2,195.42	57.5%
600 CAPITAL OUTLAY	$	2,000.00	.00	.00	2,000.00	.0%
TOTAL	$	251,162.66	107,561.23	1,497.08	142,104.35	43.4%
TOTAL SPECIAL INSTRUCTION	$	251,162.66	107.561.23	1,497.08	142,104.35	43.4%
1300 VOCATIONAL INSTRUCTION						
1310						
100 SALARIES	$	3,416,634.00	1,485,770.85	.00	1,930,863.15	43.5%
200 BENEFITS	$	892,207.00	356,169.53	28.44	536,009.03	39.9%
400 PURCHASED SERVICES	$	63,095.00	10,387.17	19,506.14	33,201.69	47.4%
500 SUPPLIES & MATERIALS	$	467,266.44	169,267.23	61,722.90	236,226.31	49.4%
600 CAPITAL OUTLAY	$	98,087.47	27,624.56	5,163.40	65,299.51	33.4%
700 REPLACEMENT-CAPITAL EXPND	$	98,991.34	49,355.76	11,848.69	37,786.89	61.8%
800 OTHER OBJECTS	$	1,100.00	195.74	.00	904.26	17.8%
TOTAL	$	5,037,381.25	2,098,70.84	98,319.57	2,840,290.84	43.6%
1330						
100 SALARIES	$	579,786.00	216,042.71	.00	363,743.29	37.3%
200 BENEFITS	$	152,141.00	52,091.11	.00	100,049.89	34.2%
400 PURCHASED SERVICES	$	8,721.19	312.75	1,913.50	6,494.94	25.5%
500 SUPPLIES & MATERIALS	$	18,941.17	3,562.07	902.39	14,476.71	23.6%
600 CAPITAL OUTLAY	$	5,152.97	399.00	53.97	4,700.00	8.8%
TOTAL	$	764,742.33	272,407.64	2,869.86	489,464.83	36.0%
1340						
100 SALARIES	$	233,580.00	91,567.02	.00	142,012.98	39.2%
200 BENEFITS	$	53,652.00	18,142.33	.00	35,509.67	33.8%
400 PURCHASED SERVICES	$	14,495.00	1,257.00	1,878.00	11,360.00	21.6%
500 SUPPLIES & MATERIALS	$	5,934.24	863.21	28.00	5,043.03	15.0%
600 CAPITAL OUTLAY	$	2,500.00	.00	.00	2,500.00	0%
TOTAL	$	310,161.24	111,829.56	1,906.00	196,425.68	36.7%

Account Description		Appropriation	Expenditure	Encumbrance	Balance	Spent
1390						
100 SALARIES	$	25,000.00	5,975.10	.00	19,024.90	23.9%
200 BENEFITS	$	7,350.00	2,216.34	.00	5,133.66	30.2%
400 PURCHASED SERVICES	$	2,000.00	.00	.00	2,000.00	.0%
500 SUPPLIES & MATERIALS	$	1,200.00	.00	.00	1,200.00	.0%
600 CAPITAL OUTLAY	$	1,000.00	.00	.00	1,000.00	.0%
TOTAL	$	36,550.00	8,191.44	.00	28,358.56	22.4%
TOTAL VOCATIONAL INSTRUCTION	$	6,148,834.82	2,491,199.48	103,095.43	3,554,539.91	42.2%
TOTAL INSTRUCTION	$	7,851,964.18	3,325,938.02	110,569.65	4,415,456.51	43.8%

Table 11:4

A Summary Financial Report of an Ohio School District for the Month of November, 1995

Balance:	November 1, 1995	$4,741,120.52
Add:	Receipts	959,745.52
	Total cash available	$5,700,866.04
Less:	Expenditures	1,404,148.14
	Cash balance as of November 30, 1995	$4,296,717.90
Less:	Encumbrances	711,319.76
	Unencumbered balance	$3,585,398.14
Bank balances:	Bank One	$ 0.00
	Central Trust	2,326.41
	Society Bank	0.00
	Cash on hand	1,400.00
	Investments	4,382,960.90
	Total	$4,386,687.31
Less:	Outstanding checks	89,969.41
	Balance as of November 30, 1995	$4,296,717.90

1. The total receipts for operating expenses of the district exceeded the disbursements by over $1,000,000.
2. The unreserved fund balance, after encumbrances have been considered, is $5,751,152.34 which is substantially greater than at the end of the previous fiscal year.
3. A simple calculation indicates that over 50.52% of its total receipts, for this column of data, came from Ohio; 44.9% from local and miscellaneous sources; 3.68% from federal sources; and .9% from investments.
4. It should also be noted that the assessed valuation of the district is $414,166,061 with the inside millage rate being 6.8 mills and the voted millage rate of 45.73 mills. The total 52.53 mills do not reflect the effective millage. The effective millage is considerably smaller.
5. Finally, there were 7,863 pupils in average daily membership. Among the 629 staff members, 406 were certified and 223 noncertified. The number of those employed full time is not indicated.

Table 11:5
A 1992 Annual Financial Report of an Ohio School District Combined Financial Report of the Board of Education For the Fiscal Year Ended June 30, 1995

Source Description	Governmental Funds	Expendable Trust Funds	Proprietary Funds	Non-Expendable Trust Funds	Agency Fund	Totals
Receipts:	Revenue Receipts			Operating Receipts		
Taxes	12,375,254.24	0.00	0.00	0.00	0.00	12,372,254.24
Tuition	64,601.96	0.00	3,003.75	0.00	0.00	67,605.71
Transportation Fees	47,081.63	0.00	0.00	0.00	0.00	47,081.63
Earnings on Investments	286,883.82	0.00	0.00	0.00	0.00	286,883.82
Food Service Sales	0.00	0.00	1,042,607.18	0.00	0.00	1,042,607.18
Extracurricular Activities	331,501.83	0.00	10,481.53	0.00	144,791.57	486,774.93
Class Materials & Fees	18,329.37	0.00	270,003.40	0.00	0.00	288,332.77
Misc. Receipts Grants in Aid	69,580.23	0.00	0.00	0.00	0.00	69,580.23
State Sources	16,169,372.99	0.00	0.00	0.00	0.00	16,169,372.99
Federal Sources	1,176,483.34	0.00	0.00	0.00	0.00	1,176,483.34
Total Receipts-(Operating)	30,536,089.41	0.00	1,326,095.86	0.00	144,791.57	32,006,976.84
Disembursements:	Expenditure Disbursement			Operating Disbursements		
Instruction	18,050,321.18	0.00	0.00	0.00	0.00	18,050,321.18
Supporting Services	8,416,381.61	60.00	0.00	0.00	0.00	8,416,441.61
Community Services	219,874.29	0.00	0.00	0.00	0.00	219,874.29
Extracurricular Activities	322,344.46	0.00	0.00	0.00	0.00	322,344.46
Facilities Acquisition	556,744.96	0.00	0.00	0.00	0.00	556,744.96
Debt Services	1,853,854.96	0.00	0.00	0.00	0.00	1,853,854.96
Employees Salaries & Wages	0.00	0.00	523,655.38	0.00	0.00	523,655.38
Employees Retirement Benefits	0.00	0.00	151,517.71	0.00	0.00	151,517.71
Purchased Services	0.00	0.00	38,538.13	0.00	0.00	38,538.13
Supplies & Materials	0.00	0.00	695,627.68	0.00	0.00	695,627.68
Capital Outlay	0.00	0.00	1,052.20	0.00	0.00	1,052.20
Capital Outlay - Replacement	0.00	0.00	3,086.65	0.00	0.00	3,086.65
Other Objects	0.00	0.00	15,598.73	0.00	136,703.87	152,302.60
Total Disbursements-(Operating)	29,419,521.46	60.00	1,429,076.48	0.00	136,703.87	30,985,361.81
Exc. Rcpts. Over/(Under) Disb.	1,116,567.95	(60.00)	(102,980.62)	0.00	8,087.70	1,021,615.03
Other Financing Sources (Users)			Non-Operating Receipts (Disbursements)			
Contributions & Donations	115,000.00	0.00	0.00	0.00	0.00	115,000.00
Prem. & Accrued Int. on Bonds	417.07	0.00	0.00	0.00	0.00	417.07
Proceeds from Sale of Notes	1,850,000.00	0.00	0.00	0.00	0.00	1,850,000.00
State Sources	0.00	0.00	12,212.22	0.00	0.00	12,212.22
Federal Sources	0.00	0.00	242,967.92	0.00	0.00	242,967.92

Source Description	Governmental Funds	Expendable Trust Funds	Proprietary Funds	Non-Expendable Trust Funds	Agency Fund	Totals
Refund of Prior Years Expend.	159,369.72	0.00	0.00	0.00	0.00	159,369.72
Refund of Prior Years Receipts	(14,574.58)	0.00	0.00	0.00	0.00	(14,574.58)
Total Other Fin. Sources (Uses)	2,110,212.21	0.00	255,180.14	0.00	0.00	2,365,392.35
Excess Receipts/Sources Over/(Under) Disbursements & Other Uses/Net	3,226,780.16	(60.00)	152,199.52	0.00	8,087.70	3,387,007.38
Beginning Fund Cash Balance	3,651,282.95	198.57	315,494.94	0.00	37,065.51	4,004,041.97
Ending Fund Cash Balance	6,878,063.11	138.57	467,694.46	0.00	45,153.21	7,391,049.35
Reserved for Encumbrances	1,126,910.77	0.00	41,098.83	0.00	7,929.20	1,175,938.80
Unreserved Fund Balance	5,751,152.34	138.57	426,595.63	0.00	3,7224.01	6,215,110.55
				Cash in Banks (Net)		(2,950.65)

I certify the following report to be correct and true, to the best of my knowledge:

....

Treasurer of the Board of Education

....

Type Name

....

Telephone Number

Summary Indebtedness Bonds

Balance Beginning of Period	1,768,000.00
New Issues-During Fiscal Period	0.00
Redeemed-During Fiscal Period	289,000.00
Balance 6-30-95	1,479,000.00

Summary Indebtedness Notes Long & Short Term

Balance Beginning of Period	1,768,000.00
New Issues-During Fiscal Period	1,100,000.00
Redeemed-During Fiscal Period	671,271.00
Balance 6-30-95	1,100,000.00

Petty Cash/Change Cash	0.00
Investments	7,394,000.00
Total Fund Balance	7,391,049.35
Memoranda Data	
Assessed Valuation	414,166,061
Property Tax Levies	
Inside 10 Mill	6.8000
Outside 10 Mill	45.7300
ADM	7,863.00
No. of Non Cert. Employees	223.00
Number of Cert. Employees	406.00

A more detailed analysis of the complete annual financial report may reveal additional information that might be useful to persons who have a special and/or particular interest in the field of school finance.

11.6-6 Annual Progress Reports

Annual Progress Reports are a part of *Senate Bill 170*, which was passed by the legislature in 1975 and evolved into Section 3313.94 of the Ohio Revised Code. Section 3313.94 was amended in 1979 through the enactment of *Senate Bill 59*. Although not strictly a financial report it certainly can be useful in maintaining a fiscally sound school system as it provides a valuable opportunity for district officials to explain certain financial aspects of school finance. As amended the law now states:

> The board of education of each school district shall issue an annual report of school progress for each school under its control and for the district according to guidelines established by the state board of education. The reports shall contain a ten-year projection of its enrollment, by year and by grade level; the names, addresses,

and home telephone numbers of the members of the state board of education, the Ohio house of representatives, and the Ohio senate elected from districts within which the school district has territory; and information about the achievements, problems, plans, and improvements in the school district. The guidelines shall be developed in consultation with representatives of the education profession, local boards of education, and other residents of the state and shall require some information common to all schools and school districts, permit reporting of information particular to each school and district and permit schools and school districts to take maximum advantage of reports already required by their board of education and other governmental units. The reports shall be issued to the local community of each school and district and shall be made in formats useful for parents and residents of the district.[8]

The Annual Progress Report Guidelines, required by the above law, were amended by the State Board of Education. These amended "Guidelines" became effective for fiscal year 1989. The guidelines now require the publication be completed by November 15 of each year. A copy must be filed with the Ohio Department of Education by December 1, of the same year.[9]

The financial data required by the guidelines are described as follows:

1. Average per-pupil costs
2. Total dollars and percentages of general fund operating expenditures in either:
   A. The six major functions code categories defined by the most current "Uniform School Accounting System (USAS)," including instruction, supporting services, operation of noninstructional services, extracurricular activities, facilities acquisition and construction services, and debt services; or
   B. The major categories defined in the most recent "Costs Per Pupil Report" published by the Ohio Department of Education.[10]

The careful design of a progress report, developed in a narrative style, helps keep the citizens better informed. An informed citizenry should be more willing to provide the financial support necessary when needs arise. The Annual Progress report provides opportunities for personnel in the district to emphasize achievements of the schools during the past year and address problems that they faced during the year and those perceived to be confronting them in the future.

11.7 Summary

This chapter, dealing with many aspects of school finance, can be briefly summarized by the following statements:

---

[8] Ohio Rev. Code Ann. at § 3313.94.

[9] Ohio Department of Education, *Annual Progress Reports Guidelines* (Columbus, Ohio: Ohio Department of Education, n.d.), at 1.

[10] *Id.* at 5.

1. The efficient and effective management of school funds is one of the most important tasks facing members of boards of education, school superintendents, and school treasurers. Sound management strategies conducted on a regular basis will help school districts avoid financial crises.
2. Members of boards of education have the final responsibility for the approval of: (1) levies to be submitted to voters, (2) budgets, and (3) appropriations.
3. Members of boards of education have the responsibility to be aware of the financial health of their district at all times. The careful review and analysis of required financial reports is one of the ways they can fulfill this responsibility.
4. It behooves superintendents and treasurers of school districts to keep the members of their board of education cognizant of the financial condition of the school district through documents and reports and explanations of the contents of the papers. Forthright answering of all questions that may arise is also very beneficial.
5. No other political subdivision in Ohio has to report on its finances as required by school districts.

Chapter 12: Court Cases and Related Issues for Ohio

12.1 Introduction

The courts have played an important role in the funding of education. This chapter reviews a number of significant cases originating in Ohio and in other states. Some of these have been decided by state supreme courts and others have been decided by the United States Supreme Court. One of the first issues brought to the courts dealt with the right of a school district to tax for the support of high schools.

12.2 Stuart v. School District of the Village of Kalamazoo

This early Michigan case involved a challenge to the attempted collection of taxes that had been voted for and assessed in order to support the local high school.[1] The court noted that the complainants (plaintiffs) were, in essence, objecting to the use of their tax dollars to support a classical curriculum-based high school education.[2] The court disagreed with the complainants' argument that those who wanted a classical education should pay for it individually. As such, the court validated the tax and dismissed the case, noting:

If these facts [as presented in the presentations made to the Court] do not demonstrate clearly and conclusively a general state policy, beginning in 1817 and continuing until after the adoption of the present constitution, in the direction of free schools in which

[1] *Stuart v. School District No. 1 of Kalamazoo*, 30 Mich. 70 (1874).
[2] *Id.* at 71.

education, and at their option the elements of classical education, might be brought within the reach of all the children of the state, then, as it seems to us, nothing can demonstrate. . . . We content ourselves with the statement that neither in our state policy, in our constitution, or in our laws, do we find the primary school districts restricted in the branches of knowledge which their officers may cause to be taught, or the grade of instruction that may be given, if their voters consent in regular form to bear the expense and raise the taxes for the purpose. Having reached this conclusion, we shall spend no time upon the objection that the district had no authority to appoint a superintendent of schools, and that the duties of superintendency should be performed by the district board. . . .[3]

12.3 Adequacy of Funding of Public Schools

Since the late 1960's, the focus on court cases dealing with adequacy of funding public elementary and secondary education has been on two central questions. The basis for these questions is to be found in most of the constitutions of the states.

The first question is, what is required of the state to provide a "thorough and efficient system of common schools"? Most of the states, like Ohio, have what are known as minimum standards, but do these standards provide a thorough and efficient system for all of the school age children? In each of the cases discussed next, "thorough and efficient" has been a central issue.

The second question is, what does the funding of education have to do with the statement "All political power is inherent in the people. Government is instituted for their equal protection and benefit"?

The real issue in cases responding to both of these questions is the toleration by the legislatures of the great disparities that exist in dollars available for the education of children in the local school districts in the states.

12.4 Financial Inequalities Between Ohio's School Districts

Tables 12:1 and 12:2 present data exemplifying the financial inequalities between Ohio's school districts. Data in Table 12:1 shows the reader the parameters of the disparities that exist in property valuations for the regular (Joint Vocational Districts excluded) school districts of Ohio. The highest valuation per pupil of a district in 1991 was found in a district that had an average daily membership of 1,531 pupils (ranked 338th in pupil size). If this district levies the 20 mills required to participate in the Foundation Program it would locally raise over $17,500 for each one of its pupils in ADM. In addition to the $17,500, this district would receive the guaranteed amount for its categorical programs as all other districts in Ohio. If this district was to levy an additional mill it would raise over $850 for each of its pupils.

A district with a $16,048 valuation, with an ADM of 1,227 could raise only slightly more than $320 from the 20 mill levy required for its participation in the State's Foundation

---

[3] *Id.* at 84–85.

Program. This amount added to the allowance made by the basic portion of the Foundation Program would provide the district with a total of about $2,670 to expend for each of its pupils. If it was to levy an additional mill, it would receive slightly over $16 for each of its pupils.

During the 1991 fiscal year there were 74 districts with assessed valuations of more than $100,000 per pupil in ADM and 26 districts with assessed valuations of less than $30,000. Nine districts had valuations in excess of $200,000 per pupil.

Table 12:1

The Low, Average, and High Per Pupil Property Valuations (assessed) for the School Districts of Ohio for the Fiscal Year 1990-91

Classification of districts	Low	Valuations Average	High
City	$22,123	$73,870	$293,290
Exempted village	22,329	63,611	209,969
Local	16,048	63,729	894,883
All districts	$16,048	$69,693	$894,883

Source: *Costs Per Pupil in 1990-1991*, an annual publication of the Division of Computer Services, of the State of Ohio Department of Education, Columbus, Ohio. See Table 12:3, on p. 72.

Table 12:2

The Low, Average, and High for the Current Expenditures Per Pupil for *General Funds* and *All Funds* for Ohio School Districts for the Fiscal Year 1991

Classification of districts	Low	Average	High
	General Fund		
City	$2,854	$4,500	$11,144
Exempted Village	2,835	3,791	6,681
Local	2,600	3,961	25,323
All districts*	2,600	3,961	25,323
Joint Vocational	4,200	7,005	9,823
	All Funds		
City	3,003	4,781	11,409
Exempted Village	3,077	3,941	6,717
Local	2,822	3,815	25,535
All districts*	2,822	4,390	25,535
Joint Vocational	4,784	7,389	10,457

Source: See Table 12:1. Table 12:1, pp. 26 - 27.
* These data do not include the Joint Vocational School Districts costs.

Another factor that affects "equal protection and benefit" is the amount of money that a district expends for each of its pupils in a year's time. Table 12:2 presents data pertaining to these expenditures for different types of school districts. It should be pointed out that the expenditure of $25,323 per pupil in ADM is an exception in that it is an island district having an ADM of only two pupils. However, there were 54 districts that spent more than $5,000 per pupil during the school year 1990-91, from their general fund accounts. At the other end of the continuum there were 29 districts that spent less than $3,000 per pupil from their general funds.

The facts presented in the above tables for Ohio, for the 1990-91 school year, are similar to those that formed the basis for the court actions taken in the states of California, Texas, West Virginia, and Kentucky, and for the Ohio cases presently being reviewed.

12.5 Serrano v. Priest

This litigation involved a constitutional challenge to the California public school financing system. Initially, the court remanded the case to the trial court with directions that the case proceed to trial.[4] In so doing, the court held that:

> [T]he facts alleged in plaintiffs' complaint were sufficient to constitute the three causes of action there set forth, and that if such allegations were sustained at trial, the state public school financing system must be declared invalid as in violation of state and federal constitutional provisions guaranteeing the equal protection of the laws.[5]

The state public school financing system then in existence relied heavily upon local district taxes on real property. Under such a system:

> [S]chool districts with a low value of taxable property per child cannot levy taxes at high enough rates to compete with more affluent districts; in many instances they cannot provide funds for a minimum [thorough and efficient] program of education. . . .[6]

The California Legislature responded to the court's decision and enacted legislation attempting to cure the constitutional defect. This legislation was enacted during the pendency of the trial on remand.[7] The trial court included, in its consideration, the changes made by the new legislation and held that the state public school financing system was invalid as a violation of state constitutional provisions guaranteeing equal protection of the law. On appeal, the California Supreme Court affirmed, holding that:

> [T]he California public school financing system for public elementary and secondary schools, . . . while not in violation of the equal protection clause of the Fourteenth Amendment to the United States Constitution, is invalid as being in violation of former article I, sections 11 and 21 (now art. IV, § 16 and art. I, § 7, respectively) of the California Constitution, commonly know[n] as the equal protection of the laws provisions of our state Constitution."[8]

---

[4] *Serrano v. Priest*, 5 Cal. 3d at 584, 487 P.2d at 1241 (1971).

[5] *Serrano v. Priest*, 18 Cal. 3d at 728, 735, 557 P.2d at 929, 930 (1976). *See Serrano v. Priest*, 5 Cal. 3d at 618–19, 487 P.2d at 1266.

[6] Percy Burrup and Vern Brimley, Jr., *Financing Education in a Climate of Change* (Boston, Mass.: Allyn and Bacon, Inc., 1982), at 211.

[7] *Serrano v. Priest*, 18 Cal. 3d at 728, 736, 557 P.2d at 929, 931.

[8] *Serrano v. Priest*, 18 Cal. 3d at 775, 557 P.2d at 957–58.

The funding system was found to be in violation of California state equal protection laws because it conditioned availability of school revenues upon district wealth, which resulted in disparities in school revenue, and because it made the quality of education dependent upon the level of district expenditure. In fact, the Court held so notwithstanding the State's contention that the California State Constitution authorized the essential elements of the invalid funding system.[9]

12.6 San Antonio Independent School District v. Rodriguez

The 1971 *Serrano v. Priest*[10] decision provided the backdrop for the *Rodriguez*[11] case, filed in federal court. *Rodriguez* was a class action initiated by Mexican-American parents whose children attended the elementary and secondary schools in an urban school district and was filed on behalf of minority school children and school children who reside in school districts having a low property tax base.[12] The suit alleged that the Texas system of financing public education violated the Equal Protection Clause of the Fourteenth Amendment of the United States Constitution.[13] A divided supreme court concluded that Texas legislative scheme for financing public education satisfied the constitutional standard under the Equal Protection Clause and was, therefore, constitutional.[14]

The majority opinion in *Rodriguez* recognized the imperfections of the challenged statutory scheme, not only in Texas, but in other states as well. A finding of unconstitutionality, however, would not only result in "an unprecedented upheaval in public education,"[15] but would violate the principles of federalism.[16]

> The consideration and initiation of fundamental reforms with respect to state taxation and education are matters reserved for the legislative processes of the various States, and we do no violence to the values of federalism and separation of powers by staying our hand. . . . The need is apparent for reform in tax systems which may well have relied too long and too heavily on the local property tax. And certainly innovative thinking as to public education, its methods, and its funding is necessary to assure both a higher level of quality and greater uniformity of opportunity. . . . But the ultimate solutions must come from the lawmakers and from the democratic pressures of those who elect them.[17]

The Supreme Court, therefore, was unwilling to disturb similar state systems for financing public education but recognized the need for change. This change, however, was to be brought about by the people at the ballot boxes and by the respective state legislatures.

---

[9] *Serrano v. Priest*, 18 Cal. 3d at 770–72, 557 P.2d at 954–955.
[10] *Serrano v. Priest*, 5 Cal. 3d at 584, 487 P.2d at 1241 (1971).
[11] *San Antonio Independent School District v. Rodriguez*, 411 U.S. 1 (1973).
[12] *Id.* at 4–5.
[13] *Id.* at 6.
[14] *Id.* at 55.
[15] *Id.* at 56.
[16] *Id.* at 58.
[17] *Id.* at 58–59.

12.7 Board of Education v. Walter

This case challenged the constitutionality of Ohio's system of financing public elementary and secondary education.[18] Although this case is important to Ohio, very little has been written and said about it. It was initiated by the Cincinnati Board of Education in 1976. The plaintiffs in the case were members of the Board of Education, the Superintendent, the Clerk-Treasurer, parents on behalf of their students and themselves, and as representatives of all similarly situated school districts in Ohio. The defendants in the case were the State Superintendent of Public Instruction, the State Board of Education, the Department of Education, and the Controlling Board (an instrument of the State Legislature).[19]

The trial officially began on December 6, 1976 in the Common Pleas Court of Hamilton County with Judge Riley, a visiting Judge hearing the case. The trial lasted 78 days, with the court hearing over seventy witnesses and reviewing over 2300 exhibits. The record of the case in the Common Pleas Court consists of 7500 pages.[20]

Some of the witnesses for the defendants testified to facts about their school districts that could not be substantiated from the required reports which they had filed with the State Department of Education. Many of the witnesses for the plaintiffs were school officials from districts having financial problems. The annual reports required by Section 3313.94 of the Ohio Revised Code were subpoenaed from these districts. This law states:

> The reports shall contain . . . information about the achievements, problems, plans and improvements in the school district.[21]

Only one of the subpoenaed reports contained information that could be construed that the district was having financial problems and it only mentioned that a consideration in the future would have to be given for raising additional taxes.

Judge Riley, in his three page opinion ruled in favor of the plaintiffs declaring Ohio's funding system for its public schools to be in violation of the Ohio Constitution, namely Article VI, Section 2, the Thorough and Efficient Clause, and Article I, Section 2, the Equal Protection and Benefit Clause.[22] In addition he ruled that certain portions of the School Foundation Program were inoperative and void.[23] Finally, and in recognition of the difficulty of changing the funding system, the Judge delayed the effects of his ruling until July 1, 1978.[24]

The defendants filed an appeal with the Court of Appeals of Hamilton County.[25] This court held that the lower court was correct in declaring that the funding plan violated the

---

[18] *Board of Education v. Walter*, No. A7602725 (C.P. Hamilton County, Ohio, Dec. 5, 1977), *aff'd in part and rev'd in part*, 10 Ohio Op. 3d 26 (Ct. App. 1978), *aff'd in part and rev'd in part*, 58 Ohio St. 2d 368, 390 N.E.2d 813 (1979), *cert. denied*, 444 U.S. 1015 (1980). *See supra* Chapter 2.

[19] *Id.*

[20] *Board of Education v. Walter*, 10 Ohio Op. 3d 26, 36 (Ct. App. 1978), *aff'd in part and rev'd in part*, 58 Ohio St. 2d 368, 390 N.E.2d 813 (1979), *cert. denied*, 444 U.S. 1015 (1980).

[21] Ohio Rev. Code Ann. at § 3313.94.

[22] *Board of Education v. Walter*, 10 Ohio Op. 3d 26, 39 (Ct. App. 1978), *aff'd in part and rev'd in part*, 58 Ohio St. 2d 368, 369, 390 N.E.2d 813 (1979), *cert. denied*, 444 U.S. 1015 (1980).

[23] *Id.*

[24] *Id.*

[25] *See Board of Education v. Walter*, 10 Ohio Op. 3d 26, 39 (Ct. App. 1978), *aff'd in part and rev'd in part*, 58 Ohio St. 2d 368, 390 N.E.2d 813 (1979), *cert. denied*, 444 U.S. 1015 (1980).

Equal Protection and Benefit Clause of Ohio's Constitution, but declared that the lower court had erred when it found that the system violated the Constitution's Thorough and Efficient Clause.[26]

Both parties in this case were dissatisfied with the Appellate Court's decision and both filed appeals to Ohio's Supreme Court.[27] This Court, in its 5 to 1 decision stated:

> The judgment of the court of appeals that the Ohio statutory system for financing elementary and secondary education violates Section 2, Article I [the Equal Protection and Benefit Clause] of the Ohio Constitution is reversed. The judgment of the court of appeals that the Ohio statutory system for financing elementary and secondary education does not violate Section 2, Article VI [the Thorough and Efficient Clause] of the Ohio Constitution is affirmed.
>
> For the reasons stated herein, the judgment of the court of appeals is reversed in part and affirmed in part.[28]

Judge Locher, dissenting to the opinion of the majority of the Court, stated from his view the system violated both the Equal Protection and Benefit and the Thorough and Efficient Clauses of Ohio's Constitution. He supported his view with a lengthy discussion of the matter that had been presented to the Court.[29]

The Ohio Supreme Court's decision did not end the Cincinnati case. The Cincinnati Board of Education (the plaintiffs) made one more effort, this time it was an appeal for an injunction with the United States District Court, Southern District of Ohio, Eastern Division. The State, (the defendant) filed an action to dismiss. Judge Timothy Hogan conducted this hearing in Cincinnati on November 1, 1979. In his twenty page decision, Judge Hogan stated that:

> . . .the motion of the defense to dismiss is sustained. The motion for an injunction is denied, and, thereupon, proceedings in this action will be stayed pending repair to the State Court to iron out the whole problem in the State Court first.[30]

The Judge used the *Rodriguez* decision as the basis for his reasoning in arriving at the above statement, noting that education is a function of state government not a function of the federal government.

This case cost the Cincinnati Board of Education in excess of $1,000,000. There are no details of the cost to the State of Ohio. After such costs, it is most unfortunate that this case failed to yield any recognizable positive results. The State of Ohio has made little more progress towards equalizing educational opportunities for its elementary and secondary school children than it did prior to the initiation of this case. However, two cases are now progressing through the Ohio courts. One has been initiated by a coalition

[26] *Id.*, 10 Ohio Op. 3d at 39.

[27] *Board of Education v. Walter*, 58 Ohio St. 2d 368, 390 N.E.2d 813 (1979), *cert. denied*, 444 U.S. 1015 (1980).

[28] *Id.*, 58 Ohio St. 2d at 388–89, 390 N.E.2d 813–829 (1979), *cert. denied*, 444 U.S. 1015 (1980).

[29] *Id.*, 58 Ohio St. 2d at 339, 390 N.E.2d 813–827 (1979) (Locher, J., dissenting), *cert. denied*, 444 U.S. 1015 (1980).

[30] *Findings*, United States District Court, Southern District of Ohio, Eastern Division, Case No. C-278-1004, Honorable Timothy S. Hogan, at 3.

of financially distressed districts. The other case was filed by the Cleveland City Board of Education.

12.8 Pauley v. Bailey

This case, originally filed in 1975, alleged that public school students were being denied a "thorough and efficient system of free schools," in violation of the West Virginia Constitution, as a result of the existing discriminatory mechanism for financing the State's educational system.[31] After the case was initially dismissed, the West Virginia Supreme Court of Appeals remanded the case back to the Kanawha County Circuit Court, reasoning that a more intense inquiry into the issue was required because education is a fundamental and constitutionally protected right in West Virginia by virtue of the state constitutional provision mandating a "thorough and efficient system of free schools."[32]

On remand, the circuit court found broad and comprehensive constitutional inadequacies in West Virginia's educational system.[33] The 244-page decision issued by the circuit court was substantially different, in length and substance, from the decision rendered by the Hamilton County Court of Common Pleas in *Board of Education v. Walter.*[34]

> In the opinion, the circuit court outlined, based upon the voluminous expert evidence gathered during the lengthy proceedings, the core elements of a "thorough and efficient" educational system. The elements were classified into broad categories of curriculum, personnel, facilities and materials and equipment. By comparison, the circuit court found systems now in existence in Lincoln County and other counties across the State to be "woefully inadequate." The circuit court further found that some counties, mostly those with greater property wealth, had educational systems that come close to "thorough and efficient," however, the court determined that all county systems required improvement.[35]

The circuit court's pronouncement regarding the core elements of a "thorough and efficient" educational system provided that:

> A high quality program consistent with. . .the West Virginia Constitution requires that all direct and indirect costs of educational programs must be fully included in the financing structure, i.e. curriculum costs, instructional, support and administrative staff salaries, benefits, supplies and equipment costs, and facility costs. Further, in order to develop thorough and efficient programs, the state has a duty to provide that the counties have the ability to:
>
> (a) attract, employ, and retain a high quality staff of sufficient size to perform the educational tasks, including sufficient administrative staff;

---

[31] *Pauley v. Bailey*, 324 S.E.2d 128, 129–30 (W. Va. 1984).

[32] *Pauley v. Kelly*, 255 S.E.2d 859, 863 (W. Va. 1979). *See Pauley v. Bailey*, 324 S.E.2d at 130 (W. Va. 1984).

[33] *See Pauley v. Bailey*, 324 S.E.2d at 131.

[34] *Board of Education v. Walter*, No. A 7602725 (C.P. Hamilton County, Ohio, Dec. 5, 1977), *aff'd in part and rev'd in part*, 10 Ohio Op. 3d 26 (Ct. App. 1978), *aff'd in part and rev'd in part*, 58 Ohio St. 2d 368, 390 N.E.2d 813 (1979), *cert. denied*, 444 U.S. 1015 (1980). *See supra* Section 12.7.

[35] *Pauley v. Bailey*, 324 S.E.2d at 131.

(b) provide high quality, well maintained educational facilities; and

(c) provide high quality textbooks, workbooks, and instructional supplies and equipment. To support the educational program, the state has a duty to provide that the counties are able to provide high quality support services in the areas of counseling and guidance, health, food preparation, and transportation.[36]

The significance of this case is that for the first time, a court actually defined what a "thorough and efficient system of education" should include. In so doing, the circuit court indicated that the education of the children of West Virginia should be the real priority of the State. The court recognized the need for funding and encouraged the Kanawha County Court to implement the beleaguered statewide reappraisal program. The court seemingly reflected the attitude of the people throughout the education community. The tax reappraisal program would be a panacea for the financial ills.

Thirteen years after the initial action to bring about changes to adequately fund the financial system in West Virginia, the issue was back before the courts.[37] At issue were the excess levy provisions of the state constitution which are designed to help finance the public school system.[38] The circuit court had determined that the excess levy provision violated the Equal Protection Clause of the Constitution because: "[D]ependence on county funds, particularly excess levies, promoted unequal treatment of students in poor and wealthy counties."[39] The circuit court therefore ordered that a portion of the state school funding be withheld from counties with excess levies, and that these sums be distributed equitably to other counties.[40] The Supreme Court of Appeals disagreed with the lower court. The excess levy provisions were held to be constitutional and the Supreme Court refused to permit the lower court's order to be enforced.[41]

12.9 Rose v. Council for Better Education

This case began August 4, 1987 and was concluded June 8, 1989 as the Supreme Court of Kentucky handed down its decision in favor of the plaintiffs, the Council for Better Education.[42]

The Council for Better Education, formulated in early 1985, was comprised mainly of persons in 66 property-poor districts. The Council also included a former associate State Superintendent of Public Instruction and former Governor of the State, a nationally recognized specialist of school finance, and three lawyers. A great deal of work was done by the plaintiffs in preparation for the trial. Not only did they collect a great amount of data but they also carefully crafted the complaint that helped to assure them success for

---

36 Kern Alexander and David W. Alexander, *American Public School Law*, 2nd ed. (St. Paul, Minn.: West Publishing Co., 1985), at 501–02 [hereinafter American Public School Law].

37 *State ex rel. Boards of Education v. Chafin*, 376 S.E.2d at 113 (W. Va. 1988).

38 *Id.*, 376 S.E.2d at 115.

39 *Id.*

40 *Id.*

41 *Id.*

42 *Rose v. Council for Better Educ., Inc.*, 790 S.W.2d at 186 (Ky. 1989) [hereinafter *Rose v. Council for Better Education, Inc.*]. *See also* Woody Barwick, "A Chronology of the Kentucky Case," *Journal of Education Finance* (Fall 1989), at 136–40.

their efforts. This extensive work was one of the important keys that helped the plaintiffs secure a positive answer in the Courts.

The Kentucky Supreme Court held that the General Assembly "has failed to establish an efficient system of common schools throughout the Commonwealth," as is mandated by the Kentucky Constitution.[43] In so deciding, the Court articulated the essential and minimal characteristics of an efficient system of common schools:

1. The establishment, maintenance and funding of common schools in Kentucky is the sole responsibility of the General Assembly.
2. Common schools shall be free to all.
3. Common schools shall be available to all Kentucky children.
4. Common schools shall be substantially uniform throughout the state.
5. Common schools shall provide equal educational opportunities to all Kentucky children, regardless of place of residence or economic circumstances.
6. Common schools shall be monitored by the General Assembly to assure that they are operated with no waste, no duplication, no mismanagement, and with no political influence.
7. The premise for the existence of common schools is that all children in Kentucky have a constitutional right to an adequate education.
8. The General Assembly shall provide funding which is sufficient to provide each child in Kentucky an adequate education.
9. An adequate education is one which has as its goal the development of the seven capacities recited previously.[44]

The Court emphasized that its finding of unconstitutionality applied to the entire system of public schools:

> This decision applies to the entire sweep of the system—all its parts and parcels. This decision applies to the statutes creating, implementing and financing the *system* and to all regulations, etc., pertaining thereto. This decision covers the creation of local school districts, school boards, and the Kentucky Department of Education to the Minimum Foundation Program and Power Equalization Program. It covers school construction and maintenance, teacher certification the whole gamut of the common school system in Kentucky.[45]

This case has been the exception to state court cases for resolving financial problems dealing with both adequacy and equity. The Governor of Kentucky signed the remedial legislation in April, 1990, and current evidence is that substantial improvements are being made in this state. However, in most cases the states have not met the constitutional mandates that require them to have "thorough and efficient" school systems and that such systems are for the "equal protection and benefit" for all children.

---

[43] *Rose v. Council for Better Educ., Inc.*, at 215.
[44] *Id.* at 212–213.
[45] *Id.* at 215.

12.10 Robinson v. Cahill

Both of Ohio's court cases on school financing have referenced the "thorough and efficient" clause in the Ohio Constitution. This was true with the New Jersey court case[46] as well.

Regarding *Robinson v. Cahill,* Alexander and Salmon[47] stated:

> The education provision of a state constitution may, without support or complement from any other constitutional source, require substantial uniformity in the allocation of school funds. The New Jersey Supreme Court in Robinson v. Cahill first expressed this view by indicating that the system of school financing could be held unconstitutional solely on the basis of the positive mandate of the education provision of the state constitution. Unlike the Kentucky case, Robinson did not find that education was fundamental, nor did it need to. Rather, the New Jersey court found that unconstitutionality could be determined even though education is not fundamental for equal protection purposes. The court in Robinson held simply that the affirmative mandate of the New Jersey Constitution had not been fulfilled by the legislature, and that "a system of instruction in any district of the state which is not thorough and efficient falls short of the constitutional command."

As a result of this New Jersey Supreme Court case, the court directed the New Jersey legislature to rectify the financial deficiencies in the state. The court stated that substantially equivalent per-pupil expenditure must be required, but did not specify specific remedies. From 1976 to 1990, the New Jersey legislature changed the school funding mechanisms several times, but none withstood court challenge.[48]

Continued inequities resulted in the second New Jersey suit, that of *Abbott v. Burke*.[49] Therefore, even though the plaintiffs won at the state supreme court level with the Robinson case, further compliance litigation resulted with *Abbott v. Burke*.[50]

In July of 1990, legislators in New Jersey enacted a new school funding system called the Quality in Education Act that established a foundation amount. Each district was given a state local "fair share" which represented an amount to be raised by local property taxes in order to qualify for a maximum level of foundation aid. The amount was determined by formula that gives equal weight to property wealth and personal income in each district. Within specified limits, districts could spend more than their foundation level, but received no additional state foundation aid for spending above this level. This still resulted in wide disparities in school district expenditures, and caused legislators to limit districts as to how much they could spend per child above the foundation level.

As mentioned earlier (12.7 Board of Education v. Walter), the thorough and

---

[46] *Robinson v. Cahill,* 62 N.J. 473, 030 A.2d 273 (1973).

[47] Alexander, Kern and Salmon, Richard G., *Public School Finance* (Needham Heights, Mass.: Allyn and Bacon, Inc)., 1995, at 35 [hereinafter Public School Finance].

[48] *Robinson v. Cahill,* 62 N.J. 473, 303 A.2d 293 (1973).

[49] *Abbott v. Burke,* 119 N.J. 297, A.2d 359 (1990).

[50] *Id.*

efficient clause of the Ohio Constitution was not pervasive, as was experienced in this New Jersey case, for both the Court of Appeals of Hamilton County[51] and the Ohio Supreme Court.[52] This same clause (thorough and efficient), was found to have merit in the current Ohio lower court case.[53] However, on August 30, 1995 the 5th District Court of Appeals in Canton, Ohio rejected Ohio's lower court opinion that found the current funding system unconstitutional.[54]

12.11 Edgewood v. Kirby

The operative term in the Texas Supreme Court Case,[54] just as occurred in Ohio's[55] two school finance cases, Kentucky's[56] and New Jersey's,[57] was "efficient." The facts in this case were quite similar to an earlier Texas case[58] but this case was ruled on by the Texas Supreme Court rather than the U.S. District Court.

According to Alexander and Salmon[59] there was considerable disparity in property wealth of Texas public school districts. They stated:

> In Texas, the evidence presented in the Edgewood case, 1989, showed that the highest-capacity school district had over $14,000,000 of property wealth per pupil while the poorest district had about $20,000, a wealth disparity ratio of approximately 700 to 1.

Alexander and Salmor,[60] went on to state:

> In Texas school finance case *Edgewood v. Kirby*, the Supreme Court of Texas noted that: "the lower expenditures in the property-poor districts are not the result of lack of tax effort. Generally, the property-rich districts can tax low and spend high while the property-poor district must tax high merely to spend low." In Texas, the court found that the 100 poorest school districts had an average tax rate of 74.5 cents and spent only $2,975 per pupil, while the rich districts had an average tax rate of 47 cents and spent an average of $7,233, per pupil.

This Texas Supreme Court case did not speak to the "fundamental rights" issues. Rather,

---

[51] *Board of Education v. Walter,* 10 Ohio Op. 3d 26, 39 (Ct. App. 1978), *aff'd in part,* 58 Ohio St. 2d 368, 390 N.E.2d 813 (1979), *cert. denied,* 444 U.S. 1015 (1980).

[52] *Board of Education v. Walter,* 58 Ohio St. 2d 368, 390 N.E.2d 813 (1979), *cert. denied,* 444 U.S. 1015 (1980).

[53] *DeRolph v. State of Ohio,* No. 22043 (Perry County, July 1, 1994) 463 [hereinafter *DeRolph v. State of Ohio*].

[54] *Id.* see 12.12.

[54] *Edgewood v. Kirby,* 777 S.W.2d 391 (1989).

[55] *Board of Education v. Walter,* No. A7602725 (C.P. Hamilton County, Ohio, Dec. 5, 1977) *aff'd in part and rev'd in part,* 10 Ohio Op. 3d 26 (Ct. App. 1978), *aff'd in part and rev'd in part,* 58 Ohio S. 2d 368, 390 N.E.2d 813 (1979), *cert. denied,* 444 U.S. 1015 (1980); *DeRolph v. State of Ohio,* No. 22043 (Perry County, July 1, 1994) 463.

[56] *Rose v. Council for Better Education, Inc.,* 790 S.W.2d 186 (Ky. 1989).

[57] *Robinson v. Cahill,* 62 N.J. 473, 303 A.2d 273 (1973); *Abbott v. Burke,* 119 N.J. 287, 575 A.2d 359 (1990).

[58] *San Antonio Independent School District v. Rodriquez,* 411 U.S. (1973).

[59] Public School Finance at 167.

[60] *Id.* at 186.

the decision rested on the basis of "equity." The state's portion of dollars provided for public schools went up significantly, just as it did in California, New Jersey, and Kentucky with resulting Supreme Court decisions. In Texas, it also led to the noted "Robin Hood" affect—that of taking from wealthier school districts and giving to poorer districts. In a sense, this principle is already applied to a degree in Ohio as many property-rich districts also have high personal income. Therefore, more money is sent from high-personal income districts to the Ohio General Revenue Fund, which is then redistributed (from funds applied to elementary and secondary education) through the State Foundation program with a higher percentage going to poorer school districts.

12.12 DeRolph v. State of Ohio

Almost two decades passed following the *Board of Education v. Walter* case before Nathan DeRolph and others filed suit in the Court of Common Pleas of Perry County, Ohio. The Ohio Coalition for Equity and Adequacy of School Funding, under the leadership of Executive Director William Phillis, was instrumental in gathering factual information pertaining to both adequacy and equity issues regarding school funding. The Coalition identified several individuals and school districts to act as plaintiffs in the trial on behalf of 500 local, city, exempted village, joint vocational, and county school districts.

At the time of the trial, Nathan DeRolph was a student in the Northern Local School District of Perry County, Ohio. He brought his action through his father Dale DeRolph. Other plaintiffs included students, teachers, school administrators, parents, board of education members, and school districts. The plaintiffs charged that the system of funding elementary and secondary public education, at the time of the proceedings and the trial, failed to comply with mandates of the Ohio Constitution.

Although several sections of the Ohio Constitution were cited, the provisions of "equal protection and benefit" and "thorough and efficient system of common schools" were most notable. Article I, section 2 of the Ohio Constitution states in part:

> All political power is inherent in the people. Government is instituted for their equal protection and benefit. . . .[61]

The thorough and efficient clause is addressed in Article VI, of the Ohio Constitution which provides:

> The general assembly shall make such provisions, by taxation, or otherwise, as, with the income arising from the school trust fund, will secure a thorough and efficient system of common schools throughout the state; but no religious or other sect, or sects shall ever have an exclusive right to, or control of, any part of the school funds of this state.[62]

Judge Linton D. Lewis, Jr. ruled in favor of the plaintiffs, and in so doing, held that Ohio's property-based school funding system for elementary and secondary schools, violated

---

[61] Ohio Const. art. I at § 2.
[62] Ohio Const. art. VI at § 2.

the Ohio Constitution.[63] This opinion is currently under appeal and will ultimately conclude when ruled by the Ohio Supreme Court.

The court directly linked the fundamentality of education to the "inalienable right" of "enjoying and defending life and liberty, acquiring, possessing and protecting property and seeking and obtaining happiness and safety" set forth in Article I, section 1[64]. . . . Upon finding education to be a fundamental right, the court found that the disparities in funding amount directly deny plaintiffs the "equal protection and benefit" of the law as guaranteed by Article 1, section 2.[65]

Concerning the "thorough and efficient" clause, the court found the argument (that the guaranteed yield foundation program was thorough and efficient because all districts met certain minimum standards) was invalid as the current standards were not even being monitored. The court also cited plaintiff districts' failure to meet ninth grade proficiency test standards as evidence of the General Assembly's failure to provide "thorough and efficient" schools.[66]

In addition to other issues relating to a "thorough and efficient" system, the court delineated State responsibilities in this matter:

> The State is obligated by law to provide a thorough and efficient system of education for all students within the state. To ensure that end, the state is likewise obligated to provide sufficient funds to meet that requirement within the constraints of the Ohio Constitution. The State's current funding system which transfers major obligations for funding from the State to the local school districts does not operate within those constraints.[67]

Thus, in *DeRolph v. State of Ohio*, the court determined that Ohio's current funding system violates both the "equal protection and benefit" and "thorough and efficient" clauses of the Ohio Constitution. This lower court decision was overturned on August 30, 1995 when the 5th District Court of Appeals ruled that it is the General Assembly's responsibility to determine funding levels and only the Ohio Supreme Court can determine if it is constitutional. The Appellate Court ruling has been appealed and awaits a Supreme Court decision in 1996.

12.13 A Related Problem—Aid to Non-public Schools

An area of Ohio school finance that has taken on importance in recent years, is in the funding of non-public schools. Many proposals continue to be offered that would use public funds for the education of children in non-public schools. The early 90's has seen the national administration advocate such use. Governor Voinivich is urging the expansion of Ohio's contribution to non-public schools even though this state currently has one of

---

[63] *DeRolph v. State of Ohio,* at 463.

[64] *Id.* at 469. See Hawk, Morris L., As Perfect as Can Be Devised: *DeRolph v. State of Ohio* and the Right of Education in Ohio, *Case Western Reserve Law Review* (Vol. 45, No. 2, winter, 1995), at 689 [hereinafter As Perfect as Can Be Devised].

[65] *DeRolph v. State of Ohio* at 469. See "As Perfect as Can Be Devised" at 690.

[66] *DeRolph v. State of Ohio* at 473. See "As Perfect as Can Be Devised" at 691.

[67] *DeRolph v. State of Ohio* at 476. See "As Perfect as Can Be Devised" at 692.

the most extensive programs in the nation. (See Table 5 in Chapter 2 for the amounts of the annual appropriations of the Ohio Legislature for such schools.)

Several cases pertain to non-public school aid and provide some background for Ohio's experience. *Pierce* is remotely related to school finance but does provide information about the tension that existed between the public and non-public schools in the 1920's and continues, to some extent, to the present time.

12.14 Pierce v. Society of Sisters

The Oregon Legislature expanded its education law, with certain exceptions, to require parents and others who had control of children between the ages of eight and sixteen years of age to send them to the district public school in which they resided.[68] This law was to take effect in 1926. The United States Supreme Court held that while the state may regulate all schools and require that all children attend some school, it cannot deny them the right to attend non-public schools.[69]

The Supreme Court reasoned that the legislation in question "unreasonably interferes with the liberty of parents and guardians to direct the upbringing and education of children under their control."[70] The business and property owned by the corporate entity challenging the legislation is "threatened with destruction through the unwarranted compulsion which appellants are exercising over present and prospective patrons of their schools."[71] As such, the corporate party to the lawsuit is afforded constitutional protection.[72] The Supreme Court, therefore, affirmed the lower court's ruling and enjoined enforcement of the legislation, relying upon the Due Process Clause of the Fourteenth Amendment.[73]

12.15 Cochran v. Louisiana State Board of Education

This 1930 decision is one of the earliest to address the question of state aid to non-public schools.[74] The challengers alleged that a recently enacted state statute requiring that state funds be used to provide "school books for school children free of cost to such children"[75] violated various provisions of the Louisiana Constitution and violated the Due Process Clause of the Fourteenth Amendment of the United States Constitution.[76] The Supreme Court affirmed the decision of the Louisiana Supreme Court, holding that the challenged statute did not violate the constitutional provisions in question.[77] It should be noted that in this case, as in subsequent decisions addressing the issue of state aid to non-public schools, the United States Supreme Court permitted states to provide some funding to non-public schools, but did not mandate such funding.

---

[68] *Pierce v. Society of Sisters*, 268 U.S. 510 (1924).
[69] *Id.* at 536.
[70] *Id.* at 534–35.
[71] *Id.* at 535.
[72] *Id.*
[73] *Id.* at 536.
[74] *Cochran v. Louisiana State Board of Education*, 281 U.S. 370 (1930).
[75] *Id.* at 374.
[76] *Id.* at 373–74.
[77] *Id.* at 375.

Cochran announced the "child benefit" theory—the theory that state funding directly benefitting school child, and not the schools, is not violative of the constitution. The Supreme Court quoted the state court decision, noting that:

> The appropriations were made for the specific purpose of purchasing school books for the use of the school children of the state, free of cost to them. It was for *their benefit* and the resulting benefit to the state that the appropriations were made. True, these children attend some school, public or private, the latter, sectarian or nonsectarian, and that the books are to be furnished them for their use, free of cost, whichever they attend. The schools, however, are not the beneficiaries of these appropriations. They obtain nothing from them, nor are they relieved of a single obligation because of them. The school children and the state alone are the beneficiaries.[78]

12.16 Everson v. Board of Education

The Legislature in New Jersey passed a law authorizing local school districts to provide transportation for children to and from public and nonprofit schools. The Ewing Township Board of Education began reimbursing parents for the transportation to sectarian schools. Everson, a taxpayer of the district, challenged the constitutionality of such practice.[79] In reaching its decision in 1947 the United States Supreme Court addressed not only the Fourteenth Amendment Due Process Clause but also the First Amendment Establishment Clause. In its 5 to 4 decision the Court stated that this law was constitutional and did not violate the Fourteenth or the First Amendments. Justice Black, in concluding the Court's decision, made the following statement concerning the question of the constitutionality of the New Jersey law under the First Amendment:

> Of course, cutting off church schools from these services so indisputably marked off from the religious function, would make it far more difficult for the schools to operate. But such is obviously not the purpose of the First Amendment. That Amendment requires the state to be a neutral in its relations with groups of religious believers and non-believers; it does not require the state to be their adversary. State power is no more to be used so as to handicap religions than it is to favor them.
>
> * * *
>
> The First Amendment has erected a wall between church and state. That wall must be kept high and impregnable. We could not approve the slightest breach. New Jersey has not breached it here.[80]

In his dissent, joined in by all four dissenting justices, Justice Rutledge argued that the legislation should be ruled unconstitutional because transportation was as important to the total cost of education as any other segment.[81]

The concept of "a wall between church and state" along with the "child benefit" theory

---

[78] *Id.* at 374–75.
[79] *Everson v. Board of Education*, 330 U.S. 1 (1946).
[80] *Id.* at 18.
[81] *Id.* at 56 (Rutledge, J., dissenting). *See also* Edmond Reutter, Jr., *The Law of Public Education,* 3d ed. (Mineola, N.Y.: The Foundation Press, Inc., 1985), at 48.

have both been used in a number of other cases dealing with aid to non-public schools since the *Cochran* and *Everson* cases. These concepts will undoubtedly be used in future cases which may develop. As of 1982, 28 states, including Ohio, provided transportation for pupils to non-public schools.[82]

Ohio's law providing for the transportation of non-public school children was enacted in 1967. This law is embodied in Section 3327.01, of the Ohio Revised Code, which mandates the transportation of children in grades kindergarten through grade eight to schools in the district of residence if they live two miles or more from the school.

This same law permits boards of education, at their discretion, to provide transportation for pupils in grades nine through twelve. However, the state reimburses local districts when they transport pupils from kindergarten through grade 12 if the pupils live a mile or more from the school of attendance. This section also states that a board of education need not provide the transportation of pupils to non-public schools if it would require more than thirty minutes travel time to the school from the collection points.[83]

No court action, to date, has been sought in Ohio contesting the transportation of pupils to non-public schools. However, several Ohio cases, all related to "auxiliary services," have dealt with aid to non-public schools. Benson Wolman, Executive Director of the American Civil Liberties Union in Ohio, was the chief plaintiff and the Superintendent of Public Instruction was the chief defendant in *Wolman v. Essex I.*

12.17 Wolman v. Essex

This case[84] involved a constitutional challenge to the former Ohio educational grant statute which authorized grants to reimburse parents of non-public school children for a portion of tuition paid by them.[85] The federal district court held that the challenged portion of the statute violated the Establishment Clause of the First Amendment of the United States Constitution.[86] In addressing the constitutional challenge, the court employed a three-pronged test adopted by the United States Supreme Court. In order to pass constitutional muster under this test: (1) the statute must express a valid secular purpose;[87] (2) "the principal or primary effect of the statute, as opposed to its purpose, must not be one that either advances or inhibits religion"[88]; and (3) the statute must not "foster an excessive government entanglement with religion."[89]

The court noted that although the statutory parental reimbursement program providing for transportation expenses at issue in *Everson v. Board of Education*[90] was upheld as constitutional, that statute:

[was] not upheld merely because [it] provided reimbursement aid to parents and

[82] Kern Alexander and David W. Alexander, *American Public School Law*, at 144.
[83] Ohio Rev Code Ann. at § 3327.01.
[84] *Wolman v. Essex*, 342 F. Supp. 390 (S.D. Ohio 1972).
[85] Ohio Rev. Code Ann. at § 3317.062 (repealed in 1975).
[86] *Wolman v. Essex*, 342 F. Supp. at 419.
[87] *Id.* at 411.
[88] *Id.* at 412.
[89] *Id.* at 413.
[90] *Everson v. Board of Education*, 330 U.S. 1 (1946).

students, but because the aid provided was ideologically neutral and supplied in common to the entire class of students of public and parochial schools alike.[91]

The court reasoned that the statutory scheme in question fails to provide any mechanism to insure that public monies provided to parents of non-public school children will not ultimately be used for religious purposes. The statute, therefore, fosters an excessive government entanglement with religion and, as such, runs afoul of the Establishment Clause.

> The Ohio plan contains the seeds for increased political involvement along religious lines at every level of government, from the local school boards to the General Assembly. This, of course, is the ultimate evil to be protected against by the [constitution]. Money under the state statute is being given directly to parents of non-public school children, who are overwhelmingly of one religious sect, in the form of a state subsidy.[92]
>
> * * *
>
> We have not breached the "wall of separation" [between church and state] by providing safe transportation for all children to all schools. We have neither breached that wall by making available the use of textbooks to all children at all schools, nor by providing tax relief to non-public schools as well as patriotic, cultural and charitable organizations. But when special relief is granted to solely non-public schools, a breach does in fact occur.[93]

12.18 Wolman v. Walter

The constitutionality of Ohio's statutory scheme which authorized various forms of state aid to students in church-related elementary and secondary schools was revisited in 1977.[94] The Ohio legislature enacted Revised Code Section 3317.06 in response to a 1975 United States Supreme Court decision.[95] The new statute provided state aid for textbooks, testing and scoring, diagnostic services, therapeutic services, instructional materials and equipment, and field trips.[96] The Supreme Court held that, with the exception of the statutory provisions related to instructional materials and equipment and to field trips, the Ohio statute did not violate the Establishment Clause of the First Amendment.[97]

The court noted that although the legislature attempted to cure the constitutional defect related to the instructional materials and equipment by authorizing the loan of material and equipment directly to the non-public schools, this provision is still unconstitutional: "In view of the impossibility of separating the secular education function from the sectarian, the state aid inevitably flows in part in support of the religious role of the schools."[98]

---

[91] *Wolman v. Essex*, 342 F. Supp. at 415.
[92] *Id.* at 417.
[93] *Id.* at 419.
[94] *Wolman v. Walter*, 433 U.S. 233 (1977).
[95] *Id.* at 232 (making reference to *Meek v. Pittenger*, 421 U.S. 349 (1975)).
[96] *Wolman v. Walter*, at 233.
[97] *Id.* at 255.
[98] *Id.* at 250.

In addressing the constitutionality of the statutory provision related to field trips, the court noted that because the non-public school controls the timing, frequency, and destination of the field trips, "the schools, rather than the children, truly are the recipients of the service."[99] The court also noted that this statutory provision fostered an excessive government entanglement with religion because "the public school authorities will be unable adequately to insure secular use of the field trip funds without close supervision of the non-public teachers."[100] Finally, the court noted that:

> [I]t is the individual teacher who makes a field trip meaningful. The experience begins with the study and discussion of the place to be visited; it continues on location with the teacher pointing out items of interest and stimulating the imagination; and it ends with a discussion of the experience. The field trips are an integral part of the educational experience, and where the teacher works within and for a sectarian institution, an unacceptable risk of fostering of religion is an inevitable byproduct.[101]

These cases, and Ohio's legislative responses to the decisions, have resolved the constitutional challenges in Ohio. In 1981, the General Assembly promulgated a law providing for the annual reimbursement of non-public schools "for the actual mandated service administrative and clerical costs incurred."[102] This law, codified at Revised Code Section 3317.063, limits the annual reimbursement payment to the non-public school to a maximum of $150 per enrolled student.[103] An interesting feature of this program is that the money goes directly to the non-public school. In the case of state funding for auxillary services and transportation, however, the money is provided to the local board of education.

Section 3317.063 also provides that the State Superintendent of Public Instruction "may, from time to time, examine any and all accounts and records of a non-public school which have been maintained pursuant to this section in support of an application for reimbursement."[104] Note that this audit is neither mandatory nor the responsibility of the State Auditor, as is the case for all public schools.

12.19 Mueller v. Allen

This 1983 decision involved a constitutional challenge to a Minnesota statute.[105] The statute permitted parents, in calculating their state income tax, to deduct expenses incurred in providing tuition, textbooks, and transportation for their children attending either public or private elementary and secondary schools.[106] The United States Supreme Court held that the statute did not violate the Establishment Clause of the First Amendment.[107]

The dissenting Justices argued that the Minnesota statute was, in fact, aid to parochial

---

[99] *Id.* at 253.
[100] *Id.* at 254.
[101] *Id.* at 253–54.
[102] Ohio Rev. Code Ann. at § 3317.063.
[103] *Id.*
[104] *Id.*
[105] *Mueller v. Allen*, 463 U.S. 388 (1983).
[106] *Id.* at 391.
[107] *Id.* at 404.

schools disguised as a tax deduction to all parents of school children.[108] The dissent concluded that: "[T]he Court has upheld financial support for religious schools without any reason at all to assume that the support will be restricted to the secular functions of those schools and will not be used to support religious instruction."[109]

12.20 Summary

The questions raised by the cases presented here have not, in most situations, been resolved in a manner that has resulted in the curtailment of state money for non-public schools. Similar cases are currently being brought to the courts in a number of states. Such actions can be expected as long as legislators fail to meet the mandates of their state constitutions that require thorough and efficient schools for all children and a higher degree of equity in the financial resources available to school districts.

In relation to the court cases dealing with aid to the non-public schools, the courts have usually been favorable to the non-public schools. It may be that if further expansion in the aid to non-public schools continues, additional consideration should be given to requiring such schools to adhere to the same rules as apply to the public schools such as maximum class size, detailed academic and financial reports, minimum salaries, negotiations, and acceptance of all students.

---

108 *Id.* 463 U.S. at 404 (Marshall, J., dissenting). *See also American Public School Law,* at 177–78.
109 *Mueller v. Allen*, at 416–17.

Chapter 13:

Funding in Other States

13.1 Introduction

A common thread exists regarding the funding of public schools among the fifty states; all states provide some revenue for the funding of schools. Also, all states' public schools receive some funds from the federal government.

The past decade has seen some changes in the percentage of funds provided from local, state, and federal sources. There has been a movement away from local funding dependence toward reliance upon state funding for the support of elementary and secondary schools. This shift has occurred as the result of societal anxieties. Studies have revealed that United States public schools have lost their supremacy in the international economic system. Charges that students are falling behind, especially in mathematics and science proficiency, have created new demands on state legislators who have perceived a need to respond to these charges. As a result, reform initiatives have been created. More state funds have been expended and additional state mandates have occurred. In other words, state legislators have gone on record to increase state revenues for schools, and they have mandated more accountability.

Monies derived from state governments increased from 47.7% in 1982-83 to 49.8% in 1987-88. During that same time period, the percentage of monies from the federal government was reduced from 7.2% to 6.2%. Local revenues decreased from 45.2% to 44.0%.[1]

It appears that states, through mandates and some increases in revenue, have provided an important thrust in educational reform during the decade of the 1980's.

13.2 Conceptual Portrayal of Public School Finance

Whereas fiscal responsibilities have been developed by each state, most state finance

---

[1] *National Education Association*, Estimates of School Statutes, 1987-88 (1988), at 61.

Figure 13:1
A Conceptual Portrayal of Public School Finance

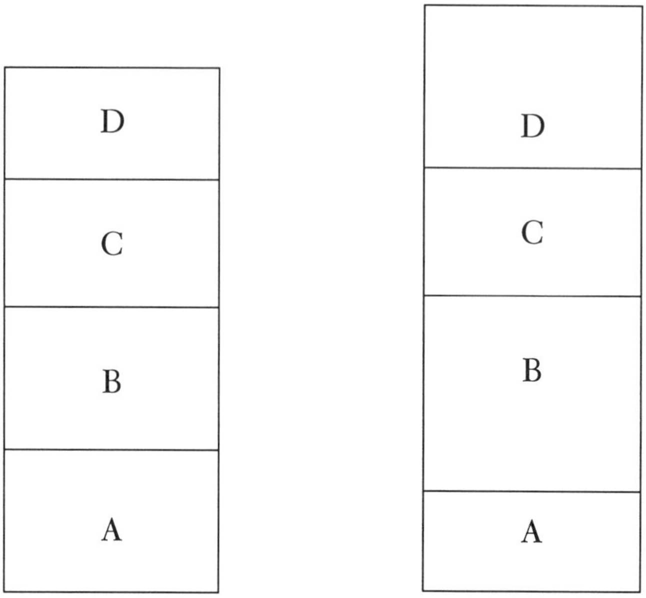

Poor School Districts — Wealthy School Districts

A = State Aid (Foundation or Guaranteed Level)
B = Local Funds (Local Effort Required to Get State Aid)
C = Flat or Matching Grants
D = Extra Local Effort

systems can be conceptually described as illustrated in Figure 13:1.

While Figure 13:1 is intended to serve as an example of state funding in the United States, it does not represent any particular state, and in fact, it does not accurately represent a limited number of states. These differences will be described later in the chapter.

Most state finance programs represent some semblance of equalization based on the ability to support the public schools with a minimal required effort at the local level. States then guarantee a certain basic level of funding above the minimum local level. For Ohio, the guaranteed amount of basic funding was $3315 per pupil for Fiscal Year 96. The state of Ohio actually provides the difference between the guarantee and the yield represented when the local district's assessed valuation is multiplied by 22 mills. Much more detail is provided relative to Ohio's funding formula in chapters four and five.

Most states also permit school districts to raise additional funds at the local level depending on the local support received. The property tax continues as the main source of local revenue for public schools. In Ohio, however, the local school income tax option has begun to make an impact as a source of funds for local districts. Refer to Figure 13:1.

13.3 Categorization of State Public School Finances

State public school finance programs were categorized in 1990-91, according to equalization programs, flat grant programs, and fully state-funded programs. Equalization programs can be broken down into five sub-categories. These are as follows:

1. Foundation programs with required local effort. (Ohio's school foundation program falls into this category with a minimum required local effort of 20 levied mills.)
2. Foundation programs with no required local effort.
3. Percentage-equalization programs with required local effort.
4. Percentage-equalization programs with no required local effort.
5. Guaranteed tax base/yield.

13.4 Foundation Programs

There were 38 states incorporating foundation programs in 1990-91. Ohio and 22 other states required a minimum fiscal effort by local districts while 15 states did not require any fiscal effort. Refer to Table 13:1.[2]

Table 13:1

States Incorporating Foundation Programs in 1990-91

Required Local Effort	*No Effort Required*
Alabama	Arizona
Alaska	Arkansas
California	Georgia
Colorado	Idaho
Florida	Illinois
Indiana	Maryland
Iowa	Montana
Kentucky	Nebraska
Louisiana	New Hampshire
Maine	New Jersey
Minnesota	North Dakota
Mississippi	Oregon
Missouri	South Dakota
Nevada	Vermont
New Mexico	West Virginia
Ohio	
Oklahoma	
South Carolina	
Tennessee	
Texas	
Utah	
Virginia	
Wyoming	

[2] Steven D. Gold, David M. Smith, et al., *Public School Finance Programs of the United States and Canada* (Albany, N.Y.: Center for the Study of the States, Rockefeller Institute of Government, 1992), at 18 [hereinafter *Public School Finance Programs*].

During the four-year time period from 1986-87 to 1990-91, the number of states incorporating foundation programs grew from 30 to 38. Massachusetts offered a foundation program in 1986-87 and then changed to a percent equalization program in 1990. Nine states began foundation programs during this four-year time interval. Of these nine states, Alabama, Alaska, California, Colorado, Kentucky and New Mexico now have foundation programs with mandatory local effort while Nebraska, New Jersey and South Dakota do not require mandatory local effort.[3]

13.5 Percent Equalization Programs

Another category for basic support programs is percent-equalization. A per unit expenditure is mandated by the respective states utilizing this method[4] as identified in Table 13:2.

In 1986-87, New York, Rhode Island, Alaska, Kansas and Pennsylvania used percent-equalization programs with mandated per unit expenditures. The required unit expenditures used by these five states had characteristics of the foundation program that Ohio uses.

Table 13:2

States Incorporating Percent Equalization Programs in 1990-91

Required Local Effort	*No Effort Required*
Connecticut	Kansas
	Massachusetts
	New York
	Pennsylvania
	Rhode Island

In 1990-91, the total number of states using percent-equalization programs grew to six. Connecticut and Massachusetts were added to the list incorporating this method of basic support while Alaska moved to a foundation program. Five of these six states now have non-mandatory local effort required for the percent-equalization program. Connecticut is the only state incorporating mandatory local effort for this method of funding.[5]

13.6 Guaranteed Tax Base/Yield Programs

Only two states in 1990-91 used a state aid program identified as guaranteed tax base/yield. These states guarantee local school districts a per pupil dollar amount up to a predetermined local effort. For example, a state incorporating this program guarantees a uniform dollar amount for each mill levied at the local level up to an authorized revenue base. Table 13:3 reveals the states utilizing this state aid program and according to Gold, Smith and others, these states have essentially neutralized the effects created by the variance in wealth among local school districts.[6]

---

[3] *Id.*
[4] *Id.*
[5] *Id.*
[6] *Id.*

Table 13:3

States Incorporating Guaranteed Tax Base/Yield Programs in 1990-91

Michigan
Wisconsin

In 1990-91, only two states, Michigan and Wisconsin, continued to use guaranteed tax base/yield programs. As was mentioned previously, Colorado, New Jersey and South Dakota changed during this four-year time interval to foundation programs while Connecticut incorporated the percent-equalization program.[7]

13.7 Flat Grant Programs

Flat grant programs represent another way some states support local educational programs. Presently only two states use this means which provides a fixed amount of state revenue based on a per-unit amount to all local school districts. Consideration for variances in local district wealth is not taken into account with flat grant programs. States incorporating flat grant programs in 1990-91 are shown in Table 13:4.[8]

Table 13:4

States Incorporating Flat Grant Programs in 1990-91

Delaware
North Carolina

Note that while Kentucky had used flat grant funding, in June, 1989, the Kentucky Supreme Court declared its system of public schooling inequitable and unconstitutional. In March of 1990 the Kentucky legislature passed a bill aimed at removing the inequities between wealthy and poor local school districts. The legislature increased taxes by $1.26 billion and established a minimum spending level of $2,900 for each Kentucky public school student.

Kentucky, along with Alabama and Nebraska moved from flat grant programs by 1990-91 to foundation-type programs. Thus, only Delaware and North Carolina remain, in 1992, as states using flat grant programs.[9]

13.8 Full State Funding

The last major state aid category is one in which all educational funds are raised by statewide taxes. This method is classified as full state funding. Table 13:5 shows those states so designated in 1990-91 as receiving basically all funds from the state level.[10]

---

[7] *Id.*
[8] *Id.*
[9] *Id.*
[10] *Id.*

Table 13:5

States Incorporating Full State Funded Programs in 1990-91

Hawaii
Washington

Initially Hawaii, with its single state-administered school district, was the only state classified as a fully state funded system for public school districts. However, as various state supreme court cases have spotlighted the inequities in funding between wealthy and poor school districts, the trend has progressed toward increased state fiscal effort.

In 1990-91, Hawaii provided 99.9% of district funds. Due to a court ruling, Washington became obligated by 1990 to take full responsibility for funding basic support programs. Therefore, Washington was classified as full state funding even though local districts provide taxes for supplementary support for non-basic programs.[11]

13.9 Determination of Local Fiscal Capacity

Most states use property valuation, either singularly or with some other measures, to

Table 13:6

States Using Just Property Evaluation to Measure Local Fiscal Capacity in 1986-87

Equalized Valuation	*Assessed Valuation*
Arizona	Alaska
Colorado	California
Florida	Delaware
Georgia	Iowa
Idaho	Louisiana
Indiana	Montana
Kentucky	New Mexico
Maine	Ohio
Massachusetts	Tennessee
Michigan	Wyoming
Minnesota	
New Jersey	
North Dakota	
South Carolina	
South Dakota	
Texas	
Utah	
Washington	
West Virginia	
Wisconsin	

[11] *Id.* at 25.

measure local fiscal capacity. Only two states, Hawaii and North Carolina, do not measure fiscal capacity. In 1986-87, 30 states, including Ohio, used property valuation solely in determining school district wealth. This information is shown in Table 13:6.[12]

Multiple ways of determining fiscal capacity were used in 1986-87 according to Salmon and others for the remaining states. Six states (Connecticut, Maryland, New York, Pennsylvania, Rhode Island, and Vermont) used a combination of property valuation and personal income. The remaining states used more than two indices for determining state fiscal equalization aid to local school districts.[13]

13.10 Determination of Fiscal and Educational Needs

States generally distribute monies to local school districts through an allocation of units. Student unit determination is based on pupil enrollment or attendance. Ohio's system is based on average daily membership as detailed in Chapter 5. Most states use student units when distributing state funds. Eight states, however, used teacher units in 1986-87 rather than pupil units for allocating state aid to local districts. These eight states were Alabama, Alaska, Delaware, Kentucky, Mississippi, North Carolina, Washington, and Wyoming.[14]

Most of the states that allocate state aid based on student enrollment or attendance use a "weighted pupil" system to provide some balance for different student needs. Program weights include grade level, special education, vocational education, compensatory education, population sparsity or density, cost indices such as Ohio's cost of doing business factor, and others.

13.11 Trends and Observations of Other States' Funding

As was mentioned at the beginning of this chapter, the last decade has evidenced considerable pressure from educational reformers including Congress and state legislators throughout the country. In some states, drastic revisions in public school finance programs have occurred. Some of these changes are the result of the aforementioned pressures while others have occurred as the result of recent state supreme court actions based on challenges of fiscal disparities between poor and wealthy school districts.

Texas serves as a prime example of changes resulting from supreme court action. In 1989, the Texas Supreme Court unanimously declared that state's system of funding schools to be unconstitutional, stating that the Texas Constitution requires that the legislature establish, support, and maintain an efficient system of public free schools.[15] The court ordered the legislature to come up with a plan to reduce the wide differences in funding between poor and wealthy school districts.

Similar situations to the Texas scene have occurred, or are now occurring in Alabama,

---

[12] Richard Salmon et al., *Public Programs of the United States and Canada*, (Blacksburg, Va.: American Education Finance Association and Virginia Polytechnic Institute and State University, 1988), at 4.

[13] *Id.* at 6.

[14] *Id.* at 8.

[15] *Kirby v. Edgewood Indep. Sch. Dist.*, 761 S.W.2d 859 (Tex. Ct. App. 1988).

Alaska, Arkansas, California, Connecticut, Idaho, Illinois, Indiana, Kentucky, Massachusetts, Michigan, Minnesota, Mississippi, Montana, New Jersey, North Dakota, Oregon, Tennessee, Washington, West Virginia, and Wyoming. Political impact from state and federal supreme court decisions will eventually change the degree of reliance upon the local property tax. Court cases such as *Kirby v. Edgewood* (Texas, 1988), *Serrano v. Priest* (California, 1971)[16], *Rodriguez v. San Antonio Independent School District* (Texas, 1973)[17], and *Robinson v. Cahill* (New Jersey, 1973)[18] all paved the way for state supreme court cases and for other legally or politically mandated changes in the way schools are funded. Although the Ohio Supreme Court gave judicial sanction to Ohio's method of funding schools (*Wolman v. Walter*, 1976)[19], changes will likely occur as of result of *DeRolph v. State of Ohio*.[20]

There has been a shift from the reliance upon property valuation as the single measure of fiscal capacity to more use of multiple measures. Salmon pointed out that in 1978-79, 34 states used only property valuation to determine local fiscal capacity.[21] By 1986-87, four of these 34 changed to incorporate multiple measures to assess fiscal ability. It would appear that income might be considered in conjunction with property for properly determining a district's wealth. With additional Ohio school districts utilizing the income tax as a means for supporting schools, income began to be considered along with property valuations in FY 96 for determining fiscal capacity in this state.

There is a trend for states to rely more upon pupil allocation units rather than teacher allocation units. From 1978 to 1986, the number of states using pupil allocation units for determining state funding increased from 37 to 42. Also, average daily membership and enrollment limits were used more to determine the pupil count while the number of states utilizing average daily attendance decreased in number.[22]

As states seek new models for school funding, Michigan serves as a prime example of a state to do so without the mandate of a state supreme court ruling. In 1993, the Michigan legislature was in disagreement over taxes and how to fund schools. The partisan disagreement resulted in the repeal of $6.3 billion in local property taxes that helped finance Michigan public schools. Without deciding how to replace some or all of the lost revenue, Republican Governor John Engler signed the legislation in August of 1993 to eliminate property taxes as a source of public school funding.

The rationale behind the Michigan legislative action, according to an editorial in the Dayton Daily News,[23] was:

---

[16] *Serrano v. Priest*, 18 Cal. 3d 728, 557 P.2d 929 (1976).

[17] *Rodriguez v. San Antonio Indep. Sch. Dist.*, 411 U.S. 1 (1973).

[18] *Robinson v. Cahill*, 303 A.2d 273 (NJ 1973), *supplemental op.*, 306 A.2d 65, *cert. denied, Dickey v. Robinson*, 414 U.S. 976 (1973).

[19] *Wolman v. Walter*, 433 U. S. 229 (1977).

[20] *DeRolph v. State of Ohio*, No. 22043 (Perry County, July 1994) 463 [hereinafter *DeRolph v. State of Ohio*].

[21] Richard Salmon et al., *Public Programs of the United States and Canada* (Blacksburg, Va.: American Education Finance Association and Virginia Polytechnic Institute and State University, 1988), at 10.

[22] *Id.* at 12.

[23] Editorial, "Michigan found way to equalize school funding," *Dayton Daily News* (Dayton, Ohio), January 11, 1994.

> The Michigan legislature—with the urging of the state's Republican governor-last year abolished the taxes that fund schools. The goal was to create a crisis.
>
> If there was not money for schools, the hope was that fact would force lawmakers to work something out and maybe simultaneously equalize the amounts of money school districts have for their students. (Republicans also were hoping they could use the opportunity to push for a school-choice plan, even school vouchers.)
>
> Under a compromise worked out on Christmas Eve, Michigan's schools will get more money. And it also appears that schools won't have such wildly differing amounts to spend per student.
>
> The legislature's solution is to put a constitutional amendment on the ballot that would raise the state sales tax from 4 percent to 6 percent, and a few other taxes would be increased as well. If amendment doesn't pass, then Plan B automatically takes effect. Plan B would increase the state income tax from 4.6 percent to 6 percent, among other things.
>
> The big change for taxpayers, under both proposals - would be a cut in their property taxes. Both funding formulas rely substantially less on that tax. This is something many homeowners - and especially senior citizens - have been crying for."

Public surveys prior to the vote on the two plans to provide needed funds for Michigan schools showed that the people favored the property tax cut but also wanted the lost revenue returned to their schools. They seemed divided over which tax they favored as a replacement. The 1994 vote resulted in the majority of voters favoring the state sales tax increase from 4 to 6 percent.

Sales taxes continued as the number one source of all state revenues. It was also observed that sales taxes increased fifty times from 1983 to 1987 and the United States median rate rose from 4.0% to 5.0%. Although Ohio's sales tax rate stayed the same (5.0%) during this five-year time frame, a total of 12 states recorded rate increases.[24] Ohio has since increased its rate from 5.0% to 6.0% in 1990.

Individual income taxes are used more extensively as a source of state revenue. During the time period 1983-87, there were a total of 35 income tax increases in 24 different states. It is interesting that of all the major taxes not being used by various states, the only ones given serious consideration are personal income tax and corporate income taxes. It would appear likely that future state revenue increases might use these two sources as well.[25]

Corporate income taxes were increased slightly more than individual income taxes during the 1983-87 period. In fact, business taxes increased 37 times in the 1983-85 time frame. Restructured corporate taxes were used in the late 1980s to finance education reform in Kentucky and Florida while Indiana used both corporate taxes and increased personal income taxes to fund its education spending program adopted in 1987.[26]

A variety of sources are used by states to fund local school districts. In addition to

---

[24] *Ibid.* at 28–30.
[25] *Id.* at 37.
[26] *Id.*

individual income and business taxes, various states use sales, cigarette, alcohol and motor fuel taxes. Miscellaneous taxes used at the state level include severance, motor vehicle, excise, insurance premium, gift and inheritance, and license.

13.12 Capital Outlay and Debt Service of Other States' Funding

In addition to evidence submitted about operating problems in Ohio's recent Perry County case,[27] data were related and examples were provided to the court regarding construction and repair needs of Ohio schools. Some states have addressed these needs differently than Ohio. For example, the neighboring state of Indiana permits local school boards to issue bonds without the vote of the electorate. These bonds, combined with outstanding bonded debt, may not exceed 2.0 percent of the district's assessed valuation. Additional debt may be incurred through lease rental agreements with private or public holding corporations.[28]

Another neighboring state, Pennsylvania, provides subsidies to school districts for the construction or renovation of facilities. According to Gold et al.[29], the process for state aid building projects is as follows:

> In order to qualify for state subsidy for the construction, renovation or purchase of a school building, each school district must go through a substantial approval process called PLANCO. This process includes but is not limited to justification, site acquisition information, calculation of project costs, calculation of related pupil capacity, and full documentation at each stage of the project's development.

Following approval, the maximum cost reimbursable to districts provided by the state for 1991-1992 for new construction or renovation was $3,900 for an elementary building, $5,100 for a secondary building, and $6,300 for a vocational facility, all multiplied by the rated pupil capacity. Additional allowances are permitted for architect's fees, sanitary sewage disposal and rough grading for the building site.[30]

While many states have capital outlay and debt service programs that resemble Ohio's, a few states provide considerably more financial aid. Alaska, although geographically quite different from Ohio, reimburses schools' debt service payments by almost 80 percent. According to Gold et al.[31], prior to 1990, Alaska promised to pay 80 percent of debt service costs of construction projects, which were approved by the Alaska Department of Education, until the debt was retired. However, in 1990 the Alaska legislature curtailed the debt reimbursement program so new construction projects cannot be included, although they still pay obligations under the prior law for existing school debt. Current Alaska law (AS14.11.100(b)) does distribute state cigarette tax proceeds to school districts

---

[27] *DeRolph v. State of Ohio,* No. 22043 (Perry County, July 1, 1994), at 463.

[28] Steven D. Gold, David M. Smith, Stephen B. Lawton, and Andrea C. Hyary, *Public School Finance Programs of the United States and Canada, 1990-1991*, Volume One (Albany, New York, American Education Finance Association and Center for the Study of the States, The Nelson A. Rockefeller Institute of Government, 1992), at 213 and 218.

[29] *Id.*, Volume Two, at 465.

[30] *Id.* at 465.

[31] *Id.*, Volume One, at 96.

which can apply the proceeds for new construction, renovations and repairs, or debt service.

California, a state which had the first successful supreme court case to attack property tax for operating schools, provides significant funding for school construction. Gold et al.[32] state:

> California has operated a program to help school districts finance school construction since the late 1940's. The program used state general obligation bonds to pay for the construction of schools. These facilities were then leased to local school districts for $1.00 a year for 40 years. After 40 years, the school facility became the property of the district. Prior to passage of Proposition 13, this program was used as a last resort by school districts. However, Proposition 13's elimination of all ad valorem taxes, made reliance on the state more critical. Even since 1986 when local taxing districts were granted the authority to levy property taxes for general obligation bonds (Proposition 49), the state has been the largest source of funds for new school construction. . . .

An interesting provision for schools in California occurred in 1986 when the California legislature passed AB2926. This bill authorized the levying of fees on new homes and commercial and industrial projects. As a result, school districts were prohibited from levying most other kinds of fees for school construction or modernization projects.[33]

Two of the smaller states in the United States, Connecticut and Delaware, provide much more aid for capital outlay and debt service than does Ohio. Connecticut[34] does not give local districts the power to issue bonds for school construction. Approved school construction bonds, instead, are issued by the municipality. The maximum value of all school construction bonds is 4.5 times the municipality's total tax revenues for the previous year. The state then makes between 20 and 80 percent of principal and interest payments to the municipality. Payments are made according to each town's wealth per capita, with poorest schools receiving the highest reimbursement percentage.

For the state of Delaware[35], funding for capital outlay financing is provided by the state at a ratio of as much as 60 percent state and 40 percent local for wealthier school districts. Based on an ability-to-pay index, poorer school districts could pay as little as 20 percent of construction costs. All construction costs for vocational and special education schools may be paid by the state with the exact percentage based on the ability to pay of the county in which the school is located.

Florida[36] offers a capital outlay and debt service plan much different from Ohio's. Revenues for capital outlay are provided by the state from taxes on utilities. State bonds that have been approved through the legislative process are then issued by the Florida State Department of Education. Capital outlay aid is allocated via formula under Public Education Capital Outlay Funds. In addition, certain revenues from the licensing of motor

---

32 *Id.* at 123.
33 *Id.* at 123–124.
34 *Id.* at 146.
35 *Id.* at 154.
36 *Id.* at 167.

vehicles are allocated to local school districts for both capital outlay funding and debt service.

While Ohio does provide financial assistance for poorer districts in this state, it is obvious that many construction/renovation needs are unmet. Technology update needs are also sorely neglected for some districts. Perhaps a critique of the capital outlay and debt service plans for those states mentioned here, plus a review of a few other states, would provide ideas for improved capital outlay funding processes in Ohio.

Chapter 14:
Related Issues

14.1 Introduction

This chapter includes a listing and brief discussion of issues related to school finance. These subjects are illustrative of the types of ongoing concerns that impact the financial operations of a school district. The various issues could well serve as brief suggestions for further in-depth study by students of school finance. These topics are primarily related to Ohio but may be applicable to other states as well.

14.2 Local Issues

1. *Lack of significant revenue growth when property values increase.* Only districts at the minimum millage level realize any increase in funds due to sexennial reappraisal or triennial update except from inside millage.
2. *Approval of effective millage rates.* Effective rates are established by the Ohio Department of Taxation based upon information provided by each county auditor. No formal procedure exists for a board of education to appeal or approve these effective rates.
3. *Local taxes collected on a calendar-year basis; school districts budget and appropriate on a fiscal year.* Confusion exists when the fiscal year and the tax collection year are not similar.
4. *Property taxes are not related to personal or family income.* In some states a circuit breaker relates property taxes to income whereby taxes, above a certain percent of income, are forgiven and paid by the state to political subdivisions.
5. *Levies and public relations.* The frequent need to promote local tax measures detracts from the primary mission of the schools.
6. *Capital improvements funded by disparate local tax base.* Quality of capital improvements varies widely among school districts due to varying ability to raise taxes.
7. *Variability of assessment practices.* Assessment practices of county auditors vary

widely on issues such as the timing of adding new construction to the duplicate, or the determination of market value.

8. *Assessment rate on real property*. Ohio's assessment rate is lower than in many other states. Higher assessment rates would result in greater revenue per mill for all political subdivisions.
9. *Budget, appropriation, and public hearing*. The appropriation measure could serve in place of the budget for purposes of the public hearing and subsequent submission to the county budget commission.
10. *Personal tangible tax's unpredictability*. Personal tangible property tax is collected in the current year and few school districts know what their revenue will be at the beginning of the fiscal year. The reduction in the assessment rate for personal tangible property has resulted in a substantial loss of revenue in many school districts. Some states tax heavy equipment and machinery as real property and not as personal property.
11. *New construction produces additional revenue*. Unless new construction is abated, or not assessed on a timely basis, it produces additional revenue to school districts. Some variation exists as to how new construction is treated, such as, improvements to land or additions to duplicate.
12. *General tax abatement and economic development*. Schools must be involved in decisions that will create greater economic development and an eventual greater tax base to fund public services.
13. *Additional local income sources*. Additional private sources of support such as business partnerships and foundations will receive more attention.
14. *User fees*. User fees may be implemented by more school districts. Examples of user fees are student lab and activity fees. This could be expanded to include instructional fees where parents pay for curricula beyond basic courses.
15. *Minimum local effort*. Many sources have suggested that the minimum required effort of 20 mills be increased if a true sharing of tax responsibility is to be realized.
16. *Tax credits considered state aid to public schools*. Some schools have experienced difficulty when Ohio's reimbursement for property tax credits has been certified as both local and state revenue, thus overstating revenue expectations.
17. *Telecommunications Assessed Valuation Reduced*. The telecommunications industry obtained major changes in assessment rate in recent years. In many cases the rate was lowered to 25% from 88% of value.
18. *Public Utility Assessment Rates*. Other public utility industries are trying to obtain lower assessment rates to better compete.
19. *Impact Fees*. Impact fees are being discussed by high growth districts. The impact fee would be assessed new properties to pay for additional and/or operating expenses.

14.3 State Issues

1. *Funding assistance for capital improvements*. With few exceptions, very little

state assistance is available to fund capital projects. This is a major concern in light of a recent study which recommended that more than $10 billion be spent to improve/expand Ohio's school facilities.

2. *Earmarking funds for education.* The concept of designating certain taxes or a predetermined portion of the state budget for schools continues to be discussed widely by educators.
3. *Lottery funds.* Lottery profit funds are earmarked for education and provide a substantial amount of state revenue. Considerable misunderstanding occurs when citizens believe the lottery funds provided additional funds to defer property tax increases. In practice such funds have generally been used to supplant state general fund revenue. Detailed reports should be required of the lottery commission. Such reports should be distributed to school district officials.
4. *State aid—grants v. foundation.* A national and state trend continues to increase funding to school districts for specific areas or programs in lieu of allocating more dollars to the foundation program. How does this relate to the equity issue?
5. *Foundation program and minimum millage.* The minimum millage of 20 mills is widely considered to be too low to represent the local share of a realistic foundation program. Also, it would help to address the equity issue if all factors would be considered before applying the charge off.
6. *Phantom revenue.* Valuation increases due to reappraisal create an "artificial" level of the local share for the foundation formula.
7. *Income factor in determining funding level.* A factor representing school district residents' ability to pay would more clearly reflect fiscal capacity than would property values alone.
8. *State loan program.* A state guaranteed loan program for school operations forestalls school closings.
9. *School district equalization factor—"Cost-of-doing-business."* Since varying costs within the state are being recognized for the basic portion of the foundation program, a more careful analysis would suggest that such a concept should be extended to the categorical portion as well.
10. *Reallocation of resources.* Considerable discussion continues regarding reallocating public utility taxes, personal tangible taxes, and those state dollars used for guarantees.
11. *Funding of line items and educational special interest.* Categorizing state funds according to programs such as vocational, special, and at risk, creates competition for revenue. This represents "implications for a weighted pupil factor."
12. *Actual foundation level must be realistic.* A state per student funding level must more realistically represent costs.
13. *Non-public school accountability.* Non-public schools do not have the same review and accountability for state revenue received as that required for public schools.
14. *Financial incentives v. disincentives.* It is generally believed to be more effective

to fund public policy beliefs by providing financial incentives than by deducting funds, when standards are not met.

15. *Expenditures and achievement.* The measuring of outputs based on financial inputs remains a very difficult issue.
16. *Funding state ordered mandates.* When the state mandates additional services/ programs which require increased expenditures, additional state funds should be made available.
17. *New state income sources.* Potential sources of additional dollars include lotteries, expansion of sales taxes, increasing personal income and corporate franchise taxes, and license and severance taxes.
18. *Grants-Entitlement v. Competitive.* The trend appears to be away from entitlement to competitive grants putting a premium on the quality of the grant application.
19. *Choice.* The growing arena of choice includes home schooling, open enrollment, vouchers, charter schools, tuition tax credits and post-secondary options.
20. *Cost of Doing Business.* The varying regional costs to conduct educational business must be reflected in any fund distribution system.
21. *Income Factor.* Income can be used to better reflect capacity of local school district when used in conjunction with property valuation.
22. *Adequacy.* A system of determining the adequate number of dollars per student or other definitions must be codified and routinely updated.
23. *Technology.* Access to adequate technology must not be left to local wealth or effort.
24. *Training for Work.* What agencies must collaborate to better deliver all the training for work necessary in the 21st century?
25. *Regionalization of Services.* How much of the existing state services to education can be regionalized and what will the service delivery system look like?

14.4 Federal Issues

1. *Voucher system.* Vouchers would permit students to transfer from one district to another (public or private) school district without paying tuition or with a reduction of tuition costs. The financial impact upon the school district from which students transfer could be significant, especially if such district has to make staff and program cuts due to the loss of students.
2. *Tuition tax credit.* Credit is given for tuition to another school district in the form of reduced federal taxes paid by individuals. Tuition tax credit can have the same net effect for school districts as the voucher plan.
3. *Grants/basic aid.* The federal government allocates discretionary money to fund project grants. Many allocations are made on a competitive basis and all are for a specific timeline. School districts that submit applications for federal funds are competing with each other, and often with other local government and other agencies/organizations. If a grant is made to a profit-making organization, the award is in the form of a contract since a fee is involved.

4. *Revenue sharing*. At this time general revenue sharing does not exist for federal grants.
5. *Arbitrage profits*. Arbitrage laws prevent taking advantage of the investment of tax exempt bonds at a rate greater than the current interest rate on such bonds. The possible penalty is the loss of the tax exemption status for school bonds.
6. *Local/state taxes deducted from income*. The amount of local taxes and state taxes paid for the support of public schools is deductible from federal income tax. One advantage of this process is that it can be used as a strategy to pass local tax levies (for example, the increased cost of a levy for the taxpayer can be reduced due to permissible deduction from federal taxes).
7. *Taxing school bonds*. Some bonds may be taxed by the federal government even though dividends are tax-exempt for Ohio.
8. *Block Grants*. Should federal funds be given to states in block amounts in order for local decisions to be made regarding spending? Will block grants eventually diminish as they will no longer represent specific funding priorities?
9. *Rescission Laws*. Laws have been passed that rescind previously approved funding levels for education. Reliable funding is no longer always possible.
10. *Funding Vocational/Technical Education*. How can we be sure that dollars allocated for manpower preparation are used for their intended purpose?

14.5 Constitutional Issues

1. *Ohio*. A suit was filed in early 1991 on the constitutionality of Ohio's school funding system. A previous case, *Board of Education v. Walter*,[1] declared Ohio's system constitutional.
2. *Other states*. Since 1970, 10 states have declared their school funding systems unconstitutional. From 1980 to 1983, California, New Jersey, Connecticut, Washington, Wyoming, West Virginia and Arkansas were so declared. Litigation on constitutional aspects of school funding did not occur from 1983 through 1987. From 1988 through 1990, Montana, Kentucky, Texas, and New Jersey (again) had their school funding systems declared unconstitutional. In addition, litigation was being discussed or initiated in 1991 in Alabama, Alaska, Idaho, Illinois, Indiana, Massachusetts, Minnesota, Mississippi, North Dakota, Oregon and Tennessee.
3. *Basic theories behind litigation*.
   a. Amount of money spent is an indicator of quality.
   b. Education is a fundamental interest in the state constitution.
   c. Wealth, as measured by income and/or property, may be a factor in quality of education.
4. *Tax effort*. States are being questioned as to whether their funding systems recognize the tax effort put forth by local constituencies.
5. *Thorough and efficient*. A funding system may be *equitable*, but it may not

---

[1] *Board of Education v. Walter*, 58 Ohio St. 2d 368 (1979), *cert. denied*, 444 U.S. 1015 (1980).

generate enough revenue to be *thorough* in meeting society's expectations.

6. *Defense of funding system.* Arguments such as "Money doesn't make a difference," "Enough money already exists," "Differences are reflected by local control," "Differences are a result of poor management," and "Education is not a fundamental interest," are often used to defend an established funding system.
7. *DeRolph v. Ohio.* A current case pending before the Supreme Court has declared Ohio's system of funding unconstitutional and that education is a fundamental right.

14.6 Accountability Issues with Financial Implications

1. *Delivery of services.* Will fewer units of delivery (consolidation) result in savings?
2. *Support services.* Will regional support services for instructional programs result in savings?
3. *Marginal utility.* As dollar increases are obtained will there be a resultant increase in results? For example, as the graduation rate is increased, a greater per unit cost might result.
4. *Commissions/Committees.* Will new commissions such as Ohio's Legislative Oversight Commission, Education Improvement Commission, or the Government Efficiency and Management Committee improve education or just increase expenditures?

14.7 Choice

1. *Voucher.* It has been argued by some that parents (and students) should have a choice on the school of attendance. Should Ohio offer this choice and provide tuition reduction via a voucher plan?
2. *Tuition tax credit.* Tuition to another school district, public or private, could be offered via a state tax credit.
3. *Post-secondary options.* Eleventh and twelfth grade students may enroll full-or part-time at colleges or universities. If courses are taken for high school credit, a proportionate share of the district's state financial aid is transferred to the college or university.
4. *Intra-district.* Amended Substitute Senate Bill 140[2] provided choice for school of attendance for students by requiring intra-district plans (that is, a plan must be developed establishing procedures for students to transfer from one school to another school in the district that houses students of the same grade level).
5. *Inter-district.* Local school boards must adopt a policy before July 1993, either prohibiting or permitting open enrollment with physically adjacent districts.
6. *Private/public.* The choice between attending private or public schools was affirmed by the *Pierce v. Society of Sisters*[3] case. How much does limited funding by some parents restrict choice? Should support for non-public schools be

[2] Ohio Rev. Code Ann. at § 3301.07.
[3] *Pierce v. Society of Sisters*, 268 U.S. 510 (1925).

increased in Ohio?

7. *Home instruction*. Some parents in Ohio have chosen to teach their children in their homes. How does (could) this affect a district's finances?
8. *Program implications*. Programs for special students (such as advanced placement, academically gifted, and programs for "at-risk" students) all have a price tag attached. What portion of the costs of these state-mandated programs should be absorbed by state funds?

14.8 Social Issues with Financial Implications

1. *Health care costs*. Health care costs for employees have risen sharply for several years. This is often a priority item in negotiations with bargaining units. What recommendations would keep this benefit more affordable for school districts?
2. *Importance/value of education*. Senate Bill 140[4] indicates that Ohio legislators are concerned about the value of education. They want, and have mandated, changes to occur that may help our state surface as a leader for student achievement. Other states have made comparable mandates. How does such legislation improve student achievement?
3. *Dysfunctional homes*. Many student social ills can be traced directly to dysfunctional homes. Who should pay the bill for these added expenses?
4. *Dropouts*. The importance of a literate America is stressed by encouraging students to remain in school; nevertheless, some students continue to "fall through the cracks." What incentives would be appropriate to discourage dropouts from school?
5. *Parenting classes*. Some districts have school psychologists meet with parents to help improve parenting skills. Ways to encourage, control, motivate, and set limits are all items of discussion as ways in which parents can help their children in the learning process. Is this a wise expenditure of school funds and the use of professional educators' time and talent?
6. *"Crack babies."* Experts indicate that we have just begun to see the problems associated with the drug, "crack." These problems will surface as obstacles to the teaching/learning process and will have to be reckoned with. What additional costs will be likely associated with these problems?
7. *Pre-school*. Pre-school programs are being viewed by many as essential to educational programs. This need is especially important for at-risk children so they will have a greater opportunity for success.

14.9 Mandates

1. *Senate Bill 140.*[5] State mandates have been created with the passage of Senate Bill 140. Required testing, publication of test results, intra-district choices, and post-secondary options are a few of the legislated requirements which

---

[4] Ohio Rev. Code Ann. at § 3301.07.
[5] *Id.*

impact on a district's finances.

2. *Federal.* Relatively few mandates have been created by the Federal government. Will this change in the future?
3. *Required course offerings.* State legislators have mandated specific requirements for course offerings from kindergarten through high school. Requirements were increased in recent years (for example, all students are now required to have gone to kindergarten prior to entering the first grade, Carnegie unit requirements have been increased at the high school level, and courses have been added to cope with some of today's social ills).
4. *Class size.* While the state has a maximum pupil/teacher ratio established for kindergarten through grade four programs, negotiated agreements have been reached by school districts throughout Ohio that have set caps on class numbers. Will lower per pupil/teacher ratio enhance the teaching/learning process? What would be the financial impact on school districts if all classes were capped at a 15 to 1 ratio?
5. *Mentoring.* Mentoring was recently added as a requirement for Ohio's schools. Should mandates include increased funds in the state budget to affect increased local costs due to mandates?

14.10 Competition for Resources

1. *Economic development.* It must be recognized that school districts are often in competition with other governmental entities for resources. The public may be placed in a position of prioritizing its programs when requests are being made for additional property or income taxes.
2. *Tax abatements.* Tax abatements for a given number of years are common in many communities. This is done to entice business and industry to locate in a community or to expand operations. A few communities have offered tax abatements to residential home owners to improve their homes and/or sites. What are some advantages and disadvantages to this practice?
3. *Restructure of infrastructure.* The infrastructure of most government agencies is in need of improvement. These unmet needs create extensive competition for resources. As a result, great difficulties exist for schools to improve their infrastructure.
4. *Priority of educational funding.* Educators question whether society really puts education as a priority item in its thinking.

14.11 Summary

In conclusion, these related issues are intended as catalysts for further discussion and study. They do not represent an exhaustive list, but rather input from the authors as to topics with funding implications.

Chapter 15:
Concluding Comments

15.1 Introduction

Modern school administrators must keep abreast of trends concerning education in general and give attention to a broad spectrum of factors that impact the financing of schools. This is based on the principle that a quality educational program can be achieved only through fiscal adequacy and stability. Administrators, as well as students of school finance must remember that concepts of school finance are constantly changing. To remain knowledgeable administrators must read current literature on the subject, attend seminars, pursue additional courses pertaining to school finance, and participate in organizations which address problems of funding education. By participating in such educational activities they become more acutely aware of what is being written and discussed in the area of school finance. Such participation also presents them with a forum to test new concepts about the subject under consideration.

Accepting the above principle of fluidity of school finance, administrators must be involved in the legislative process if they want to help shape this important aspect of their profession. Productive involvement is accomplished through a continuing relationship with state legislators and congressmen who represent their respective school districts. Professional organizations (that is, American Association of School Administrators, Buckeye Association of School Administrators, National School Boards Association, and Ohio School Boards Association) also help keep administrators aware of pending educational legislation at both the state and federal levels.

15.2 Involvement in State and Federal Legislation

Major emphasis is focused on interaction with state officials and legislators since they often determine what local schools can do with the financial resources made available to them. By maintaining a close relationship with legislators, administrators can more readily have a positive influence on any proposed legislation. This relationship can be enhanced through direct talks, correspondence, and visits to legislators' offices as well as by personal contacts when the legislators are in the administrators' respective communities. Another way to keep abreast of legislative matters is for administrators to attend legislative committee meetings which deal with educational matters. Administrators may find it important to make presentations to legislative committees that are dealing with particular education finance subjects. In such cases, it is essential that all testimony be presented in a clear, correct and verifiable form.

In communicating with legislators, administrators must know the facts about proposed legislation—how it will affect their individual districts and how it would impact on public education throughout the state. To proceed without such facts leads to loss of credibility and embarrassment for the person(s) testifying and to the district(s) being represented.

Legislators should be encouraged to visit schools. They should also be on the mailing lists of school districts to receive publications and reports to help keep them informed about the school district which they are elected to represent.

Once enacted, legislation is immediately subject to interpretation and implementation. It is essential that administrators not only read the law but also attend workshops, sponsored by the Ohio Department of Education and/or professional organizations where further explanations of the law are presented. This approach will enable administrators to understand the interpretations which are being given to the new legislation and to discover its impact on the financing of their individual districts when the law is fully implemented.

15.3 Leadership in the Local Setting

Funds coming to school districts from local taxes help maintain the adequacy and stability of a district's financial resources. It is imperative that administrators assume the lead in seeing that local funds are adequate to meet the needs of all students in the district. To accomplish this task they must not only work closely with the members of their boards of education and staffs but also with the "power brokers" of their communities. This implies that these individuals and groups must be continually kept informed concerning the following: 1) needs of the school system; 2) effects of the enactments of the new laws; and 3) current financial condition of the district. This can be accomplished through the board meetings, staff meetings, personal contacts, printed word, and electronic media.

Today's school administrators must possess a broad spectrum of skills and abilities, particularly in dealing with criticism. They must also be aware of persons who will likely help them in maintaining the stability of the district's financial base and of those who might threaten that stability. When dealing with most professions, and even the trades, clients tend to defer to the "expert" for solutions and remedies. However, in education this relationship is quite different. This is due to the fact that most adults have participated in the process/product aspects of the educational enterprise over varying time periods. They come away from these experiences with certain perceptions as to how schools should be operated. Though such perception may frequently be wrong it should be remembered that "perceptions" usually carry the weight of "facts" in the eyes of the perceiver.

15.4 Meeting Criticism in the Local Community

When considering increased local funding for schools, critics have a tendency to equate "what is" with "what was." This approach tends to be based on statements such as, "If it was good enough for us when we were in school, it is certainly good enough for the students today." One of the major fallacies in this statement is that critics may have experienced an educational program that had inadequate funding. The resultant educational programs could have lacked breadth of educational options. However, these same critics may not have encountered any serious drawbacks in terms of obtaining gainful employment. People with such experiences often fail to realize that the advancements in knowledge and the resultant changes in workplace technology have occurred at such a rapid pace that an education comparable to theirs would likely be inadequate to prepare today's youth for college entrance or even entry-level employment in skilled occupations.

School administrators must influence persons who normally are positive towards school issues as well as critics. It is essential for all citizens to realize that skills and abilities needed for gainful employment and/or access to higher education programs demand more funds for education than were needed in the past.

15.5 Cooperation With Business and Industrial Leaders

Another observation of the current and emerging school finance picture is the more active role being played by business and industry. *Amended Substitute Senate Bill 140,*[1] enacted by the Ohio Legislature in 1989, mandates that public schools become more actively involved with the leaders of business and industry. It should be noted however, that even before the enactment of this bill such leaders were expressing concern that the returns on their financial investment (taxes) in public education, were inadequate and, in many instances, unacceptable.

W.R. Timken, Jr., Chairman of the Board of Directors of the Timken Company of Canton, addressing the participants at the statewide conference on school/business relationships, held in Columbus on November 28, 1990, said:

> No longer can those of us in business ignore this complex problem. The private sector cannot be content to simply pay taxes and depend on school boards, administrators, and teachers to determine the product of our K-12 system. We must work together with educators for improvement. There are plenty of solutions; we just have to roll up our sleeves and get on with it. . . . Some might wonder what businesses can bring to the table. Are we expected to be only the banker? Just bring the money? Or are we expected to be true partners, bringing ideas and experiences to the table. . . . Unless we are asked to be true partners, we won't be at the table long, nor will much be achieved.[2]

A major thrust of his remarks was that we cannot continue with the philosophy that all we need to do in order to solve education's problems is to spend more money. To underscore this fact he also stated in the previously mentioned address:

> Totally committed people throughout the ages have accomplished incredible things with virtually nothing. Defying expectation, human will power has triumphed again

---

[1] Ohio Rev. Code Ann. at § 3301.07.

[2] William R. Timken, Jr., "Education in Ohio—Unlimited Opportunities" (a paper presented at the School-Business Partnership Conference II, Columbus, Ohio, November 28, 1990), at 3–4.

> and again where few resources existed. Yet here we are, the citizens in Ohio, spending $8 billion on education for our young people in K-12 and we are unhappy with the results. . . . The fact remains K-12 education seems to be adequately financed. We have to use the dollars more effectively.[3]

Although Mr. Timken conceded that there are great disparities in the financial resources available per pupil in Ohio's school districts and that the problem has to be resolved, he insisted that the current level of funding was adequate (as is indicated in the above quotation).

Business and industry can be helpful in a number of ways but the authors hesitate to equate the products of the school with the products of industry. Business and industry select the raw materials with which they work and reject those that do not meet their standard of quality required to produce the end product. In addition, once the raw materials are received by companies, they then control those materials until the product is completed. In contrast, schools cannot reject any of the raw material (children) sent to them nor do they have complete control of the children throughout the production process. In fact, children are under the supervision of the schools less than 20% of the total hours available in a given year. In other words, children come under the influence of those aspects of society which are beyond the schools' control 80% of the time. All educators need to elicit help from the business community, but in so doing they must retain the right to direct the educational enterprise as they seek the best educational program that can be provided for each child who comes into their sphere of responsibility.

15.6 School Finance and the Small School District

An additional issue that should be brought to the attention of the students of Ohio school finance is the cost of maintaining small (in terms of student population) school districts. Can a small district provide, through Ohio's current system of public school funding, a quality education program? The answer depends chiefly on the district's tax base. There are a number of districts in Ohio that have fewer than 1,000 pupils but possess a tax valuation in excess of $100,000 per pupil. In one county, during the 1990-91 school year, the three smallest districts had average daily memberships of from 733 to 800 and per-pupil assessed valuations ranging from $151,000 to $549,000. These same districts had average per-pupil costs ranging from $6,238 to $9,406 (including expenditures from all funds).[4] Such districts, excluding island districts, should have little difficulty in providing quality educational programs for all of their pupils.

Ohio does have a substantial number of small K-12 districts. One hundred eighteen school districts, or 19.3% of the 612 school districts, fell within this category during the 1989-1990 school year. Table 15-1 presents data pertaining to the size of districts.[5]

---

[3] *Id.* at 4, 7.

[4] Division of Computer Services and Statistical Reports, *Costs Per Pupil–1990-1991* (Columbus, Ohio: Ohio Department of Education, n.d.), at 9 and 55.

[5] *Financing Education in Ohio* (Columbus, Ohio: A Report of the League of Women Voters of Ohio Education Fund, 1990), at 2.2.

Table 15:1

Size of Ohio School Districts According to Enrollments and Type of District for the School Year 1989-90

	Enrollment ranges						Total Districts	
Type of District	0 - 499	500- 999	1000- 2599	2500- 9999	10000- 24999	Over 25000	Number	Percent
City	—	2	60	144	9	6	191	31.21
Exempted Village	—	8	34	6	1	—	49	8.01
Local	14	94	198	65	1	—	372	60.78
Totals	14	104	292	185	11	6	612	100.00
% in each enrollment	2.30	16.99	47.71	30.33	1.8	0.98	100.00	—

The authors believe that size alone does not determine the quality of a school district's educational program. However, the breadth of programs usually is not as comprehensive as those in large systems. Small districts cannot normally afford to offer courses with very low class enrollments. This limitation can be ameliorated, in most circumstances, through cooperative programs with neighboring districts and/or by using any of a number of the new communication techniques.

The Ohio Legislature has been very hesitant to force consolidation or reorganization of districts to create larger districts. There has been very little action in this direction since the early 1970s. To the contrary, a comparatively small district that enrolled fewer than 2,500 pupils was permitted to de-consolidate in the 1980s. This resulted in two districts each of which reported their 1994-1995 enrollment to be less than 1,200 pupils.[6]

In fact, as recently as 1987, the Ohio Legislature's action discouraged reorganization by changing Section 3318.03 of the Ohio Revised Code. This revision reduced the number of pupils required to be enrolled in grades 7 through 12 for participation in Ohio's school facilities program. The school facilities program is a non-interest bearing loan program that is available to districts that do not have the money to construct adequate facilities.

Whether Ohio's legislative leaders will move towards more consolidation and reorganization remains to be seen. However, during the 1995 legislative session, they did move to expand the possibilities for collaboration between and among school districts. N.C. Holmes, writing in the November issue of *The School Administrator*, noted the following regarding Ohio's public school administrators:

> School administrators from various sectors would like to work together. That law, supported by both rural and large-city systems makes it possible for 88 county school systems—Ohio's version of a regional agency—to engage in service agreements with 190 city districts and 49 village districts that previously were excluded or exempted from the county systems.
>
> The same legislation broadened the opportunity for two or more districts to join

[6] *Ohio Educational Directory—1994-1995* (Columbus, Ohio: Ohio Department of Education, n.d.), at 200.

together to, in effect, create a larger financing base to support an initiative, such as a math/science program or a performing arts program.[7]

15.7 Concluding Comments

In summary, administrators and aspiring administrators are urged to take active roles in the legislative process and to become engaged in their communities' organizations. All data supporting school issues must be prepared and presented in a clear, concise manner or form that can be readily verified and understood.

Business and industry's increased interest in the schools will bring new challenges for administrators. However, the final decisions concerning the educational programs of schools will, to a large degree, remain in the hands of educators, boards of education and legislators.

Whether the legislative body will take a more active role in the reorganization of Ohio's school districts remains to be seen. Regardless of the legislation that may occur concerning this area of public education, with equitable and adequate funding and interdistrict cooperation, smaller districts can provide quality programs for their pupils.

---

[7] Natalie C. Holmes, "Consolidate, Cooperate or Collaborate: Dilemmas of Rural Schools," *The School Administrator* 10 (Nov. 1990), at 8 and 14.

APPENDIX CONTENTS

Selected Ohio Administrative Code Provisions

Chapter 3301-11 Annual Educational Assessment

Chapter 3301-14 Education Management Information System

Chapter 3301-35 Standards for Kindergarten through Twelfth Grade

Chapter 3301-38 County School District Plans

Chapter 3301-40 Rules on Nonpublic Schools Administrative Cost Reimbursement

Chapter 3301-11
Annual Educational Assessment

3301-11-01 Definitions.

Data to be reported in the annual report shall indicate achievements, problems, plans, and improvements, utilizing the following definitions:

(A) For rules 3301-11-02 to 3301-11-05 of the Administrative Code:

(1) "Achievements" are measurable student accomplishments. Achievements may include, but are not limited to, the reporting of curricular goals attained, awards/recognition, competency test results, standardized achievement test scores or post high school graduation data about students. Whenever test results are reported, factors necessary for proper interpretation should be reported, including, but not limited to, the time of year tests were administered; proportion of students tested at each grade; and to what comparison group, if any, test results were referenced.

(2) "Problems" are either specific shortcomings in programs or special factors bearing adversely upon the operation of schools. Problems may include, but are not limited to, reasons for failing to achieve goals on schedule, inadequate financing, low attendance, vandalism, violence or low level of community support. Problems are things that stand in the way of attaining the basic objectives of each district and school.

(3) "Plans" are steps for attaining stated goals. They may include, but are not limited to, provisions for research, special assignment of personnel, use of outside resources, new or remodeled facilities and special costs.

(4) "Improvements" are the actual results achieved in attaining specific goals. Improvements may include, but are not limited to, new programs, higher student achievement, higher rates of attendance, fewer dropouts, reduced vandalism, new or remodeled facilities, expanded media centers, laboratories, shops, or classrooms, etc.

(B) For paragraph (B)(2)(b) of rule 3301-11-02 and paragraph (B)(2)(b) of rule 3301-11-05 of the Administrative Code:

(1) "Instruction" includes the activities dealing directly with the teaching of pupils or the interaction between teacher and pupil(s). Included in this definition are regular, special, vocational and other instruction, as defined in the most current "Uniform School Accounting System User Manual."

(2) "Supporting services" include administrative, technical, and logistical support to facilitate and enhance instruction, and to a lesser degree, community services. Included in this definition are pupil and instructional staff services, board of education and administration services, fiscal and business services, operation and maintenance of plant services, pupil transportation services and central services, as defined in the most current "Uniform School Accounting System User Manual."

(3) "Operation of noninstructional services include food service operation, community services, enterprise operations, and other operation of noninstructional services, as defined by the most current "Uniform School Accounting System User Manual."

(4) "Extracurricular activities" include student activities under the guidance or supervision of qualified adults, designed to provide opportunities for pupils to participate on an individual basis, in small groups or in large groups. Participation is usually not required and credit is usually not given.

(5) "Facilities acquisition and construction services" includes the acquisition of, or addition to, fixed assets, as defined in the most current "Uniform School Accounting System User Manual."

(6) "Debt services" includes any transaction primarily for the purpose of discharging the school district's commitment for interest and principal on general obligation debts, as defined in the most current "Uniform School Accounting System User Manual."

(C) For rules 3301-11-02 to 3301-11-05 of the Administrative Code:

(1) "Classroom personnel" includes all certificated staff members who provide direct instruction to pupils on a regularly scheduled basis. Included in this definition are elementary and secondary teachers, kindergarten teachers, ungraded primary teachers, head teachers and any others so defined by the most current certificated staff report form (CS-1). Excluded from this definition are educational service personnel, special education and vocational personnel, and personnel funded from federal sources and from disadvantaged pupil program fund.

(2) "Administrative and supervisory personnel includes the superintendent, assistant superintendents, principals, assistant principals, administrative specialists, supervisors and directors, the audio-visual staff, and any others so defined by the most current certificated staff report form (CS-1).

(3) "Educational service personnel" includes visiting teachers, counselors, librarians, school nurses, and elementary art, physical education and music teachers.

(4) “Special education personnel" includes psychologists and interns, special education supervisors and coordinators, therapists, special education teachers who address identified target populations, and any others so defined by the most current certificated staff report form (CS-1).

(5) "Vocational personnel" includes teachers in the respective areas of agriculture, business education, marketing or distributive education, home, economics

trade and industrial education and any other teachers of classes meeting current department of education vocational education standards.

(6) "Other personnel" includes those serving federal programs, auxiliary service personnel, disadvantaged pupil program fund (D.P.P.F.) personnel and others defined by the current certificated staff report form (CS-1).

History: Eff. 6-7-76; 8-1-88

3301-11-02 City, exempted village, and local district reports

(A)(1) Each school district shall devise a procedure for releasing to the public on a yearly basis a report indicating the achievements, problems, plans and improvements made by the district in meeting the educational goals established by the district board of education for either:

(a) The school district; or

(b) The individual buildings.

(2) This report shall contain information presented in two ways: narrative and appropriate statistical data.

(3) The narrative report shall include the names, addresses and home telephone numbers of persons elected to the following state offices from districts within which the school district has territory:

(a) State board of education;

(b) Ohio house of representatives; and

(c) Ohio senate.

(4) This narrative report may also deal with the areas of attendance, budget, curriculum, extracurricular activities, facilities, pupil achievement, staffing, staff development, special services, transportation, etc.

(B) In addition to the preceding information, the annual progress reports for each city, exempted village and local school district shall include the following statistical information:

(1) Ten-year enrollment projections, by year and by grade level.

(2) Financial data, including:

(a) Average per-pupil costs.

(b) Total dollars and percentages of general fund operating expenditures in either:

(i) The six major function code categories defined by the most current "Uniform School Accounting System (USAS)," including instruction, supporting services, operation of noninstructional services, extracurricular activities, facilities acquisition and construction services, and debt services; or

(ii) The major categories defined in the most recent "Costs Per Pupil Report" published by the Ohio department of education.

(3) Staff data, including:

(a) Number of full-time equivalent classroom personnel per one thousand students.

(b) Number of full-time equivalent special education personnel per one thousand students.

(c) Number of full-time equivalent vocational education personnel per one thousand students.

(d) Number of full-time equivalent educational service personnel per one thousand students.

(e) Number of full-time equivalent administrative and supervisory personnel per one thousand students.

(f) Number of full-time equivalent paid instructional aides per one thousand students.

(g) Average classroom teacher experience and training based on data reported in form CS-1, "Report of Certificated Staff."

(h) Average classroom teacher salary based on data reported in form CS-1, "Report of Certificated Staff."

(i) Percentage breakdown of total certificated staff by race and sex based on data reported in form CS-1, "Report of Certificated Staff."

(4) Pupil data, including:

(a) Average daily membership as reported in form OCCD-5, "Superintendent's Annual Closing Report."

(b) Beginning the first school year following implementation and every year thereafter, the data included in the achievement and ability test report prepared for each district by the department of education in accordance with division (I) of section 3301.078 of the Revised Code.

History: Eff. 6-30-76; 8-1-88

3301-11-03 Building reports.

(A)(1) Each school district, in accordance with the procedure established by the district board of education, shall devise a procedure for releasing to the public on a yearly basis, a report that indicates the achievements, problems, plans and improvements for each building in meeting the educational goals established by the district board of education for either:

(a) The school district; or

(b) The individual building.

(2) The narrative section of the report may deal with the areas of attendance, budget, curriculum, extracurricular activities, facilities, pupil achievement, staffing, staff development, special services, transportation, etc.

(B) In addition to the preceding information, the annual progress reports for each building shall include the following statistical information.

(1) Staff data, including:

(a) Full-time equivalent classroom personnel, special education personnel and vocational education personnel/pupil ratio.

(b) Number of full-time equivalent other personnel as reported in form CS-1, "Report of Certificated Staff."

(c) Number of full-time equivalent administrative and supervisory personnel.

(d) Number of full-time equivalent paid instructional aides.

(e) Number of full-time equivalent volunteers.

(f) Average classroom personnel experience and training based on data reported in form CS-1, "Report of Certificated Staff."

(g) Percentage breakdown of total building certificated staff, by race and sex, based on data reported in form CS-1, "Report of Certificated Staff."

(2) Pupil data, including:

(a) Total average daily membership, by grade and sex, as reported in form ADM-1, "Report of Average Daily Membership."

(b) Ethnic composition that is the proportion of the total average daily membership for each ethnic group included in form ADM-1, "Report of Average Daily Membership."

(c) One or more of the following economic status indices may also be reported: rate of unemployment; percentage receiving aid to dependent children; or percentages receiving free or reduced-price lunches.

(3) Total expenditures for the past three years for library-media center materials including library books, periodicals, newspapers and nonprint materials.

(C) Annual progress reports shall also include a statement describing the standardized test and competency test data which are available for individual students in the building and describe the procedure by which parents may review those data for their own children.

History: Eff. 6-30-76; 8-1-88

3301-11-04 County board reports.

(A)(1) Each county board of education shall devise a procedure for releasing to the public on a yearly basis a report indicating the achievements, problems, plans and improvements made by the district in meeting the educational goals and/or mission statement established by the county board of education.

(2) This report shall contain information presented in two ways: narrative and appropriate statistical data.

(3) The narrative report shall include the names, addresses and home telephone numbers of persons selected to the following state offices from districts within which the county school district has territory:

(a) State board of education;

(b) Ohio house of representatives; and

(c) Ohio senate.

(4) The narrative section of the report may deal with the areas of attendance, budget, curriculum, pupil achievement, staffing, staff development, special services, transportation, etc.

(B) In addition to the preceding information, the annual progress reports for each county school district shall include the following statistical information:

(1) Financial data, including percentage breakdown of total revenues showing contributions from local districts as well as state, federal and other resource agencies. Local district revenue should be identified by the district from which it is derived.

(2) Staff data, including:

(a) Number of full-time equivalent personnel as reported in form CS-1, "Report of Certificated Staff."

(b) Average staff experience and training based on data reported in form CS-1, "Report of Certificated Staff."

(c) Average staff salary based on data reported in form CS-1, "Report of Certificated Staff."

(d) Percentage breakdown of staff by race and sex, based on data reported in form CS-1, "Report on Certificated Staff."

(3) If direct instructional services are provided to students, pupil data, including:

(a) A description of the services provided.

(b) Total average daily membership data by grade.

(c) Percentage breakdown of ethnic composition by the groups included in form ADM-1, "Report of Average Daily Membership."

(d) Cost per pupil of instruction, as defined by the current "Uniform School Accounting System User Manual."

History: Eff. 6-30-76; 8-1-88

3301-11-05 Joint vocational school district reports.

(A)(1) Each joint vocational school board of education shall devise a procedure for releasing to the public on a yearly basis a report indicating the achievements, problems, plans and improvements made by the district to meet the educational goals established by the district board of education.

(2) This report shall contain information presented in two ways: narrative and appropriate statistical data.

(3) The narrative report shall include the names, addresses and home telephone numbers of persons elected to the following state offices from districts within which the school district has territory:

(a) State board of education;

(b) Ohio house of representatives; and

(c) Ohio senate.

(4) The narrative section of the report may also deal with the areas of attendance, budget, curriculum, extracurricular activities, facilities, pupil achievement, staffing, staff development, special services, transportation, etc.

(B) In addition to the preceding information, the 00000annual progress reports for each joint vocational school shall include the following statistical information:

(1) Ten-year enrollment projections, by year and by grade level.

(2) Financial data, including:

(a) Average per-pupil costs.

(b) Total dollars and percentages of general fund operating expenditures in either:

(i) The six major function code categories defined by the most current "Uniform School Accounting System (USAS)," including instruction, supporting services, operation of noninstructional services, extracurricular activities, facilities acquisition and construction services, and debt services; or

(ii) The major categories defined in the most recent "Costs Per Pupil Report" published by the Ohio department of education.

(3) Staff data, including:

(a) Number of full-time equivalent classroom personnel per one thousand students.

(b) Number of full-time equivalent special education personnel per one thousand students.

(c) Number of full-time equivalent vocational education personnel per one thousand students.

(d) Number of full-time equivalent administrative and supervisory personnel per one thousand students.

(e) Average teacher experience and training based on data reported in form CS-1, "Report of Certificated Staff."

(f) Percentage breakdown of total certificated staff by race and sex based on data reported in form CS-1, "Report of Certificated Staff."

(4) Pupil data, including:

(a) Total closing enrollment, including sex data, as reported in the "Vocational Education Closing Report Form VE-22."

(b) Total closing enrollment, including race data, as reported in the "Vocational Education Closing Report Form VE-22."

(c) Average daily membership as reported in form OCCD-5, "Superintendent's Annual Closing Report."

(d) Number of academic courses offered at the joint vocational school; number of students receiving their full academic preparation at the joint vocational school.

(e) One or more of the following economic status indices may be reported: rate of unemployment; percentages receiving aid to dependent children; percentages receiving free or reduced-price lunches.

History: Eff. 6-30-76; 8-1-88

3301-11-06 Report format and distribution.

(A) Annual progress reports shall be prepared and distributed on or before November fifteenth of each successive year. The reporting period shall be the preceding school year (July first through June thirtieth).

(B) Annual progress reports for city, county, exempted village, joint vocational school, and local districts shall be made available in printed form and in such language as to be useful to citizens. The report shall be issued to the local community of each district. Districts shall be permitted maximum flexibility in the manner of distribution. Reports may be published in the local news media, be on file in the school library, be sent home with each student, etc.

(C) Annual building reports shall be made available in printed form and in such language as to be useful to citizens. The report shall be issued to the local community of each building. Buildings shall be permitted maximum flexibility in the manner of distribution. Reports may be published in the local news media, be on file in the school library, be sent home with each student, etc.

(D) The rules included in this chapter are minimum requirements. They are not restrictive. School districts are encouraged to go beyond the requirements.

History: Eff. 6-30-76; 8-1-88

Chapter 3301-14
Education Management Information System

3301-14-01 Rule for the operation of the education management information system.

(A) As used in this rule, the following definitions apply:

(1) "Education management information system" means an integrated system of statewide data collecting, reporting, and compiling for school districts, including the publication of guidelines as defined in paragraph (A)(4) of this rule and as required by section 3301.0714 of the Revised Code.

(2) "Department" means the Ohio department of education.

(3) "Designated data acquisition site" means a data processing installation pursuant to section 46.01 of

Amended Substitute House Bill 111 of the 118th General Assembly, capable of collecting, preparing and transmitting to the department in machine-readable form those data required by the department and the auditor of state.

(4) "Ohio education management information system: definitions, procedures, and guidelines," hereafter referred to as the "EMIS guidelines," means the publication issued by the department containing the school district student, staff, and financial information to be collected and reported, along with data-element definitions, procedures, and guidelines necessary to implement the education management information system.

(B) The provisions of this rule shall apply to all city, county, local, exempted village, and joint vocational school districts and Ohio's designated data acquisition sites pursuant to section 3301.0714 of the Revised Code.

(C) The education management information system shall contain, but not be limited to, automated school district student, staff, and financial information. The information to be collected and reported shall be defined in the "EMIS guidelines". This publication shall be developed by the department and shall include, but not be limited to:

(1) Definitions of all data pursuant to divisions (A)(1), (B), and (C) of section 3301.0714 of the Revised Code.

(2) Procedures for collecting, transferring, and reporting data to the department pursuant to divisions (A)(2) and (D) of section 3301.0714 of the Revised Code.

(3) Procedures for the security, privacy, and retention of school district data records collected pursuant to section 3301.0714 of the Revised Code.

(4) Procedures for compiling the data pursuant to divisions (A)(3) and (E) of section 3301.0714 of the Revised Code.

(5) Procedures for annually reporting the data to the public pursuant to divisions (A)(4) and (F) of sections 3301.0714 of the Revised Code; sections 3319.32 and 3319.321 of the Revised Code; and 20 U.S.C. 1232(G). In accordance with these statutes, no data, such as a social security number, shall be used to release personally identifiable student information to the department.

(6) Procedures for user access to the education management information system data.

(D) School districts shall provide all data required by section 3301.0714 of the Revised Code as set forth in the "EMIS guidelines".

(E) Data shall be maintained within the education management information system pursuant to division (I) of section 3301.07 of the Revised Code.

(F) The "EMIS guidelines" shall be periodically reviewed by the department in consultation with a committee of education practitioners and concerned individuals, consisting of no more than fifteen members. The department shall update this document in a manner consistent with changes in law and recommendations from the committee to the state superintendent of public instruction.

History: Eff. 4-1-91

Chapter 3301-35
Standards for Kindergarten through Twelfth Grade

3301-35-01 Definitions.

The following terms are defined as they are used in these rules.

(A) "Board of education" - the elected governing body of a school district or the governing body of a nonpublic school.

(B) "Certificated staff" - school personnel who have been assigned positions which require a certificate in accordance with section 3319.30 of the Revised Code.

(C) "Classified staff" - school personnel who are assigned to positions under section 3317.12 of the Revised Code.

(D) "Educational option" - experiences or activities which may be provided in accordance with board policy to supplement the regular school program scheduled for pupils. Such options may include:

(1) "Correspondence course" - systematic instruction by mail or electronic media between a pupil and instructor in accordance with board policy.

(2) "Educational travel" - an educational activity involving travel in accordance with board policy under the direction of a person approved by the board and parent.

(3) "Independent study" - an educational activity involving advanced or indepth work by an individual pupil under the direction of a certificated member of the school staff in accordance with board policy.

(4) "Mentor program" - an educational activity including advanced or indepth work by an individual pupil in accordance with board policy under the direction of a noncertificated individual. Mentors shall be individuals selected in accordance with board criteria and subject to parent approval.

(5) "Tutorial program" - an educational activity involving work by an individual pupil under the direction of a certificated teacher in accordance with

board policy.

(E) "Intervention" - alternative or supplemental action designed to remediate, reinforce, or support pupil learning relative to specified performance objectives.

(F) "Parent" - a person or government agency having responsibility for a child as defined by section 3321.01 of the Revised Code.

(G) "Policies" - principles governing the operation of the school. Policies shall be established and adopted by the board of education.

(H) "Procedures" - an administrative course of action specified in writing.

(I) "Pupil activity programs" - school sponsored noncredit activities which are beyond the scope of the prescribed courses of study but are provided school supervision and support. Pupil activity programs include but need not be limited to performance groups, interscholastic activities, and school clubs.

(J) "Pupil performance objectives" - statements derived from prescribed goals and objectives delineating expected student outcomes as observable behaviors or products of behavior.

(K) "Superintendent" - chief administrative officer of a school district or the chief administrative officer of a nonpublic school.

History: Eff. 9-1-83

3301-35-02 Educational program.

The kindergarten through twelfth grade educational program shall be implemented in accordance with adopted policies which cover paragraphs (A) to (E) of this rule. Board policies shall be available to parents, pupils, and school personnel.

(A) A written philosophy of education and educational goals shall give direction to the educational program and shall provide a basis for daily operations.

(1) The educational program shall be provided without discrimination on the basis of color, national origin, race, or sex.

(2) The philosophy of education and educational goals shall reflect pupil interests and needs identified by broad representation of community, pupils, and staff.

(B) Curriculum and instruction shall be characterized by systematic planning, articulation, implementation, and evaluation.

(1) Courses of study shall establish the basis for curriculum and instruction.

(a) A course of study shall be adopted for each subject taught. Each course of study shall:

(i) Comply with the provisions of section 3313.60 of the Revised Code;

(ii) Be based on the philosophy of education and educational goals;

(iii) Prescribe what is to be taught;

(iv) Specify subject matter objectives;

(v) Establish a scope and sequence;

(vi) Provide a basis for pupil evaluation.

(b) Courses of study shall provide for the following topics to be a part of the curriculum: career education, citizenship, human relations education, multicultural education, energy and resource conservation education, and instruction in study skills.

(c) Courses of study shall be reviewed and updated at least once every five years.

(2) Locally developed competency based education programs shall be implemented for English composition, mathematics, and reading.

(a) Pupil performance objectives shall be established for English composition, mathematics, and reading.

(b) Provisions shall be made for periodic assessment of pupil performance, including testing at least once in grades one through four, grades five through eight, and grades nine through eleven.

(c) Guidelines shall be established for the use of assessment results for instruction, evaluation, intervention, guidance, and promotion decisions.

(d) Intervention shall be provided according to pupil needs.

(e) Written policies and procedures shall be adopted by the board of education regarding the participation of handicapped pupils in locally developed competency based education programs. Provisions may be made for exemption of individual handicapped pupils from the requirements of the locally developed competency based education programs.

(f) Implementation of competency based education in English composition, mathematics, and reading shall begin no later than the 1984-85 school year, with full implementation to be completed no later than the 1989-90 school year.

(g) Competency based education programs shall be reviewed and updated at least once every five years.

(3) Daily lesson plans shall give direction for instruction and implementation of courses of study.

(4) Pupil achievement shall be monitored according to established procedures.

(a) Reports of pupil progress shall be made to parents at established intervals.

(i) An interim report shall be made to parents when pupil progress is unsatisfactory.

(ii) Parents shall be notified of problems with pupil conduct or attendance according to established procedures.

(b) Pupil records shall be safeguarded according to sections 1347.99 and 3319.321 of the Revised Code.

(5) Criteria for decisions on pupil promotion and

retention shall include a requirement that pupils complete one year of American history and one-half year of Ohio studies for promotion from the eighth grade.

(6) Requirements for high school graduation shall include eighteen units earned in grades nine through twelve and shall be distributed as follows:

(a) English language arts, three units;

(b) Health, one-half unit;

(c) Mathematics, two units;

(d) Physical education, one-half unit;

(e) Science, one unit;

(f) Social studies, two units which shall include:

(I) American history, one-half unit, and

(ii) American government, one-half unit;

(g) Elective units, nine.

(h) Each pupil shall be required to complete three units in another subject in addition to the English requirement stated in paragraph (B)(6)(a) of this rule.

The effective date of this requirement shall be September 1, 1987.

(7) Diplomas shall be issued to pupils who complete graduation requirements in accordance with the provisions of paragraph (B)(6) of this rule and section 3313.61 of the Revised Code.

(8) Requirements for awarding credit to pupils who successfully complete courses in grades nine through twelve:

(a) Shall specify that a minimum of one hundred twenty hours be scheduled for one unit of credit with the following exceptions:

(i) Laboratory courses shall be scheduled for a minimum of one hundred fifty hours for one unit of credit;

(ii) Physical education courses shall be scheduled for a minimum of one hundred twenty hours for one-half unit of credit;

(b) Shall specify that credit courses have at least two meetings per week;

(c) Shall specify that a fractional unit of credit be awarded on a proportionate basis for a course scheduled to meet less than the minimum time required for one unit of credit;

(d) May permit more than one unit of credit to be awarded on a proportionate basis for a course scheduled for more than one hundred twenty hours;

(e) May permit pupils below the ninth grade to take advanced work for credit, but such credit may not be considered in calculating the eighteen units required for high school graduation in paragraph (B)(6) of this rule.

(9) Each building shall be open for instruction with pupils in attendance according to sections 3313.48 to 3313.482, 3313.484, and 3313.485 of the Revised Code, whichever section is applicable.

(10) Scheduled classes, supervised activities, or approved educational options for kindergarten pupils shall be provided for the equivalent of at least two and one-half hours a day throughout the year.

(a) A minimum of two hundred minutes per week shall be allocated for readiness activities in handwriting, mathematics, and reading.

(b) The balance of time shall be allocated for art, English language arts, health, music, physical education, science, and social studies.

(11) The school day for pupils in grades one through six shall consist of scheduled classes, supervised activities, or approved educational options for at least five hours exclusive of the lunch period.

(a) A minimum of eleven hundred minutes per week shall be allocated at each grade level for planned instruction in English language arts, health, mathematics, reading, science, and social studies. Foreign language instruction may be included in the eleven hundred minutes.

(b) A minimum of two hundred minutes per week shall be allocated at each grade level for planned instruction in art, music, and physical education.

(c) Weekly time allocations may be modified, except for English language arts, mathematics, and reading, provided pupils complete an equivalent amount of time on an annual basis as specified in paragraphs (B)(11)(a) and (B)(11)(b) of this rule.

(12) The school day for pupils in grades seven and eight shall consist of scheduled classes, supervised activities excluding interscholastic athletics, or approved educational options for at least five and one-half hours exclusive of the lunch period.

(a) Seventh and eighth grade pupils shall be scheduled for planned instruction the equivalent of at least one thousand minutes per week for the following:

(i) English language arts;

(ii) Mathematics;

(iii) Reading or foreign language;

(iv) Science;

(v) Social studies.

(b) Seventh and eighth grade pupils shall be scheduled for planned instruction the equivalent of at least eighty minutes per week in physical education.

(c) Seventh or eighth grade pupils shall be scheduled for planned instruction the equivalent of at least eighty minutes per week in each of the following:

(i) Art;

(ii) Health;

(iii) Music.

(d) The remainder of the minimum school week for seventh and eighth grade pupils may be allocated for planned instruction in subjects specified in paragraphs (B)(12)(a) to (B)(12)(c) of this rule or in subjects such as:

(i) Business education which may include typewriting or keyboarding;

(ii) Computer science;

(iii) Home economics;

(iv) Industrial arts.

(13) The school day for pupils in grades nine through twelve shall consist of scheduled classes, supervised activities excluding interscholastic athletics, or approved educational options for at least five and one-half hours exclusive of the lunch period.

(a) A minimum of forty-five units shall be scheduled and operated in separately organized classes each year.

(b) The forty-five units shall be distributed as follows:

(i) Business or vocational business, two units of which at least one-half unit shall be typewriting or keyboarding;

(ii) Economics, one-half unit;

(iii) English language arts, four and one-half units;

(iv) Fine arts, four units of which at least one unit shall be art and one unit shall be music;

(v) Foreign language, three units if one foreign language is scheduled; or two units each if two foreign languages are scheduled;

(vi) Health, one-half unit;

(vii) Home economics or vocational home economics, two units;

(viii) Industrial arts, two units;

(ix) Mathematics, four units;

(x) Physical education, one-half unit;

(xi) Reading, one-half unit;

(xii) Science, four units, including at least two laboratory courses;

(xiii) Social studies, two and one-half units, including one-half unit of American history and one-half unit of American government;

(xiv) Fifteen units unspecified which may include twelve units which pupils may earn in vocational courses either at the home school or a vocational school.

(C) Educational options may be made available to pupils.

(1) The superintendent may approve an educational option upon evidence that:

(a) The parent has approved participation for any pupil under the age of eighteen;

(b) An instructional plan has been submitted prior to pupil participation. The instructional plan shall include:

(i) Instructional objectives;

(ii) An outline including major instructional activities, materials, and environments;

(iii) A description of criteria and methods for assessing pupil performance;

(c) A certificated teacher shall provide instruction and evaluate pupil performance in tutorial programs and independent studies;

(d) A certificated teacher shall evaluate pupil performance in correspondence courses, educational travel, and mentor programs.

(2) Promotion and retention decisions regarding pupils in kindergarten through eighth grade shall consider pupil performance relative to the objectives of an option.

(3) A maximum of six units of credit may be applied toward the eighteen units required for graduation in paragraph (B)(6) of this rule. No more than four of the six units may be applied toward requirements specified in paragraphs (B)(6)(a) to (B)(6)(f) of this rule.

(D) An experimental program may be provided to meet the identified needs of pupils subject to prior approval by the Ohio department of education.

(E) The educational program provided in accordance with paragraphs (A) to (E) of this rule shall be evaluated at least once every five years. Evaluation procedures shall be conducted according to professionally recognized criteria and procedures.

History: Replaces part of rule 3301-31-01, 3301-31-02, 3301-31-03, 3301-31-04, 3301-31-05, 3301-31-06, 3301-31-07, 3301-31-08, 3301-31-09, 3301-35-01, 3301-35-02, 3301-35-03, 3301-35-04, 3301-35-05, 3301-35-06, 3301-35-07, 3301-35-08, 3301-37-01, 3301-37-02, 3301-37-03, 3301-37-04, 3301-37-05, 3301-37-06, 3301-37-07, 3301-37-08; Eff. (Amended) 7-1-70; (Amended) 7-1-68; 9-1-83

3301-35-03 Educational resources.

Resources for implementation of the educational program shall be allocated in accordance with adopted policies which cover paragraphs (A) to (K) of this rule. Board policies shall be available to parents, pupils, and school personnel.

(A) Certificated and classified staff shall be recruited, employed, assigned, evaluated, and provided inservice education without discrimination on the basis of age, color, national origin, race, or sex.

(1) Certificated and classified staff shall be assigned responsibilities in accordance with written position descriptions commensurate with their certification and qualifications, respectively.

(2) Each certificated staff member shall hold the appropriate type certificate with respect to assigned position in accordance with section 3319.22 or 3301.071 of the Revised Code. Copies of certificates appropriate to assignments shall be on file in the administrative office.

Certificated staff holding elementary certificates

may be assigned to grades seven and eight. Certificated staff holding secondary certificates may be assigned to grades seven and eight to teach the subjects for which certification is held.

(3) The ratio of teachers to pupils on a districtwide basis shall be at least one full-time equivalent classroom teacher per twenty-five pupils in average daily membership. Said ratio shall be calculated in accordance with sections 3317.02 and 3317.023 of the Revised Code.

The ratio of teachers to pupils in kindergarten through fourth grade on a districtwide basis shall be at least one full-time equivalent classroom teacher per twenty-five pupils in average daily membership. Said ratio shall be calculated in accordance with sections 3317.02 and 3317.023 of the Revised Code. The effective date of this requirement shall be September 1, 1986.

(4) A minimum of five full-time equivalent educational service personnel shall be employed on a districtwide basis for each one thousand pupils in average daily membership. Said ratio shall be calculated in accordance with sections 3317.02 and 3317.023 of the Revised Code.

Educational service personnel shall be assigned to at least five of seven areas: counselor, librarian, school nurse, visiting teacher, and elementary art, music, and physical education. Educational service personnel assigned to elementary art, music, and physical education shall hold the special teaching certificate in the subject assigned.

(5) Each school shall be provided the services of a principal. Each school with fifteen or more full-time equivalent classroom teachers shall be assigned the services of a full-time principal. A principal shall be assigned to no more than two schools.

(6) Curriculum supervision shall be provided to assist in the improvement of the instructional program.

(7) Each school shall be provided clerical and custodial services.

(8) Certificated and classified staff shall be supervised and evaluated according to a planned sequence of observations and evaluation conferences.

(9) Certificated and classified staff shall have opportunities to participate in inservice education, which shall include:

(a) Cooperative planning, implementation, and evaluation;

(b) Job-related training in areas of need identified in personnel evaluations;

(c) Orientation activities for new employees.

Annual inservice education for certificated staff shall include instructional methods, subject matter updates, and strategies for preventing and correcting disruptive behavior.

(10) Records shall be maintained on staff participation in inservice education and educational program development.

(11) Staff shall have access to a professional library.

(12) The schedule for each full-time equivalent classroom teacher, who is assigned to a school with a teacher day of six hours or longer exclusive of the lunch period, shall include at least two hundred minutes per week for instructional planning and evaluation and conferences.

(B) Instructional materials and equipment shall support attainment of objectives specified in courses of study.

(1) Instructional materials, textbooks, and equipment shall be available for teacher and pupil use at each grade level.

(a) Instructional materials, textbooks, and equipment shall be selected according to adopted policies with the involvement of certificated staff.

(b) Instructional materials, textbooks, and equipment shall be current.

(2) A library shall be provided in each school.

(a) The library collection shall:

(i) Be selected according to adopted policies with the involvement of certificated staff;

(ii) Include materials which support attainment of objectives specified in courses of study;

(iii) Include materials appropriate to pupil ages, interests, and educational needs;

(iv) Include current reference materials with at least one set of encyclopedia having a copyright date within the past five years;

(v) Be inventoried and cataloged centrally according to a nationally recognized system;

(vi) Be organized for convenient accessibility.

(b) Each library shall be staffed by a certificated librarian or by an aide or volunteer supervised by a certificated librarian. Library services shall be available throughout the school day.

(c) Library services shall include provisions for:

(i) Instruction of pupils in library skills;

(ii) Instruction of certificated staff in the use of library services and the production of instructional materials.

(d) Annual school year district expenditures for library materials and equipment shall amount to at least one-half of one per cent of the total general fund expenditures for regular instruction for the previous school year as entered on "Form 625, Ohio Common Core Data."

(C) Facilities shall accommodate the enrollment and the philosophy of education and educational goals of the school.

(1) Facilities shall be of a quality and quantity to support pupil learning relative to objectives specified in courses of study. Facilities for guidance and counseling shall be of a quality and quantity to implement the district plan for guidance services. First aid facilities and space for temporary placement or isolation of injured or ill pupils shall be provided.

(2) Facilities shall be available to support the work of certificated staff and shall include work space, filing facilities, access to a telephone, and access to a room for private conferences.

(3) School facilities and grounds shall be well-maintained, free from hazards, and in compliance with fire and safety laws and regulations as evidenced by:

(a) Reports of annual school fire inspections as conducted by the appropriate local authority;

(b) Reports of annual school health inspections as conducted by the appropriate local authority;

(D) Pupil health and safety shall be safeguarded by an organized program of school health services designed to identify pupil health problems and to coordinate school and community health resources for pupils, as evidenced by but not limited to:

(1) Compliance with immunization requirements of section 3313.67 of the Revised Code;

(2) Compliance with emergency medical authorization requirements of section 3313.712 of the Revised Code;

(3) Screening procedures to identify pupils with vision and hearing problems and a program of health counseling, referral, and follow-up;

(4) Procedures for emergency situations including fire drills, rapid dismissals, and tornado drills in accordance with section 3737.73 of the Revised Code;

(5) Records of monthly fire drills or rapid dismissals and records of tornado drills;

(6) Emergency procedures posted in classrooms and available to parents, pupils, and school personnel;

(7) Emergency telephone numbers posted by each telephone;

(8) Supervision of school grounds, play areas, and other facilities when scheduled for pupil use;

(9) First aid facilities and materials.

(E) Pupil cumulative records shall be maintained.

(F) Pupil admission, placement, and withdrawal shall be processed according to established procedures.

(1) Admission of pupils to kindergarten and grade one shall be in accordance with section 3321.01 of the Revised Code.

(2) Grade placement and units of credit shall be accepted for pupils transferring from any school in the state of Ohio which is in compliance with Chapter 3301-35 of the Administrative Code and from any out-of-state school approved by a state department of education or the equivalent for schools attended in a foreign country.

Credit for foreign exchange studies may be assigned in accordance with paragraph (B)(8) of rule 3301-35-02 of the Administrative Code.

(G) Pupil attendance and conduct shall be administered according to established objectives and procedures.

(1) Pupil attendance shall be administered in accordance with section 3321.04 of the Revised Code.

(2) Pupil conduct shall be governed by a code of conduct. The code of conduct shall:

(a) Specify expectations for pupil attendance and conduct;

(b) Specify procedures, corrective measures, and penalties regarding code of conduct violations;

(c) Safeguard pupil due process rights;

(d) Be available to parents, pupils, and school personnel;

(e) Be posted in accordance with section 3313.661 of the Revised Code.

(H) School guidance services shall be provided for pupils in kindergarten through twelfth grade in accordance with a written plan adopted by the board of education.

(1) School guidance services shall include:

(a) Systematic aid to pupils regarding educational, career, civic, personal, and social concerns including the harmful effects of drugs, alcohol, and tobacco;

(b) Appraisal, counseling, educational and career planning, referral, and staff consultations.

(2) Counseling services shall be provided by a certificated school counselor.

(I) Pupil activity programs shall be operated in accordance with the philosophy of education and educational goals and shall safeguard the interests of the school, participants, and spectators. Schools shall not sponsor interscholastic athletics for pupils in kindergarten through sixth grade.

(J) A planned community relations program shall be implemented to encourage citizen participation in and support for the educational program. The community relations program shall give evidence of efforts to:

(1) Encourage citizen participation in school functions in accordance with the philosophy of education and educational goals;

(2) Communicate educational program goals, strengths, and needs;

(3) Provide information regarding school activities and pupil accomplishments;

(4) Enlist community resources to support the educational program;

(5) Utilize the services of volunteers who are

assigned responsibilities consistent with their qualifications and experience and who are supervised by appropriate school personnel.

(K) Educational resource allocation in accordance with paragraphs (A) to (J) of this rule shall be evaluated at least once every five years. Evaluation procedures shall be conducted according to professionally recognized criteria and procedures.

History: Replaces part of rule 3301-31-01, 3301-31-02, 3301-31-03, 3301-31-04, 3301-31-05, 3301-31-06, 3301-31-07, 3301-31-08, 3301-31-09, 3301-35-01, 3301-35-02, 3301-35-03, 3301-35-04, 3301-35-05, 3301-35-06, 3301-35-07, 3301-35-08, 3301-37-01, 3301-37-02, 3301-37-03, 3301-37-04, 3301-37-05, 3301-37-06, 3301-37-07, 3301-37-08; Eff. (Amended) 7-1-70; (Amended) 7-1-68; 9-1-83

3301-35-04 Nonpublic school.

A nonpublic school chartered by the state board of education shall comply with rules 3301-35-01 to 3301-35-03 of the Administrative Code, with the following modifications:

(A) Paragraph (B)(12) of rule 3301-35-02 of the Administrative Code, school day for grades seven and eight, shall apply as follows:

The school day for pupils in grades seven and eight shall consist of scheduled classes, supervised activities excluding interscholastic athletics, or approved educational options for at least five hours exclusive of the lunch period.

(B) Paragraph (B)(13) of rule 3301-35-02 of the Administrative Code, school day for grades nine through twelve, shall apply as follows:

(1) The school day for pupils in grades nine through twelve shall consist of scheduled classes, supervised activities excluding interscholastic athletics, or approved educational options for at least five hours exclusive of the lunch period.

(2) A minimum of thirty-three units shall be scheduled and operated in separately organized classes each year. The thirty-three units shall be distributed as follows:

(a) Business or vocational business, two units of which at least one-half unit shall be typewriting or keyboarding;

(b) Economics, one-half unit;

(c) English language arts, four and one-half units;

(d) Fine arts, four units of which at least one unit shall be art and one unit shall be music;

(e) Foreign language, three units if one foreign language is scheduled; or two units each if two foreign languages are scheduled;

(f) Health, one-half unit;

(g) Home economics or vocational home economics, two units;

(h) Industrial arts, two units;

(i) Mathematics, four units;

(j) Physical education, one-half unit;

(k) Reading, one-half unit;

(l) Science, four units, including at least two laboratory courses;

(m) Social studies, two and one-half units, including one-half unit of American history and one-half unit of American government;

(n) Electives, three units.

(C) Paragraphs (A)(3) and (A)(4) of rule 3301-35-03 of the Administrative Code, pupil-teacher ratio and educational service personnel, shall not apply.

(D) Paragraph (B)(2)(d) of rule 3301-35-03 of the Administrative Code, library expenditures, shall not apply.

(E) Paragraph (J) of rule 3301-35-03 of the Administrative Code, community relations, shall not apply.

History: Replaces part of rule 3301-31-01, 3301-31-02, 3301-31-03, 3301-31-04, 3301-31-05, 3301-31-06, 3301-31-07, 3301-31-08, 3301-31-09, 3301-35-01, 3301-35-02, 3301-35-03, 3301-35-04, 3301-35-05, 3301-35-06, 3301-35-07, 3301-35-08, 3301-37-01, 3301-37-02, 3301-37-03, 3301-37-04, 3301-37-05, 3301-37-06, 3301-37-07, 3301-37-08; Eff. (Amended) 7-1-70; (Amended) 7-1-68; 9-1-83

3301-35-05 Special purpose school.

A special purpose school may be established provided it complies with minimum standards specified in rules 3301-35-01 to 3301-35-03 of the Administrative Code with the following modifications:

(A) College preparatory high school.

(1) A school district may establish a college preparatory high school provided pupils have the option of attending a high school which operates in accordance with rules 3301-35-01 to 3301-35-03 of the Administrative Code.

(2) The number of graduates admitted to degree granting institutions shall equal or exceed ninety-five per cent of the graduates for a period of three consecutive years immediately preceding the request.

(3) Paragraph (B)(2) of rule 3301-35-02 of the Administrative Code, competency based education, shall not apply.

(4) Paragraph (B)(13) of rule 3301-35-02 of the Administrative Code, units of credit scheduled, shall apply as follows:

Courses shall be scheduled and operated in separately organized classes each year to permit pupils to meet graduation requirements specified in paragraph (B)(6) of rule 3301-35-02 of the Administrative Code.

(B) Alternative school.

(1) A school district may establish an alternative school provided pupils have the option of attending a school which operates in accordance with rules 3301-35-01 to 3301-35-03 of the Administrative Code.

(2) Courses shall be scheduled and operated in separately organized classes each year to permit pupils to meet graduation requirements specified in paragraph (B)(6) of rule 3301-35-02 of the Administrative Code.

(C) A nonpublic school for special needs pupils may be chartered in accordance with minimum standards specified in rules 3301-35-01 to 3301-35-04 of the Administrative Code subject to such exceptions as may be approved by the state board of education on the basis of recommendations by the superintendent of public instruction.

(D) An adult high school may be chartered in accordance with minimum standards specified in rules 3301-35-01 to 3301-35-03 of the Administrative Code, subject to such exceptions as may be approved by the state board of education on the basis of recommendations by the superintendent of public instruction.

(E) A school provided by a state institution may be chartered in accordance with minimum standards specified in rules 3301-35-01 to 3301-35-03 of the Administrative Code subject to such exceptions as may be approved by the state board of education on the basis of recommendations by the superintendent of public instruction.

History: Replaces part of rule 3301-19-01, 3301-19-02, 3301-19-03, 3301-31-01, 3301-31-02, 3301-31-03, 3301-31-04, 3301-31-05, 3301-31-06, 3301-31-07, 3301-31-08, 3301-31-09, 3301-35-01, 3301-35-02, 3301-35-03, 3301-35-04, 3301-35-05, 3301-35-06, 3301-35-07, 3301-35-08, 3301-37-01, 3301-37-02, 3301-37-03, 3301-37-04, 3301-37-05, 3301-37-06, 3301-37-07, 3301-37-08; Eff. (Amended) 4-30-77; (Amended) 7-1-70; (Amended) 7-1-68; 9-1-83

3301-35-06 Procedures for beginning a new school and when changing location or ownership of a school.

(A) A new school may be established and operated for a specified period in accordance with the following procedures, provided the school has at least three grade levels or fifteen pupils.

(1) The superintendent shall initiate contact with the Ohio department of education regarding plans for beginning a school.

(2) The Ohio department of education shall provide copies of minimum standards and procedures for beginning a school.

(3) The superintendent shall submit a plan for attaining compliance with minimum standards to the Ohio department of education. The plan shall include:

(a) Objectives related to minimum standards;

(b) A timeline for attaining compliance with minimum standards.

Nonpublic schools shall comply with rules 3301-39-01 to 3301-39-04 of the Administrative Code, "Rules On Racially Nondiscriminatory Policies And Practices For Nonpublic Schools."

(4) A new school may operate under a letter of approval issued by the Ohio department of education subsequent to an onsite evaluation of the school relative to a school plan. A new school may be approved to operate according to a plan for a period not to exceed four years.

(5) The superintendent of public instruction may recommend to the state board of education that a charter be granted when an onsite evaluation indicates that a school is in compliance with minimum standards.

(B) A change in location or ownership of any school shall be reported to the Ohio department of education. A change in location or ownership shall render a charter null and void.

History: Eff. 9-1-83

3301-35-07 Procedures for evaluations.

(A) A school shall be evaluated at least once every five years to determine compliance with rules 3301-35-01 to 3301-35-06 of the Administrative Code.

(1) The superintendent shall be informed of evaluation dates and procedures.

(2) A written report of the results of the school evaluation shall be mailed to the superintendent, the principal, and the president of the board of education. The evaluation report shall specify any deficiencies and dates by which corrections will be required.

The principal shall notify parents and other interested parties of a public meeting to be held within thirty days of receipt of the evaluation report. The purpose of the meeting would be to discuss the results of the school evaluation.

(3) A plan to correct deficiencies shall be prepared and submitted to the Ohio department of education.

(4) Onsite verification may be conducted to review progress regarding the correction of deficiencies.

(5) An extension of the timeline or alternate means

for correction of deficiencies may be approved by the state board of education.

(6) The Ohio department of education shall make public notice of any deficiencies which have not been corrected by the times specified in the evaluation report. Failure to comply with rules 3301-35-01 to 3301-35-06 of the Administrative Code shall be cause for initiating charter revocation proceedings in accordance with section 3301.16 of the Revised Code and Chapter 119. of the Revised Code.

(B) Exceptions to the provisions of rules 3301-35-01 to 3301-35-06 of the Administrative Code may be granted by the state board of education upon evidence of good and sufficient reason.

History: Eff. 9-1-83

3301-35-08 Non-chartered, non-tax supported school.

A school, which is not chartered or seeking a charter from the state board of education because of truly held religious beliefs, shall annually certify in a report to the parents of its pupils that the school meets Ohio minimum standards for non-chartered, non-tax supported schools cited in paragraphs (A) to (H) of this rule. A copy of said report shall be filed with the Ohio department of education on or before the thirtieth of September of each year.

(A) School year. The school shall be open for instruction with pupils in attendance for not less than one hundred eighty-two days each school year according to section 3313.48 of the Revised Code.

(B) School day. The school day for pupils in grades one through twelve shall be no less than five hours exclusive of the noon recess according to section 3313.48 of the Revised Code.

(C) Pupil attendance. Pupil attendance shall be reported to facilitate administration of laws relating to compulsory education and the employment of minors. Parents shall be responsible for reporting their child's school enrollment or withdrawal. An individual in charge of the non-chartered, non-tax supported school may, as a matter of convenience, provide the report for the parent.

(1) The attendance report shall include the name, age, and place of residence of each pupil below eighteen years of age.

(2) The report shall be made to the treasurer of the board of education of the city, exempted village, or local school district in which the pupil resides.

(3) The report shall be made within the first two weeks of the beginning of each school year. In the case of pupil withdrawal or entrance during the school year, notice shall be given to the treasurer of the appropriate board(s) of education. Such notice shall be given within the first week of the next school month.

(D) Teacher and administrator qualifications. Teachers and administrators shall have received a bachelor's degree or the equivalent thereof from a recognized college or university.

(E) Courses of study. Each non-chartered, non-tax supported school shall have courses of study for the following subjects:

(1) Language arts;

(2) Geography, the history of the United States and Ohio, and national, state, and local government;

(3) Mathematics;

(4) Science;

(5) Health;

(6) Physical education;

(7) The fine arts, including music;

(8) First aid, safety, and fire prevention;

(9) Other subjects as prescribed by the non-chartered, non-tax supported school.

(F) Pupil promotion. Each non-chartered, non-tax supported school shall follow regular procedures for promotion from grade to grade of pupils who have met the school's educational requirements.

(G) Pupil health and safety. Each non-chartered, non-tax supported school shall comply with state and local health, fire, and safety laws.

(H) Pupils attending a non-chartered, non-tax supported school are not entitled to pupil transportation as provided pursuant to section 3327.01 of the Revised Code, and pupils attending a non-chartered, non-tax supported school are not entitled to auxiliary services as provided pursuant to section 3317.06 of the Revised Code.

A non-chartered, non-tax supported school is not entitled to nonpublic administrative cost reimburse-ment provided pursuant to section 3317.063 of the Revised Code.

History: Eff. 9-1-83

Chapter 3301-38
County School District Plans

3301-38-01 Definitions.

(A) "County school district" means the territory within the territorial limits of a county, exclusive of the territory embraced in any city school district or exempted village school district, and excluding the territory detached therefrom for school purposes and including the territory attached thereto for school purposes.

(B) "County board of education" means the board of education which consists of five members who are resident electors of the county school district as provided by section 3313.01 of the Revised Code.

(C) "County school district office of education" means the staff and facilities of the county board of education for the purpose of providing educational services.

(D) "County school district plan" means a written document approved by the county board of education and the state board of education which states how the responsibilities of the county school district shall be implemented and which details the scope of services to be provided to the member school districts of the county school district and/or agencies, as well as to contract districts. The plan shall be developed in cooperation with the superintendent and/or designees of the districts served and shall contain the elements required in the rules in this chapter.

3301-38-02 Program.

(A) A statement of philosophy shall be adopted by the county board of education.

(B) The mission of the county school district shall be determined by the county board of education in a policy statement and shall be promulgated through the county school district plan.

(C) The mission statement shall be based on the following principles:

(1) Provision of leadership and service to meet the individual and collective needs of the districts served;

(2) Promotion of cost-effective educational programs that are responsive to the current and future social and economic trends;

(3) Establishment of the county school district as an integral part of the education network;

(4) Link between the local school district and the Ohio department of education;

(5) Responsibility of monitoring Chapter 3301-35 of the Administrative Code, the minimum standards for elementary and secondary schools; and

(6) Implementation of services as required by the Revised Code, the county board of education, or requested by the Ohio department of education.

History: Eff. 2-1-89

3301-38-03 Facilities.

The county school district plan shall address the provision of physical facilities consistent with the mission statement, the services provided, and the required staff in accordance with adopted policies which cover the following:

(A) Facilities shall be of quality and quantity to support staff.

(B) Facilities shall:

(1) Include work space, professional library, filing facilities, access to telephones, conference space, and restrooms;

(2) Have access to a meeting room to accommodate county board of education meetings and other assemblies in accordance with section 3319.19 of the Revised Code; and

(3) Be adequately equipped.

(C) Facilities and grounds shall be well maintained and free from hazards and in compliance with fire and safety laws and regulations as evidenced by reports of required fire and health inspections by the appropriate local authority.

(D) Physical facilities shall be evaluated according to the following criteria:

(1) The evaluation shall be conducted according to professionally recognized criteria and procedures; and

(2) The physical facilities shall be in compliance with Pub. L. 94-142 and Section 504 of the Rehabilitation Act of 1973.

(E) The county commissioners or their equivalent governmental body have responsibility to provide and equip facilities in accordance with section 3319.19 of the Revised Code. A meeting shall be initiated by the Ohio department of education with the county commissioners within forty-five days of receipt of the evaluation to review the findings. A plan to correct any existing deficiencies shall be developed. The results of the plan shall be submitted in writing and shared with all parties.

History: Eff. 2-1-89

3301-38-04 Fiscal monitoring.

The county school district plan shall prescribe the role of the county school district office of education in the fiscal monitoring of the local school districts. The plan shall incorporate the following:

(A) Consultation and review by the county superintendent regarding the local budget document, appropriation measure, school district tax levy, and local bond issues prior to adoption;

(B) Access to all completed Ohio department of education fiscal management information;

(C) Consultation with the Ohio department of education on fiscal matters pertaining to the local school districts, including requests for staffing and financial analysis and involvement in the emergency school advancement fund process;

(D) Evidence that selected service(s) have been subjected to a cost-benefit analysis to determine if service(s) are best provided by individual school districts or by cooperative arrangements between/among the districts; and

(E) Equitable division of funds between the districts involved when a county board of education creates a new local school district from one or more districts or parts thereof and when a county board of education transfers a part of a school district to an adjoining school district in accordance with section 3311.22, 3311.231, or 3311.26 of the Revised Code.

History: Eff. 2-1-89

3301-38-05 Personnel in the county office of education.

The county school district plan for county office of education personnel shall include policies and procedures to ensure that:

(A) The county office of education provides supervisory services to local school districts in accordance with section 3317.11 of Revised Code;

(B) The staff is adequate in order to implement its mission;

(C) The staff shall possess the qualifications of preparation, experience, and attitude to carry out the mission;

(D) The county school district staff are paid salaries commensurate with training, experience, and expectations of the county school district;

(E) The staff is supervised and evaluated;

(F) The county superintendent acts as treasurer of the county board of education, unless the county board has taken action to become its own fiscal agent in accordance with sections 135.01 and 3313.22 of the Revised Code;

(G) The county superintendent serves as executive officer of the county board of education and may serve as treasurer of a joint vocational school district in accordance with section 3311.19 of the Revised Code; and

(H) The county superintendent serves as the chief school administrator of the county school district.

History: Eff. 2-1-89

3301-38-06 Personnel under the supervision of the county school district.

The county school district plan shall include procedures that assure there is an ongoing program of:

(A) Nominating teachers, principals, and local superintendents for employment by local boards of education in accordance with sections 3319.02, 3319.07, and 3319.11 of the Revised Code;

(B) Directing and assigning teachers and other employees of the schools under their supervision in accordance with section 3319.01 of the Revised Code;

(C) Classroom supervision and evaluation for the purpose of improving the quality of education;

(D) Recommending which contract shall be suspended when a local board of education finds it necessary to suspend teacher contracts because of decreased enrollment or for other reasons set forth in section 3319.17 of the Revised Code;

(E) External and internal communication with classified and certificated personnel;

(F) Inservice for all school district personnel and school board members;

(G) Inservice for newly assigned personnel;

(H) Continuing education units;

(I) Processing teacher certificates for the local school districts in the county in accordance with section 3319.36 of the Revised Code;

(J) Providing for physical examination of school bus drivers in accordance with section 3327.10 of the Revised Code;

(K) Issuing certificates of qualification to school bus drivers in accordance with section 3327.10 of the Revised Code;

(L) Acting in the place of a local board of education and performing its duties in the case where the local board does not fill a vacancy as required by law or fails to perform a duty imposed upon it by law in accordance with section 3313.85 of the Revised Code; and

(M) Certifying to the treasurer of each local board of education the correct salary to be paid to each teacher as related to the adopted salary schedule in accordance with section 3317.14 of the Revised Code.

History: Eff. 2-1-89

3301-38-07 Curriculum.

The county school district plan shall provide for the maximum involvement of local school districts and shall include the following required services:

(A) An adopted graded course of study in accordance with section 3313.60 of the Revised Code;

(B) Assistance in implementing a graded course of study, including inservice;

(C) Adoption of a textbook list in accordance with section 3329.08 of the Revised Code;

(D) Assistance with compliance of the requirements to develop and implement competency-based education;

(E) Assistance with implementing state-mandated testing programs;

(F) Research and analysis of test data for instructional improvement and intervention;

(G) A handbook of curriculum development procedures;

(H) Maintenance of a professional library;

(I) Assistance in the development of educational options which are in compliance with Chapter 3301-35 of the Administrative Code, minimum standards for elementary and secondary schools;

(J) Curriculum services to city, exempted village, and local school districts as mutually agreed to; and

(K) Facilitation and assistance to the Ohio department of education with the evaluation of schools.

History: Eff. 2-1-89

3301-38-08 Planning and development.

The county school district plan shall include the following:

(A) Scope of the program;

(B) Inclusion of local school district participation;

(C) Method of funding;

(D) Guidelines for the distribution of educational and statistical information; and

(E) Systematic study of fringe benefits and salaries.

History: Eff. 2-1-89

3301-38-09 Communications.

The county school district plan shall provide for the establishment of a communications program that will include the following:

(A) Regular contact with local and area news media;

(B) Annual report in accordance with section 3313.94 of the Revised Code;

(C) Publishing appropriate, informative bulletins and brochures;

(D) Assistance to local school districts in development of comprehensive programs of school and community relations;

(E) Communication with local school district staff and board members on a regular basis;

(F) Assistance in communications to local school districts in crisis situations;

(G) Establishment of a speakers bureau; and

(H) Facilitation and interaction with persons, programs, and agencies affecting the county and local school districts.

History: Eff. 2-1-89

3301-38-10 State school building assistance program as provided in Chapter 3318. of the Revised Code.

The county school district plan shall include the following areas of assistance to local school districts:

(A) Development of a course of action based on an analysis of current and anticipated conditions within the community and school;

(B) Definition of the purpose of the school and the policy and practices surrounding the program implementation;

(C) Development of architectural and educational specifications;

(D) Selection of an architect;

(E) Site selection; and

(F) Project budget and cost control.

History: Eff. 2-1-89

3301-38-11 Pupil personnel.

The county school district plan shall ensure the following:

(A) Certification of all data required to be submitted to the Ohio department of education;

(B) Employment of a county attendance officer, or with the consent of the judge of the appropriate juvenile court, designate a probation officer as such, in accordance with section 3321.15 of the Revised Code;

(C) Establishment and maintenance of special education classes as required to meet the needs of handicapped children;

(D) Provision for the transportation of handicapped children;

(E) Provision of facilities for handicapped classes;

(F) Provision for ruling on the need for private transportation in accordance with section 3327.02 of the Revised Code;

(G) Provision for forwarding information to the superintendent of schools of a district to which a child moves in accordance with section 3321.13 of the Revised Code;

(H) Provision for the assignment of pupils to the proper schools and grades within the district in accordance with section 3319.01 of the Revised Code;

(I) Provision for the issuance of age and schooling certificates in accordance with Chapter 3331. and section 4109.02 of the Revised Code;

(J) Provision for authorizing the excuse of pupils

from attendance in accordance with section 3321.04 of the Revised Code;

(K) Provision for the filing and preservation of school membership records of all local school districts in accordance with section 3317.031 of the Revised Code; and

(L) Certification of all student data, including average daily membership, nonresidents, and unauthorized attendance in accordance with section 3317.03 of the Revised Code.

History: Eff. 2-1-89

3301-38-12 Ancillary services.

Services deemed appropriate may be provided in accordance with the county school district plan, which shall include the following areas:

(A) Scope of the program;

(B) Opportunity for school districts and other agencies to participate in ancillary services provided by the county school district; and © Method of funding.

History: Eff. 2-1-89

3301-38-13 County school district evaluation.

(A) The evaluation process should be an experience leading to improvements in the services offered by the county school district and shall be conducted once every five years by the Ohio department of education.

(B) The evaluation program shall consist of three major components;

(1) Preevaluation conference;

(2) On-site evaluation; and

(3) Postevaluation activities.

(C) A report of the evaluation shall be prepared and shall include a physical facilities report and a summary of recommendations. The superintendent of the county school district shall hold a public meeting within thirty days of the receipt of the evaluation report to discuss the results of the evaluation. The county superintendent is responsible for notifying the Ohio department of education of the date on which the public meeting will be held. A copy of the evaluation shall be sent to the school districts identified in the plan prior to the public meeting.

(D) It is the responsibility of the county superintendent to submit a plan, including a time line, to the Ohio department of education for correcting any violations specified in the evaluation report. The plan must be submitted within ninety days of receipt of the evaluation report. The time line for corrections indicated in the plan must be consistent with the date established in the evaluation report or consistent with the new date approved by the Ohio department of education.

(E) Evidence of the implementation of the mission policy statement shall be maintained.

History: Eff. 2-1-89

3301-38-14 County school district charter.

Each county board of education shall, within one hundred eighty days of the effective date of the rules in this chapter, submit to the state board of education a plan of service that meets this chapter. The state board of education shall, upon the approval of any such plan, issue a charter to that county school district.

History: Eff. 2-1-89

Chapter 3301-40 Rules on Nonpublic Schools Administrative Cost Reimbursement

3301-40-01 Purpose.

Pursuant to the provisions of section 3317.063 of the Revised Code, annual reimbursement to each chartered nonpublic school shall be made for the actual mandated service administrative and clerical costs incurred by such school during the preceding school year in preparing, maintaining, and filing reports, forms, and records, and in providing such other administrative and clerical services that are not an integral part of the teaching process as may be required by state law or rule or by requirements duly promulgated by city, exempted village, or local school districts.

The mandated service costs reimbursed shall include, but are not limited to, the preparation, filing and maintenance of forms, reports, or records and other clerical and administrative services relating to state chartering or approval of the nonpublic school, pupil attendance, pupil health and health testing, transportation of pupils, federally funded education programs, pupil appraisal, pupil progress, teacher certification, unemployment and workers' compensation, transfer of pupils, and such other education related data which are now or hereafter shall be required of such nonpublic school by state law or rule, or by requirements of the state department of education, other state agencies, or city, exempted village, or local school districts.

History: Eff. 6-1-82

3301-40-02 Eligibility.

Only nonpublic schools chartered by the state board of education shall be eligible to receive administrative cost reimbursement pursuant to the provisions of section 3317.063 of the Revised Code.

History: Eff. 6-1-82

3301-40-03 Procedures.

(A) A nonpublic school requesting administrative cost reimbursement shall submit an application to the Ohio department of education in the form and at such time as the superintendent of public instruction shall require.

(B) A nonpublic school requesting administrative cost reimbursement shall maintain at least the following records in support of a claim for reimbursement:

(1) A separate account or system of accounts for the expenses incurred in rendering the required services for which reimbursement is sought. These shall include accounts for salaries, fringe benefits, contractual expenses, and supplies and materials.

(2) A time record for each employee involved in providing services for which reimbursement is requested. This record shall clearly indicate the amount of time devoted to each service.

(3) Salary records for each employee involved in providing services for which reimbursement is requested. These records shall show gross salary, payroll deductions, and net salary by payroll period.

(4) A voucher file to include all paid vouchers, in whole or in part, used to substantiate costs included in the request for reimbursement.

History: Eff. 6-1-82

3301-40-04 Employees.

(A) The required services for which nonpublic schools are reimbursed for administrative costs shall be performed by school employees. Any reimbursement shall be made on the basis of the salary of the employee actually performing the service.

(B) Employee services shall be performed in accordance with the state law or rule, or school district requirements which mandate that such services be performed.

History: Eff. 6-1-82

3301-40-05 Reimbursement.

(A) Upon approval of the required application for reimbursement by the Ohio department of education and the release of funds by the controlling board, reimbursement payments to nonpublic school for administrative costs pursuant to section 3317.063 of the Revised Code shall be paid to, and in the name of, the nonpublic school as chartered by the state board of education.

(B) Reimbursement payments to a nonpublic school shall not exceed an amount for each school year equal to one hundred dollars per pupil enrolled in that nonpublic school.

History: Eff. 6-1-82

3301-40-06 Audit.

The superintendent of public instruction may, from time to time, examine any and all accounts and records of a nonpublic school which have been maintained pursuant to section 3317.063 of the Revised Code and rule 3301-40-03 of the Administrative Code in support of an application for reimbursement, for the purpose of determining the costs to such school of rendering the services for which reimbursement is sought. If after such audit it is determined that any school has received funds in excess of the actual cost of providing such services, said school shall immediately reimburse the state in such excess amount.

History: Eff. 6-1-82

3301-40-07 Appeals.

Any nonpublic school may appeal the findings of an audit conducted by the superintendent of public instruction pursuant to the provisions of rule 3301-40-06 of the Administrative Code to the state board of education within thirty days after receipt of said audit, and the state board of education shall hear such appeal pursuant to the provisions of Chapter 119. of the Revised Code.

History: Eff. 6-1-82

Chapter 3301-44
Post-Secondary Enrollment Options

3301-44-01 Definitions.

The following terms are defined as they are used in this chapter.

(A) "College" means any state-assisted college or university described in section 3333.041 of the Revised Code and any nonprofit institution holding a certificate of authorization pursuant to Chapter 1713. of the Revised Code.

(B) "School district" means the school district to which a student is admitted under section 3313.64, 3313.65, 3317.08, or 3313.98 of the Revised Code.

(C) "Parent" has the same meaning as in section 3313.64 of the Revised Code.

(D) "Participant" means a student enrolled in a college under the post-secondary enrollment options program established by this chapter.

(E) "Secondary grade" means the eleventh and twelfth grades.

(F) "Locally determined" means official action by district boards of education.

(G) "Carnegie unit" means the basic unit of credit used to meet high school graduation requirements. One Carnegie unit is awarded for courses scheduled for one hundred twenty instructional hours. Exceptions are: (1) laboratory courses must be scheduled for one hundred fifty instructional hours; and (2) physical education must be scheduled for two hundred forty instructional hours for one Carnegie unit. Proportionate credit must be awarded for courses scheduled for fewer than the number of instructional hours required and may be awarded for courses scheduled for more than the requisite number of instructional hours for a Carnegie unit.

(H) "School foundation payments" means the amount required to be paid to a school district for a fiscal year under Chapter 3317. of the Revised Code.

(I) "Tuition base" means, with respect to a participant's school district, the formula amount specified in section 3317.022 of the Revised Code multiplied by the district's equalization factor specified in division (E) of section 3317.02 of the Revised Code.

(J) "Educational program" means enrollment in one or more school districts or in a college under division (B) of section 3365.04 of the Revised Code.

(K) "Nonpublic school" means a chartered school for which minimum standards are prescribed by the state board of education pursuant to division (D) of section 3301.07 of the Revised Code.

History: Eff. 3-15-90 (Emer.); 10-1-90

3301-44-02 Statement of purpose.

The purpose of the rules in this chapter is to prescribe conditions governing the post-secondary enrollment options program under section 3365.02 of the Revised Code, which provides that a secondary grade student may enroll at a college, on a full- or part-time basis, and complete nonsectarian courses for high school and college credit.

The program is intended to provide expanded opportunities for appropriately qualified high school students to experience coursework at the college or university level. Any high school student admitted to a course by an institution of higher education will be expected and required to perform at the same level as the institution's regular students. High schools continue to be responsible for providing a comprehensive and challenging college preparatory curriculum, including advanced placement and other advanced level courses, for their students. College courses should either contribute to or supplement the broad academic preparation needed by high school students. Credit for highly specialized content college courses generally should not substitute for important broader content college preparatory courses.

History: Eff. 3-15-90 (Emer.); 10-1-90

3301-44-03 Information and counseling.

(A) The chief administrator of a nonpublic school wishing to participate in the post-secondary enrollment options program shall notify the Ohio department of education by the first day of April prior to the school year in which the school's students will participate.

(B) Each school district or participating nonpublic school shall provide information about the post-secondary enrollment options program to all students enrolled in grades ten and eleven and to their parents prior to the first day of March.

(C) The information provided to students and their parents by school districts and participating nonpublic schools shall include:

(1) Program eligibility, including:

(a) Junior status as locally determined;

(b) Acceptance by college.

(2) Program options, including:

(a) Enrollment in college courses for college credit, or both high school graduation and college credit; and

(b) Financial arrangements for tuition, books, materials, and fees for each option.

(D) A student or his parent shall inform the district board of education or the nonpublic school administrator by the thirtieth day of March of the student's intent to participate in the post-secondary enrollment options program. Failure to do so will result in ineligibility to participate in the program during the next academic school year without permission of the district superintendent or the nonpublic school administrator.

(E) School districts shall provide counseling services, after the thirtieth day of March, to students in grades ten and eleven and to their parents. Such counseling services must be provided before any student may participate in the program to ensure that students and parents are fully aware of the advantages, possible risks and consequences of participation. Counseling information shall include without limitation:

(1) Program eligibility, including:

(a) Junior status as locally determined;

(b) Acceptance by college. In considering the admission of any secondary student, a college shall give priority to its other students regarding enrollment in courses. However, once a student has been accepted in a course as a participant, the institution shall not displace the participant for another student.

(2) The options required by section 3365.04 of the Revised Code;

(3) Financial arrangements for tuition, books, materials, and fees;

(4) The process for granting academic credits;

(5) Criteria for any transportation aid;

(6) Available support services;

(7) Scheduling;

(8) The consequences of failing or not completing a course in which the student enrolls and the effect of the grade attained in the course being included in the student's grade point average, if applicable;

(9) The effect of program participation on the student's ability to complete the district's graduation requirements;

(10) The academic and social responsibilities of students and parents under the program;

(11) Information about and encouragement to use the counseling services of the college in which the student intends to enroll;

(12) Information confirming the fact that students can take college courses at no cost;

(13) Encouragement to all students who have the ability to undertake college work, especially gifted students, to seriously consider the program.

(F) The chief administrator of any participating nonpublic school shall provide counseling to students in grades ten and eleven and to their parents before the students participate in the program to ensure that they and their parents are aware of the possible risks and consequences of participation.

(1) Such counseling shall include explaining the fact that funding may be limited and that not all students who wish to participate may be able to do so and the effect of program participation on the student's ability to complete the nonpublic school's graduation requirements.

(2) Participating nonpublic schools shall provide students and their parents with a form which shall be signed as an indication that they have received the counseling required and that they understand the responsibilities they must assume in the post-secondary enrollment options program.

(G) The school district shall provide the student and his parent with a form which shall be signed as an indication that they have received the counseling required by paragraph (E) of this rule and that they understand the responsibilities they must assume in the post-secondary enrollment options program.

History: Eff. 3-15-90 (Emer.); 10-1-90

3301-44-04 Notification.

(A) Notwithstanding any other provision of law, a student enrolled in a school district or participating nonpublic school may apply to a college to enroll in it during his eleventh or twelfth grade school year. If a college accepts the student, it shall send written notice to the student, his school district or nonpublic school, and the superintendent of public instruction within ten days after acceptance.

(B) The college shall, within ten days after each enrollment for a term, also send the student, his school district or nonpublic school, and the superintendent of public instruction a written notice indicating the courses and hours of enrollment of the student and the option elected by the student under section 3365.04 of the Revised Code and rule 3301-44-05 of the Administrative Code.

History: Eff. 3-15-90 (Emer.); 10-1-90

3301-44-05 Enrollment options.

(A) The student may elect at the time of enrollment to receive post-secondary credit from the college for the course(s) taken at college.

(B) The student may elect at the time of enrollment for each course to receive credit for the course toward fulfilling the graduation requirements of his school district or nonpublic school as well as post-secondary credit for the course.

History: Eff. 3-15-90 (Emer.); 10-1-90

3301-44-06 College and high school graduation credit.

(A) If a student successfully completes a course in which he was enrolled under paragraph (B) of rule 3301-44-05 of the Administrative Code, the board of education or nonpublic school administrator shall award him appropriate credit toward high school graduation in accordance with paragraph (B) of this rule.

(B) High school credit awarded for courses successfully completed under this chapter shall count toward the graduation requirements and subject area requirements of the school district or nonpublic school when the student has elected to receive high school credit under rule 3301-44-05 of the Administrative Code.

(1) If a course comparable to one a student completed at a college is offered by the district or nonpublic school, the board or nonpublic school administrator shall award comparable credit for the course completed at the college.

(2) If no comparable course is offered by the district or nonpublic school, the board or nonpublic school administrator shall grant an appropriate number of credits in a similar subject area to the student.

(3) If there is a dispute between the board and the student regarding high school credits granted for a course, the student may appeal the decision to the state board of education. The state board's decision regarding any high school credits granted under this rule is final.

(C) Evidence of successful completion of each course and the high school credits awarded by the district or nonpublic school administrator shall be included in the student's record. The record shall indicate that the credits were earned as a participant of the post-secondary enrollment options program and shall include the name of the college at which the credits were earned.

(D) The district board or nonpublic school administrator shall determine whether and the manner in which the grade achieved in a course completed at a college, and for which high school graduation credit is awarded will be counted in the student's cumulative grade point average.

History: Eff. 3-15-90 (Emer.); 10-1-90

3301-44-07 Calculating full-time enrollment.

(A) A student in grade eleven may not enroll in college courses for which he elects to receive credit toward high school graduation for more than the equivalent of two academic school years.

(B) A student in grade twelve enrolling for the first time in college courses for which he elects to receive credit toward high school graduation may not enroll for more than the equivalent of one academic school year.

(C) The restrictions specified in paragraphs (A) and (B) of this rule shall be reduced proportionately for any such student who enrolls in the program during the course of a school year.

(D) The method for determining whether a student is enrolled full-time in his high school and/or joint vocational school shall be that he is scheduled at the high school and/or joint vocational school for the total number of courses that might be scheduled using the total number of periods available during an official school day at the home district or nonpublic high school, less the standard lunch period.

(E) The maximum number of Carnegie units that constitutes a student's educational program during an academic school year shall be the sum of the Carnegie units scheduled at the high school, joint vocational school, and college, and shall not exceed the number of Carnegie units that might be scheduled using the total number of periods available at the high school during an official school day, less the standard lunch period.

(F) Conversion of units of high school graduation credit earned through successful completion of joint vocational school programs to Carnegie units required for high school graduation shall be accomplished as follows:

(1) The joint vocational school will determine the full-time equivalency in the joint vocational school of each participating student and report such information to the student's home school district.

(2) The home school district will multiply the full-time equivalency for each student (as reported by the joint vocational school) by the total number of periods (excluding the standard lunch period) available at the high school to determine the number of Carnegie units earned at the joint vocational school.

(G) Conversion of units of high school graduation credit earned through successful completion of college courses elected for such credit as specified in paragraph (B) of rule 3301-44-05 of the Administrative Code to Carnegie units required for high school graduation shall be accomplished using one of the following methods:

(1) College courses for which five semester hours (seven and one-half quarter hours) of credit are earned shall be awarded one Carnegie unit toward high school graduation; fractional Carnegie units shall be awarded proportionately.

(2) College courses shall be substituted for courses required for high school graduation based upon comparability of content and without regard to instructional time. The Carnegie units awarded shall be the same as if the comparable course were taught in the district school.

(3) A locally developed alternative method approved by the state superintendent of public instruction.

(H) The home school district shall confirm with the Ohio department of education, the joint vocational school, and with each college in which a student from the home school district enrolls, the percentage of full-time equivalency the student represents for the district, the joint vocational school, and the college as calculated in rule 3301-44-08 of the Administrative Code.

History: Eff. 3-15-90 (Emer.); 10-1-90

3301-44-08 Financial responsibilities.

(A) If the student elects to enroll under paragraph (A) of rule 3301-44-05 of the Administrative Code, the college shall notify the student about payment of tuition and fees in the customary manner followed by the college, and the student shall be responsible for payment of all tuition, textbooks, materials, and fees associated with the course.

(B) If, at the time of enrollment, the student elects to enroll under paragraph (B) of rule 3301-44-05 of the Administrative Code, the college shall be reimbursed in accordance with section 3365.07 of the Revised Code. A college that expects to receive or receives reimbursement under section 3365.07 of the Revised Code shall furnish to a participant all textbooks and materials directly related to a course taken by the participant under paragraph (B) of rule 3301-44-05 of the Administrative Code. No college shall charge such participant for tuition, textbooks, materials, or other fees directly related to any such course.

(C) Financial support for students participating in the program will be determined as follows:

(1) Participating students enrolled full-time in a joint vocational school will have appropriate tuition, books, materials, and fees paid for by the joint vocational school (seventy-five per cent) and the appropriate city, local, or exempted village school district (twenty-five per cent) of the amount due the college as determined by paragraph (C)(2)(j) of this rule.

(2) Participating students enrolled in a joint vocational school and a city, local, or exempted village school district will have appropriate costs for tuition, books, materials, and fees shared by the home school district and the joint vocational school using the following procedures:

(a) The sum of the home school district, joint vocational school, and college units represent a student's total educational program.

(b) The percentage of full-time equivalency a student represents for the home school district is equal to the units scheduled at the high school over the maximum units possible to constitute the student's educational program.

(c) The percentage of full-time equivalency a student represents for the joint vocational school is equal to the units scheduled at the joint vocational school over the maximum units possible to constitute the student's educational program.

(d) The percentage of full-time equivalency a student represents for a college is equal to the units scheduled at the college over the maximum units possible to constitute the student's educational program.

(e) The sum of the home school district, joint vocational school, and college percentages of full-time equivalency constitutes the total full-time equivalency for the student's educational program.

(f) The percentage of the school day a student represents for the home school district is equal to the units scheduled at the high school over the sum of the units scheduled at the high school, joint vocational school, and college.

(g) The percentage of the school day a student represents for the joint vocational school is equal to the units scheduled at the joint vocational school over the sum of the units scheduled at the high school, joint vocational school, and college.

(h) The percentage of the school day a student represents for the college is equal to the units scheduled at the college over the sum of the units scheduled at the high school, joint vocational school, and college.

(I) To determine the percentage of time for which the home school district and joint vocational school are responsible, calculate the following:

(i) For the home school district, divide the units scheduled at the home school by the sum of the units scheduled at the home school and the joint vocational school;

(ii) For the joint vocational school, divide the units scheduled at the joint vocational school by the sum of the units scheduled at the home school and the joint vocational school.

(j) The amount owed the college is calculated by multiplying the full-time equivalency obtained in paragraph (C)(2)(e) of this rule by the tuition base as defined in paragraph (I) of rule 3301-44-01 of the Administrative Code. Multiply that amount by the percentage obtained in paragraph (C)(2)(h) of this rule.

(k) The home school district share of this amount is equal to the sum of the percentage obtained for the home school district in paragraph (C)(2)(i)(i) of this rule plus twenty-five per cent times the percentage obtained for the joint vocational school in paragraph (C)(2)(i)(ii) of this rule times the amount owed to the college as calculated in paragraph (C)(2)(j) of this rule.

(1) The joint vocational school share is equal to the difference between the amount owed the college and the home school district share of that amount.

(D) If the student enrolls under paragraph (B) of rule 3301-44-05 of the Administrative Code, such reimbursement is contingent upon the student's completing each course for which credit toward fulfilling the graduation requirements of his school district or nonpublic school is requested. Failure to complete the course, whether through a formal "class-drop" process, or nonattendance other than for reasons generally accepted by the school district or nonpublic school, may result in any or all financial obligations for that course defaulting to the student or his parent as determined locally.

(E) It is the responsibility of any college participating in the post-secondary enrollment options program for high school graduation credit to notify the student, parent, school district or nonpublic school, and superintendent of public instruction of a participating student's failure to complete the course as a result of a formal "class-drop" process, or failure to attend classes regularly. Such notification shall be made in a timely manner, but no later than fourteen calendar days of such determination.

(F) Each July, the department of education shall pay each college for any participant enrolled in the college in the prior school year under paragraph (B) of this rule, the lesser of:

(1) The amount computed in paragraph (C)(2)(j) of this rule;

(2) The actual costs that would have been the responsibility of the student had he elected to enroll under paragraph (A) of rule 3301-44-05 of the Administrative Code, as verified by the department, of tuition, textbooks, materials, and fees directly related to any courses elected by the student during the prior school year under paragraph (B) of rule 3301-44-05 of the Administrative Code.

(G) The department shall not reimburse any college for any course taken by a student under paragraph (A) of rule 3301-44-05 of the Administrative Code.

(H) No student enrolled under this chapter in a course for which credit toward high school graduation is awarded is eligible for any financial aid under Chapter 3351. of the Revised Code.

(I) If a school district provides transportation for resident school students in grades eleven and twelve under section 3327.01 of the Revised Code, a parent of a pupil enrolled in a course under paragraph (B) of rule 3301-44-05 of the Administrative Code may apply to the board of education for full or partial reimbursement for the necessary costs of transporting the student between the secondary school he attends and the college in which he is enrolled. Reimbursement may be paid solely from funds received by the district under division (K) of section 3317.024 of the Revised Code, based on financial need, in accordance with paragraph (J) of this rule.

(J) Full or partial reimbursement for transporting students enrolled in college courses for high school graduation credit shall be calculated on the basis of the provisions of the National School Lunch Act, 42 U.S.C. 1758, and the income eligibility scale for free or reduced-price meals as established annually by the United States department of agriculture under said act.

(K) Paragraphs (B) and (I) of this rule do not apply to any college course in which a student is enrolled if, during the term such student is enrolled in the college course, he is also a full-time student in his home school district and joint vocational school, or nonpublic school.

(L) If the participant was not enrolled in a participating nonpublic school, the amount paid under paragraph (F) of this rule for each student shall be subtracted from the payments under Chapter 3317. of the Revised Code made to the student's school district.

History: Eff. 3-15-90 (Emer.); 10-1-90

3301-44-09 Participation by nonpublic schools.

(A) Nonpublic school students in grades eleven and twelve may participate in the post-secondary enrollment options program as provided in rules 3301-44-01 to 3301-44-08 of the Administrative Code except as such provisions are modified by this rule.

(B) Each nonpublic school student who wishes to become a participant in any school year shall send to the Ohio department of education a copy of his acceptance from a college and an application. The application shall include information about the student's proposed participation, including:

(1) The school year in which he wishes to participate;

(2) The semesters or terms the student wishes to enroll during such year;

(3) The student's expected full-time equivalency percentage for each such semester or term;

(4) The percentage of the school day each such semester or term that the student expects to be enrolled in programs provided by a college for both college and nonpublic school credit.

(C) Paragraph (C) of rule 3301-44-08 of the Administrative Code does not apply to participating nonpublic schools. The percentage of the school day a student represents for the nonpublic school is equal to the units scheduled at the nonpublic school divided by the sum of the units scheduled at the nonpublic school and the college. The percentage of the school day a student represents for the college is equal to the units scheduled at the college divided by the sum of the units scheduled at the nonpublic school and the college. The sum of the units taken at the nonpublic school and at the college, divided by the maximum number of units possible to constitute a student's educational program represents full-time equivalency for the student.

(D) Upon receipt of an application, the Ohio department of education shall record the date and time of receipt and shall calculate the amount owed the college by multiplying the full-time equivalency obtained in paragraph (C) of this rule by the tuition base as defined in paragraph (I) of rule 3301-44-01 of the Administrative Code. The amount obtained should be multiplied by the percentage of the school day a student represents for the college which is equal to the units scheduled at the college over the sum of the units scheduled at the nonpublic school and college.

(E) Paragraph (L) of rule 3301-44-08 of the Administrative Code does not apply to participating nonpublic schools. A base amount for each school year (the year beginning on the first day of July and ending on the thirtieth day of June) of one million dollars will be available to support nonpublic school student participation in the post-secondary enrollment options program.

(F) The reimbursement amount owed colleges for nonpublic school students participating in the post-secondary enrollment options program shall be subtracted from the remaining base amount for that school year.

(G) Applications will be processed in the order of receipt. The Ohio department of education will notify each applicant for whom financial support is available, within three weeks of the receipt of his application, that he may participate in the post-secondary enrollment options program.

(H) The Ohio department of education will notify each applicant for whom financial support is not available, within one week of the receipt of his application, the applicant's nonpublic school, and the college accepting the applicant that funds will not be available for the applicant's participation in the program during the year for which the application was made.

(I) No applicant receiving notification that funds are not available may participate in the post-secondary enrollment options program for both college and nonpublic school credit in the year for which he applied and no college will be paid for participation by any such applicant.

History: Eff. 10-1-90

Chapter 3301-48
Open Enrollment Programs

3301-48-01 Intradistrict open enrollment programs.

(A) General provisions.

(1) Each city, local, and exempted village board of education must adopt an intradistrict open enrollment policy, effective with the school year that begins July 1, 1993, allowing district students to enroll in an alternative school. A copy of this policy, or of any revised policy, shall be sent to the Ohio department of education within thirty days after the adoption.

(2) A board of education may adopt an intradistrict open enrollment policy before the school year which begins July 1, 1993. Any district adopting an intradistrict open enrollment policy before July 1, 1993, shall send a copy to the Ohio department of education within thirty days after the effective date of this rule or within thirty days after the adoption of the policy.

(3) The intradistrict open enrollment policy shall be adopted pursuant to section 3313.97 of the Revised Code.

(4) Before July 1, 1991, the Ohio department of education shall conduct an evaluation of selected school districts that choose to adopt an intradistrict open enrollment policy before July 1, 1993. The evaluation will determine the effects or consequences of permitting intradistrict movement of students.

(B) Student application and admitting procedures and records.

(1) Each school district adopting an intradistrict open enrollment policy shall be required to include in the policy, but shall not be limited to, the following provisions:

(a) A district-wide time line for parental information, application process, and notification of acceptance;

(b) Criteria for prioritizing applications for participation in intradistrict open enrollment;

(c) Criteria for establishing district capacity limits by grade level, school building, and educational program; and

(d) Procedures to ensure that appropriate racial balance is maintained in the district schools.

(2) Each school district with an intradistrict open enrollment policy shall maintain, but shall not be limited to, the following records:

(a) Individual student applications and a summary of those student applications for a school year;

(b) Evidence of parental informational meetings; and

(c) Evidence of the notification of parents and school building administrators.

(C) School district monitoring.

(1) School districts participating in intradistrict open enrollment shall be monitored by the Ohio department

of education. The monitoring process shall determine that the policies, agreements, procedures, and guidelines developed by the school districts are implemented as specified in section 3313.97 of the Revised Code.

(2) For monitoring purposes, each school district shall provide the Ohio department of education the following:

(a) Written application and admission procedures and the application form used by the district;

(b) Written procedure for establishing district capacity limits by grade level, school building, and education program;

(c) Written procedure to ensure that an appropriate racial balance is maintained in the district schools; and

(d) Access to records as described in paragraph (B)(2) of this rule.

(3) The Ohio department of education monitoring process shall consist of the following:

(a) Collection of all intradistrict open enrollment policies;

(b) On-site inspection completed as part of the evaluation of a school district under Chapter 3301-35 of the Administrative Code, relating to minimum standards for elementary and secondary schools; and

(c) The development of guidelines to deal with conflicts and concerns arising out of the implementation of this rule.

History: Eff. 7-1-90

3301-48-02 Interdistrict open enrollment programs.

(A) General provisions.

(1) The board of education of each city, local and exempted village school district shall adopt a resolution, prior to the school year which begins July 1, 1993, which either entirely prohibits the enrollment of students from adjacent districts or permits the enrollment of students, admitted under section 3313.98 of the Revised Code, tuition free, from all adjacent districts in accordance with a policy contained in the resolution. A copy of the resolution, or of any revised resolution, shall be sent to the Ohio department of education within thirty days of the adoption of the resolution.

(2) Two or more adjacent school districts may, by the adoption of identical resolutions prior to the school year which begins July 1, 1993, enter into an agreement to permit interdistrict enrollment among the students of the districts. Any such agreement shall:

(a) Contain the enrollment policy of each district entering into the agreement;

(b) Comply with the requirements of divisions (B) to (F) of section 3313.98 of the Revised Code; and

(c) Remain in effect for at least twelve months or until July 1, 1993, whichever occurs first. Such agreements shall expire on or before July 1, 1993.

(3) A copy of each agreement entered into prior to July 1, 1993, shall be furnished to the Ohio department of education at least thirty days prior to the effective date of the agreement.

(4) The state board of education shall make the payments and deductions required by section 3313.981 of the Revised Code for interdistrict enrollment permitted before July 1, 1993.

(5) Before July 1, 1991, the Ohio department of education shall make an evaluation of selected districts adopting an interdistrict open enrollment policy before July 1, 1993. The evaluation will determine the effects or consequences of interdistrict movement of students.

(B) Student application and admitting procedures.

(1) Each school district adopting an interdistrict open enrollment policy allowing the enrollment of adjacent school district students tuition free pursuant to section 3313.98 of the Revised Code shall be required to include, but shall not be limited to, the following provisions:

(a) A district-wide time line for parental information, the application process, and notification of student acceptance;

(b) Criteria for prioritizing applications for participation in interdistrict open enrollment;

(c) Criteria for establishing district capacity limits by grade level, school building and educational program; and

(d) Procedures to ensure that appropriate racial balance is maintained in the district schools.

(2) Each school district with an interdistrict open enrollment policy shall maintain, but not be limited to, the following records:

(a) Individual student applications and a summary of those student applications for a school year;

(b) Evidence of parental informational meetings; and

(c) Evidence of notification of parents and school building administrators.

(C) School district monitoring.

(1) School districts participating in interdistrict open enrollment shall be monitored by the Ohio department of education. The monitoring process shall determine that the policies, agreements, procedures, and guidelines developed by school districts are implemented as specified in section 3313.98 of the Revised Code.

(2) For monitoring purposes, each school district shall provide the Ohio department of education the following:

(a) Written application and admission procedures and the application form used by the district;

(b) Written procedure for establishing district capacity limits by grade level, school building, and education program; and

(c) Written procedure to ensure that an appropriate racial balance is maintained in the district schools.

(3) The Ohio department of education monitoring process shall consist of the following:

(a) Collection of all interdistrict open enrollment policies;

(b) An on-site inspection completed as part of the evaluation of a school district under Chapter 3301-35 of the Administrative Code, relating to minimum standards for elementary and secondary schools; and

(c) The development of guidelines to deal with conflicts and concerns arising out of the implementation of this rule.

(D) Interdistrict reporting.

(1) A school district that has adopted a resolution permitting adjacent district students to enroll, shall report, by the first day of September of each year, both the number of adjacent district students enrolled and the classes or grade levels assigned, to the superintendent of the student's native district. Students enrolling after said day shall be reported in a like manner.

(2) No school district shall count any adjacent district student in its average daily membership certified under section 3317.03 of the Revised Code. However, each school district shall count in its average daily membership any native students enrolled in the schools of an adjacent district admitted under section 3313.98 of the Revised Code.

(E) Financial reporting. All city, local, and exempted village school districts shall report, by the fifteenth day of June of each year, to the Ohio department of education, the number of native students enrolled in adjacent school districts and the number of adjacent school district students enrolled pursuant to section 3313.98 of the Revised Code. Student average daily membership shall be reported on the basis of full-time equivalence.

(F) Financial calculation for the educating school district. The full-time equivalence reported by the educating district is multiplied by the dollar formula amount specified in section 3317.022 of the Revised Code and by the district's equalization factor as defined in division (E) of section 3317.02 of the Revised Code. The total so calculated is credited to the educating district.

(G) Financial calculations for the resident school district. The full-time equivalence reported by the native district is multiplied by the dollar formula amount specified in section 3317.022 of the Revised Code and by the district's equalization factor as defined in division (E) of section 3317.02 of the Revised Code. The total so calculated is deducted from the native district.

(H) Excess cost for handicapped students. This calculation shall be made in accordance with sections 3323.14 and 3313.981 of the Revised Code.

(I) Transportation of students.

(1) Upon the request of a parent, and provided the school board offers transportation to native students of the same grade level and distance from school under section 3327.01 of the Revised Code, a school board enrolling an adjacent district student shall provide transportation for the student within the boundaries of the board's district, except that the board shall be required to pick up and drop off a nonhandicapped student only at a regular school bus stop designation.

(2) A school board enrolling an adjacent district student whose family has an income below the federal poverty line, may reimburse the parent from funds received under division (K) of section 3317.024 of the Revised Code for the reasonable cost of transportation from the student's home to the designated school bus stop. For the purpose of this rule "poverty line" means the poverty line established in accordance with section 673(2) of the "Community Services Block Grant act," 95 Stat. 1609, 42 U.S.C.A. 9902, as amended.

History: Eff. 7-1-90

Chapter 3301-49
Competency Guarantees

3301-49-01 Rule relating to guarantee of competency of certain high school graduates.

(A) The purpose of this rule is to establish guidelines and procedures whereby city, local, exempted village, or joint vocational school districts may establish a policy to guarantee that certain graduates of the district have attained a specific level of competency.

(B) "Graduate" means a person who has received a diploma from a district pursuant to section 3313.61 of the Revised Code.

(C) The board of education of any city, local, exempted village, or joint vocational school district may establish a policy to guarantee a specific level of competency for certain graduates.

(D) Such guarantee policies shall proclaim that any graduate meeting criteria established by the board is capable of performing specified functions at an established level.

(E) The guarantee policy shall include:

(1) Any criteria that must be met by a graduate of the district to be eligible for consideration;

(2) A list of specific functions that are guaranteed;

(3) A performance level for each guaranteed function;

(4) Indication of an employer's right to submit a written statement to the board of education, when appropriate, stating that a guaranteed graduate of its district does not meet the level of competency specified in the district's guarantee policy;

(5) A statement assuring that additional educational opportunities will be provided, without regard to age or place of residence, to the district's graduates whose competencies have been guaranteed, until the graduate attains the competency level specified in the policy; and

(6) Assurance that no fee will be charged to any person or government entity for such additional education.

(F) School funds may be expended for a guarantee program.

(G) Guaranteed graduates receiving additional education may not be counted in the district's average daily membership, nor may such individuals be included as a participant in any other program that would result in additional state funds to the school district.

(H) The educational program specified for returning guaranteed graduates shall be determined by the district superintendent and shall provide the help needed for the individual to achieve the guaranteed level of competency.

History: Eff. 10-29-90

Chapter 3301-53
Special Education Programs for the Mentally Retarded

3301-53-01 Minimum standards for chartering county board of mental retardation and developmental disabilities special education programs.

(A) Definitions. All terms used in this rule shall be considered as defined in rules 3301-35-01 and 3301-51-01 of the Administrative Code. Rule 3301-35-01 of the Administrative Code sets forth the definitions for the minimum standards for elementary and secondary schools and rule 3301-51-01 of the Administrative Code sets forth the definitions for the rules governing the education of handicapped children.

(B) Responsibilities of the county board of mental retardation and developmental disabilities. The county board of mental retardation and developmental disabilities ("board") shall provide a special education program ("program") for eligible pupils appropriately placed in such programs pursuant to rules 3301-51-02 and 3301-51-07 of the Administrative Code.

(C) Eligible pupils. The board shall provide a program to serve:

(1) School-age developmentally handicapped and/or multihandicapped children.

(2) Preschool children who are eligible for a program according to rule 3301-51-07 of the Administrative Code.

(D) Educational program requirements

(1) All programs shall comply with the following statutes and related rules:

(a) Section 3313.48 of the Revised Code, minimum school year.

(b) Section 3313.661 of the Revised Code, suspension or expulsion.

(c) Section 3313.67 of the Revised Code, required immunizations.

(d) Section 3313.712 of the Revised Code, emergency medical authorization.

(e) Section 3313.72 of the Revised Code, contract with health district for services of physician, dentist, or nurse.

(f) Section 3319.321 and Chapter 1347. of the Revised Code, safeguarding of pupil records.

(g) Section 3321.04 of the Revised Code, pupil attendance.

(h) Chapter 3323. of the Revised Code, education of handicapped children.

(i) Section 3707.26 of the Revised Code, inspection of schools by the board of health.

(j) Section 3737.73 of the Revised Code, drills and rapid dismissals.

(k) Rule 3301-35-01 of the Administrative Code, the definitions rule for elementary and secondary schools.

(l) Paragraph (D) of rule 3301-35-03 of the Administrative Code, pupil health and safety.

(m) Paragraph (G) of rule 3301-35-03 of the Administrative Code, pupil attendance and conduct.

(n) Rule 3301-51-01 of the Administrative Code, definitions for education of handicapped children.

(o) Rule 3301-51-02 of the Administrative Code, procedural safeguards for handicapped children.

(p) Rule 3301-51-03 of the Administrative Code, continuum of program options for handicapped children.

(q) Paragraph (A) of rule 3301-51-04 of the Administrative Code, program for multihandicapped children.

(r) Paragraph (F) of rule 3301-51-04 of the Administrative Code, program for developmentally handicapped children.

(s) Rule 3301-51-05 of the Administrative Code,

related services for handicapped children.

(t) Rule 3301-51-06 of the Administrative Code, funding of special education and related services.

(u) Rule 3301-51-07 of the Administrative Code, rule for the education of preschool children and for supervisory services in county boards of mental retardation and developmental disabilities.

(2) The program shall be guided by written policies of the board which are consistent with applicable statutory requirements contained in the Revised Code and rules adopted by the state board of education. Such policies and rules shall include, but not be limited to:

(a) Staff;

(b) Cumulative records;

(c) Curriculum and instruction;

(d) Health and safety;

(e) Instructional materials and equipment;

(f) Pupil activity programs;

(g) Pupil admission;

(h) Pupil attendance and conduct;

(i) Selection of materials, textbooks, equipment, and instructional resources; and

(j) Use of behavior management procedures.

(3) A written philosophy of education and educational goals shall give direction to the educational program and shall provide a basis for daily operation.

(4) Courses of study, methods of instruction, and other procedures shall effectively promote the needs, interests, and abilities of each school-age developmentally handicapped and multihandicapped pupil. The program shall be designed to raise the level of functioning in all areas of development.

(5) The program for school-age multihandicapped pupils shall be organized and operated pursuant to paragraph (A) of rule 3301-51-04 of the Administrative Code relating to special education programs for multihandicapped children.

(6) The program for school-age developmentally handicapped pupils shall be organized and operated pursuant to paragraph (F) of rule 3301-51-04 of the Administrative Code relating to special education programs for developmentally handicapped children.

(7) The program for preschool children shall be organized and operated pursuant to paragraph (A)(2) of rule 3301-51-07 of the Administrative Code relating to special education of preschool children in county boards of mental retardation and developmental disabilities.

(8) Curriculum and instruction shall be characterized by systematic planning, articulation, implementation, and evaluation.

(9) Courses of study for school-age programs shall establish the basis for curriculum and instruction.

(a) A course of study shall be adopted which describes the domains, life spaces, developmental sequences or other appropriate approaches which meet the needs of pupils.

(b) Courses of study shall be reviewed and updated at least once every five years.

(10) A current individualized educational program shall be on file for each handicapped pupil in the program and available to appropriate staff.

(11) Pupil achievement shall be monitored according to established procedures. Reports of pupil progress shall be made to parents at established intervals. All reporting shall be according to established procedures of the board.

(12) The school day.

(a) The school day for school-age pupils shall consist of scheduled classes or supervised activities for at least five hours, exclusive of the lunch period.

(b) Preschool children may attend programs for an entire official school day for five days per week, or any prorated portion of a day or week.

(13) An experimental educational program may be provided to meet the identified needs of pupils subject to prior approval by the department of education.

(E) Educational resources

(1) Staff shall be recruited, employed, assigned, and provided inservice education without discrimination on the basis of age, color, national origin, race or sex.

(a) Staff shall be assigned responsibilities in accordance with written position descriptions commensurate with their certification and qualifications respectively.

(b) A special class teacher for school-age developmentally handicapped and multihandicapped pupils shall hold a valid special education teacher's certificate for the area in which instruction is being provided. A preschool class teacher shall hold a valid special education or prekindergarten teacher's certificate with validation in early education of handicapped children.

(c) Related services personnel defined by rule 3301-51-05 of the Administrative Code governing related services for handicapped children shall meet the certificate requirements.

(2) The program shall be provided clerical and custodial services.

(3) Staff shall be supervised and evaluated according to a planned sequence of observations and evaluation conferences.

(4) Staff shall have opportunities to participate in inservice education, which shall include:

(a) Cooperative planning, implementation, and evaluation;

(b) Job-related training in areas of need identified in personnel evaluations; and

(c) Orientation activities for new employees.

(5) Records shall be maintained on staff participation in inservice education and educational program development.

(6) Instructional materials and equipment shall support attainment of objectives specified in courses of study. Such materials and equipment shall be current, selected according to adopted policies with the involvement of staff, and be available for teacher and pupil use.

(7) Facilities shall accommodate the enrollment and the philosophy of education and educational goals of the program.

(8) Pupil activity programs shall be operated in accordance with the philosophy of education and educational goals and shall safeguard the interests of the program, participants, and spectators.

(F) Evaluation and chartering.

(1) The program shall be evaluated by the department of education to determine if such program is in compliance with this rule. Such evaluation shall take place at least once every five years.

(2) The program shall be recommended to the state board of education for chartering if the program meets the requirements of this rule and those set forth in Chapter 3301-51 of the Administrative Code relating to education of handicapped children.

History: Eff. 6-10-88; 11-1-77; 7-1-89

3301-53-02 Rule for distribution of transportation operating subsidy to county boards of mental retardation and developmental disabilities.

(A) The purpose of this rule is to establish a basis for distribution of the transportation operating subsidy to county boards of mental retardation and developmental disabilities.

(B) The provisions of this rule shall apply to all county boards of mental retardation and developmental disabilities that provide services under Chapter 3323. of the Revised Code.

(C) As used in this rule, the following definitions apply:

(1) "Average daily membership (ADM)" means the average of the number of eligible individuals actually enrolled during the first full week of October of any given year. Amendments to the ADM shall be submitted to the Ohio department of education by February first of the following year.

(2) "County board" means a county board of mental retardation and developmental disabilities.

(3) "Department" means the Ohio department of education.

(D) In calculating the transportation operating subsidy, the following procedures apply:

(1) County boards shall submit an annual cost report for transportation expenditures to the department no later than June thirtieth of each year.

(2) The transportation reports shall be verified, signed and dated by the superintendent or his designee of a county board.

(3) Subject to the appropriations of the general assembly, the department shall calculate and distribute the transportation subsidy July through June of each fiscal year on a monthly basis.

(4) The department shall distribute to each county board an amount based upon the ADM for the designated twelve-month reporting period and the number of individuals receiving transportation services. Final adjustments for transportation service shall be made within the first quarter following the close of the fiscal year.

(5) The payment of subsidy for transportation operating costs for individuals who are enrolled in programs and services operated by a county board shall be calculated at a rate of up to three dollars per day per individual and one-half of the actual cost in excess of three dollars per day.

History: Eff. 7-1-89

3301-53-03 Rule for excess cost charges for county boards of mental retardation and developmental disabilities special education programs.

(A) As used in this rule, the following definitions apply:

(1) "Excess cost" means the average per-pupil educational cost for educating school-age children incurred by the educating county board of mental retardation and developmental disabilities that is in excess of the per-pupil amount received by the county board of mental retardation and developmental disabilities under Chapter 3317. of the Revised Code.

(2) "Individualized education program" means a written statement for a handicapped child that is developed and implemented in accordance with paragraph (E) of rule 3301-51-02 of the Administrative Code.

(3) "Certified excess cost" means the cost calculated under this rule approved by the Ohio department of education which is the maximum amount of money a county board of mental retardation and developmental disabilities may charge a public school district responsible for tuition of a nonresident student enrolled in a county board of mental retardation and develop-

mental disabilities program.

(4) "County board" means a county board of mental retardation and developmental disabilities.

(B) County boards may charge the school district responsible for tuition an amount of excess cost calculated under this rule when the following occurs:

(1) The school district places or has placed a child with the county board for special education, but another district is responsible for tuition under Chapter 3313. of the Revised Code; and

(2) The child is not a resident of the territory served by the county board.

(C) Contracts shall be established between the public school district being assessed excess cost and the educating county board prior to the completion of the individualized education program or thereafter.

(D) Excess cost calculations shall be the average cost per student of all school-age students enrolled in the county board. The calculation of excess cost shall be completed by June thirtieth and shall include costs incurred for the fiscal year just completed.

(E) Payment of excess cost by the public school district shall be made directly to the educating county board.

(F) Public school districts assessed excess cost charges shall not be included as a tuition deduction on form SF-169.

(G) Excess cost calculations completed by a county board shall be based on the following and shall apply only to school-age programs:

(1) Expenditures for direct services of the teachers and aides, ancillary services excluding food service costs, program supervision, building services and maintenance, administrative, and transportation costs; and

(2) Classroom unit, ancillary service, and transportation reimbursement shall be deducted by the Ohio department of education, and the certified excess cost shall be reported to the county board.

History: Eff. 6-10-88; 11-1-77; 7-1-89

Chapter 3301-54
Payment for Contracted Special Education Units

3301-54-01 Rule for determining the amount of payment for contracted special education units.

(A) "Contracted special education units" are those funds which a school district or county board of mental retardation and developmental disabilities intends to use for services under division (C) of section 3317.05 of the Revised Code by contracting out such services under section 3323.08 or 5126.05 of the Revised Code.

(B) As provided in section 3317.052 of the Revised Code, the following contracted special education units are eligible for payment:

(1) Child study;

(2) Occupational therapy services;

(3) Physical therapy services; and

(4) Speech and language services.

(C) This rule shall apply to public school districts and county boards of mental retardation and developmental disabilities as provided by section 3317.052 of the Revised Code.

(D) A school district or a county board of mental retardation and developmental disabilities may be approved for a contracted special education unit. The following criteria applies:

(1) The contracted special education unit must have been approved by the division of special education, Ohio department of education, as a special education unit;

(2) The contracted special education unit must be in operation during the first full week of October and reported on the school district's or county board of mental retardation and developmental disabilities' "certificated staff-1" (CS-1 form);

(3) A request to convert the approved special education unit to a contracted special education unit must be made to the division of special education in accordance with established unit instructions and timelines; and

(4) The division of special education approval will be based upon a school district's or county board of mental retardation and developmental disabilities' ability to meet the above-mentioned criteria. Notification of this approval will be in accordance with established unit procedures.

(E) The amount paid for each approved contracted special education unit shall be calculated as follows:

(1) State minimum salary allowance for each approved contracted special education unit, or fraction of such unit, based upon the information submitted on the school district's or county board of mental retardation and developmental disabilities' CS-1 form;

(2) Fifteen per cent of the salary allowance; and

(3) Applicable unit allowance.

(F) The payment shall be made not later than the thirty-first day of December of the calendar year in which the fiscal year for which the units were approved ends.

(G) The personnel employed and approved for contracted special education units must hold the appropriate certification from the Ohio department of education.

History: Eff. 10-1-90

Chapter 3301-61
Vocational Education

3301-61-01 Statutory requirements.

All school districts shall comply with the Revised Code of the state of Ohio in matters relating to, but not limited to, operation and control of the school. Significant statutes concerning vocational education programs are the following:

(A) Section 3313.90 of the Revised Code, vocational education programs.

(B) Section 3313.91 of the Revised Code, purchase of vocational education from a private source.

(C) Section 3313.911 of the Revised Code, the state board may assign a district to a joint vocational district; petition against assignment; referendum.

(D) Section 3313.92 of the Revised Code, joint school building projects including school for handicapped children.

History: Replaces rule 3301-61-01, 3301-61-02; Eff. 1-30-75; 4-1-89

3301-61-02 Job training approval and ongoing compliance.

Each school district shall provide through an approved plan for vocational education job-training programs for eligible students based upon the following percentages:

Percentage of Graduates Entering College or Vocational Degree-Granting Higher Education Programs	Minimum Percentage of Students 16 Years of Age or Older for Whom Job-Training Programs Shall be Offered
50% or less	40%
51% - 60%	30%
61% - 70%	20%
71% - 80%	10%
81% or more	5%

History: Replaces rule 3301-61-03; Eff. 1-30-75; 4-1-89

3301-61-03 Criteria for job-training programs.

Each school district shall provide, through an approved plan for vocational education, a minimum of twelve different vocational education job-training offerings and twenty classes of vocational education under Chapter 3317. of the Revised Code. No more than four of the twelve offerings shall be provided by cooperative education methods. All job-training programs shall meet criteria and standards for vocational offerings established by the state board of education with consideration of present and future labor market trends. State/federal funds may be withdrawn from any approved vocational education job-training offering where, for three consecutive years, program completers fail to meet specified levels of accountability in terms of gainful employment, the military, or postsecondary education.

All approved vocational education job training offerings shall also have active local board-approved advisory committees that are composed of employers from any relevant industry or occupation for which the committee is established; trade or professional organizations representing any relevant occupations; and organized labor and other community representatives where appropriate. Each advisory committee shall meet at least once annually and the minutes of all official advisory committee meetings shall be kept on file as a part of each school district's official records.

History: Replaces rule 3301-61-04; Eff. 1-30-75; 4-1-89

3301-61-04 Allocation of funds.

Allocation of construction funds shall be made only to the district which has a minimum enrollment of one thousand five hundred students in grades nine through twelve and which provides the minimum required programs in an individual, joint, contractual or compact type arrangement. Because of the limitation of funds, districts or combination of districts with a minimum of three thousand students in grades nine through twelve will be given priority.

History: Replaces rule 3301-61-05; Eff. 1-30-75; 4-1-89

3301-61-05 Approval of request for funds.

State board procedures for the approval of requests for construction and equipment funds and for the submission of these requests for approval of the state controlling board shall be as follows:

(A) Funds shall not be allocated until the district or area plan for vocational education has been approved by the state board of education.

(B) After approval of a request for funds by the state board of education, a request for state funds shall be made to the state controlling board for release of funds for the project.

(C) Any district adversely affected by the determination of the division of vocational education or action of the state board of education may follow the procedure for appeal as outlined in Chapter 119. of the Revised Code.

(D) Procedures for applying for allocation of state and federal funds to match funds from the bureau of vocational rehabilitation shall follow the same procedure as for the allocation of construction and equipment funds.

History: Replaces rule 3301-61-06; Eff. 1-30-75; 4-1-89

3301-61-06 Criteria for contractual agreement between school districts.

Any contractual agreement between school districts for vocational offerings shall include:

(A) The provisions for physical facilities for the vocational offerings by one or more of the boards of education with one participating school district providing for no less than ten job-training offerings and sixteen classes.

(B) The tax source for building-needed vocational facilities and an agreement that each district will guarantee to pay a participation fee for students annually to the district which will be offering the vocational education program based upon the following formula:

(1) Districts enrolling sixty per cent or less of graduates in degree-granting higher education programs will guarantee to pay a participation fee to the district which will be offering the required scope of the vocational education program for a minimum of twenty per cent of the eleventh and twelfth grade enrollment.

(2) Districts enrolling sixty-one to seventy per cent of graduates in degree-granting higher education programs will guarantee to pay a participation fee to the district which will be offering the required scope of the vocational education program for a minimum of fifteen per cent of the eleventh and twelfth grade enrollment.

(3) Districts enrolling seventy-one to eighty per cent of its graduates in degree-granting higher education programs will guarantee to pay a participation fee to the district which will be offering the required scope of the vocational education program for a minimum of ten per cent of the eleventh and twelfth grade enrollment.

(4) Districts sending eighty-one per cent or more of its graduates to degree-granting higher education programs will guarantee to pay a participation fee to the district which will be offering the required scope of the vocational education program for a minimum of five per cent of the eleventh and twelfth grade enrollment.

(5) Districts that develop a creative or exemplary plan or plans for providing vocational education job-training offerings, in which provisions other than paragraphs (B)(1) to (B)(4) above are desirable, may establish mutually agreeable fiscal arrangements which shall be stated in such plan or plans.

(6) In districts operating under the provisions of paragraphs (B)(1) to (B)(4) above, a participation fee will be established. Participating districts are responsible to pay participation fees based upon the formula above even though less than the formula number of students participate in vocational classes in the vocational center.

(7) The amount due from the participating district shall be the product of the cost per pupil less the amount of state reimbursement per pupil to the receiving district times the number of students attending the vocational programs in the receiving district for no less than the per cent established by guaranteed percentages as listed in paragraphs (B)(1) to (B)(4) of this rule.

(8) In those cases where the superintendent of public instruction determines either that the approved vocational offerings of the district that is to pay the fee are of sufficient breadth to warrant a lower annual fee or that other factors warrant a lower annual fee, the superintendent of public instruction may recommend a lower fee to the state board of education.

(C) A plan for no less than five years, renewable on the basis of five-year periods. In cases where a board of education offering the required scope of the vocational education offerings has obligated funds for the construction and for equipping vocational facilities, the contract between the boards of education must cover a period of years necessary to amortize the obligation. Such contracts shall be with the approval of the state department of education.

(D) Arrangements for change in contractual relationships as contracts expire and new ones are written, or modification to such contractual arrangements during the life of the contract, must have approval of all participating districts and the state department of education.

(E) A guarantee that vocational education fees will be no more than those calculated by using the uniform school accounting system of the bureau of inspection and supervision of public offices of the auditor of state, as identified in the subject dimension of expenditures plus the proportional share of debt retirement in the fund dimension. If school district accounting records do not encompass the subject dimension, the procedure guide for secondary vocational education program costs established by the division of vocational and career education, state department of education, shall be used.

History: Replaces rule 3301-61-07; Eff. 10-1-80; 1-30-75; 4-1-89

3301-61-07 Revisions of vocational plans.

Revisions of plans for a vocational education planning district, individual district, or combination of districts, shall be submitted to the state board of education for approval at any meeting. Proposed amendments are to be submitted to the state department of education, division of vocational education, by the twentieth of the month prior to the month in which they are to be considered by the state board of education. In accordance with section 3313.90 of the Revised Code, in approving the organization for vocational education, the state board of education shall provide that no school district is excluded in the statewide plan.

History: Replaces rule 3301-61-08; Eff. 1-30-75; 4-1-89

3301-61-08 Prohibitions on grant programs.

In grant programs which support the provision of health, education or welfare services, discrimination in the selection or eligibility of individuals to receive the services, and segregation or other discriminatory practices in the manner of providing them, are prohibited. This prohibition extends to all facilities and services provided by the grantee under the program or, if the grantee is the state, by a political subdivision of the state. It extends also to services purchased or otherwise obtained by the grantee or political subdivision, and to the facilities in which such services are provided, subject, however, to the provisions of Title VI of the Civil Rights Act of 1964, 78 Stat. 252; Title IX of the Education Amendments of 1972, 86 Stat. 373; and section 504 of the Rehabilitation Act of 1973, 87 Stat. 394, as written on the effective date of this rule.

History: Replaces rule 3301-61-09; Eff. 1-30-75; 4-1-89

3301-61-09 Exemptions to enrollment requirement and job-training programs.

Exemptions to the minimum requirement of one thousand five hundred students in grades nine through twelve may be made by the state board of education based on sparsity of population or other factors indicating that comprehensive educational and vocational programs can be provided through an alternate plan. School districts enrolling forty per cent or more of their eligible students in vocational education job-training programs may be exempt from offering twelve programs and twenty classes but must provide no less than ten job-training programs and sixteen classes.

History: Replaces rule 3301-61-10; Eff. 1-30-75; 4-1-89

3301-61-10 Provisions for nonpublic school students.

Each vocational education planning district shall provide the opportunity for all eligible nonpublic school students with legal residence within the geographic boundaries of the public school district to participate in the vocational job-training programs without financial assessment, charge, or tuition to such student, except such assessments, charges, or tuition paid by resident public school students in such programs. The nonpublic school students shall be included in the average daily membership of the school district maintaining the vocational education program as a part-time student in proportion to the time spent in the vocational education program.

History: Replaces rule 3301-61-11; Eff. 1-30-75; 4-1-89

3301-61-11 Compliance.

Except for good and sufficient reason established to the satisfaction of both the state board of education and the state controlling board, if the state board of education determines that a school district has failed to comply with section 3313.90 of the Revised Code, such school district shall be subject to a ten per cent reduction of funds as provided by section 3317.023 of the Revised Code and computed under section 3317.022 of the Revised Code. In making such determination, the state board of education shall observe the requirements of the Administrative Procedure Act, Chapter 119. of the Revised Code.

History: Replaces rule 3301-61-12; Eff. 1-30-75; 4-1-89

3301-61-12 Full-time equivalent students for vocational education.

Full-time equivalent vocational students shall be determined by multiplying the number of hours per week in vocational programs by the number of students enrolled full time in the total instructional program and dividing the product by thirty (the number of educational hours possible in the school week). The resulting quotient is the number of full-time equivalent students to be reported as full-time equivalents for vocational units.

History: Replaces rule 3301-61-13; Eff. 4-1-89

3301-61-13 Standard for extended service for vocational education.

The following provisions shall be applied in determining and granting extended service funding for vocational programs:

(A) All approved vocational education instructional programs are eligible for extended service consideration and may be approved for state subsidy support based upon application from a local education agency.

(B) Extended service shall be granted for vocational education instructional programs required by licensing agencies or boards to provide instruction that exceeds the time allotments within the regular school year.

(C) Extended service shall be provided for those vocational education programs in which instruction is required beyond the school year:

(1) Agricultural education:

(a) Agricultural production and farm management--For approved programs, twelve weeks of extended service shall be provided and may be approved for funding. The twelve weeks shall be prorated when offered in combination with other programs which qualify for less extended service.

(b) Animal production and care--For all two-year programs, an extended service period of four weeks shall be provided and may be approved for funding.

(c) Agriculture resource conservation and recreation--For all two-year programs, twelve weeks of extended service shall be provided and may be approved for funding.

(d) Horticulture--For all two-year programs, an extended service period of eight weeks shall be provided and may be approved for funding. No more than two eight-week periods of extended service may be funded in a three-year horticulture program.

(e) Forestry--For all two-year programs, an extended service period of twelve weeks shall be provided and may be approved for funding provided that such programs consist of an eleventh grade laboratory and a twelfth grade cooperative course.

(f) Agricultural-industrial equipment and mechanics--For all two-year programs, an extended service period of four weeks shall be provided beyond the regular school year and may be approved for funding.

(g) Agricultural products processing--For all two-year programs, two weeks of extended service shall be provided and may be approved for funding.

(h) Environmental management--For all two-year programs, two weeks of extended service shall be provided and may be approved for funding.

(2) Home economics:

(a) Consumer homemaking--For all teachers with .75 to 1.00 units, an extended service period of two weeks shall be provided and may be approved for funding. For all teachers with less than .75 units, an extended service period of one week shall be provided and may be approved for funding.

(b) Impact--For all programs, an extended service period of two weeks shall be provided and may be approved for funding.

(c) GRADS (graduation, reality, and dual role skills)--For all programs, an extended service period of two weeks shall be provided and may be approved for funding.

(D) Extended service for cooperative programs shall be provided beyond the regular school year:

(1) Employment shall be continuous and immediately prior to the opening and/or immediately following the closing of the school year. Employment immediately following the school year shall be limited to a maximum of one week.

(2) A minimum of four weeks for new teacher-coordinators in a community and/or for the initiation of new programs in a community.

(3) A minimum of three weeks for teacher-coordinators in programs that exclusively serve at-risk, disadvantaged, and handicapped students.

(4) A minimum of two weeks for all other teacher-coordinators.

(E) Approved extended service for vocational teachers shall not be in conflict with other school-related education-sanctioned duties and/or assignments, including professional education requirements for teacher certification.

History: Replaces rule 3301-61-15; Eff. 1-1-83; 8-1-80; 1-1-83; 4-1-89

3301-61-14 Rule for the provisions for the vocational school building assistance fund.

(A) Any school district which is designated as the

primary provider of secondary job training programs and which offers the minimum scope of twelve programs and twenty classes as set forth in state board of education standards for vocational education is eligible to make application for loan funds.

(B) The applicant district shall demonstrate financial need for the loan with reference to levels of assessed valuation, enrollment levels and enrollment changes, ability of the district to maintain minimum education standards, and show a good faith effort to secure funds from sources other than the state.

(C) Loan funds shall not be allotted until the district or area plan for vocational education has been approved by the state board of education.

(D) Districts with an approved construction and equipment proposal filed prior to March 1, 1990, shall receive priority for fund distribution.

(E) The division of vocational and career education, department of education shall prepare uniform procedures including the loan application and loan agreement.

(F) Applicant school districts may file loan applications between the first day of July and the thirtieth day of June in any fiscal year.

(G) Only after verification of funds availability, agreement to terms by the eligible recipient, state board of education approval, and release of funds by the state controlling board shall the state board of education enter into a loan agreement.

(H) The applicant district shall demonstrate the ability to repay the loan, and the repayment of loans shall not exceed fifteen years for construction loans and five years for equipment loans with the repayment schedule not to exceed semiannual payments as specified in the loan agreement.

(I) If any district defaults on the repayment plan by more than sixty days and cannot reach accord for a revised repayment plan approved by the state department of education, the state department of education shall proceed to withhold an amount equal to the annual repayment schedule from the state foundation payment or other state subsidy programs in effect at the time of defaultation.

(J) All repayments to said loan fund and any interest earned on moneys deposited with the state shall be deposited in the vocational school building loan fund for reallocation by the state board of education.

(K) Loans made through this fund shall be interest free and shall not be considered in calculating the net indebtedness of the school district for purposes of section 133.06 of the Revised Code.

(L) Loan approval procedures and criteria for prioritization shall include:

(1) The innovative and creative approaches to the implementation of the modernization plan for vocational education pursuant to section 3313.901 of the Revised Code.

(2) The articulation agreements of applicant districts with technical colleges and other institutions of higher education and post-secondary technical education programs or the sharing of facilities and equipment.

(M) Any district adversely affected by the determination of the division of vocational and career education, department of education, or action of the state board of education may follow the procedure for appeal as outlined in Chapter 119. of the Revised Code.

History: Eff. 4-1-91

3301-61-15 Rule for the maintenance of records and reporting district membership of adult students whose enrollment is used to calculate unit reimbursement in secondary vocational education occupationally specific programs.

(A) Section 3317.053 of the Revised Code permits the state board of education to count persons not otherwise to be included in school districts average daily membership (ADM) towards the calculation of unit funding. This rule specifies the recordkeeping and reporting of any individuals enrolled under the aforementioned section of the Revised Code.

(B) Definitions.

(1) "Record of district membership" is all items required in the education management information system (EMIS) including all demographic, attendance, and course elements as reported in the October and June student counts.

(2) "Person" means an adult who is a resident of the state of Ohio who has graduated or reached his twenty-second birthday and who is either a resident of the district or an in-state non-resident paying tuition.

(3) "Not eligible to be included in a district average daily membership" means one who is unable to be included in the ADM under section 3317.05 of the Revised Code.

(4) "Participation" means enrolled in the total program of vocational education including laboratory and related instruction with the expressed intention of completing the entire program for the purpose of occupational preparation.

(5) "Secondary vocational education job training unit" means occupationally specific job training programs.

(C) General provisions.

(1) School districts wishing to enroll persons under the provisions of section 3317.053 of the Revised Code

must maintain the following records:

(a) Student records for each person in EMIS including all demographic, attendance, and course elements as reported in the October and June student counts.

(b) Each person must be reported in a grade level as an "adult, non-high school completor" or "adult, high school completor."

(c) Each person must be identified as having a student status as a "resident," "in-state non-resident tuition," or "in-state, non-resident, vocational contract student."

(d) Student percentage of time in the vocational program.

(e) Joint vocational school districts (JVSD's) must also furnish information as if the student were coming from one of the JVSD membership districts. Information required includes district of residence, attending/home indicator, and attending/home district information retrieval number (IRN).

(2) School districts enrolling persons under the provisions of section 3317.053 of the Revised Code shall annually report to the state board of education the number of persons for whom a record is maintained through the appropriate EMIS reports submitted by the school district.

History: Eff. 10-1-94

Chapter 3301-67
Distribution of Funds to Joint Vocational Schools for Academics

3301-67-01 Criteria for distribution of funds to joint vocational schools for academics.

(A) Definitions.

(1) "Board of education" is a board of a school district as defined by section 3311.01 of the Revised Code and refers to city, local, exempted village, county, joint high school, and joint vocational school districts.

(2) "Joint vocational school" is a school district formed under section 3313.90 of the Revised Code with the major goal of providing vocational education program opportunities for persons to gain the skills and knowledge required for employability.

(3) "Academics" are those nonelective courses required for high school graduation as identified by Chapter 3301-35 of the Administrative Code relating to minimum standards for elementary and secondary schools.

(B) General provisions.

(1) A joint vocational school district may receive a payment for educational courses, other than vocational education unit-funded courses, necessary to meet the requirements for graduation from a participating school district of the joint vocational school by meeting the criteria defined in this rule.

(2) Such reimbursement is to be allocated for the sole purpose of financially supporting state-required academic courses offered on-site at joint vocational schools which:

(a) Enhance technological and occupational competencies of vocationally enrolled students sixteen years of age and older; and/or

(b) Are required for graduation under Chapter 3301-35 of the Administrative Code.

(3) A minimum of twelve academic classes must be offered in a joint vocational district to be eligible for this funding.

(4) The formula for distribution of funds is based on a per vocational unit add-on for those joint vocational schools which meet the eligibility requirements set forth in paragraphs (B)(2) and (B)(3) of this rule, and is calculated at eight per cent of the value of the secondary vocational units.

(C) Limitations on funds.

(1) Annually, a priority obligation for funding the specified number of vocational education units is to be met with any remaining dollars thereafter allocated for eligible courses on the formula basis as outlined in this rule.

(2) If available dollars are insufficient to meet formula obligations, a uniform percentage reduction to joint vocational schools shall be made.

History: Eff. 8-1-88

Chapter 3301-81
Driver Education

3301-81-01 Availability of driver and traffic safety education programs.

(A) Each public board of education shall make a driver education course available to each resident pupil and/or school-age youth during the semester or term of the pupil's sixteenth birthday or the immediate succeeding semester or term. It is recommended that the driver education course be made available during the regular school day; however, additional classes may be conducted after school, on weekends and during summer school.

Each public board of education shall develop a driver and traffic safety education course of study which shall include rules 3301-81-02 and 3301-81-03 of the

Administrative Code.

(B) Pupils enrolled in driver education shall be provided instruction in both classroom and laboratory phases in the same semester or the following semester. The complete course must be completed within nine months. Pupils shall be sixteen years of age on or before actual behind-the-wheel instruction is started. Behind-the-wheel instruction shall not begin until nine hours of classroom instruction is completed. The summer term shall mean semester for purposes of this rule.

(C) The Ohio department of education shall subsidize fifty dollars times the number of pupils completing the approved course. Students must complete the entire course pursuant to rule 3301-81-02 of the Administrative Code to be claimed for the driver education subsidy.

(D) Such courses may be provided as follows: (1) By a school for which the state board of education prescribes minimum standards as stated in rules 3301-35-01 to 3301-35-08 of the Administrative Code. The course shall consist of the standard sixty-hour course.

(2) One public school contracting with another public school.

(3) Through contract by a public school with a commercial driver training school licensed under section 4508.03 of the Revised Code for the purpose of providing instruction under section 3301.17 of the Revised Code and meets length of course as set forth in rule 3301-81-02 of the Administrative Code and course content standards as set forth in rule 3301-81-03 of the Administrative Code. Teachers teaching the classroom phase shall hold a provisional or higher grade certificate with driver education endorsed on the certificate.

Such course shall be taught in classrooms of a high school meeting minimum standards as stated in paragraph (D)(1) of this rule, and to the extent practicable, shall be provided to pupils at their school of attendance.

(4) Through contractual arrangements negotiated and supervised by the Ohio department of education area coordinators.

(5) By state-supported and special purpose schools which have been approved by the Ohio department of education. No state subsidy, pursuant to section 3301.17 of the Revised Code, shall be made for these students.

(E) Public boards of education are responsible for providing a course of driver education to all resident youth through twenty-one years of age including, but not limited to, the following:

(1) Those individuals twenty-one years of age who have graduated from high school and who could not enroll in driver education while in high school.

(2) Those individuals who have dropped out of high school and could not enroll in driver education while in high school.

(3) Those individuals who moved into Ohio from another state and have not completed an approved driver education course in another state.

(4) Those individuals who are handicapped.

(F) To ensure availability of driver education to all resident pupils, the high school principal may release a student to attend a commercial driver training school licensed under Chapter 4508. of the Revised Code, by confirming that the pupil(s) could not enroll in a course of driver education in the regular high school program due to scheduling difficulties, or because the course was not available, pursuant to paragraph (A) of this rule, or the student is employed or involved in a hardship pursuant to section 3301.17 of the Revised Code.

(G) Public boards of education may employ a teacher to teach driver education in the nonpublic school as a full-time or part-time teacher. The public board of education may claim the nonpublic students for subsidy payment under section 3301.17 of the Revised Code. Nonpublic students enrolled in a course of driver education may be included in the average daily membership on form ADM-1 for foundation calculation under section 3317.03 of the Revised Code.

(H) County or joint vocational school district boards of education may conduct approved driver education courses.

History: Eff. 8-15-77; 8-1-72; 10-1-88

3301-81-02 Length of course.

(A) Each board of education shall make the standard high school driver education course available to all eligible students and school-age youth which shall consist of a minimum of sixty hours. A request for an exception to this paragraph may be approved by the Ohio department of education.

The courses shall be as follows:

(1) The standard sixty-hour course shall include thirty-six hours of classroom instruction and twenty-four hours of laboratory instruction of which six hours shall be actual behind-the-wheel instruction, or forty-two hours of classroom instruction and eighteen hours of laboratory instruction of which six hours shall be actual behind-the-wheel instruction.

(2) The standard sixty-hour high school driver education course shall be a minimum of four weeks duration.

(B) The following also applies to the instruction and laboratory phases of driver education:

(1) When a multimedia programmed learning

system is included as a phase of the standard sixty-hour driver education course, it shall replace no more than twenty hours of classroom instruction.

Special permission for multimedia programs shall be secured from the Ohio department of education. When state-owned driving simulation and multimedia equipment is leased to a school district, it shall be used a minimum of four hours a day during the time school is in regular session.

(2) When simulation is included as a phase of the standard sixty-hour driver education course, twelve hours of simulation may substitute for two hours of behind-the-wheel instruction, and six hours of observation time.

(3) Multiple car off-street driving ranges may be used to substitute for a designated number of hours of behind-the-wheel instruction. The number of hours of substitution shall be determined by the Ohio department of education and shall depend upon the size and design of the range. Simulation and multimedia systems may be used in conjunction with driving range facilities. Written approval from the Ohio department of education shall be required for the district to establish and maintain a driving range.

When multiple car off-street driving range facilities are provided by the Ohio department of education, they shall be used a minimum of four hours a day during the time school is in regular session.

(4) A pupil may not be enrolled in more than four hours of in-car instruction of which no more than two hours are behind-the-wheel instruction during one calendar day.

(5) At no time shall a driver education teacher or laboratory aide instructor conduct behind-the-wheel instruction with fewer than two students in the car.

History: Eff. 8-15-77; 8-1-72; 10-1-88

3301-81-03 Course content.

Course content shall include, but not be limited to, instruction and evaluation in the following areas:

(A) Basic and advanced driving techniques including development of perceptual skills and interpretation of driving situations and techniques for handling emergencies.

(B) Rules of the road and other federal, state and local motor vehicle laws and ordinances, including the current Ohio publications relative to traffic laws.

(C) Critical vehicle systems and subsystems which require preventive maintenance.

(D) The vehicle, highway and community features:

(1) That aid the driver in avoiding crashes.

(2) That protect the driver and passengers in crashes.

(3) That aid in the prompt and proper care of the injured.

(E) Signs, signals, highway markings and highway design features which require understanding for safe operation of motor vehicles.

(F) Differences in the characteristics of urban, suburban and rural driving, including safe use of modern multilane expressways.

(G) Pedestrian safety.

(H) Bicycle, motorcycle, and other two-wheel vehicle safety.

(I) School crossing, railroad crossing, and other critical areas.

(J) School bus passenger safety.

(K) Accident causation, analysis and reporting.

(L) Attitudes and responsibilities which contribute to highway safety.

(M) Alcohol and drugs and their relation to highway safety.

(N) Vision, fatigue and other impairments relating to safe driving.

(O) Sharing the roadway with school buses, trucks, slow-moving and emergency vehicles.

(P) Danger of objects being dropped from overhead passes.

(Q) Recreational vehicles, all-terrain vehicles and the towing of trailers.

(R) Consumer economics: purchase, maintenance, and insurance of a vehicle.

(S) Energy conservation information.

(T) Front-wheel and four-wheel drive vehicles.

Textbooks shall be reviewed every five years for applicability to current driver education practices.

History: Eff. 8-15-77; 8-1-72; 10-1-88

3301-81-04 Teachers and laboratory aide instructors.

(A) Classroom teacher qualifications. Teacher qualifications shall apply to all teachers providing classroom instruction under rule 3301-81-01 of the Administrative Code. These qualifications do not apply to courses operated under Chapter 4508. of the Revised Code or paragraph (D)(3) of rule 3301-81-01 of the Administrative Code.

(1) Teachers providing classroom, simulation, multimedia and/or range instruction shall hold a provisional or higher grade certificate with driver education endorsed on the certificate. This certificate shall be issued by the division of teacher education and certification of the Ohio department of education

pursuant to rule 3301-23-20 of the Administrative Code.

(2) Each driver education teacher shall meet the following criteria:

(a) Have a minimum of five years driving experience;

(b) Hold a valid driver's license;

(c) Have no felony convictions;

(d) Have good physical health as evidenced by a health certificate signed by a doctor of medicine, licensed in the state of Ohio, upon the request of the board of education;

(e) Teachers seeking certification under this rule shall present evidence of successful completion of six semester or nine quarter hours of college credit in driver and traffic safety education.

(3) Teachers meeting the qualifications of paragraphs (A)(1) and (A)(2) of this rule are qualified to teach all phases of the driver education curriculum. (4) Substitute teachers for driver education must meet all qualifications of the regular certified driver education teacher as prescribed in paragraph (A) of this rule.

(B) Laboratory aide instructor qualifications. In addition to the classroom driver education teacher, a board of education may employ laboratory aide instructors to teach the behind-the-wheel phase of driver education. The laboratory aide instructor shall meet the following:

(1) Have a high school diploma or a statement of high school equivalence issued by the division of guidance and testing, Ohio department of education;

(2) Have a minimum of five years driving experience;

(3) Hold a valid driver's license;

(4) Have no felony convictions;

(5) Have good physical health as evidenced by a health certificate signed by a doctor of medicine in the state of Ohio within six months of the time of application;

(6) Complete a forty-hour driver education course prior to employment:

This pre-employment course shall be conducted by an educational institution approved by the driver education section, Ohio department of education, and shall include methods of behind-the-wheel instruction.

(7) Complete eighty additional hours of inservice instruction during the first two years of employment, forty hours each year:

The eighty hours of inservice instruction shall be conducted by an educational institution approved by the driver education section, Ohio department of education, and shall include methods of behind-the-wheel instruction.

(8) Hold an educational aide permit, valid for one year, issued upon evidence of completion of the forty-hour inservice instruction requirement.

Individuals meeting the criteria of paragraphs (B)(1) to (B)(8) of this rule will be issued an educational aide permit. This permit will be renewed upon written request from the superintendent of the district employing the laboratory aide instructor. The request shall include evidence of completion of the required additional inservice training. These permits will be issued by the division of teacher education and certification, Ohio department of education.

(C) Divisions (J) and (K) of section 4507.40 of the Revised Code shall disqualify any driver education teacher or any laboratory aide instructor from teaching any phase of the course in driver education. In addition, prior to being judged qualified, and annually thereafter, the Ohio department of education shall supply the names of all driver education teachers to the motor vehicle licensing agency, and shall in return receive the driving record of each person for evaluation to help determine their suitability to continue to serve as teachers of driver education.

(D) No person shall be permitted to teach any phase of driver education within two years from the date of a driving while intoxicated (DWI) conviction.

(E) The department of education shall notify a school district superintendent when a driver education teacher or instructor accumulates six or more points on their driving record within a two-year period. The superintendent will evaluate the report and determine continued use of the teacher or instructor.

History: Eff. 8-15-77; 8-1-72; 10-1-88

3301-81-05 Course credit.

Driver and traffic safety education courses shall carry credit toward graduation when conducted entirely by the public or nonpublic school. Whether completed as a separate course or part of another course in a school for which the state board of education prescribes minimum standards, pupils shall be granted credit under the same standards that credit is granted for the satisfactory completion of any other course. Pupils completing driver training courses provided wholly or in part by commercial driver training schools shall not be granted credit.

Upon satisfactory completion of a driver education course in another school district, the pupil's record and course credit shall be transferred to the resident school district.

History: Eff. 8-1-72; 8-15-77; 10-1-88

3301-81-06 Parental consent.

No pupil shall be enrolled for the behind-the-wheel phase of a driver education course without the written consent of parent or guardian.

(A) The parental consent shall state that the parent or guardian is knowledgeable of and consents to the student enrolling in a driver education course.

(B) A temporary driving permit shall be in the possession of the pupil during behind-the-wheel instruction.

History: Eff. 8-15-77; 8-1-72; 10-1-88

3301-81-07 Driver training vehicles.

(A) Cars provided for all behind-the-wheel instruction shall be in safe mechanical condition, equipped with dual controls, instructor's inside mirror, seat belts for all occupants, and outside rear view mirrors installed on the right and left sides of the vehicles.

(B) All vehicles used for driver education shall be so marked with a rooftop sign visible at a distance of three hundred feet.

(C) All vehicles used for driver education shall be properly registered on an inventory form provided by the Ohio department of education.

(D) Vehicles obtained or used in driver education shall be used exclusively for that purpose.

(E) Public boards of education are authorized to pay a service or lease charge for driver education vehicles and include such charge when reporting annual cost.

History: Eff. (Amended) 8-1-72; 8-15-77

3301-81-08 Subsidy payment.

No subsidy payment will be made to public boards of education prior to annual course approval and/or for failure to file designated forms on the dates established by the Ohio department of education.

Public schools will be subsidized fifty dollars for each student who completes the driver education course. Such funds shall be used solely for the purpose of promoting highway safety through driver education.

(A) Two copies of all subsidy forms, as supplied by the Ohio department of education area coordinator's office, shall be filed in the Ohio department of education area coordinator's office on the required date in order for a school district to be eligible for subsidy payment.

(B) Public boards of education may include the nonpublic pupils in the average daily membership on form ADM-1 who are enrolled in a course of driver education during the first full week of October.

(C) Districts may include teachers who are teaching driver education during the summer for purposes of extended service calculations.

(D) Section 3301.17 of the Revised Code and the Ohio attorney general's opinion no. 76-019 restricts payment of funds by a local board of education to a commercial driver training facility prior to the actual receipt of school funds from the Ohio department of education.

History: Replaces rule 3301-81-09; Eff. 8-15-77; 8-1-72; 10-1-88

3301-81-09 Driver education certificate of completion.

(A) The high school driver education certificate of completion will be distributed to school districts from the Ohio department of education area coordinator's office.

(B) All certificates shall be correctly completed and typed for acceptance by the Ohio highway patrol driver examiner.

(C) The driver education certificate of completion shall not be duplicated. A copy of a certificate shall be invalid.

(D) Replacement driver education certificates will be issued from the Ohio department of education area coordinator's office upon receipt of a replacement request for a lost driver education certificate.

The replacement request for a lost driver education certificate shall be verified by a school official, signed by the student and notarized.

(E) Out-of-state transfer driver education certificates will be issued to the school district from the Ohio department of education area coordinator's office upon verification of a pupil's satisfactory completion of an approved driver education course in another state.

(F) An out-of-state student shall furnish the receiving school district in Ohio a transcript or certificate of completion from the former school, which indicates successful completion of a driver education course in that state. The course must be approved by the department of public instruction in that state.

History: Replaces rule 3301-81-10; Eff. 8-15-77; 8-1-72; 10-1-88

3301-81-10 Purchase of liability insurance.

For purposes of driver education courses, a board of education of any school district may procure a policy or policies of insurance pursuant to section 3313.201 of the Revised Code.

History: Replaces rule 3301-81-11; Eff. 8-15-77; 8-1-72; 10-1-88

3301-81-11 Driver education program approval.

Driver education courses for which the state board of education prescribes minimum standards shall be evaluated and approved annually by the Ohio department of education, field service section. The accumulated information shall be forwarded to the national highway traffic safety administration as required by "Highway Safety Program Standard 4" for driver education.

History: Replaces rule 3301-81-12; Eff. 8-15-77; 8-1-72; 10-1-88

3301-81-12 Maximum consecutive hours to be spent in behind-the-wheel phase of instruction by the teacher.

A teacher instructing the behind-the-wheel on-street phase of a driver education course shall spend no more than four consecutive hours at a time teaching in the car. After a teacher has spent four consecutive hours engaged in behind-the-wheel instruction, a minimum period of one-half hour shall elapse before additional instruction is given.

History: Replaces rule 3301-81-13; Eff. 8-15-77; 8-1-72; 10-1-88

3301-81-13 Applicability of driver education rules.

This chapter applies solely to pupils enrolled in driver education courses which are regulated and approved by the Ohio department of education. This chapter does not pertain to adult education classes.

History: Replaces rule 3301-81-15; Eff. 8-15-77; 8-1-72; 10-1-88

3301-81-14 Compliance.

Any school district not complying with all the rules in this chapter shall not receive course approval for the driver education curriculum and shall not receive a driver education subsidy payment.

History: Replaces rule 3301-81-16; Eff. 8-15-77; 8-1-72; 10-1-88

Chapter 3301-83
Pupil Transportation

3301-83-01 Calculation of pupil transportation operation payments.

(A) Authority - Pupil transportation operation payment amount for each school district may be determined as prescribed the General Assembly, in section 3317.024 of the Revised Code.

(B) Eligibility - Fiscal year payment for pupil transportation operation shall be made to all city, exempted village, and local school districts eligible for school foundation funding as provided for by Chapter 3317. of the Revised Code.

(C) Formula for calculation of payment amounts

(1) Type I (board-owned and operated school buses) - The greater of:

(a) An amount for the number of eligible pupils transported, as determined by multiplying the number of eligible pupils by a per pupil amount approved by the state board of education; or

(b) An amount for the approved total annual miles traveled as determined by multiplying the total annual miles by a per mile amount approved by the state board of education.

(2) Type II (contractor-owned and operated school buses) - The greater of:

(a) An amount for the number of eligible pupils transported, as determined by multiplying the number of eligible pupils by a per pupil amount approved by the state board of education; or

(b) An amount for the approved total annual miles traveled, as determined by multiplying the total annual miles by a per mile amount approved by the state board of education.

(3) Type III (public utility) - An amount for the number of eligible pupils transported, as determined by multiplying the number of eligible pupils by a per pupil amount approved by the state board of education.

(4) Type IV (payment to parent or guardian) - Payment shall be determined by multiplying the number of eligible pupils by a per pupil amount approved by the

state board of education.

(5) Type V (board-owned vehicles other than school buses) - An amount for the approved total annual miles traveled, as determined by multiplying the total annual miles by a per mile amount approved by the state board of education.

(6) Type VI (privately owned vehicles other than school buses) - An amount for the approved total annual miles traveled, as determined by multiplying the total annual miles by a per mile amount approved by the state board of education.

(D) Reporting and annual adjustments

(1) Each school district shall file annual reports of all pupils transported, miles traveled, actual costs, and other necessary information for the purposes of calculation and adjustments in amount due. Pupils transported and miles traveled shall be reported by vehicle for any one day during the first full week of October that school is in session. Actual cost shall be reported by vehicle on or before the twentieth of July following the close of the fiscal year.

(2) All adjustments by transportation service type shall be made within the first quarter following the close of the fiscal year.

(E) Vehicles approved for use and operational payment

(1) Board-owned and operated school buses - A vehicle operated by a qualified driver meeting the definition of a school bus successfully passing the annual state highway patrol safety inspection assigned a school bus identification number and painted national school bus chrome with proper black lettering. Vehicle met or exceeded Ohio school bus minimum standards at the time of construction.

(2) Contractor-owned school buses - A vehicle meeting all the requirements of a board-owned school bus and requirement of licensing by the Ohio department of highway safety and bonding as required by law.

(3) Public transit vehicles - Vehicles owned and operated by regional transit authorities, community transit authorities, or privately owned, under contract with a board of education and operated on routes designed for the purpose of transporting fare-paying passengers and eligible students simultaneously.

(4) Board-owned vehicles other than school buses - A vehicle, nine-passenger or less, not including driver, with no school bus identification other than school district name.

(5) Privately owned vehicle other than school buses - A vehicle, nine-passenger or less, not including driver, used for transportation of pupils from the place of residence to the nearest pick-up point on a regular school bus route. Residence must be five-tenths of one mile or more from the pick-up point and inaccessible by regular school bus.

(F) Vehicles approved for activity use only

(1) A "school activity bus" is a school bus which meets all the requirements of the Ohio school bus minimum construction standards, Chapter 3301-87 of the Administrative Code.

(2) School activity buses are permitted to use the following items which are not permitted on route buses: interior book racks, coach type seats, exterior roof luggage racks, and independent auxiliary engine-powered air-conditioning.

(3) School activity buses may be used as the board of education or county board of mental retardation/developmental disabilities policy permits. Use of the activity bus shall not conflict with commercial bus operations. Use of the activity bus shall comply with all applicable state and federal laws and rules.

(4) Activity buses shall not be used on regular routes.

(5) Activity buses are not eligible for school bus purchase assistance.

(6) Any activity bus currently in use shall comply with these rules.

(G) Operational regulations

(1) An "eligible pupil," for payment purposes:

(a) Is one whose place of residence is one mile or more from the school of assignment for public school pupils and school of attendance in case of nonpublic pupils when measured in the following manner: "Measurement of distance originates at a point on the traveled portion of the roadway nearest the primary entrance to the place of residence and then along the most direct route traversable by motor vehicle to the school bus loading area nearest and opposite the entrance door used by pupils transported"; and

(b) Is transported from a pick-up point one-half mile or less from the place of residence, to a school of assignment in the case of public school pupils, and to the school of attendance in the case of nonpublic school pupils and who is returned from the school of assignment or attendance to the designated pick-up point; and

(c) Is enrolled in grades kindergarten through twelve and regularly transported to and from a public school; or

(d) Is enrolled in grades kindergarten through twelve and regularly transported to and from a nonpublic school chartered by the state board of education and eligible for transportation service.

(2) Nonresident non-open enrollment pupils regularly transported may be reported for payment purposes only when such pupils are released by the district of residence.

Miles traveled to transport eligible pupils participating in an open enrollment program may be reported for payment purposes by the resident district from home to the designated border pick-up point and by the educating school district from the border pick-up point to the building of attendance in the educating district. If the educating district or the resident district provides all the open enrollment transportation for a student, the miles may be reported by the district providing the service.

(3) Miles traveled from bus storage location or school building to first student pick-up, all route miles, and return to storage both a.m. and p.m., including kindergarten miles, are approved for payment purposes.

(4) Miles traveled to and from storage locations outside the county or counties of the school district location are not approved miles for payment purposes. Miles traveled from county line to first pick-up and return to county line are approved miles.

(5) Total annual miles for payment purposes shall be calculated by multiplying total daily miles by one hundred eighty days.

(6) Recalculation of pupil transportation operation payment amount due may be approved when:

(a) Local board policy or routing is revised to provide transportation service for additional pupils or increased miles on or before the first of February, and providing such change in policy is to continue in effect for the remainder of the school year.

(b) A nonpublic school is chartered for operation subsequent to the initial reporting period.

(c) School district erroneously reports or Ohio department of education errs in actual calculation of amount due.

(7) School districts contracting with transit authorities for the purpose of transporting eligible pupils to and from school shall require the transit authority director to file with the board of education actual operational costs in excess of, or less than, reimbursement as provided for by paragraph (C)(3) of this rule. Such report shall be filed with the board of education at the close of each fiscal year. Each board of education shall file with the Ohio department of education all transit authority and local board costs on or before the twentieth day of July of each year.

(8) Type IV, payment to parent or guardian in lieu of transportation service for eligible pupils whose transportation is deemed impractical by school conveyance, must be declared as being impractical by board of education resolution. Payment under this type will not be made for pupils who live within two miles of their school of attendance.

Post-secondary transportation shall be reported as Type IV when pupils are eligible for such reimbursement under law and any rules adopted by the state board of education.

(9) For payment purposes, all school districts providing transportation service to nonpublic or vocational schools on days public schools are not in session and shuttle service to joint vocational schools may report on forms provided by the Ohio department of education such additional miles.

History: Eff. 11-1-75; 12-28-77; 12-28-79; 3-22-82; 4-1-84; 5-1-86; 4-1-88; 4-27-90; 5-1-92; 5-6-94

3301-83-03 Purpose.

The purpose of these rules is to reduce and prevent, to the greatest extent possible, death of or injury to pupils and to ensure uniform, economical and efficient pupil transportation operations.

History: Eff. 10-22-84

3301-83-04 Scope.

The rules in this chapter are designed to establish minimum requirements for a safe pupil transportation program, including management, general operation, maintenance of school buses, training of personnel, pupil management, driver qualifications and emergency procedures.

These rules shall apply to all transportation operations and services to pupils transported by county boards of mental retardation and developmental disabilities and any school or school district chartered or approved by the state board of education.

History: Eff. 10-22-84; 7-1-91

3301-83-05 Administration.

(A) The state agencies responsible for pupil transportation may assist in pupil transportation operation and safety by providing:

(1) Leadership;

(2) Management;

(3) Safety programs;

(4) Training programs.

(B) The state agencies responsible for pupil transportation shall assist in pupil transportation operation and safety by providing:

(1) Disbursement of state funding;

(2) Minimum standards for school bus construction;

(3) Minimum standards for pupil transportation operations;

(4) Forms and reports.

(C) The board of education or county board of mental retardation and developmental disabilities may designate a transportation supervisor to administer the transportation program and shall be responsible for the management and supervision of:

(1) Personnel;

(2) Safety;

(3) Training;

(4) Operations;

(5) Maintenance.

History: Eff. 10-22-84; 7-1-91

3301-83-06 Personnel qualifications.

(A) The transportation supervisor

The pupil transportation supervisor and/or private operator should have an understanding of the educational process and the role of transportation in this process.

Qualifications shall include:

(1) A satisfactory driving record as revealed through checks made by the employing agency.

(2) A satisfactory work history as verified through professional references.

(3) A report of the state bureau of criminal identification and investigation and/or local law enforcement agency.

(4) Post-high school education or work experience in education, business administration, management or transportation as determined by the board of education or county board of mental retardation and developmental disabilities.

(5) The ability to work with a broad range of individuals and organizations.

(6) The ability to manage personnel and resources to achieve a desired objective.

(B) The school bus driver

The school bus driver should have an understanding of the role of pupil transportation in the educational program and meet all the physical, mental and moral requirements established by state laws and these regulations.

Qualifications shall include:

(1) Being of legal age (section 3327.10 of the Revised Code).

(2) Being physically qualified (rule 3301-83-07 of the Administrative Code).

(3) An annual driver record check 3301-83-07 of the Administrative Code).

(4) Being licensed as a school bus operator.

(5) Holding school bus driver certification by a city or exempted village superintendent or by a county board of education or county board of mental retardation and developmental disabilities.

(6) Completing pre-service and inservice training (rule 3301-83-10 of the Administrative Code).

(7) Physical capability of appropriately lifting and managing handicapped pupils when necessary.

(8) Ability to cope with stressful situations.

(9) Possessing or upgrading skills through formal and/or inservice training.

(10) A report of the state bureau of criminal identification and investigation and/or county or local law enforcement agency shall be required prior to the hiring of an individual. For currently employed school bus drivers, a new report shall be required every two calendar years.

(C) Maintenance Personnel

Personnel employed for vehicle maintenance duties shall be qualified to perform quality preventive and regular maintenance programs and shall understand the relationship of vehicle maintenance to a safe pupil transportation program.

Qualifications as determined by the employer shall include:

(1) Work history;

(2) Education and training;

(3) Inservice attendance;

(4) Testing;

(5) On-the-job performance evaluations.

(D) Aides for handicapped pupils

Qualifications shall include:

(1) Physical capability of appropriately lifting and managing handicapped pupils when necessary.

(2) Ability to cope with stressful situations as related to handicapped pupils.

(3) Possessing or upgrading skills through formal and/or inservice training related to transportation of the handicapped.

History: Eff. 10-22-84; 7-1-91

3301-83-07 School bus driver physical qualifications rule.

(A) A person who meets the physical qualifications set forth in this rule as certified by a proper medical authority may be authorized to operate a school bus, as defined by division (F) of section 4511.01 of the Revised Code, for the purpose of transporting pupils.

(B) One or more licensed doctors of medicine or osteopathy will be appointed annually by all county boards of education and superintendents of city and exempted village school districts or county boards of mental retardation and developmental disabilities to conduct the examinations in compliance with this rule.

(C) Physical examination time schedule.

(1) School bus driver medical examinations will be scheduled after May first and must be accomplished before drivers will be qualified to operate a school bus with passengers on board for the next school year.

(2) Persons employed as new drivers before January first must meet the physical qualifications as defined in paragraph (E) of this rule prior to operating a school bus with passengers on board and be re-examined if re-employed as a school bus driver for the next school year.

(3) Persons employed as new drivers on or after January first must be examined prior to operating a school bus with passengers on board and the examination will remain valid throughout the following school year. Re-examination will be required if the driver is to be employed as a school bus driver for the second complete school year.

(D) All persons certified as physically qualified to operate a school bus will be required to request, obtain, and present to the county board of education, county board of mental retardation and developmental disabilities, or the appropriate superintendent an abstract of their driving record. This abstract can be obtained upon written request to the bureau of motor vehicles and accompanied by the prescribed fee. On receipt of the abstract, the appropriate board or superintendent will make and retain a copy of the abstract and attach the original abstract to the department of education copy of the completed physical examination. All costs connected with obtaining abstracts of driving records are the responsibility of the driver applicant.

(E) A person may be certified by the appointed examiner as physically qualified to operate a school bus if the person:

(1) Has no loss of a foot, a leg, a hand, or an arm.

(2) Has no impairment of the use of a foot, a leg, a hand, fingers, or an arm, and no other structural defect or limitation which is likely to interfere with a person's ability to control and safely operate a school bus.

(3) Has no established medical history or clinical diagnosis of diabetes mellitus currently requiring insulin for control.

The Ohio department of education may grant waivers to insulin-using individuals under the following conditions:

(a) The individual possesses a currently valid commercial driver license (CDL).

(b) The individual has had a driving record for a three-year period immediately preceding the date of application for a waiver which:

(i) Contains no suspensions or revocations of their drivers' licenses of the operation of any motor vehicle, including their personal vehicle except for suspensions or revocations due to nonpayment of fines;

(ii) Contains no involvement in a reportable accident for which a citation for a moving traffic violation while operating a commercial motor vehicle (CMV) was issued, or more than two commercial citations for any other moving traffic violations while operating a CMV; and

(iii) Contains no involvement in more than one serious traffic violations while operating a CMV.

(c) The individual has provided a licensed endocrinologist with a complete medical history including, but not limited to, the date insulin use began, all hospitalization reports, consultation notes for diagnostic examinations, special studies pertaining to the diabetes, and follow-up reports and reports of any hypoglycemic insulin reactions within the last three years;

(d) The individual has been examined by a licensed endocrinologist and a complete medical evaluation concerning their medical history and current status has been made, including, at a minimum:

(i) Fasting blood studies (glucose, glycosylated hemoglobin/Hb A1c, including lab reference range) and urinalysis performed during the last six months; and

(ii) A detailed report of insulin dosages and types, diet utilized for control and any significant factors such as smoking, alcohol use, and other medications or drugs taken.

(e) The individual submits a signed statement prepared by the examining endocrinologist whose license status is indicated. The signed statement must include separate declarations indicating the following medical determinations:

(i) The endocrinologist is familiar with the applicant's medical history for the past three years either through actual treatment over that time or through consultation with a physician who has treated the applicant during that time;

(ii) The applicant has been using insulin to control his/her diabetes on the date of the application.

(iii) The applicant does not have severe hypoglycemia or episodes of altered consciousness requiring the assistance of another person to regain control;

(iv) The applicant does not have hypoglycemia unawareness or the inability to recognize the early symptoms of hypoglycemia such as sweating, anxiety, forceful heartbeat and lightheadedness;

(v) Within the past three years, the applicant has not had a hypoglycemic reaction, at any time, that resulted in any change in mental status that would have been, in the endocrinologist's opinion, detrimental to safe driving;

(vi) The applicant's diabetic condition will not adversely affect his/her ability to operate a CMV or a school bus;

(vii) The applicant has been educated in diabetes and its management, thoroughly informed of and understands the procedures which must be followed to monitor and manage his/her diabetes and what procedures should be followed if complications arise; and

(viii) The applicant has the ability and has demonstrated willingness to properly monitor and manage his her diabetes.

(f) The individual submits a separate statement from an examining ophthalmologist that the applicant has been examined after January 1994, and that the applicant does not have unstable proliferative diabetic retinopathy or unstable advancing disease of blood vessels in the retina and has stable visual acuity (at least 20/40 (Snellen) in each eye separately, with or without corrective lenses.)

(g) The following special conditions are required for the issuance of any waiver to an insulin-using diabetic driver. Each driver must:

(i) Carry, use, and record, in a log, the readings from a portable self-monitoring blood glucose device (SMBG) that is equipped with a computerized memory. Blood glucose monitoring must be performed one hour prior to and approximately every four hours while on duty. Paper tapes generated by SMBGs having a printing capability may be used in lieu of a log prepared by the waived driver. Make log records of blood glucose values available to any authorized enforcement official upon request;

(ii) Carry upon your person and use, as necessary, a source of rapidly absorbable glucose;

(iii) Carry insulin and the equipment/materials necessary for administering the medication;

(iv) Report, in writing, any citation for a moving violation involving the operation of a CMV or a school bus to the Ohio department of education no later than fifteen days following the issuance of such citation. A photostatic copy of the citation issued must accompany the written report;

(v) Report, in writing, the judicial/administrative disposition of any citation for a moving violation involving the operation of a CMV or a school bus to the Ohio department of education no later than fifteen days following the notice of disposition;

(vi) Report, in writing, involvement in any accident whatsoever while operating a CMV or a school bus to the Ohio department of education no later than fifteen days following the accident (include state, insurance company, and/or motor carrier accident reports);

(vii) Report, in writing, any change of residence, address, or telephone number to the Ohio department of education no later than fifteen days after such a change.

(viii) Report, in writing, any change of employer, including name, address, and telephone number, or type of vehicle operated to the Ohio department of education no later than fifteen days after such a change.

(ix) Submit any medical information derived from medical assistance or treatment arising from any accident involvement to the Ohio department of education no later than fifteen days following the accident. A copy of the attending medical specialist's and laboratory reports will meet the reporting requirement.

(x) Submit log records of your blood glucose values for a twenty-four hour period immediately prior to any accident involvement to the Ohio department of education no later than fifteen days following the accident.

(xi) Submit a signed statement from the licensed endocrinologist who conducted the initial medical evaluation to the Ohio department of education no later than fifteen days before each six-month anniversary of the waiver issuance date, that you have been examined and your diabetic condition is currently stable and under control. This semiannual examination must be conducted within the six-week period immediately preceding each six-month anniversary of the waiver issuance date. You must make your log records of your blood glucose values for the preceding three months available to the examining endocrinologist at the time of the required examination;

(xii) Waived drivers who use a medical specialist, other than the specialist who conducted the initial medical evaluation, must be re-examined by an endocrinologist, using the criteria and procedures established for the pre-qualification examination and submit a signed statement from that licensed endocrinologist;

(xiii) Submit a signed statement from an ophthalmologist to the Ohio department of education, no later than fifteen days before each anniversary of the waiver issuance date, that you have been examined and that you do not have unstable proliferative diabetic retinopathy, and that you continue to have stable visual acuity (at least 20/40 (Snellen) in each eye, corrected or uncorrected). This annual examination must be conducted within the six-week period immediately preceding the anniversary of the waiver issuance date.

(h) All documentation described in paragraphs (E)(3)(g)(iv) to (E)(3)(g)(xiii) of this rule must be mailed to the Ohio department of education, division of school finance, pupil transportation section, 65 South Front street, Columbus, Ohio 43266-0308. Failure to submit timely reports may be cause for revocation of the waiver.

(i) Any individual school bus driver granted a waiver under this rule remains subject to the provisions of section 3327.10 of the Revised Code, including the reporting requirements of division (D) of section 3327.10 of the Revised Code.

(j) Applicants for a waiver from the insulin-using diabetes mellitus qualification requirement are required to submit their applications on plain paper, include all supporting documents, and include the information set forth below. Each information item must be completed by an appropriate answer or marked "none", if not applicable.

(i) Vital statistics

(a) Name of applicant (first name, middle initial, last name);

(b) Address (street number and name);

(c) City, state, and zip code;

(d) Telephone number (area code and number);

(e) Sex (male or female);

(f) Date of birth (month, day, and year);

(g) Age;

(h) State driver's license number (list all licenses held during the three-year period either immediately preceding the date of application to operate a CMV or school bus);

(i) Issuing state;

(j) Driver's license expiration date; and

(k) Driver's license classification code.

(1) Your employer's/prospective employer's name, address and telephone number;

(ii) Experience

(a) Number of years driving buses, and approximate number of miles driving buses; and

(b) Approximate number of years driving a CMV other than a school bus, and the approximate number of miles driving such other CMV.

(iii) Experience factor

(a) Unless the Ohio department of education is satisfied otherwise, you must have accumulated at least three years experience operating a CMV on a regular basis and that experience must be recent enough to reflect your capabilities.

(b) To qualify for a waiver, you must have a clean driving record as described in paragraph (E)(3)(b) of this rule for the three years immediately preceding the date of your application.

(iv) Supporting documents

Your application must include supporting documents for the requirements set forth in paragraph (E)(3) of this rule and any other documents deemed necessary by the Ohio department of education.

(k) A waiver issued by the Ohio department of education is valid for three years from the date of issuance unless revoked by the department for cause or based on a change in statute or rules.

(4) Has no current clinical diagnosis of myocardial infarction, angina pectoris, coronary insufficiency, thrombosis, or any other cardiovascular disease of a variety known to be accompanied by syncope, dyspnea, collapse, or congestive cardiac failure. A person with a history of cardiovascular surgery or abnormality shall be given a more stringent examination (example: stress testing, holter monitoring, angiography or other examinations) to determine whether or not the surgery or abnormality will degrade the ability to control, inspect, and safely operate a school bus. If it is determined that the surgery or abnormality will not degrade the ability, the examining physician will provide certification to that effect with the examination report.

(5) Has no established medical history or clinical diagnosis of respiratory dysfunction likely to interfere with a person's ability to control and safely operate a school bus.

(6) Has normal blood pressure below 160/90 mmHg or held below 160/90 mmHg by prescribed non-mood modifying medication. An examining physician determining a person's blood pressure to be above 160/90 mmHg may establish that the person's medical history demonstrates control within standard limits. In every instance of determined controlled blood pressure, the examining physician shall attach certification to the medical examination report that the blood pressure and prescribed medication will not interfere with the control and safe operation of a school bus or shall reject that person. Any school bus driver having a doctor's certificate related to controlled blood pressure attached to this medical examination report shall submit a six-month update certificate issued by the examining physician which demonstrates tested blood pressure less than 160/90 mmHg.

(7) Has no established medical history or clinical diagnosis of rheumatic, arthritic, orthopedic, muscular, neuromuscular, or vascular disease which interferes with the ability to control and operate a school bus safely.

(8) Has no established medical history or clinical diagnosis of epilepsy or any other condition which is likely to cause loss of consciousness or any loss of ability to control and safely operate a school bus.

(9) Has no mental, emotional, nervous, organic, or functional disease or psychiatric disorder likely to interfere with the ability to control and operate a school bus safely.

(10) Has distant visual acuity of at least 20/40 (SNELLEN) in each eye without corrective lenses or visual acuity separately corrected to 20/40 (SNELLEN) or better with corrective lenses, distant binocular acuity of at least 20/40 (SNELLEN) in both eyes with or without corrective lenses, field of vision of at least seventy degrees in the horizontal meridan in each eye,

and the ability to recognize the colors of traffic signals and devices showing standard red, green, and amber. Persons may use corrective lenses to attain these standards. If eyeglasses are used, they must be secured about the head by a restraining device independent of the eyeglasses themselves.

(11) When tested with a screening audiometer, does not have an average hearing loss in the better ear greater than forty decibels at five hundred Hz, one thousand Hz, and two thousand Hz with or without a hearing aid when the audiometric device is calibrated to "American National Standard" (formerly ASA standard) Z24.5.

(12) Has no current clinical record of use of amphetamines, amphetamine-like derivatives, narcotic, psychotropic, or any habit-forming drug.

(13) Has no recent history of alcohol abuse and has no current clinical diagnosis of alcoholism.

(14) Has no neurologic deficit that would impair ability to operate a school bus safely.

(15) Does not show evidence of active pulmonary tuberculosis, or other communicable diseases, and has taken the tuberculin test as required by rules of the Ohio public health council.

(16) Has speech capabilities to give clear and understandable directions or commands.

(F) Administration

(1) School bus drivers who have experienced a prolonged period of absence due to illness may be required by the appropriate superintendent to be re-examined in accordance with this rule.

(2) Currently employed school bus operators disqualified by the appointed examining physician shall be notified by the local, city, exempted village, or county board of mental retardation and developmental disabilities superintendent within fifteen days following receipt of the examination report. Currently employed school bus operators desiring to appeal a disqualification shall file the appeal in writing within fifteen days with the local, city, exempted village, or county board of mental retardation and developmental disabilities superintendent.

(3) Upon receipt of an appeal, the county board of education or the city or exempted village or the county board of mental retardation and developmental disabilities superintendent shall arrange for a medical re-examination. The re-examination may be conducted by a public health board or private physician. The re-examining physician shall not be the physician administering the original examination.

(4) All re-examinations shall be based on the school bus driver physical qualification rule and shall be final.

(5) Physical qualification examination reports shall contain a release authorization to be signed by the examinee for purposes of evaluation by constituted authorities.

(6) Costs for examinations required to the extent of compliance with this rule shall be the responsibility of the county, city, and exempted village boards of education, or county boards of mental retardation and developmental disabilities.

(7) Physical examination reports for persons certified by the examining physicians as meeting this rule shall be retained for a period of five years by the employing school district or county board of mental retardation and developmental disabilities. The employing school district and county board of mental retardation and developmental disabilities shall file the examination report with the department of education, pupil transportation section, within thirty days following the examination.

History: Eff. 3-31-75; 8-1-80; 10-22-84; 10-11-85 (Emer.); 1-1-86; 4-1-88; 7-1-91; 3-4-94 (Emer.); 7-1-94

3301-83-08 Pupil transportation management policies.

Board of education and county board of mental retardation and developmental disabilities adopted pupil transportation management policies should be developed cooperatively by school administrators and transportation personnel. Policies should be designed to ensure the safety and welfare of all school bus passengers and shall include:

(A) The school bus driver's authority and/or responsibility to maintain control of the pupils (section 3319.41 of the Revised Code).

(B) The pupil's right to "due process" as provided for by the local board of education or the county board of mental retardation and developmental disabilities policies and procedure.

(C) Pupil management and safety instruction policies shall include the following:

(1) Pupils shall arrive at the bus stop before the bus is scheduled to arrive.

(2) Pupils must wait in a location clear of traffic and away from the bus stops.

(3) Behavior at school bus stop must not threaten life, limb or property of any individual.

(4) Pupils must go directly to an available or assigned seat so the bus may safely resume motion.

(5) Pupils must remain seated keeping aisles and exits clear.

(6) Pupils must observe classroom conduct and obey the driver promptly and respectfully.

(7) Pupils must not use profane language.

(8) Pupils must refrain from eating and drinking on

the bus except as required for medical reasons.

(9) Pupils must not use tobacco on the bus.

(10) Pupils must not have alcohol or drugs in their possession on the bus except for prescription medication required for a student.

(11) Pupils must not throw or pass objects on, from or into the bus.

(12) Pupils may carry on the bus only objects that can be held in their laps (see paragraph (I) of rule 3301-83-20 of the Administrative Code).

(13) Pupils must leave or board the bus at locations to which they have been assigned unless they have parental and administrative authorization to do otherwise.

(14) Pupils must not put head or arms out of the bus windows.

(15) Guidelines will be formulated for the use and storage of equipment and other means of assistance required by handicapped pupils.

(16) Proper steps will be taken to collect, store and use medical information related to pupils known to have medical problems which may require driver attention.

(D) Suspension, expulsion or immediate removal from bus

(1) The provisions of section 3313.66 of the Revised Code shall apply to suspension, expulsion and immediate removal of a pupil from school bus riding privileges.

(2) The superintendent or superintendent designees, or principals are authorized to suspend or remove pupils from school bus riding privileges.

(3) Immediate removal of a pupil from transportation is authorized. A pupil removed immediately from transportation must be given notice as soon as practicable of a hearing which must be held within seventy-two hours of the removal. The notice shall also include the reason for removal. Immediate removal is authorized when the pupil's presence poses a danger to persons or property or a threat to the safe operation of the school bus. Length of time removed from ridership shall be in accordance with school district or county board of mental retardation and developmentally disabilities policy but not more than ten days.

(4) Suspension of riding for rule violation or conduct not considered a danger to persons or property or a threat to the safe operation of the school bus may not exceed the ten days. Suspension of riding privileges by the superintendent, superintendent designee, or principal, shall be in accordance with section 3313.66 of the Revised Code and school district or county board of mental retardation and developmentally disabilities policy related to due process.

(5) Expulsion of a pupil from riding privileges shall be by the superintendent and in compliance with divisions (B), (D) and (E) of section 3313.66 of the Revised Code.

(6) School bus drivers shall report in writing to the appropriate administrator all rule violations or conduct that justify immediate removal, suspension or expulsion.

(7) Suspension or immediate removal or handicapped pupils may require a modification of the above procedures and shall be accomplished in accordance with the law.

History: Eff. 10-22-84; 9-1-70; 7-1-91

3301-83-09 Pupil instruction.

(A) Safety instruction shall be given to all pupils in grades kindergarten through three regularly transported within two weeks after the commencement of classes each school year (see section 3327.16 of the Revised Code). The program shall include but not be limited to:

(1) Safe walking practices to and from the bus stop.

(2) Wearing of light-colored or reflective clothing when going to and from the bus stop in darkness.

(3) How and where to wait safely for the bus including how to avoid personal risks involving strangers.

(4) What to do if the bus is late or does not arrive.

(5) How to enter and leave the bus safely, including the use of a notebook, backpack, or equivalent which contain items that could be dropped around the bus.

(6) Safe riding practices (including instruction on rule 3301-83-08 of the Administrative Code, pupil transportation management policies).

(7) Safely crossing the highway before boarding and after leaving the bus.

(8) Proper respect for the rights and privileges of others.

(B) Pupils enrolled in grades kindergarten through three who may be transported on non-routine type trips only must be given a general orientation annually on school bus riding safety procedures.

(C) Pupils enrolled in grades four through twelve and regularly transported should be properly instructed in safety procedures on and around the school bus.

History: Eff. 10-22-84; 10-22-84; 7-1-91

3301-83-10 Personnel training program.

(A) Minimum school bus driver training requirements

Each school district or county board of mental retardation and developmental disabilities shall assign one or more persons to be trained and responsible for the on-the-bus instruction of beginning school bus drivers. A school bus driver training program shall be completed by each beginning driver in compliance with the following:

(1) On-the-bus instruction of eight hours, or as required to achieve an acceptable level of competence, shall be completed prior to a driver being assigned to operate a school bus with pupils on board and shall consist of:

(a) Pre-trip inspection;

(b) dentification of unacceptable driving techniques;

(c) Starting the engine;

(d) Position of hands for steering;

(e) Shifting standard transmissions;

(f) Shifting automatic transmissions;

(g) Starting into traffic: entering and leaving the freeway;

(h) Speed control;

(i) Changing lanes;

(j) Passing;

(k) Stop streets;

(l) Left and right turns;

(m) Turn-arounds;

(n) Loading and unloading pupils;

(o) Railroad crossings;

(p) Miscellaneous items:

(i) Special driving situations;

(ii) Special trips;

(iii) Regular trip restrictions.

(2) Fifteen hours minimum of pre-service classroom instruction shall be completed prior to operating a school bus with pupils on board and shall consist of the following:

(a) School bus and commercial driver license requirements;

(b) Public relations;

(c) Pre-driving instructions;

(d) Driving the bus;

(e) Defensive driving;

(f) Pupil management;

(g) Safety and emergency procedures;

(h) First aid;

(i) Transporting the handicapped;

(j) Fuel conservation;

(k) Radio communication;

(l) Motor vehicle laws;

(m) School district policies.

(3) In unusual circumstances, with the exception of safety and emergency procedures, pupil management and school district or county board of mental retardation and developmental disabilities policies, the fifteen hours of classroom instruction may be completed within the first three months of employment. A temporary certificate may be issued for operation of a school bus during the training period.

(B) School bus driver inservice training

The county, city, exempted village, local or county board of mental retardation and developmental disabilities superintendent shall provide and require all regular and substitute bus drivers to attend an annual inservice training program based on a needs assessment which includes a minimum of four hours of classroom instruction that must include one or more of the following:

(1) School bus and commercial driver license requirements;

(2) Public and staff relations;

(3) Equipment and care;

(4) Driving the bus;

(5) Defensive driving;

(6) Pupil management;

(7) Safety and emergency procedures;

(8) First aid;

(9) Transporting the handicapped child;

(10) Motor vehicle laws;

(11) Signs, signals and pavement markings;

(12) Fuel conservation;

(13) Radio communications.

(C) Pupil transportation supervisor training

School districts or county boards of mental retardation and developmental disabilities should encourage and support supervisors of pupil transportation to attend local, regional, state and national workshops and conferences devoted to the management, supervision, organization and technical components of pupil transportation.

(D) School bus mechanic training

Each school district or county board of mental retardation and developmental disabilities shall provide the opportunity for school bus maintenance personnel to participate in a yearly workshop or training seminar, a minimum of two hours of instruction, as is available through and approved by the Ohio department of education or as locally developed in one or more of the following areas:

(1) Preventive maintenance procedures;

(2) Repair procedures for each type of vehicle in the fleet and its special equipment;

(3) Servicing procedures for equipment;

(4) Inspection of the vehicle and its equipment;

(5) Recovery procedures for vehicles involved in an accident or breakdown;

(6) Preparation of maintenance records;

(7) Parts and equipment purchasing and storage;

(8) Establishment of parts inventory control procedures.

History: Eff. 10-22-84; 9-1-70; 7-1-91

3301-83-11 School bus inspections.

(A) Ohio state highway patrol safety inspection

The school district or county board of mental retardation and developmental disabilities administrator and/or the private contractor shall be responsible for presenting all school buses for the annual Ohio state highway patrol safety inspection. The administrator and/or the private contractor will be responsible for the pre-inspection, repair and preparation of each school bus for inspection.

(B) School bus driver inspection of the school bus

It is the responsibility of the school bus driver to make a daily pre-trip inspection of the school bus before leaving storage. It is the responsibility of the school district or county board of mental retardation and developmental disabilities to provide each driver with all inspection forms, which include the following, for reporting purposes.

(1) Stationary inspection

(a) Pre-starting inspection:

(i) Observe the bus for evidence of oil, fuel, or coolant leaks and vandalism.

(ii) Raise the hood and check the safety latch or hinges, then check oil, water, belts, hoses and wiring for frayed, cracked and/or deteriorated conditions.

(b) Walk-around inspection:

Place the transmission in neutral and set the parking brake. Start the engine and check the following:

(i) Tires: underinflated, flat, excessive wear or damaged.

(ii) Wheels: loose or missing nuts, excessive corrosion, cracks or other damage and sanders if installed.

(iii) Fluid leaks: evidence of oil on wheels and tires.

(iv) All school bus windows should be clean.

(v) All outside mirrors: clean, properly aimed and tightly adjusted.

(vi) Warning systems: headlights, back-up lights, clearance and marker lights, all signals and signs, reflectors, turn signals, stop lights and warning flashers clean and working properly.

(vii) Exhaust system: check for sagging exhaust pipes, short and leaky tailpipes and defective mufflers.

(viii) Exits: check service and emergency doors for ease of operation.

(ix) Check wheelchair lift operation if installed.

(c) Inside safety check:

(i) Check driver's seat and seat belt adjustments.

(ii) With the engine running check or inspect the following instruments and controls:

(a) Vacuum or air pressure gauge or hydraulic indicator lights.

(b) Oil pressure gauge.

(c) Indicator lights, if installed:

(i) Oil pressure warning light.

(ii) Service brake warning light.

(iii) Alternator/generator warning light.

(iv) Ammeter and/or voltmeter.

(v) Water temperature gauge or warning light.

(d) Dome lights.

(e) Horn.

(f) Heaters, fans and defrosters.

(g) Mirrors and sunshade.

(h) Wipers and washers.

(iii) Check passenger seats, frames, emergency exits and windows.

(iv) Check emergency equipment: fusees, fuses, first-aid kit, fire extinguisher, wrecking bar and emergency reflectors.

(2) Operation inspection

A planned road pre-check when driving between storage and first pupil pickup enables the driver to evaluate the steering, suspension, clutch, transmission, driveline, engine and brakes. The following items shall be checked and, if found in need of repair, a written report shall be submitted to the designated school official:

(a) Parking brake: check by slowly engaging the drive train while the parking brake is on. (In air brake systems, the parking brake will remain applied if there is a partial or complete air pressure loss in the service brakes.)

(b) Transmission operation: an automatic transmission should not slip and a manual transmission should allow for easy and smooth gear changes throughout the entire shifting range.

(c) Clutch: the clutch should engage easily and smoothly without jerking, slipping excessively or "chattering." A properly adjusted clutch should have some "free play" when the pedal is fully released.

(d) Service brakes: test at low speeds and bring the bus to a complete stop. The bus should stop in a straight line without skidding, swerving or pulling to one side.

(e) Engine: listen for unusual engine noises.

(f) Steering: check for any unusual handling characteristics.

(g) Suspension: check for any unusual ride or handling characteristics.

History: Eff. 10-22-84; 7-1-91

3301-83-12 Safety procedures.

(A) Warning lights

(1) Alternately flashing amber and red signal lamps

(a) Alternately flashing amber lamps are to be used to warn motorists that the bus is stopping to take on or to discharge passengers (or red if the bus is equipped with four red lights only).

(b) Alternately flashing red lights are to be used to inform motorists that the bus is stopped on the roadway to take on or discharge passengers.

(2) Stop arm shall be operated simultaneously with flashing red signal lamps.

(3) A white flashing strobe light, individually switched, may be used when approaching and at stop locations, turn-arounds, and railroad crossings, when unfavorable atmospheric conditions or time of day limit visibility (i.e., fog, rain, snow, darkness). Strobe lights may also be used when approaching and at stop locations, turn-arounds, and railroad crossings when visibility is limited due to conditions other than weather or darkness.

(4) Four-way hazard lights shall be activated at railroad crossings and turn-arounds unless prohibited by local ordinance.

(B) Railroad grade crossings

(1) General

(a) The driver of any school bus, with or without passengers, shall come to a complete stop,no closer than fifteen feet, and within fifty feet from the rails nearest the front of the bus.

(b) Drivers making stops at railroad crossings shall observe traffic and reduce speed far enough in advance of the stop to avoid trapping other motorists in panic stops or rear-end collisions with the bus. On multiple roadways, all stops must be made in the far right lane whenever possible and practical.

(c) Four-way hazard signals shall be activated, unless prohibited by local ordinance. No other signs or signals will be activated from the bus while stopped or stopping at the railroad crossing.

(d) When the bus is stopped the driver shall shift to neutral, turn off the warning lamp switch if necessary, fully open the service door, and listen and look in both directions along the track or tracks for approaching engines, trains, or train cars (section 4511.63 of the Revised Code).

(e) For improved vision and hearing, a window at the driver's left shall be opened and radios and other noisy equipment (fans, etc.) shall be turned off on approaching the crossing and remain off until the bus has cleared the crossing.

(f) If the view of the track or tracks is obstructed for one thousand feet in either direction, no portion of the bus may be driven onto the tracks until the driver has made certain that no train is approaching. Although railroad signals may indicate the tracks are clear, the driver must develop and use visual and audible senses to determine whether or not it is safe to proceed.

(g) The school bus driver shall shift the bus into gear, look and listen, close the service door and drive across the tracks in an appropriate gear without shifting (section 4511.63 of the Revised Code).

(h) After crossing the tracks, the driver shall turn on the alternating flashing signal lamp master switch, if necessary.

(i) After a train has passed the crossing, the bus driver shall not drive the bus onto any tracks until the driver is certain that no train, hidden by the first train, is approaching on an adjacent track.

(2) At crossing controlled by signals

(a) The driver of a school bus which has stopped at any railroad track or tracks where there is in operation any flashing red lights and/or bell shall not proceed across such track unless by authorization from a law enforcement officer, flagperson or school employee authorized by local law enforcement officials (section 4511.62 of the Revised Code).

(b) At crossings controlled by traffic signals (usually on freeways), the bus driver shall obey the traffic signals.

(c) Crossing when flashing or audible signals malfunction is permitted when authorized by a school district policy that specifies the procedures for drivers.

(3) At crossings controlled by crossing gate or barrier

(a) No bus driver shall drive the bus through, around or under any crossing gate or barrier at a railroad crossing while such gate or barrier is closed or being opened or closed (section 4511.62 of the Revised Code).

(b) The bus driver must never assume that automatic signals or other devices are completely reliable.

(4) Weather conditions

During wet, stormy or foggy weather, before placing part of the bus on the tracks, the driver must know that the crossing can be made in safety.

(5) Behavior of passengers at railroad crossings

When any school bus is stopped for any railroad track, all passengers must be silent until the crossing is completed. A signal for silence shall be given by the school bus driver approximately three hundred feet from the crossing.

(C) School bus turn-around

(1) Whenever possible, the bus shall be clearly visible to the other motorists five hundred feet in both directions.

(2) Whenever possible, the school bus shall back into an intersecting area to the right to make a turn-around.

(3) Four-way hazard lights shall be activated unless prohibited by local ordinance.

(4) The driver shall not back the school bus at

pick-up or discharge locations while pupils are outside the vehicle.

(D) Loading and unloading at school facilities

(1) When it is necessary to load or unload pupils off the school grounds, the bus shall be stopped and positioned so that pupils do not cross the roadway to get to or from the bus.

(2) Warning flasher lights shall be deactivated when loading and unloading on school grounds or when loading and unloading from a school bus stopped off the traveled portion of the roadway adjoining the school grounds (division (B) of section 4511.75 of the Revised Code).

(3) Parking for loading or unloading on school grounds shall be bumper to bumper or diagonal. Either method used shall exclude any necessity for backing the school bus.

(4) Pupils in the loading area shall be properly supervised by or arranged for by the building principal.

(5) Except when loading or unloading handicapped pupils, the driver shall remain on the bus while pupils are loading and unloading.

(E) Fueling

(1) Buses shall not be fueled while the engine is running.

(2) Smoking shall not be permitted while fueling.

(3) Buses shall not be fueled with pupils on board.

(F) Before receiving or discharging pupils, the bus shall be driven to the right side of the paved or traveled portion of the roadway and brought to a full stop.

(G) The bus driver shall be the only operator of the service entrance door. The door shall not be opened to load or unload pupils until traffic has cleared the bus or come to a complete stop in all directions.

(H) The bus driver shall not use the service door control to activate warning lights. The door must remain in a securely closed position while the bus is in motion.

(I) The bus driver shall not leave a school bus unattended with pupils on board except when loading or unloading handicapped pupils or in the event of an emergency.

(J) The driver shall not leave the bus until the brakes are set, the engine stopped and the ignition key removed, with the exception for buses equipped with wheelchair lifts or diesel engines that require the engine to be running.

History: Eff. 10-22-84; 7-1-91

3301-83-13 School bus stops.

(A) Designation of school bus stops

It shall be the responsibility of the superintendent or designee to determine the location of all school bus stops which shall be approved annually by the board of education as an integral part of the school bus routing plan within ten days following the opening of school (section 3327.01 of the Revised Code). Authority to designate or relocate subsequent school bus stops may be delegated by the board of education to the superintendent or designee.

(B) School bus stop location

(1) School bus stop locations shall provide for the maximum safety of pupils giving consideration to distance from residence, traffic volume, physical characteristics, visibility and weather conditions.

(2) School bus stops shall be established on the residence side of all four-lane highways and on the residence side of other roadways posing potential hazards to students as determined by school officials.

(3) School bus stops shall be located at a distance from the crest of a hill or curve to allow motorists traveling at the posted speed to stop within the sight distance. If the line of sight is less than five hundred feet in either direction, a school bus stop ahead sign ("Ohio Manual of Uniform Traffic Control Devices", pages five to eleven, section 5D-11) shall be installed at least five hundred feet in advance of the school bus stop.

(4) Each pupil shall be assigned and required to use a specific school bus stop except in unusual circumstances as approved by the superintendent or designee.

(5) Each bus shall have a detailed route sheet on board.

History: Eff. 10-22-84; 7-1-91

3301-83-14 Records and reports.

Each school district and county board of mental retardation and developmental disabilities shall maintain the following records for the management and reporting of the pupil transportation program.

(A) Maintenance and repair:

(1) Records to document that reported mechanical deficiencies discovered during inspections were corrected.

(2) A maintenance and repair record for each school bus.

(B) An accounting system for fuel consumption and costs for routine and non-routine uses of school buses and annual operating costs by vehicle and by fleet as prescribed by the Ohio department of education form T-2.

(C) A pupil accounting system that details assigned:

(1) School bus;

(2) School bus stop;

(3) School of attendance, student address, telephone number and grade.

(D) A record of routine and non-routine daily and annual miles driven by vehicle and by fleet.

(E) A reporting of the numbers of regular and substitute school bus drivers, mechanics, supervisors, secretaries, clerks and driver's aides.

(F) Maintain and file "School Bus Driver Medical Examination Report."

(G) Maintain and file "School Bus Accident Report" for each accident as defined:

(1) Any accident or occurrence involving a school bus operated by or under contract to a school district or a county board mental retardation and developmental disabilities which results in a fatality, an injury or damage to any motor vehicle or property.

(2) Any action taken by a bus driver employed by a school district or a county board mental retardation and developmental disabilities which contributes directly to any fatality, injury or damage to any motor vehicle or property.

(3) File with the department of education, pupil transportation section, a report of any accident which results in a fatality, an injury or motor vehicle or property damage in excess of five hundred dollars.

(H) Submit reports as required by the Ohio department of education.

History: Eff. 10-22-84; 9-1-70; 7-1-91

3301-83-15 Emergency and evacuation procedures.

(A) Emergency

Each school district or county board of mental retardation and developmental disabilities shall adopt a policy for handling emergencies on school buses while pupils are being transported. Such a policy shall include, but not necessarily be limited to, procedures for handling any medical emergencies of pupils while they are being transported. Each school district or county board of mental retardation and developmental disabilities shall provide training to all school bus drivers transporting pupils to ensure that the drivers understand the policy and their responsibilities under it. No school bus driver shall transport pupils unless the driver has received such training.

This policy shall be developed in cooperation with all those whose services would be required in the event of emergencies. The school transportation supervisor, school administrators, teachers, drivers, maintenance and service personnel and students shall be provided instruction in the procedures to be followed in the event of:

(1) Accident

The policy shall describe how to protect the accident scene; evacuate and control students; evaluate the need for medical assistance; notify the responsible law enforcement agency, school officials and emergency services; collect and record data essential to the preparation of required reports; and communicate with parents and/or guardians.

(2) Disability of driver

Procedures for handling situations in the event of injury or disability of the bus driver shall be included in the policy.

(3) School bus failure

The policy shall describe procedures for securing the bus, disposing of and controlling passengers, notifying school officials, securing alternate equipment, and repairing and recovering the disabled school bus.

(4) Inclement weather conditions

The pre-emergency policy shall provide instruction as to school closings, delayed take-ups and/or early dismissals.

(5) Tornado

The policy shall provide procedures for drivers and students in the event of tornado sightings and/or warnings.

(B) Evacuation

Superintendent or designee shall organize and conduct three emergency exit drills for all students who ride school buses to and from school.

(1) Each of the following three emergency procedures shall be conducted at least once annually:

(a) Everyone exits through the front entrance door;

(b) Everyone exits through the rear emergency door;

(c) Front half exits through the front door and rear half exits through the rear door.

(2) All drills shall be arranged and scheduled by the transportation administrator in cooperation with building principals. School bus drivers will conduct the drill sessions.

(3) Drills shall be held on school property when possible and not on the bus route.

(4) The driver shall stay in the bus during evacuation drills. The parking brake must be set, ignition turned off, and transmissions in gear or park.

(5) Children shall not take lunch boxes, books, etc., when they leave the bus.

(6) Pupils shall assemble at a distance of at least one hundred feet from the bus in an "emergency drill" and remain there until given further directions.

(7) Emergency evacuation of handicapped pupils may require modification of the above procedures.

History: Eff. 10-22-84; 7-1-91

3301-83-16 Non-routine use of school buses.

"Non-routine use of school buses" is defined as transportation of passengers for purposes other than regularly scheduled routes to and from school. School buses may be used for non-routine trips only when such trips will not interfere with routine transportation services.

(A) Approved non-routine use of buses

(1) Trips that are extensions of the instructional program as determined by school district or county board of mental retardation and developmental disabilities administration.

(2) Trips for the transportation of enrolled pupils directly participating in school-sponsored events. A "school-sponsored event" is defined as any activity in which pupils are participating and are under the direct supervision and control of a certified staff member or any advisor as designated by the superintendent.

(3) Transporting pupils taking part in summer recreation programs when such programs are sponsored by a recreation commission and there is an agreement between the board of education, and the recreation commission (OAG no. 67-081).

(4) Trips for transportation of the aged when contracted with a municipal corporation or a public or nonprofit private agency or organization delivering services to the aged (section 3327.14 of the Revised Code).

(5) Trips for transportation of pupils and/or adults, as approved by the board of education to and from events within the local community which are school or local community sponsored. Such events shall be open to the public.

(6) Emergency evacuation and/or emergency evacuation drills when such emergencies are declared by state or local directors of emergency disaster services.

(7) A civil emergency as declared by the governor.

(8) Transporting school employees engaged in board-approved employee improvement programs.

(B) Costs

No pupil charge may be made for transporting pupils to and from regular day classes and other educational field trips on school days. This applies equally to board-owned buses and privately-owned buses operated under a contract with a board of education. A fee not to exceed actual costs may be assessed for transportation to and from educational field trips on non-school days.

The board of education or county board of mental retardation and developmental disabilities shall recover an amount not to exceed the actual operational costs associated with non-routine use of school buses, with the exception of field trips that are extensions of the instructional program. These costs include:

(1) Driver salary and benefits;

(2) Fuel;

(3) Maintenance;

(4) Service;

(5) Supervision; (6) Insurance.

(C) Permits

City, exempted village, local, or county board of mental retardation and developmental disabilities superintendents or their designees shall issue a trip permit which shall accompany the driver on any non-routine trip. The permit shall provide the following information:

(1) Date of trip;

(2) Destination;

(3) Purpose of trip;

(4) Name of school district;

(5) Driver's name;

(6) Bus registration number;

(7) Total miles of trip;

(8) Superintendent or designee signature.

(D) Chaperones

One or more adult chaperones, as approved by the superintendent or designee, shall accompany each school bus required for any non-routine trip involving school-age passengers. The chaperone's responsibility shall be to assist the school bus driver in maintaining passenger control and in enforcing procedures for the safety of all passengers. A certified person licensed as a school bus driver may serve as a chaperone and driver concurrently.

(E) Out-of-state trips

Any out-of-state travel shall remain within two hundred forty miles round-trip distance from point of exit from the state to the point of entry to the state (section 3327.15 of the Revised Code).

(F) Driver selection for assignment to non-routine trips should be based upon a policy adopted by the board of education or county board of mental retardation and developmental disabilities which gives consideration to driver knowledge, skill, experience, vehicle familiarity and experience in operating a bus in the area to be traveled.

(G) A pre-trip inspection as detailed in paragraph (B) of rule 3301-83-11 of the Administrative Code shall be completed and documented immediately prior to departure of a school bus on a non-routine trip providing the bus had not received a documented pre-trip inspection during routine service on the day of the non-routine trip.

History: Eff. 10-22-84; 9-1-70; 7-1-91

3301-83-17 Authorized and unauthorized passengers.

(A) Authorized passengers:

(1) Pupils enrolled in grades kindergarten through twelve eligible for transportation services authorized or required by section 3327.01 of the Revised Code and local board of education or county board of mental retardation and developmental disabilities policy.

(2) Children attending an approved pre-school program authorized and directed by the board of education or county board of mental retardation and developmental disabilities.

(3) Resident pre-school children and parent(s) or guardian who are participating in school-sponsored special programs that require attendance of both. This includes parent and child participating in a graduation, reality, and dual-role skills (GRADS) or similar type program.

(4) School officials may authorize transportation of a school-age visitor to the home of a regular school bus passenger upon proper parental authorization on a space-available basis which does not displace regular riders.

(5) Resident pre-school children and school age pupils may be transported to pre-school programs and school-age child-care programs (for example, latchkey programs). These extra miles are not reimbursable. School age pupils may be counted for reimbursement only once if eligible for routine transportation (see rule 3301-83-01 of the Administrative Code).

(6) Resident pre-school handicapped children are to be transported to school district pre-school special education programs within the district and outside the district if assigned by the school district of residence. If transportation is necessary for pre-school handicapped children to receive a free and appropriate education it must be provided at no cost to the parent or guardian.

(7) School districts may enter into contractual agreements to provide transportation service for latchkey programs under the provisions of sections 3313.207, 3313.208, and 3313.209 of the Revised Code; and to provide transportation service for pre-school and daycare programs under provisions of paragraph (C) of section 3313.646 of the Revised Code.

(B) Unauthorized passengers:

(1) Family members of school bus drivers who are not enrolled in any of the approved school programs, unless adults appointed as chaperones on non-routine trips.

(2) School employees, on routine bus routes.

(3) Adults not enrolled in any of the approved grades kindergarten through twelve programs, unless assigned by proper school officials as bus monitors.

History: Eff. 10-22-84; 7-1-91

3301-83-18 Seating and load capacity.

(A) Seating shall be provided that will permit each regularly transported passenger to sit in a position which will provide maximum protection by the barrier.

(B) Bus routing and seating plans shall be coordinated so as to eliminate standing of pupils transported on a regular basis when a school bus is in motion.

(C) Pupils may be assigned seats to ensure maximum barrier protection and to eliminate standees.

(D) In no event shall the number of passengers exceed one hundred ten per cent of the manufacturer's rated capacity.

(E) To comply with this rule, routing and seating plans shall be adjusted within ten days following the opening of school.

History: Eff. 9-1-70; 10-22-84

3301-83-19 Authorized vehicles for transportation of pupils to and from school and school-related events.

(A) School buses

All vehicles designed to carry more than nine passengers, not including the driver, and used to transport students to and from school or school-related events shall meet or exceed all federal regulations and the Ohio school bus minimum construction standards (division (F) of section 4511.01 of the Revised Code).

(B) Public transit vehicles

This includes vehicles owned and operated by regional transit authorities or community transit authorities, or which are privately owned, under contract with a board of education or county board of mental retardation and developmental disabilities and operated on routes designed for the purpose of transporting fare-paying passengers and eligible students simultaneously.

(C) Board-owned or leased vehicles other than school buses

This includes vehicles, nine-passengers or less, as originally designed and constructed at the factory, not including the driver, used for transportation of handicapped pupils or for the transportation of pupils who are not accessible to conventional transportation services. If a van-type vehicle is used, it shall be equipped with a fire extinguisher, first-aid kit, reflectors, and wrecking bar. The vehicle shall be equipped with a road-speed control device. The vehicle shall have a rooftop sign marked "SCHOOL TRANSPOR-

TATION." These changes are effective for all vehicles manufactured or in use after the effective date of the rules in this chapter.

(D) Privately owned vehicles other than school buses

This includes vehicles, nine passengers or less, as originally designed and constructed at the factory, not including the driver, and used for transportation of pupils from the place of residence to the nearest pickup point on a regular school bus route. Residence must be one-half mile or more from the pickup point and inaccessible to a regular school bus.

(E) Vehicles not meeting the above definitions shall not be used for transportation of pupils to and from school or non-routine trips.

(F) Vehicles approved for activity use only

(1) A school activity bus is a school bus which meets all the requirements of the Ohio school bus minimum construction standards, Chapter 3301-87 of the Administrative Code.

(2) School activity buses are permitted to use the following items which are not permitted on route buses: interior book racks, coach-type seats, exterior roof luggage racks, and independent auxiliary engine-powered air-conditioning.

(3) School activity buses may be used as the board of education or county board of mental retardation and developmental disabilities policy permits. Use of the activity bus shall not conflict with commercial bus operations. Use of the activity bus shall comply with all applicable state and federal laws and rules.

(4) Activity buses shall not be used on regular routes.

(5) Activity buses are not eligible for school bus purchase assistance.

(6) Any activity bus currently in use shall comply with these rules by January 1, 1992.

History: Eff. 10-22-84; 7-1-91

3301-83-20 General rules.

(A) The use of alcohol, tobacco, and non-prescribed drugs is prohibited on the school bus.

(B) The driver shall use the established route and make stops only at points designated by the board of education or county board of mental retardation and developmental disabilities or the administrator who is authorized to designate such stops.

(C) The driver shall operate the bus on the approved time schedule and shall wait for pupils if ahead of schedule.

(D) Animals, firearms, ammunition, weapons, explosives or other dangerous materials or objects are prohibited on school buses.

(E) All buses shall be kept clean on the inside and on the outside. Front and rear windows, lights and mirrors should be clean and all markings clearly visible.

(F) All buses shall be equipped with emergency assistance cards which list three telephone numbers to call and provide space for describing the location of the school bus and the type of emergency.

(G) The school bus driver shall use the seat belt whenever the school bus is in motion.

(H) Hazards survey

School bus drivers should report regularly any pedestrian or vehicular concerns such as:

(1) Construction sites;

(2) Heavy traffic volume;

(3) Posted speeds in excess of thirty-five miles per hour;

(4) Lack of sidewalks or sidewalks in poor condition;

(5) Overpasses and underpasses;

(6) Areas of poor visibility;

(7) Restricted sight distances;

(8) On-street parking areas;

(9) Railroad crossings.

(I) Equipment such as music instruments, athletic uniforms, etc., which cannot be held by passengers in their seats, shall be stored in the rear of the bus. When it is necessary to transport such equipment concurrently with pupils, space shall be provided to comply with this rule without having standees in the bus. Equipment required in the assistance of the handicapped shall be used and stored as required by local policies. A clear aisle to the exit door must be maintained at all times.

(J) Maximum hours. The school bus driver shall operate the bus for not more than ten hours in any one twenty-four hour period. Operation means on-road driving and lay-over time does not count as operating time.

History: Eff. 10-22-84; 9-1-70; 7-1-91

3301-83-21 Supplementary provisions for county boards of mental retardation and developmental disabilities.

(A) As used in this rule, the following definitions apply:

(1) "Individualized education program" means a written statement for a handicapped child that is developed and implemented in accordance with paragraph (E) of rule 3301-51-02 of the Administrative Code.

(2) "Individualized habilitation plan" means a written plan of intervention and action that is developed

on the basis of a comprehensive evaluation.

(3) "County board" means a county board of mental retardation and developmental disabilities.

(4) "Department" means Ohio department of education.

(B) The county board shall provide transportation services for children ages three to twenty-one eligible for transportation and enrolled in department-funded programs. The nature and extent of transportation services to be provided to each individual served shall be determined through the individualized education program or individualized habilitation plan process. The determination shall be reviewed annually.

(1) When it is determined through the individualized education program or individualized habilitation plan process that transportation other than that provided by the county board is an integral part of the education or habilitation of the individual, the county board shall provide reimbursement for transportation to the parent or guardian. Under these circumstances, written agreement between the county board and the parent or guardian shall be obtained prior to the provision of such transportation services. Documentation of this agreement shall be kept on file.

(2) Reimbursement of transportation costs paid to a parent or guardian may be approved as part of the transportation operating subsidy from the department with prior written agreement between the county board and the parent or guardian.

(C) The county board shall have insurance, including, but not limited, to bodily injury, bodily liability, and property damage liability, for all transportation services operated directly by the county board.

(D) Individuals enrolled in a county board program shall not travel on a vehicle on a regularly scheduled route for more than ninety minutes one way on any day nor more than one hundred eighty minutes on any day on a regularly scheduled round trip.

(E) A school bus driver shall have a current and valid "American Red Cross" first-aid certificate.

(F) All new bus drivers, assistants, and substitutes shall attend, prior to their assignment to a bus with passengers on board, an orientation which includes a review of the vehicle operator's manual and a practical overview of the characteristics and needs of individuals to be transported.

(G) The county board shall adopt a policy and procedures that ensure assistance is provided to individuals while being transported on county board vehicles when the individualized education program or individualized habilitation plan indicates a need for such assistance.

(H) A commercial driver's license of the proper class shall be required of a person hired for the purpose of transporting individuals in alternative transportation vehicles.

(I) Individuals shall be picked up and returned to their residences unless other arrangements have been agreed upon by the county board program and the responsible parent or guardian.

(J) When alternative transportation is used, each vehicle shall annually meet the requirements of the random vehicle inspection rules and regulations of the Ohio department of highway safety.

History: Eff. 7-1-91

3301-83-22 Vehicles maintenance.

School vehicles and school buses owned and operated by school districts or county boards of mental retardation and developmental disabilities shall be maintained in safe operating condition through a systematic preventative maintenance program.

History: Eff. 7-1-91

Chapter 3301-85
Purchase of School Buses

3301-85-01 Rule for distribution of payment for the purchase of school buses.

(A) General provisions

(1) Payment to school districts for the purchase of school buses shall be based upon section 3317.07 of the Revised Code upon determination that pupils residing more than one mile from school could not be transported without such additional aid.

(2) School bus purchasing shall be in compliance with section 3327.08 of the Revised Code and applicable parts of section 3313.46 of the Revised Code.

(3) All new buses purchased must meet or exceed all current federal and state minimum standards for construction and design of school buses.

(4) All school districts and county boards of mental retardation and developmental disabilities eligible to receive department of education funding shall be eligible to receive state support for the purchase of school buses pursuant to section 3317.07 of the Revised Code.

(5) Any school district or county boards of mental retardation and developmental disabilities obtaining bus services for pupil transportation pursuant to a contract may use payments received under this rule to defray the

costs of contracting for bus services in lieu of for purchasing buses.

(B) Funding approval procedure for school buses needed to transport pupils with disabilities and nonpublic pupils.

(1) File application for bus purchasing assistance on forms provided by the department of education.

(2) Application for assistance for replacement school buses will be evaluated on the basis of need as determined by age, mileage, and cost of anticipated repairs and replacement plan of the district and county board of mental retardation and developmental disabilities.

(3) Applications for assistance for emergency replacement of school buses will be given priority on the list which is compiled for funding consideration by the department of education.

(4) Applications for assistance for additional school buses will be evaluated on the basis of need due to additional eligible riders or rerouting requiring additional buses.

(5) Applications for the bus purchasing assistance for school buses required by law to be funded at one hundred per cent of net cost will be ranked by mileage for school districts and county boards of mental retardation and developmental disabilities. Districts must maintain accurate written documentation of odometer replacement, alteration, or repair. Contracts to purchase shall become school district and county board of mental retardation and developmental disabilities responsibilities should appropriations by the legislature be insufficient.

(6) Upon delivery, the school district or county board of mental retardation and developmental disabilities will submit data certifying actual cost and delivery and the state department will request a warrant be issued in the amount due.

(7) Applications not approved for funding will be carried forward to the next succeeding fiscal year contingent upon appropriations by the legislature unless officially canceled by the submitting school school district or county board of mental retardation and developmental disabilities.

(C) Funding formula for school buses needed to transport pupils with disabilities and nonpublic pupils

(1) Funding for school buses needed and approved for transportation of eligible nonpublic school pupils shall be at one hundred per cent of net cost.

(2) Funding for school buses needed and approved for transportation of eligible pupils with disabilities shall be at one hundred per cent of net cost.

(3) Net cost shall be determined by the actual approved gross cost of the body and chassis requirements to meet state and federal minimum construction standards minus one hundred per cent of the trade-in amount.

(4) One hundred per cent of trade-in amount or insurance amount in the case of an accident for school buses needed to transport pupils with disabilities and nonpublic pupils will be deducted from the actual approved gross cost. This is only applicable when the trade-in is a department of education funded bus.

(5) School districts that contract with school bus contractors to provide transportation service shall receive a calculated amount each school year based on the average gross cost of a school bus in the prior year, the average age of school buses replaced in the prior year, and the total number of route buses needed to transport eligible nonpublic pupils and pupils with disabilities.

(a) School districts which enter into an agreement with a licensed school bus contractor to provide pupil transportation service and which sell the board-owned school buses pursuant to section 3313.41 of the Revised Code shall return one hundred per cent of the proceeds to the state of Ohio, department of education, or make the buses available without charge to other school districts as ranked in paragraph (B)(5) of this rule. The return of proceeds or use by other districts applies only when the bus was funded by the Ohio department of education.

(b) School districts that enter into an agreement with a licensed school bus contractor to provide pupil transportation service may lease the board-owned school buses to the contractor.

(D) Funding for used buses, including public, nonpublic, and handicapped used buses. To be funded, a used bus can be no more than five model years old or have sixty-five thousand miles for gasoline powered school buses or one hundred thousand miles for diesel powered school buses. Funding assistance for used school bus bodies and/or chassis will be based on the average of three independent appraisals by school bus body or chassis distributors and must meet or exceed the Ohio school bus construction standards, Chapter 3301-87 of the Administrative Code.

(E) Funding for new school bus bodies to be placed on old school bus chassis will be made when the following conditions are met:

(1) The school bus chassis meets or exceeds federal and state minimum standards for construction for the year in which it was built.

(2) The new school bus body must be the most current model available and meet or exceed federal and state minimum standards for construction.

(3) The entire rebuilt unit (older chassis with a new body) must be certified by the new school bus body installer as meeting or exceeding federal and state

standards for construction for the above chassis and body time-frames.

(F) Funding for handicapped lifts for new or used school buses will be made under the following conditions:

(1) If the school bus is not new, it shall be no more than five model years old.

(2) Funding shall include no more than one thousand dollars for installation costs if the school bus is not new.

(3) The lift must meet or exceed all current federal and state standards for handicapped lifts.

(G) Funding for all other school buses required for transportation of eligible pupils shall be based on:

(1) The number of eligible public pupils;

(2) The number of miles to transport eligible public pupils;

(3) An equity factor which shall consider valuation per pupil and median income for each school district; and

(4) A rough road factor which shall be based on the road classification system used by the Ohio department of transportation and shall consider all Type I (board-owned and operated) and Type II (contractor-owned and operated) yellow bus miles for public and nonpublic pupils, and the transportation of pupils with disabilities.

(H) Eligible pupils and eligible miles for payment purposes.

(1) Eligible pupils for inclusion in the bus purchase formula are those reported on the report of pupil transportation service.

(2) Eligible pupils are defined in paragraph (G) of rule 3301-83-01 of the Administrative Code and are those pupils who are regularly transported on yellow school buses owned and operated by school districts or by school bus contractors, excluding pupils who attend chartered nonpublic schools and pupils with disabilities who are regularly transported on yellow school buses which have been funded at one hundred per cent of net cost.

(3) Eligible miles for inclusion in the bus purchase formula are those reported on the report of pupil transportation service.

(4) Eligible miles are defined in paragraph (G) of rule 3301-83-01 of the Administrative Code, and are those miles needed to transport eligible pupils to and from school, from a pick-up point one half mile or less from the place of residence to school and return to the pick-up point.

(I) Funding formula for county boards of mental retardation and developmental disabilities.

(1) Funding for school buses required and approved for transportation of school pupils ages three through twenty-one shall be one hundred per cent of net cost.

(2) Net cost shall be determined by the base cost of the body and chassis requirements to meet state and federal minimum construction standards.

(3) One hundred per cent of trade-in amount or salvage will be deducted from actual approved gross cost to determine net cost. This is only applicable when the trade-in is a department of education funded bus.

(4) "Enrollee days" means the number of scheduled days for which adults and school pupils ages three through twenty-one are transported to county board of mental retardation and developmental disabilities programs. Annually, a count of individuals transported on school buses shall be made and shall not include those riding alternative means of transportation.

(5) Separate transportation systems for school pupils ages three through twenty-one and adults shall designate school buses accordingly and shall be eligible for reimbursement of school buses used to transport school pupils ages three through twenty-one.

(6) Combined transportation systems for school pupils ages three through twenty-one and adults shall determine the number of school buses eligible for reimbursement based on the percentage of eligible school pupil ridership and the total inventory of school buses.

(7) Percentage of eligible ridership shall be calculated by totaling the number of enrollee days of school pupils ages three through twenty-one and dividing by the enrollee days of all individuals transported on school buses by the county board of mental retardation and developmental disabilities.

(8) Percentage of eligible ridership shall be multiplied by the total school bus inventory to determine the number of school buses that would be eligible for replacement. The department of education with the county board of mental retardation and developmental disabilities shall designate actual buses eligible for department of education bus purchase procedures.

(9) The ridership and enrollee calculations shall be updated annually.

History: Eff. 9-23-74; 1-1-78; 10-22-84; 7-1-89; 1-1-93; 8-1-94

Chapter 3301-89 Transfers of Territory

3301-89-01 General policies of the state board of education in a request for transfer of territory under section 3311.06 or 3311.24 of the Revised Code.

(A) The rules under Chapter 3301-89 of the

Administrative Code apply to the request for a transfer of territory following municipal annexation under section 3311.06 of the Revised Code or a petition for transfer of territory under section 3311.24 of the Revised Code.

(B) The rules under Chapter 3301-89 of the Administrative Code do not apply to the transfer of territory following municipal annexation when the district in which the territory is located is a party to an annexation agreement with a city school district under section 3311.06 of the Revised Code. Further, the use of the term "agreement" in Chapter 3301-89 of the Administrative Code does not mean "annexation agreement" as defined in division (A)(4) of section 3311.06 of the Revised Code.

(C) The department of education shall require the boards of education affected by a request for transfer of territory to enter into good faith negotiations pursuant to sections 3311.06 and 3311.24 of the Revised Code.

(D) In situations where agreement has been reached between respective boards of education, the terms of agreement should be sent to the state board of education with reasonable dispatch. In those situations where agreement does not exist, the state board of education will thoroughly examine the facilitator's report, pursuant to paragraph (A)(8) of rule 3301-89-04 of the Administrative Code. If the state board of education determines that the negotiations were not held in good faith, the transfer request shall be remanded back to the districts for further negotiations for a period not to exceed one year. However, no transfer request will be remanded more than once to the districts. If the state board determines that negotiations were held in good faith, but no agreement reached; or if negotiations were held the second time on the same transfer request and no agreement reached, then the state board of education will thoroughly examine the stated reasons for and against the requested transfer and provide due process to all parties involved as set forth in paragraph (E) of rule 3301-89-02 of the Administrative Code.

(E) A request for the transfer of territory for school purposes which previously has been disapproved by the state board of education will be reconsidered only if significant change has taken place subsequent to the filing of the original request.

(F) A request for transfer of territory will be considered upon its merit with primary consideration given to the present and ultimate good of the pupils concerned.

(G) The file at the department of education concerning a requested transfer will be made available to any affected party or interested person at all reasonable times for inspection. Upon request, copies of documents from the file will be made available at cost and within a reasonable period of time.

History: Eff. 2-1-87; 4-27-90

3301-89-02 Procedures of the state board of education in a request for transfer of territory under section 3311.06 or 3311.24 of the Revised Code.

(A) Initial requests

(1) A school district may request a transfer of certain territory for school purposes under section 3311.06 of the Revised Code by sending an initial letter requesting the land transfer to the state board of education and including copies of:

(a) The resolution of the requesting board of education;

(b) Each annexation ordinance identified by number; and

(c) A map showing the area(s) being considered for transfer.

(2) Under the provisions of section 3311.24 of the Revised Code, if the board of education of a city or exempted village school district deems it advisable to transfer territory from such district to an adjoining city, exempted village, or county school district, then the board of education of the district in which the proposal originates shall file the request, along with a map showing the boundaries of the territory proposed to be transferred, with the state board of education prior to the first day of April in any even-numbered year.

(3) A person(s) interested in requesting a transfer of territory from one school district to another, for school purposes, pursuant to section 3311.24 of the Revised Code, may petition to do so through the resident board of education.

(a) The board of education of the district in which such a proposal originates, regardless of its position on the proposed transfer, shall file the proposal, together with a map showing the boundaries of the territories proposed to be transferred, with the state board of education prior to the first day of April in any even-numbered year.

(b) The board of education of the district in which the proposal originates by petition of qualified electors residing within the portion of the school district proposed to be transferred shall determine the sufficiency of the signatures on the petition and shall notify the state board of education of its determination.

(4) A school district or a party initiating a request for transfer of territory shall serve a copy of the request on the school district(s) affected by the proposed transfer and shall indicate such service on the request which is filed with the state board of education.

(5) Upon receipt of a request for transfer under paragraph (A)(1) or (A)(2) of this rule, the department of education shall notify all school districts involved of their responsibilities for negotiations under rule 3301-89-04 of the Administrative Code.

(6) Upon receipt of a negotiated agreement, the state board of education shall adopt a resolution of approval of the negotiated agreement or may establish a hearing if approval is not granted.

(B) Upon receipt of the initial request for a transfer of territory under section 3311.06 or division (A) of 3311.24 of the Revised Code, or upon determination by the state board of education that negotiations pursuant to rule 3301-89-04 of the Administrative Code have failed to produce an agreement, the department of education shall send to each of the school districts involved in the proposed land transfer a request for information. This request includes seventeen questions. The answers to these questions, along with other considerations, will be considered. The seventeen questions are:

(1) Why is the request being made?

(2) Are there racial isolation implications?

(a) What is the percentage of minority students in the relinquishing district?

(b) What is the percentage of minority students in the acquiring district?

(c) If approved, would the transfer result in an increase in the percentage of minority pupils in the relinquishing district?

(3) What long-range educational planning for the students in the districts affected has taken place?

(4) Will the acquiring district have the fiscal and human resources to efficiently operate an expanded educational program?

(5) Will the acquiring district have adequate facilities to accommodate the additional enrollment?

(6) Will both the districts involved have pupil population and property valuation sufficient to maintain high school centers?

(7) Will the proposed transfer of territory contribute to good district organization for the acquiring district?

(8) Does the acquiring district have the capacity to assume any financial obligation that might accompany the relinquished territory?

(9) Will the loss of either pupils or valuation be detrimental to the fiscal or educational operation of the relinquishing school district?

(10) Have previous transfers caused substantive harm to the relinquishing district?

(11) Is the property wealth in the affected area such that the motivation for the request could be considered a tax grab?

(12) Are there any school buildings in the area proposed for transfer?

(13) What are the distances between the school buildings in:

(a) The present area?

(b) The proposed area?

(14) If approved, will the requested transfer create a school district with noncontiguous territory?

(15) Is the area being requested an isolated segment of the district of which it is a part?

(16) Will the municipal and school district boundary lines become coterminous?

(17) For both the districts:

(a) What is the inside millage?

(b) What is the outside operating millage?

(c) What is the bonded indebtedness millage?

(C) When a school district completes the questionnaire and forwards the same to the department of education, the school district shall serve a copy on the other school district(s) affected by the proposed transfer and shall indicate such service on the questionnaire which is filed with the department of education.

(D) Upon receipt of completed questionnaires from both school districts concerned, the department of education will analyze the information and present its analysis to the state board of education for consideration.

(E) Upon receipt of the data from the department of education, the state board of education may declare its intention to consider the request for transfer of certain territories from one school district to another by passing a resolution of intention to consider the matter and providing the parties an opportunity for a hearing.

(F) If a request for a hearing is subsequently received by the department of education, a referee shall be appointed and a hearing date shall be established by the department.

(G) The data and documents received by the department of education under this chapter shall become part of the record of the hearing for consideration by the referee.

(H) In making a report and recommendation to the state board of education, the referee shall be governed by the provisions of Chapter 3301-89 of the Administrative Code.

(1) When the referee's report is received with its recommendation to approve or disapprove the transfer of territory, the department of education will mail such report to the school districts and any other affected parties.

(2) Upon their receipt of the referee's report, the affected parties will have ten days in which to submit written objections to the report to the department.

(3) Any party that files objections shall file a copy of the objections with the other affected parties.

(4) Any affected party may file a response to the objections. Such response must be filed with the department of education within ten days after the objections are mailed to the department of education.

(I) After the time for filing objections and responses has ended, the state board education will then consider the referee's report, objections, and responses, and adopt a resolution which approves, disapproves, or modifies the recommendation of the referee. The decision of the state board of education will be made solely on the record of the hearing, the report of the referee and any objections or responses filed by the parties.

(J) When a determination concerning a transfer of territory will be made by the state board of education, the department of education shall notify the school districts and other affected parties of the time and place the matter will be considered by the state board of education.

History: Eff. 5-1-88; 2-1-87; 4-27-90

3301-89-03 Factors to be considered by a referee appointed to hear a request for transfer of territory under section 3311.06 or 3311.24 of the Revised Code.

(A) A referee appointed to hear a transfer request under section 3311.06 or 3311.24 of the Revised Code shall consider the information provided by the school districts under paragraph (B) of rule 3301-89-02 of the Administrative Code and shall be governed by the provisions of Chapter 3301-89 of the Administrative Code.

(B) Other factors that a referee shall consider in hearing any request for a transfer of territory for school purposes include, but are not necessarily limited to:

(1) Documented agreements made by public agencies involved in municipal annexation proceedings should be honored;

(2) A previous agreement entered into by the school districts concerned should be honored unless all concerned districts agree to amend it;

(3) The statement signed by the school district boards of education after negotiations as required by paragraph (D)(4) of Rule 3301-89-04 of the Administrative Code;

(4) There should not be undue delay in requesting a transfer for school purposes after a territory has been annexed for municipal purposes;

(5) The transfer shall not cause, preserve, or increase racial isolation;

(6) All school district territories should be contiguous unless otherwise authorized by law;

(7) School district boundary lines that have existed for a long period of time should not be changed if substantial upheaval results because of long-held loyalties by the parties involved;

(8) The pupil loss of the relinquishing district should not be such that the educational program of that district is severely impaired;

(9) The fiscal resources acquired should be commensurate with the educational responsibilities assumed; and

(10) The educational facilities of districts should be effectively utilized.

(C) When a hearing officer has received and considered the information provided by representatives of the school districts, petitioners for a transfer of territory, and any other party at the hearing, particularly information under paragraph (B) of this rule and paragraph (B) of rule 3301-89-02 of the Administrative Code, and the evidence is in balance, the hearing officer may consider the preference of the residents with school-age children who live in the territory sought to be transferred to another school district. The school district preference of such residents with school-age children in the territory requested for transfer may only be considered and given weight when all other factors are equal.

History: Eff. 2-1-87; 5-1-88; 4-27-90; 1-1-95

3301-89-04 Procedures governing negotiations of school districts, other than urban school districts as defined in division (A)(3) of section 3311.06 of the Revised Code.

(A) Negotiation process

(1) Unless negotiations have been initiated, the first negotiation session shall be set within thirty days of the receipt of notification of responsibility to negotiate from the department of education.

(2) The date, time, and place of the negotiation sessions shall be mutually agreed upon by the participating districts.

(3) A record of at least the time, place, and date of each session shall be kept by each school district represented.

(4) Any board of education may request assistance from the department of education. Upon request, the superintendent of public instruction shall designate one or more department employees to provide assistance.

(5) District superintendents and/or their designees shall comprise the negotiating teams. Teams shall be limited to three persons each. By mutual consent, up to three observers for each team may be present.

(6) If agreements are not reached within one hundred twenty days, a mutually agreed upon facilitator

with a public education background and/or experience shall be selected within thirty days. The cost of the facilitator shall be shared equally by the parties involved. If the parties fail to agree upon a facilitator, the superintendent of public instruction shall name one.

(7) Agreements reached shall be adopted by each board of education involved. A copy of the resolution and the negotiated agreement shall be transmitted by each board of education to the state board of education.

(8) In the event agreements are not reached within a year from the initial negotiation session, the facilitator shall issue to the state board of education a record of the good faith efforts of all parties involved in the negotiations.

(B) The negotiations process shall strive for the realization of the following goals:

(1) Written delineation of the present and future educational needs of the pupils in each of the school districts.

(2) A written review of the educational, financial, and territorial stability of each district affected by the transfer.

(3) A statement of assurance of appropriate educational programs, services, and opportunities for all the pupils in each participating district, and adequate planning for the facilities needed to provide these programs, services, and opportunities.

(C) The following are examples of terms that school districts may agree to:

(1) Share revenues from the property included in the territory to be transferred;

(2) Establish cooperative programs between the participating districts;

(3) Establish mechanisms for the settlement of any future boundary disputes; and

(4) No tax revenue to the receiving district from the territory transferred for a period of time.

(D) Before the state board of education may hold a hearing on a transfer, or approve or disapprove any such transfer, it must receive the following items:

(1) A resolution requesting approval of the transfer, passed by at least one of the school districts whose territory would be affected by the transfer, if the transfer request is pursuant to section 3311.06 of the Revised Code;

(2) A resolution requesting approval of the transfer, passed by the school district submitting the proposal, if the transfer request is initiated by a board of education pursuant to section 3311.24 of the Revised Code;

(3) Evidence determined to be sufficient by the state board of education to show that good faith negotiations have taken place or that the district requesting the transfer has made a good faith effort to hold such negotiations; and

(4) If any negotiations took place, a signed statement is required by every school district board of education that has participated in the negotiations, listing the terms agreed upon and the points on which no agreement could be reached.

History: Eff. 4-27-90

Chapter 3301-90
Guide to Districts for Emergency Repairs to School Facilities

3301-90-01 Rule for the issuance of grants to school districts for emergency repairs to school facilities.

(A) Expenditures by a city, exempted village, local, or joint vocational school district for emergency repairs must be in one or more of the following categories:

(1) Life, safety, or health code violation;

(2) Court-ordered repairs;

(3) Unanticipated disaster; or

(4) Other unexpected repairs.

(B) School districts must have an unanticipated event requiring expenditures that have not been previously budgeted for school facilities repairs. The following must be identified:

(1) Insurance that does not cover the emergency;

(2) School district budget that does not have available funds to cover the emergency; and

(3) Other funding sources that are not available to cover the emergency.

(C) The applications for funds for emergency repairs will be reviewed by the Ohio department of education and prioritized on a first-come, first-served basis.

(D) An inspection will be done by the Ohio department of education and will include the following:

(1) On-site review of the emergency need;

(2) Review of the school district budget;

(3) Meeting with insurance adjusters, (if applicable);

(4) Meeting with life, safety, or health code violation representative (if applicable); and

(5) Review of court order to perform repairs (if applicable).

(E) An allowance of fifty thousand dollars per category may be requested. Not more than two hundred thousand dollars may be awarded to any school district.

(F) Money shall be released for emergency school repairs grants only after approval by the state controlling board.

History: Eff. 10-29-90

Glossary

abatement, tax
Refer to *tax abatement.*

accounting records
These are records that a district keeps of its actual revenue and expenditures as money is received and spent. Such documents may be able to provide more detailed information on specific items than is published in the district's financial report.

accounts
This is a descriptive heading under which are recorded financial transactions that are similar in terms of a given frame of reference (for example, purpose, object or source).

accounts payable
Accounts payable are amounts which are due to trade vendors and/or others for goods or services received by the district for which payment has not yet been made.

accounts receivable
Amounts owed to the school district by private persons, firms, governmental units or others are classified as accounts receivable.

accrual basis
This is a basis of accounting under which revenues are recorded when earned or when levies are passed. Expenditures are recorded as soon as they result in liabiliites, regardless of when the revenue is actually received or the payment is actually made. Refer also to *current expense, revenue,* and *expenditures.*

accrued interest
Interest which has accumulated between interest dates but which is not yet due is called accrued interest.

ADA
ADA is an abbreviation for average daily attendance of students.

ADC
Refer to *aid to dependent children.*

adjusted gross income (AGI)
Adjusted gross income refers to income adjusted for federal tax purposes.

ADM
ADM is an abbreviation for the average daily membership of students. It is the official measure that Ohio uses to represent the number of students in a school district for the purpose of calculating state aid. Some states use average daily attendance.

administration
In this text, administration refers to those activities which are not confined to one school building, subject, or a restricted phase of school activity, but which have as their purpose the general regulation, direction, and control of the system-wide affairs of a school district.

adopted budget
This refers to the budget which has been officially voted on and approved by a school board. The budget is normally adopted in January and represents the next fiscal year's time frame. Refer also to *budget.*

adult education
This term refers to organized public educational programs which provide opportunities for adults and out-of-school youth to further their education, regardless of their previous level of educational attainment. Only those programs which have as their primary purpose the development of skills, knowledge, habits, or attitudes are included; the programs may result in adult development through traditional, formal instruction or through means of informal group leadership directed toward specific, recognizable goals. Programs which are not considered as being within the framework of adult education include the following: regular, full-time, and summer elementary and secondary day school, community college, and college programs. Activities which are considered as being within the framework of adult education include those which are primarily social or recreational, or which have

as their primary purpose the production of goods.

AGI

This is an abbreviation for *adjusted gross income.*

aid, basic

Refer to *basic aid.*

aid, categorical

Refer to *categorical aid.*

aid to dependent children (ADC)

This term refers to children whose parents qualify for Aid to Families with Dependent Children. Depending on the number of students and/or percent of students classified as ADC children, school districts get additional aid under Ohio's foundation formula.

Aid to Families with Dependent Children (AFDC)

Refer to *aid to dependent children.*

allocation

Allocation is the actual transfer of money from a specified government fund to the unit of government for which it has been appropriated.

allocation formula

A mathematical formula is used to determine the resources to be received by a particular school. The amount allocated is based on a school's enrollment, a per-pupil guaranteed dollar amount, an equalization factor, assessed valuation yield for 20 mills, and other factors.

amortization

Amortization refers to reducing a debt through stated, periodic payments of principal and interest.

annual revaluation of property

The county auditor is obligated to make necessary changes in assessed value each year if he finds value has changed from the value at which it is listed on the tax list; but he can only be ordered to do so by the tax commissioner in years of sexennial reappraisal or triennial revaluation.

appropriation

A board of education is authorized to make expenditures and to incur financial obligations for specific purposes. This formal action is called appropriation, as funds are appropriated into various accounts in specified amounts.

appropriation expenditure

This refers to an expenditure chargeable to an appropriation.

appropriation resolution

A resolution must be approved by a school board which appropriates the funds needed to operate each department of the school system for the July 1 through June 30 fiscal year. This document revises the tax budget to balance with expected revenue. It may be amended during the fiscal year if additional revenue becomes available. Also, see *temporary appropriation resolution.*

assessed valuation

The assessed valuation is the value of taxable property as determined by a governmental agency or tax assessor. Taxes are paid on the basis of a property's assessed valuation. The assessed valuation of property in most states and localities is only a percentage of the market value of the property. In Ohio, property is assessed at 35% of the market value. The percentage of appraised value used in determining assessed value for real property is 35%. For personal property it is: public utility property—88%; electrical production equipment—100%; all other personal property—25%.

assessment ratio

The assessed valuation of property in most states is usually less than the market value of the property. In other words, owners are able to sell property for a price higher than the assessed valuation of the property. Although most states have a legal standard at which all property should be assessed, the assessed valuations are usually below even the legal level; assessed valuations may vary widely among jurisdictions in a state. The actual assessment level or assessment ratio is determined by comparing actual assessed valuations to market values.

assessor

A governmental official is responsible for the evaluation of all taxable properties located within the taxing unit. This official is known as an assessor.

assets

Assets are resources which can be used over a number of years. Assets include the following: capital assets (school buildings, major equipment, and so forth), cash, investments, accounts receivable, and inventories. Assets are often listed in the annual financial report and may be paid for by the issuing of bonds which will be paid back over a number of years.

assumption

A document prepared by district administrators early in the process of developing a proposed budget is called assumption. It sets forth the key expectations for the coming year. Expectations, for example, often include the following: the number of students to be served, the rate of inflation and so forth. An assumption includes those factors which can be expected to govern the development of a detailed financial plan.

audit

Audit is the examination of records and accounts as well as the securing of other evidence for one or more of the following purposes: (a) determining the propriety of proposed or completed transactions, (b) ascertaining whether all transactions have been recorded, and (c) ascertaining whether transactions are accurately recorded in the accounts and in the statements reflecting the accounts.

auditing

Auditing is the verification of the accuracy and completeness of financial records of an organization as well as the appraisal of the legality, efficiency, and effectiveness of the financial management of the organization. Public schools are usually audited by auditors of the state. This is done on an annual basis.

average daily attendance (ADA)

This refers to pupil enrollment measured by attendance, not membership.

average daily membership (ADM)

ADM is the official measure that Ohio uses to represent the number of students in a school district for the purpose of calculating state aid. Membership is measured by actual enrollment as of the first full week of October.

balance sheet

A summarized statement of the financial condition of a school district or fund, as of a given date is referred to as a balance sheet. The balance sheet reflects assets, liabilities, and fund balance.

basic aid

In Ohio, a basic amount of money is guaranteed by the state for the education of a pupil. The money can be used by the district for any educational purpose.

basic aid foundation formula

Refer to *foundation program.*

basis of accounting

This refers to a policy governing when revenues and expenditures are counted in a district's accounting records; possibilities include cash basis (which lists financial events only when money is actually received or paid out) and accrual basis (which counts changes when the district knows the events will occur). Ohio utilizes an accrual accounting system.

beginning balance

The amount of money that a district has on hand at the beginning of a fiscal year is the beginning balance. It consists of money remaining at the end of the previous fiscal year.

board of tax appeals

Reviews appeals of decisions by the county boards of revision and final determinations of the tax commissioner.

bond

Bond is a borrowing device used by many school districts. The buyer of the bond is entitled to receive scheduled payments before district monies are used for any other purpose. The bond holder, in effect, receives a lien against district revenues.

bonded debt

The portion of a school district's debt which

is covered by outstanding bonds is known as bonded debt. Bonded debt is also known as funded debt.

bonded indebtedness

Most states limit the ability of local governments, including school districts, to incur debt. Limits on debt associated with the sale of bonds (bonded indebtedness) are frequently tied to the source of revenue from which the debt is to be repaid. In the case of school districts, this usually is the assessed valuation of property. Bonded indebtedness can be linked to local tax rates. Also, see *debt limit.*

bond issue

Bond issues are issues placed on the ballot to raise funds for capital improvements of school facilities or to provide for the construction of new facilities. The money from such is not permitted to be used for the day-to-day operation of schools and must be used for those items identified on the ballot voted by the public.

bonds, term

Refer to *term bonds.*

budget

Budget is a financial plan of receipts and expenditures developed to reflect the needs of a school district.

budget development calendar

This refers to a schedule of steps to be taken by district administrators and the school board in the process of creating the budget for the next fiscal year. This document may identify target dates for receiving proposals from principals and division heads as well as identifying target dates for executive decisions, briefing meetings for the school board regarding the proposed budget, publication of the proposed budget, public meetings to receive citizen comments, the final school board vote, and any subsequent steps required before the budget can take effect.

capital outlay

Capital outlay refers to direct expenditures for contract or force accounts of the construction of buildings, roads, and other improvements as well as for the purchasing of equipment, land, and existing structures. Amounts for additions, replacements, and major alterations to fixed works and structures are classified as current operation expenditures.

cash and security holdings

Cash, deposits, and governmental and private securities (bonds, notes, mortgages, and so forth) are all called cash and security holdings. The term does not include interfund loans, receivables, the value of real property, the value of other fixed assets, or the holdings of agency and private trust funds.

cash basis

This is the basis of accounting under which revenues are recorded only when actually received. Only cash disbursements are recorded as expenditures.

categorical aid

In Ohio, funds are provided by the state, in addition to basic aid, that are allocated to school districts for specific categorical expenditures such as the following: pupil transportation, programs for the gifted, school lunches, special education programs, vocational programs, and so forth. Specific criteria must be met in order to receive the aid.

C.A.U.V.

C.A.U.V. refers to current agriculture use valuation. Land devoted exclusively for agricultural use may be valued according to land current use (value of what it can produce), instead of "highest and best" (market value) use. Land owners must apply for C.A.U.V. annually; if received, property taxes are reduced substantially.

classes of real property

There are two classes of real property defined in Section 2a of Article XII of the Constitution for the purpose of providing a tax reduction factor to each class. Classification of real property for other purposes is prohibited by the Uniform Rule. The classes of real property are: (1) residential/agricultural, and (2) nonresidential/agricultural.

classification

Refer to *function* [*classification*] and *object* [*classification*].

coding
Coding is a system of numbering or otherwise designating accounts, entries, invoices, vouchers, and so forth, the purpose of which is to provide symbols to reveal certain required information.

community services
Those services which are provided by a school district for the community (as a whole or as a segment) are identified as community services. Community services are outside the auspices of regular pupil education programs.

consolidation guarantee
This is a program for consolidated school districts to guarantee that their total school foundation (basic plus categorical) for three years will be no less than it was in the year that the consolidation occurred.

construction
This refers to the production of fixed works, structures, and additions as well as replacements and major alterations. Construction includes the planning and designing of specific projects as well as site improvement and the provision of equipment and facilities that form an integral part of a structure.

consumer price index (CPI)
CPI is an index measuring the change in the cost of the purchase of goods and services by a typical wage-earner. The cost is expressed as a percentage of these same goods and services in some base period. The concept is also known as "cost-of-living." The CPI annual report is based on the calendar year, January through December.

contingent liabilities
Potentialities which may become liabilities as a result of conditions undetermined at a given date, such as pending law suits, judgments under appeal, and unsettled disputed claims are classified as contingent liabilities.

contracted services
Contracted services are services rendered by personnel who are not on the payroll of the school district. Services include all related expenses covered by the contract.

controlling account
This refers to an account usually kept in the general ledger in which the postings to a number of identical, similar, or related accounts are summarized so that the balance in the controlling account equals the sum of the balance of the detailed accounts. The controlling account serves as a check on the accuracy of detailed account postings.

corporate franchise tax
A tax applied to corporations either on the net worth (book value of capital investments, capital and reserves) or on the Ohio net income (profits) is called a corporate franchise tax.

cost accounting
Cost accounting is a method of accounting which provides for the gathering and recording of all the elements of costs incurred to accomplish a purpose, to carry on an activity or operation, and/or to complete a unit of work or a specific job.

cost-of-doing-business factor
This is an equalization factor used to weight the foundation formula to take into account the differences in the costs of operating in different counties in Ohio. New factors are listed each biennium on average wages/salaries in each county.

county auditor
Responsible for assessing all real and certain personal property within his county; he prepares the general tax list and duplicate and gives the duplicate to the county treasurer for the actual collection of taxes.

current agricultural use valuation (C.A.U.V.)
Refer to *C.A.U.V.*

current expense
When accounts are maintained on an accrual basis, the term current expense includes the total charge incurred, whether paid or unpaid. When accounts are maintained on a cash basis, it includes only actual disbursements.

current operating expenditures
Current operating expenditures include expenditures for the daily operation of the school

program. Included are expenses for administration, instruction, operation, and maintenance of the plant as well as fixed charges.

current tax collections

Amounts received from taxes levied for the current fiscal year are called current tax collections.

debt

Debt refers to credit obligations of a school system or its parent government. Included are long-term and all interest-bearing short-term (repayable within one year) credit obligations. Excluded are non-interest-bearing short-term obligations, interfund obligations, amounts owed in a trust or agency capacity, advances, and contingent loans from other governmental units as well as rights of individuals to benefits from the school system employee retirement fund.

debt limit

Most states establish a maximum amount of debt that can be incurred. In Ohio, the debt limit is 9% of the total assessed valuation in respective districts.

debt, outstanding

Refer to *outstanding debt.*

debt service

The expenditures necessary to repay the borrowed money are considered as debt service expenditures. Included are both principal and interest on the loan plus any costs which are incurred in employing a bank or some financial agency to handle the details involved in retiring the loan.

deficit

The excess of the obligations of a fund over the fund's resources are classified as deficit.

delinquent tax collection

This refers to amounts received from taxes levied in prior fiscal years that were not paid on time by property owners.

depreciation

Depreciation is the reduction in the value of capital assets through wear and tear or obsolescence.

direct expenses

Elements of cost which can be easily, obviously, and conveniently indentified with specific activities are called direct expenses. They are distinguished from costs incurred for several different activities and which elements are not readily identifiable with specific activities. Refer also to *indirect expenses.*

disadvantaged pupil impact aid (DPIA)

DPIA refers to special funding provided by the State of Ohio which is designed to support the educational costs in school districts with large numbers of disadvantaged children. The monies may be used by the school districts for general operating expenses.

disadvantaged pupil program fund (DPPF)

This fund was specifically designed for school districts having programs for disadvantaged pupils. Monies from this program fund are not part of the state's foundation program and can be spent only for approved programs.

district power equalization (DPE)

This refers to a state equalization aid program that "equalizes" the ability of each school district to raise funds for education. In a pure DPE program, the state guarantees to both property-poor and property-rich school districts, the same dollar yield for the same property tax rate. In short, equal tax rates produce equal per-pupil expenditures. In the property-poor school districts, the state makes up the difference between what is raised locally and what the state guarantees. In property-rich school districts, excess funds may or may not be "recaptured" by the state for distribution to property-poor school districts. Most DPE state laws do not include recapture provisions. DPE programs are known by a variety of names throughout the states; among the names are the following: guaranteed tax base programs, guaranteed yield programs, and percentage equalizing programs. DPE programs focus on a district's ability to support the educational program; thus, DPE programs enchance the local fiscal role in education. DPE satisfies the "fiscal neutrality standard" without achieving "uniformity of expenditures" among school districts.

district wealth
See *tax base.*

dual control
Dual control is a system of administrative organization in which two or more administrators, with approximately equal administrative powers, report directly to the governing board of the organization.

due dates for real property taxes
December 31 of the year for which the taxes are levied and the following June 20; at least one-half of the taxes due must be paid at the first collection due date (December 31); in practice, extensions for the preparation of the tax list and tax bills delay the due dates until weeks or months later.

educational consumer price index (ECPI)
Refer to *consumer price index* (CPI) for general concept. ECPI differs only from CPI in that ECPI is based on a fiscal calendar of July 1 through June 30 instead of the traditional January 1 through December 31 annual calendar used by CPI.

educational service personnel (ESP)
Educational service personnel include the following: librarians, counselors, visiting teachers, nurses, and elementary school teachers of art, music, and physical education and school social workers. Districts must employ at least five ESP for every 1,000 pupils listed in the ADM; failure to comply will result in a reduction in the state basic aid amount.

effective mills
A tax rate applied to real property after adjustments have been applied which reflect a tax reduction factor is referred to as effective mills.

elasticity of tax revenues
This refers to the responsiveness of the revenue from a tax to changes in various economic factors within the state or nation. In particular, policy-makers may want to know whether tax revenues will increase more rapidly, as rapidly, or less rapidly than changes in personal income. The revenues from an elastic tax will increase by more than 1% for each 1% increase in personal income. Income taxes are usually elastic tax sources. In general, elastic tax sources have progressive patterns of incidence; inelastic tax sources have regressive patterns of incidence.

emergency levy
A tax from which the proceeds are used to avoid an operating deficit is classified as an emergency levy. It lasts no more than five years.

encumbrance
Encumbrance is an accounting device which marks certain monies as set aside for a specified purpose; the appropriate amount is entered when a purchase order or requisition is made.

ending balance
The amount remaining available to the school district after all expenditures are made during a fiscal year is called an ending balance.

equalization
This refers to the process by which the state compensates for disparities in local wealth and taxpaying ability; this is achieved by directing funds toward demonstrated educational needs.

equalization factor
Refer to *cost-of-doing-business factor.*

equalization formula aid
This refers to financial assistance extended by a higher-level governmental unit, the state, to a lower-level governmental unit, the school districts, to equalize the fiscal situation of the lower-level unit of government. Because school districts vary in their abilities to raise property tax dollars, equalization formula aid is allocated to make the ability to raise such local funds more nearly equal. In general, equalization formula aid increases as the per-pupil property wealth of a school district decreases.

equal yield formula
This is a formula used to determine how much money each school district receives from the state in basic program support. The formula insures that every district will receive a set amount of money per pupil for each mill of local support.

equipment

Equipment is a material item of a nonexpendable nature. Examples include the following: a built-in facility, a movable or fixed unit of furniture, furnishings, an instrument or apparatus, a machine (including attachments), and an instrumental skill-training device. In addition, the term includes a set of small articles which has repairable or replaceable parts, and the whole set of which retains its identity and utility over a period of time which is characteristic of, and definable for, items of its class.

equity

Fairness, impartiality, justice or anything that is fair or equitable all speak to the term equity. In a legal framework, equity is (a) the resorting to general principles of fairness and justice when existing laws are inadequate for the situation, and (b) a system of rules and doctrines supplementing statutory and common law and superseding such law when it proves inadequate for just settlement.

exemption

Some property is excluded from the application of property taxes, e.g., churches, charities, public property used for a public purpose, tax abatements, etc.

expenditures

All amounts of money paid out by a school system are expenditures. It is the net of recoveries and other correcting transactions other than those for retirement of debt, purchase of securities, extension of loans, and agency transactions.

expenditure uniformity

Expenditure uniformity is a standard in school finance requiring equal expenditures per pupil or per weighted pupil for all students in the state. Refer to *fiscal neutrality*.

expenses, direct

Refer to *direct expenses*.

expenses, indirect

Refer to *indirect expenses*.

federal authorization appropriation allocation

Components of the concept are as follows: (a) authorization is a statement, usually contained in a statute, that government funds up to a certain, specified amount may be appropriated for a given purpose; (b) an appropriation is a statement, usually contained in an appropriation bill, that a certain, specified amount shall be spent for a given purpose by some unit of government and that this amount shall be derived from a specified unit of government; and (c) allocation is the actual transfer of the money from the specified governmental fund to the unit of government for which it has been appropriated.

fidelity bond

This is a bond guaranteeing a school district against losses resulting from the dishonest actions of the treasurer, employees, or other persons of the school district. Refer also to *surety bond*.

financial ability

Financial ability is a measure in terms of some economic, social, or political indices of the ability of a unit of government to purchase a given kind, amount, and quality of goods and/or services.

financial effort

This is in reference to a measure of the degree to which a unit of government is purchasing specified goods and/or services of a given kind, amount, and quality.

financial report

An annual document published after the end of each fiscal year is called a financial report. It sets forth actual expenditures and revenues and is usually subject to outside audit to verify its accuracy.

fiscal capacity

Fiscal capacity is the capability of a locality to raise money through taxes which can be based on assessed or equalized property valuation, income wealth, or a combination of several measures.

fiscal dependence

A school district is said to be fiscally dependent when one or more outside agencies of government other than the state legislature have delegated powers which enable them to exercise final control over the budgets, taxing power, or other fiscal affairs of the school district. Refer also to *fiscal independence* which contrasts with fiscal dependence.

fiscal equity
Fiscal equity is a standard of equalization which insures that the total amount of resources available to a student is the same statewide.

fiscal independence
In contrast to a school district which is said to be fiscally dependent, a fiscally independent school district is directly responsible to the state and to the people of the district in fiscal matters. Refer to *fiscal dependence* for contrast.

fiscal neutrality
This is a court-defined equity standard in school finance. It is a negative standard stating that current operating expenditures per pupil cannot be related to a school district's adjusted valuation per pupil. It simply means that differences in expenditures per pupil cannot be related to local school wealth

fiscal period
This refers to any period at the end of which a school district determines its financial condition as well as the results of its operations; any period at the end of which a school district "closes its books."

fiscal year (FY)
A 12-month period with a starting date selected by the state and used as the period to be covered by the budget is called a fiscal year. In Ohio, the FY starts on July 1 and runs through June 30.

fixed assets
Land, buildings, machinery, furniture, and other equipment which the school district intends to hold or continue to use over a long period of time are all fixed assets. "Fixed" denotes probability of intent to continue use or possession; it does not indicate immobility of an asset.

fixed charges
Fixed charges are known, recurring expenditures such as rent, taxes, insurance premiums, and contributions to employee retirement systems.

flat grant program
A flat grant program allocates an equal sum of dollars for each public school pupil in the state. A flat grant is not an equalization aid program because it allocates the same dollar amount per pupil regardless of the property or income wealth of the local school districts. However, if no local dollars are raised for education and all school dollars come from the state, a flat grant program becomes equivalent to full-state assumption.

floating debt
This refers to liabilities (except bonds) payable on demand or at an early date; for example, accounts payable, bank loans, notes, or warrants.

food service
Activities which have as their purpose the preparation and serving of regular and incidental meals, lunches, or snacks in connection with school activities are all classified under food service.

foundation (or guaranteed) level
The level of per-pupil expenditures guaranteed to all school districts in a state through a combination of state aid and locally-raised revenue. In Ohio, the foundation level for FY 93 was $2,817 per pupil.

foundation program
Foundation program refers to a financial system that typically guarantees a certain foundation level of expenditures of basic aid for each student together with a minimum tax rate that each school district must levy for education purposes. The difference between what a local school district raises at the minimum tax rate and the foundation expenditure level is made up in state aid.

full-state assumption (FSA)
A school finance program in which the state pays for all education costs and sets equal per-pupil expenditures in all school districts is called a full-state assumption program. FSA would satisfy the "uniformity" standard of equity.

full-time equivalency (FTE)
FTE is a unit used to count the personnel assigned to a school or other administrative unit. One FTE consists either or a full-time employee or two or more part-time employees who together work a number of hours equivalent to one full-time employee.

function [classification]
An expenditure category defining a general purpose for which district money is spent is referred to as function. It is used in organizing a standard line-item budget; examples might include the following: "instruction," "administration," or "support services."

fund
This is an accounting device used to track revenue dollars which can only be used for specified purposes as well as to record the expenditures which meet those restrictions.

fund accounts
All accounts necessary to set forth the financial operations and financial condition of a fund are referred to as fund accounts.

fund, bonded debt
This term refers to the fund used to maintain a record of bonded debt.

fund, building and site
The fund, building and site, is designated for recording transactions in monies and other assets "earmarked" for use in acquiring new school sites, buildings, and equipment additions. It is also used in connection with major remodeling of, or additions to, facilities.

fund, debt retirement
A fund designated for the recording of transactions in monies and other assets "earmarked" for use in payment of principal and interest on long-term debt is called debt retirement.

fund, endowment
This is a fund from which the income may be expended, but the principal of which must remain intact.

fund, fixed assets
The fund used to maintain a record of fixed assets.

fund, revolving
A fund provided to carry out a cycle of operations is called a revolving fund.

general aid
General aid is state or federal aid to school districts which can be used for any purpose.

general expenditure
This refers to any school system expenditure other than one classified as employee retirement or other insurance trust expenditure.

general fund
General fund is the fund of a local school district from which the district's treasurer pays for the normal expenses for the district. It includes expenditures for salaries, fringe benefits, utilities, bus expenses, cleaning materials, educational supplies, maintenance materials, and so forth. This fund is often known as the operating fund.

general ledger
General ledger is a book, file, or other device in which accounts are kept to the degree of detail necessary that summarizes the financial transactions of the school district.

general property tax
This tax is levied on land and buildings located within the school district; it is essentially a real estate or property tax. Every owner of private and business property in the district including public utilities pays this tax. As a general rule, property owned by governmental, charitable and religious institutions is exempt from taxation. Refer also to *property tax.*

general revenue
All school system revenue except employee retirement or other insurance trust revenue falls under the category of general revenue.

general tax list of real and public utility property
Record maintained by the county auditor that registers the assessed value of each parcel of taxable real or public utility personal property in the county.

general tax list of tangible personal property
County auditor's record of all taxable per-

sonal property, except utility property.

gift
Money received from a philanthropic foundation, private individual, or private organization for which no repayment or special service to the contributor is expected.

grant, public
A contribution of either financial or material goods, made by one governmental unit to another and for which the contributing unit expects no repayment. Grants may be for specific or general purposes.

guarantee
This refers to a program providing for most school districts to receive state aid equal to the amount of the state aid received in the previous year. In FY 93, all Ohio school districts have a basic aid guarantee of 100% of the previous year's basic aid if they have less than $285,000 valuation per pupil. Districts that exceed $285,000 per pupil are guaranteed only 85% of the previous year's basic aid.

guaranteed support level
The dollar amount which the state guarantees will be available for each pupil regardless of where the pupil resides. The state guarantees that if 20 mills are levied by a local district, combined state and local resources will produce a given dollar amount.

guaranteed tax base program (GTB)
This is a tax base guaranteed by the state for the education of a pupil. The state guarantees that for each mill levied locally, combined state and local resources will produce the given dollar amount.

guaranteed tax yield program
This program is a tax base guaranteed by the state for the education of a pupil. The state guarantees that for each mill levied locally, combined state and local resources will produce the given dollar amount.

guarantee level
Refer to *foundation level.*

home-school counselors
Refer to *visiting teachers.*

home-school visitors
Refer to *visiting teachers.*

homestead exemption
Real estate tax reductions are given to qualified elderly and disabled homeowners. Local governments and schools are reimbursed by the state for the resultant tax loss.

impact aid
Impact aid is a program that provides assistance to school districts that serve significant numbers of children whose parents either work for the federal government or reside on property owned by the federal government.

income wealth
Income wealth refers to the tax base of a locality based on the income of the residents.

indirect expenses
Elements of cost which are not directly attributed to a particular category; for example, facilities costs.

inside mills
Refer to *millage, inside.*

instructional unit
In contrast to pupils as the base (unit) for quantifying district needs and allocating funds, some states allocate funds on the basis of the number of pupils per classroom or the number of pupils per teacher. These instructional units can be computed for specific program areas, grade levels or types of school districts (that is, urban, rural, and so forth).

intangible property tax
This term refers to a tax on dealers in intangibles; for example, stockbrokers or investment companies.

interest earnings
This term applies to interest earned on deposits and securities including amounts for accrued interest on investment securities sold; however, receipts for accrued interest on bonds issued are classified as offsets to interest expenditure. Note that interest earnings shown under general revenue do not include earnings on assets of employee retirement systems.

interfund transfer
Money which is taken from one fund under the control of the board of education and added to another fund under the board's control is classified as interfund transfer money.

intergovernmental expenditures
Intergovernmental expenditures are amounts paid to other governmental units as fiscal aid in the form of share revenues and grants-in-aid, school building authority payments, or payments in lieu of taxes. The term, however, excludes amounts paid to other governmental units for purchases of commodities, property, or utility services, as well as any tax imposed and paid as such; it also excludes employer contributions for social insurance (for example, contributions to the federal government for old-age benefits, survivors' benefits, disability benefits); and in addition, health insurance for school district employees.

intergovernmental revenue
This refers to amounts received from other governmental units as fiscal aid in the form of shared revenues and grants-in-aid, reimbursement for performance of general governmental functions, payment for specific services rendered for the governmental payer, or revenue in lieu of taxes. All intergovernmental revenue is classified as general revenue. Intergovernmental revenue excludes amounts received from other governmental units for proceeds from the sale of property or commodities.

intermediate source of revenue
An intermediate administrative unit or political subdivision which serves in a liaison capacity between a represented school district and the state; it collects revenue and distributes it to the represented school district. The amount distributed differs from that which was collected.

internal control
Internal control is a plan of organization under which employees' duties are so defined and arranged, and records and procedures are so designed as to facilitate the exercising of effective accounting control over assets, liabilities, revenues, and expenditures. For example, under such a system, the employees' work is sub-divided in order that a single employee does not perform a complete cycle of operations; an employee who handles cash would not therefore be the one who also posts the accounts receivable record. Under such a system, the procedures to be followed are administratively organized and clearly specific; the procedures require proper authorizations by designated officials before actions are taken.

inventories
Tangible items, not yet recorded under appropriate expenditure accounts of the unit which is to receive such, are called inventories. Such items are located in centralized storage areas from which the items are periodically distributed to schools, individuals, or other organizational units on the basis of appropriate requisitions.

journal
A journal is any form on which the financial transactions of the school district are formally recorded for the first time; examples include the following: a cash receipts book, a check register, and journal voucher.

judgment
Judgment is an amount to be paid or collected as the result of a court decision.

levy, tax
Refer to *tax levy*.

liability, general fund
Debt or other legal obligation arising from past general fund transactions; the obligation is payable but not necessarily due immediately.

line-item budget
This is the current, standard format for the presentation of financial plans in most public school districts. It presents figures on a district-wide basis for expected revenue listed by source; planned expenditures listed by function and object; and the resulting ending balance.

loans, short-term
Refer to *short-term loans*.

local leeway
In state aid programs, this refers to the right

of a participating district to tax itself at a rate above the mandated local tax effort or to spend above a specified expenditure level.

local yield per pupil, per mill

This is a term for the number of dollars that a school district can raise per pupil for each mill levied locally. The per-pupil valuation is divided by 1,000 to calculate the local per-pupil, per-mill yield. For example, a per-pupil valuation of $85,000 divided by 1,000 equals $85 which represents the amount of local taxes raised on a per-pupil basis when one mill is added to the tax rate.

long-term debt

Long-term debt is debt payable more than one year after date of issuance.

long-term debt issued

The par value of long-term debt obligations which are incurred during the fiscal period; it includes funding obligations. Debt obligations authorized but not actually incurred during the fiscal period are not included.

long-term debt retired

The par value of long-term debt obligations liquidated by repayments or exchange; it includes debt retired by operational funding.

maintenance of plant

Those activities which are concerned with maintaining the grounds, buildings, and equipment at their original condition in terms of completeness and/or efficiency; maintenance includes repairs to or replacements of property. Maintenance includes anything less than the complete replacement of a total building.

maintenance operation

This term refers to the maintenance of the physical plant utilized by an organization. Maintenance activities are those which are undertaken to preserve the dollar value of the capital asset; operation activities are those which are undertaken to make the plant usable from day to day.

mandamus

Mandamus is a court order requiring compliance with a specific statute.

mandated programs

Those educational programs or classes required by the state or federal government are called mandated programs.

market value

Refer to *real value.*

median family income

Assuming a rank ordering of all families residing in a school district, the median income family would be the family whose income is midway between the lowest and highest family incomes.

memorandum account

This account is an informal record of a school district transaction that is not recorded as part of the regular financial accounts but for which a record is desired.

mill

A mill is the basic unit for computing local property taxes and is equivalent to one tenth of a cent. A local tax mill is also the yield from one dollar per thousand of the total assessed value of property. For example, an individual home which is assessed at $20,000 for tax purposes would cost the owner $20.00 (less any roll-backs) for each mill in the tax rate. For the calculation of tax bills, one mill is equivalent to $.001; $25\frac{1}{2}$ mills is equivalent to $.0255; and 50 mills, $.05.

millage, inside

Ten mills of property tax may be levied by local governments without the vote of the people. A school district is allocated a portion of the 10 non-voted mills by the county budget commission. The average share of non-voted mills for schools in Ohio is 4.6 mills (.0046).

millage, outside

Outside mills are additional mills, above the inside millage. These mills must be approved by voters of a political subdivision (for example, school districts, townships, villages, cities, counties, joint vocational schools, and so forth). Outside millage does not include the millage which has been voter-approved for special projects or for the operation of a political subdivision.

millage, total current expense

This is the total of both the inside and outside millage that is designated for the current expenses (namely, the general fund) of a school district.

municipal overburden

This is a term which has been used to describe the fiscal position of large cities in relationship to the difficulties associated with providing tax monies for public education. Municipal overburden includes the large burden of non-education services that cities must provide and that most other jurisdictions do not have to provide or at least provide in the same quantity. These non-education services may include above-average services or expenses related to the following: welfare, health care, hospitalization, public housing, police, fire, and sanitation. The sum of the expenses for providing the non-education services results in a competition of public agencies and services for public tax monies; therefore, education must compete with the various agencies and services for each local tax dollar raised. This competition for tax revenue reduces the ability of large city school districts to raise education dollars. The argument for the concept of municipal overburden is, therefore, that the fiscal squeeze caused by the above-described situation coupled with the number of educationally-disadvantaged children as well as those in need of special education places large city school districts at a fiscal disadvantage in supporting public school services.

net expenditures

These are the actual outlay by a school district for a specified service or item after the deduction of any discounts, rebates, reimbursements, or revenue produced by the service or item.

object [classification]

This is an expense category used by public school districts to define specifically various types of expenditures; examples might include "personnel salaries" and "materials and supplies."

obligations

Obligations are amounts which a school district will be required to meet from its resources.

operating levy

An operating levy is used to generate a tax, the proceeds from which a school board can utilize for any legal expenditure. The bulk of funds derived from operating levies is used to pay for the daily costs associated with operating a school district; these costs, for example, include the provision of salaries for personnel, books for students, supplies and equipment for plant maintenance, and repairs for buildings. The proceeds from operating levies can also be used for permanent improvements (for example, the construction of buildings, sidewalks, and parking lots) as well as for the purchase of furniture and equipment (including buses). The funds may be used for any other expenditures which are not forbidden specifically by law.

operation of plant

Activities which are concerned with keeping the physical plant open and ready for use; the activities include the following: cleaning, lighting, heating, moving furniture, caring for grounds, operating telephone switchboards, and other "housekeeping" activities which recur on a regular (daily, weekly, monthly, or seasonal) basis. It does not include the functions associated with repairs.

outside millage

Refer to *millage, outside.*

outstanding debt

All debt obligations remaining unpaid on a specified date are classified as outstanding debt.

"Park Investment Case"

State, ex rel. Park Investment Co. v. Board of Tax Appeals, 32 Ohio St. 2d 28 (1972). This was a case in which the Ohio Supreme Court held that all real property in the state must be assessed uniformly for tax purposes.

pay-as-you-go

This approach allows districts which are in a strong financial position to pay for facilities as they are being constructed; thereby saving up to 50% of the total construction cost.

percentage equalization program

This is a program through which the state contributes a percentage of the cost involved in the education of a student. The percentage is based on locally-determined education expenditure levels.

permanent improvement levy

A tax from which the proceeds are limited to costs related to the construction of or addition to school buildings and/or improvement of school grounds. Monies can only be expended for construction/improvements which represent a normal duration life of five or more years.

per-pupil expenditure

Cost per-pupil or per-pupil expenditure both refer to the amount of money expended to provide an educational program for one student. It is calculated by dividing the total expenses of a school district by the number of pupils in that district.

petty cash

Money set aside for the provision of making change or immediate payments of comparatively small amounts is called petty cash.

phased-in levy

A tax for operating expenses; it will produce a predetermined increase in tax revenue each year.

prepaid expenditures

Portions of expenditures which are made during one fiscal year that cover services or benefits for which a recording is made in succeeding years; examples include prepaid insurance premiums and rent.

program budget

Program budget is a budgetary format organized for expenditures covering specific services or programs provided by a school system. This format provides an alternative to the traditional line-item budget statement which presents expenditures by function and object.

progressive tax

This refers to a tax that increases in percentage as taxpayers' income levels increase. Accordingly, under this system a high-income taxpayer will pay a higher percentage of his/her income than would a low-income taxpayer.

property tax

A tax conditioned on ownership of property and measured by the value of such; this form of tax includes general property taxes related to property as a whole in addition to real and personal tangible, whether taxed at a single rate or at classified rates. Real property includes all lands, buildings, and fixtures thereon and appurtenances thereto. Personal property is not included as part of the real estate and pertains only to inventories and other properties owned by commercial enterprises. Property taxation represents a system of uniform taxation of real and personal property when such is not exempt by provision of law. Refer also to *general property tax.*

property tax circuit breaker program

This is a tax relief program which is usually financed by a state. The program focuses property tax relief on particular households which are presumed, based on established criteria, to be overburdened by property taxes. It is intended to reduce a presumed regressivity of the property tax. A typical property tax circuit breaker program attempts to limit the property tax burden to a percentage of household income; it is applicable only to residential property taxpayers. The percent of taxes due usually rises as income rises to reflect an attempt to make the overall tax burden progressive. Most states initially enacted circuit breaker programs solely for senior citizens; however, a few states have extended circuit breaker benefits to all low-income households regardless of the age of the head of the household. The circuit program is based on actual or estimated taxes paid on residential property; generally a circuit breaker benefit takes the form of a credit on state income taxes.

property wealth

This term refers to the tax base of a locality based on the real and tangible property values of the locality.

proportional tax

A tax that exacts the same percentage of family income regardless of the income level.

proposed budget
This is the budget recommended, or proposed, to the school board by the superintendent or chief business officer; the recommendation is based on a process of administrative planning.

prorating
Prorating is the allocation of portions of a single expenditure to more than one account in direct proportion to the benefits provided by the expenditure for the program or purpose represented by the accounts.

pupil transportation services
Those activities which have as their purpose, the conveyance of students to and from school activities, either between home and school, or on trips for curricular or co-curricular activities.

pupil-weighted systems
A state aid system in which various types of pupils are assigned various "weights" for school funding purposes; weights are assigned based on the estimated or assumed per-pupil costs represented by the particular educational program in which they are enrolled. Aid is allocated on the basis of the total number of weighted students comprised by the system as a whole. Usually the cost of the educational programs for students enrolled in grades four through six is considered the standard program and each student is weighted as 1.0. For states such as Florida which choose to invest more funds in the earlier school years, pupils in grades kindergarten through three are assigned a weight factor greater than 1.0, typically around 1.3. In other states, high school students are weighted about 1.25; these secondary weights are, however, slowly being eliminated. The two major areas where numerous weightings have been used include special education programs and vocational education programs. Florida, for example, assigns weights for 15 different categories of special education students and six different categories of vocational education students. Weighted-pupil programs reflect the concept that the costs associated with providing an educational program for one type of student is different than for another type; students enrolled in the higher-cost programs are assigned a higher weight and, therefore, more money is received for each. State aid is calculated and distributed on the basis of the total number of weighted students in each school district. Determination of the appropriate weight for each type of student is based on a number of factors and is, therefore, a difficult matter. Pupil-weighted systems are also known as weighted-pupil programs.

purchase order
A purchase order is a document which authorizes the delivery of specified merchandise or service and the charging for such by the provider.

real property tax
The tax levied against land and buildings within a school district.

real value
Real value is the value of property if it were sold "at arm's length"; for assessment purposes, the price or cost which the property would command in the open market in its present geographical location. The concept is also known as market value, sale value, true cash value, and true market.

reappraisal
Reappraisal is the process by which all real property is valued for tax purposes; reappraisal occurs every six years.

reappraisal guarantee
This refers to a program guaranteeing school districts the same amount of aid which was received the previous year despite any variations in the property tax appraisals. It guarantees the total SF-12 amount, not just the basic aid portion.

rebates
Rebates are abatements or refunds.

recapture
Recapture is a feature in state aid funding formulas for schools whereby local school districts which raise a per-pupil amount in excess of the state-guaranteed, per-pupil expenditure amount would be required to repay the state the excess amount. The paid-back amounts are redistributed to poorer school districts (that is,

those with a lower per-pupil valuation).

receipts, revenue
Refer to *revenue receipts.*

receivable taxes
The uncollected portion of taxes which a governmental unit has received.

redetermination
The process by which all real property is adjusted in value on the third year after reappraisal.

refund
Refund is an amount returned or a credit allowed due to an over-collection or a return of a purchased item.

regressive tax
A tax that does not increase in direct proportion to the increase in taxpayer income is called regressive tax. Thus, a high-income taxpayer will pay a lower percentage of his/her income than would a low-income taxpayer.

reimbursement
A repayment (pay-back) of an expenditure made on behalf of another individual, department, firm, corporation, or governmental unit.

remodeling
Remodeling is any major, permanent, structural improvement made to a building. It includes changes in partitions, roof structures, walls, and so forth. Repairs are not included in the category of remodeling; instead, repairs are classified under maintenance.

repairs
This is the term used for the restoration of equipment, buildings, or grounds. Repair work infers restoration from a worn, damaged or inefficient status to an earlier or original state of completeness, efficiency, or condition.

replacement of equipment
An act of purchasing and substituting one complete unit of equipment for another; the replacement equipment serves the same purpose in the same way as the displaced equipment. The displaced equipment is likely sold, scrapped, or "written off."

required local effort (RLE)
State aid to school districts is based on and governed by required locally-levied taxes; local funds raised by RLE are subtracted from the total foundation funds to determine the amount of state aid the district is to receive.

required local tax rate
Mandated property tax rate required for participation in the state aid system for public school districts; the required local tax rate is usually associated with a foundation program and is often expressed in terms of mills. Refer to *mill.*

requisition
Requisition is a written demand or request for specified articles or services. A requisition is usually initiated by one department and submitted to the purchasing officer or another department.

reserve
An amount carried forward or "reserved" for the following fiscal period; this reservation of funds reflects a specific project or purpose according to the original appropriation. Amounts not separately reappropriated at the end of one fiscal period for a project or purpose extending beyond that period to another are carried forward in a "reserve" account. A reserve appears on the liability side of the balance sheet. An amount deducted from an asset, sometimes called a "reserve" can be more accurately described as an "allowance."

retirement fund system
This is a system reflecting a plan whereby funds built up through contributions from participants and/or from other sources are used to make regular payments to those who retire from active service in the educational system; the retirement is the result of age, disability, or length of service.

revenue
Revenue refers to all funds received by a school system from external sources less refunds and/or other correcting transactions—other than from issuance of debt, liquidation of investments or agency and probate trust transactions. Revenue excludes non-cash transactions such as receipt of services, commodities, or other "receipts in kind."

revenue gap

A revenue gap exists when projected expenditures exceed projected tax revenues. Although revenue gaps are not usually permitted to exist de facto in a current fiscal year, the projection of a revenue gap for an ensuing year strategically results in one of two actions—either tax rates must be increased, or expenditures must be cut in order to compensate for the projected gap. Neither action is politically easy. Revenue gaps usually occur when the elasticity of expenditures exceeds the elasticity of revenues. This often occurs at the state and local levels because state and local taxes are, in most cases, less elastic than expenditures. (If state governments want to eliminate the occurrence of revenue gaps and the resultant requirement to increase tax rates or decrease projected expenditures, attention must be focused on ways to increase the elasticity of state tax systems; a common way to accommodate elasticity in state funding systems is generally believed to include an increasing reliance on income taxes.)

revenue receipts

These are receipts which represent additions to the financial assets of a school district without any corresponding additions to the district's debt or without any decreases in the district's assets.

rollback

In Ohio, a 10% reduction is credited to each taxpayer's real property tax bill. An additional 2½% reduction is granted to resident homeowners (those who live in the houses which they own). The state reimburses the local political subdivisions for these tax revenue losses.

sales tax

This tax applies to specific retail sales. It also includes a "use" tax provision which applies to certain services regarding the rental of commercial equipment.

sale value

Refer to *real value.*

school district tax rate

This is the term which various states utilize to indicate the local school property tax rate. The tax rate often reflects the amount of property tax dollars which will be raised for each $100 of assessed valuation, or if the rate is expressed in terms of millage, the tax rate reflects the amount of property tax dollars which will be raised for each $1,000 of assessed valuation. For example, a tax rate of $1.60 per $100 of assessed valuation indicates that a taxpayer will pay $1.60 for each $100 of his/her total assessed valuation; a tax rate of 16 mills indicates that the taxpayer will pay $16 for each $1,000 of assessed valuation.

school lunch sales

This refers to gross revenue from cafeteria sales to all purchasers (children and adults).

school site

A site is a plot of ground set aside for school use inclusive of non-building improvements; the improvements may include such enhancements as grading, drainage, drives, parking areas, walkways, plantings, play courts and play fields. Buildings and structures are not included as part of the school site; instead, they are part of the school plant.

school-site budget

This is a budgetary format presenting expenditures by school buildings as opposed to the traditional district-wide line item budget format which presents expenditures by function and object. The process involved in a school-site budget requires involvement of building-level personnel.

school social workers

Refer to *visiting teachers.*

school, summer

Refer to *summer school.*

securities

Securities are formal evidences of indebtedness or of property. Examples include the following: bonds, mortgages, notes, stocks, and so forth.

serial bonds

Serial bonds are certificates, issues, or evidences of debts redeemable by installments, each of which is to be paid in full, ordinarily from revenues reflecting the fiscal year in which each matures or, in some cases, preceding years.

SF-12

An Ohio Department of Education form (School Finance Form #12) utilized to report to school districts the amount of money that each will receive from the state in a fiscal year. The report forms are prepared by the Division of School Finance and are normally distributed to each school district three times per year. The July report is based on the estimated number of pupils that will be included in the ADM; the January report is based on the actual ADM as reported by the school district to the Ohio Department of Education in the October pupil data (enrollment) report; finally, the June report is based on the October pupil data report, but in addition, it takes into account any tax valuation changes in the district.

short-term debt

This is interest-bearing debt, payable within one year from date of issuance. Examples include the following: bank loans, bond anticipation notes, tax anticipation notes, and warrants. The term also includes obligations having no fixed maturity date if payable from a tax levied for collection in the same year as that of issuance.

short-term loans

These are loans due subsequent to the current year but limited to a relatively short term of years because of their nature. Refer also to *tax anticipation notes.*

spending reserve

Spending reserve is an estimate of expenditures which cannot exceed the district's spending reserve balance. A district's spending reserve balance is the amount by which 50% of the amount the district's estimated personal property taxes to be settled in the next calendar year exceeds the amount to be received in the first half of the year. The spending reserve is available for appropriation during a current fiscal year only by means of the written approval of the state superintendent of public instruction and in compliance with *Ohio Revised Code*, § 133.301.

state aid for current operating expenses

This is the sum of the equalization formula aid and the categorical aid for vocational education, special education, bilingual education, transportation, and other categorical aid programs. Refer to *categorical aid.*

state aid ratio (SAR)

This refers to a ratio derived from positioning side-by-side a local school district's capability to raise funds based on per-pupil valuation versus a state-wide criterion. Given the assumption that the state-wide capacity to raise funds (based on the average per-pupil property valuation) is equivalent to 100% per pupil, a local school district's capacity could be expressed as a comparative percentage. A capability ratio or comparative percentage can be computed to reflect a local school district's potential for generating funds versus the state-wide standard. The derived ratio or percentage can be utilized to equalize funding on a per-pupil basis. The amount of state aid for a school district is, therefore, determined by a percentage equalization formula.

stay-at-home bond issue

This concept permits a school district to meet state payback requirements while providing a permanent improvement fund at the local level.

student body activities

Direct and personal activities which are managed or operated by the student body under the guidance and direction of adults; these activities are not an integral part of the regular instructional program. Examples include the following: interscholastic athletics, publications, clubs, bands, orchestras, class organizations, and entertainments.

student services

Activities which are carried on for the benefit of public school pupils but which are not an integral part of the regular instructional program; examples include the following: bookstores, food services, and student body activities.

summer school

A school session operated during the period between the end of the regular school term and the beginning of the next regular school term.

supervisors of instruction

Supervisors are school personnel who have been delegated the responsibility of assisting teachers in improving the learning situations and instructional methods.

supplies

Supplies are material items of an expendable nature due to the nature of their use in being consumed, worn out, or deteriorated. In addition, the term includes material items which lose their identity through processes involving fabrication and/or incorporation into different or more complex units or substances. Refer to *equipment* for contrast.

surety bond

A written promise to pay damages or to indemnify against losses caused by the party or parties named therein is called a surety bond. The indemnification is against losses, hurts or damages which may be the result of non-performance of duty or defalcation. Examples of use include the following: (a) a surety bond might be posted by a contractor against damaging an existing structure during the construction of an addition, or (b) a surety bond might be posted by an official who handles cash or securities against loss or embezzlement of such.

surplus

For purposes within this text, the term generally refers to a "fund balance" which represents a fund's excess over its liabilities and reserves.

system of accounts

This term refers to an explanation of the accounting system (practices and terms) used by a district; a district's statement of the inclusions of each budget category is normally included with each category listing in a district's budget statement as well as other, related financial documents. The statements and explanations regarding a district's system of accounts, in effect, forms a "dictionary-handbook" of how a district classifies and defines its funds, revenue source headings, function headings, and object headings.

tangible personal property tax

This is a tax levied on furniture and fixtures, equipment, supplies, inventory, and machines used in business and industry within political subdivisions, including school districts. It is not adjusted by the tax reduction factor.

tax abatement

Tax abatement refers to a tax reduction or "forgiveness" of real estate and/or personal property taxes. The tax abatement is at times granted for a limited time to a business or industry's commercial property. An abatement is intended to encourage the business or industry to locate or expand within a community since the economic growth of the community will be naturally fostered by the location or expansion therein.

tax anticipation notes

Notes (sometimes referred to as "warrants") are issued in anticipation of the collection of taxes. The proceeds from such are treated as current or short-term loans if paid back from the anticipated tax collection with the issuance of the note. The notes or warrants are usually retirable only from tax collections and frequently only from the tax collections anticipated with their issuance.

tax base

Tax base is the taxable value of real and tangible property from which a community can raise tax revenue.

tax burden

This refers to the percentage of income which is consumed by a tax or tax system; typically the term is used in reference to the income of an individual or a family. The term is frequently applied in conjunction with the determination of whether a particular tax burden is progressive, proportional, or regressive. Across the nation, taxes which are progressive seem to find a greater acceptance than those which are proportional or regressive. Refer also to *progressive tax*, *proportional tax*, and *regressive tax*.

tax collecting unit

Tax collecting unit is the unit of government responsible for the actual collection of the taxes levied. This is commonly the same unit which is responsible for the assessment of property. The actual collection, however, is carried out by the treasurer of the unit. The units include cities, townships, and villages.

tax commissioner
Chief Officer of the Department of Taxation; the commissioner administers the assessment of personal and railroad property, supervises the taxation of real property in the state, and is charged with the duty of achieving uniformity in the taxation of real property.

tax, corporate franchise
Refer to *corporate franchise tax.*

tax diversion
This refers to pooling revenues from property taxes which are levied against tangible and real business, industrial, mining, and utility property within one locality and redistributing the revenues by means of a county, a regional, or a state fund; the concept is also known as tax pooling.

tax duplicate
Tax duplicate, also known as the "general tax list," represents the sum of all taxable value of real estate, personal tangible, and public utility properties. Refer to *Ohio Revised Code*, Section 319.28.

tax effort
Taxes as a percent of local income are referred to as tax effort.

taxes
As applied to taxes for the support of public schools, taxes are compulsory contributions exacted by a school system for public purposes (with the exception of that portion utilized for employee retirement and social insurance programs which are classified as insurance trust revenue). All tax revenue is classified as general revenue and comprises amounts received (including interest and penalties but excluding protested amounts and refunds) from all taxes imposed by a governmental unit. School system tax revenues exclude amounts from shares of state-imposed-and-collected taxes which are classified as intergovermental revenue. Refer also to *intergovernmental revenue.*

taxes, receivable
Refer to *receivable taxes.*

tax exemption
This refers to immunity from taxation. Refer to *tax exempt property.*

tax exempt property
Specific classes of property are exempted from property taxation. As a general rule, included are properties owned by the government, schools, colleges, and churches. In addition, some special-use properties (for example, coal conversion facilities) are also treated as tax exempt property.

tax, flat rate
Flat rate refers to a tax in which the rate remains constant.

tax incidence
Refer to *tax shifting.*

taxing unit
Units of government are authorized and responsible for imposing a particular tax and for receiving and eventually expending the revenues. These units (political subdivisions) include the following: cities, counties, public school districts, townships, villages, and special districts established for specific purposes.

tax issues
Boards of education may choose to seek revenue from various types of property taxes. Currently four types of state property tax issues exist for Ohio's schools; they include the following: operating levies, income tax issues, permanent improvement levies, and bond issues. (The terms and their nuances often elude the general public's understanding.)

tax levy
A levy is an issue placed on the ballot which seeks voter approval for a specified amount of revenue to be raised by a particular millage rate. Such a levy may be used for a specified project; however, more commonly the revenue received from the levy is used for the general operation of the school district. Stated in another way, a tax levy is an imposition by a governmental unit as agreed to by the voting public for the provision of tax revenues or special assessments for specific purposes.

tax pooling
Refer to *tax diversion.*

tax, property
Refer to *property tax.*

tax rate
The number of mills by which taxable value is multiplied to determine the amount from which certain reductions are made to determine liability for taxes; prior to those adjustments, each mill generates $1.00 of taxes for every $1,000.

tax, real property
Refer to *real property tax.*

tax reduction factor
This refers to a provision for a tax credit. In order "to cushion" the tax burden on property owners whose properties increased in value due to inflation, the legislature afforded real property owners a tax credit by means of a reduction factor. Thus, the actual amount of taxes paid on a piece of property does not increase when the property is reappraised at a higher value; instead, the property tax due remains at nearly the same amount as when the levy was originally approved. The tax reduction factor does not apply to emergency levies or debt levies, which are approved by voters in terms of specific amounts. Due to the passage of *State Issue 1* in 1981, the tax reduction factor is computed separately for residential/agricultural property (class 1) and all other real property (class 2).

tax, regressive
Refer to *regressive tax.*

tax, sales
Refer to *sales tax.*

tax shifting
There is a phenomenon whereby a tax, which is specifically the responsibility of one party, is "shifted" to another party. For example, a store owner who may in fact be responsible for a particular tax, may shift the burden of such to the consumers who purchase products from his/her store. Taxes may be shifted both forward and backward. For example, landlords might be able to shift higher property taxes forward to tenants in the form of higher rent payments; a business might be able to shift higher property or corporate income taxes backward to employees in the form of lower wages and salaries. The ability to shift the tax burden depends on a variety of economic factors. Economists often debate with one another regarding the extent to which some taxes are shifted. It is commonly agreed, however, that sales taxes are shifted to consumers. Tax shifting is also known as tax incidence.

tax, tangible personal property
Refer to *tangible personal property tax.*

tax, value added
Refer to *value added tax.*

temporary appropriation resolution
A board of education, for a variety of reasons, may decide to adopt an appropriation resolution for a temporary period of time for a maximum of three months. Following this temporary time period, a board of education must then adopt the fiscal year appropriation no later than October 1.

ten-mill limitations
The sum of the tax rates levied against any given piece of taxable property cannot exceed ten mills unless the excess is approved by a majority of the electors voting on the issue in the taxing district that imposes the excess. It is important to note that the ten-mill limitation does not allow each subdivision to levy ten inside mills; rather, the ten-mill limitation is reached when the sum of all inside mills levied by all subdivisions equals ten-mills as applied to property in a given taxing district.

term bonds
Term bonds are bonds of the same issue, usually maturing all at one time and ordinarily to be retired from funds accumulated over a period of years for that specific purpose.

transportation services, pupil
Refer to *pupil transportation services.*

triennial update of property value
This is the process by which the value of all real property is adjusted in the third year after reappraisal.

true cash value
Refer to *real value.*

true market value
Refer to *real value.*

unappropriated surplus
That portion of the balance of a given fund which is not segregated for a specific purpose and is, therefore, available for appropriation is called unappropriated surplus.

uniform rule
Section 2 of Article XII, Ohio Constitution, requires that land and improvements be taxed uniformly; different classes of real property (e.g., residential, agricultural, commercial, industrial) may not be taxed at different levels of assessed value anywhere in the state, or at different tax rates within the same taxing district, except as expressly authorized by Section 2a of Article XII.

valuation per pupil
The assessed valuation of all property located within a school district which is taxed for school purposes, divided by the total number of pupils enrolled in the school system, equals the valuation per pupil (also referred to as "per-pupil valuation"). An equation representing another way of expressing the same concept as that above is as follows: "total assessed valuation divided by school enrollment equals valuation per pupil." The per-pupil valuation is the single, best measure of taxable wealth available for the support of a school system's educational program. The more taxable property there is per pupil, the greater the income which can be produced through a specific local tax rate for education on a per-pupil basis.

value added tax (VAT)
VAT is a tax levied against a product as it is produced and distributed because each step adds value to the product.

value, real
Refer to *real value.*

visiting teachers
Visiting teachers, sometimes known as home-school counselors, home-school visitors, and school social workers, serve to coordinate the off-grounds pupil instruction with the on-site school personnel. Off-grounds instruction takes place in a variety of places; for example, hospitals, convalescent homes, detention homes, and so forth. This category of school personnel is included under instructional personnel as teachers.

voucher
Voucher is a document which is used to authorize the payment of funds and usually indicates the accounts to be charged.

weighted-pupil programs
Refer to *pupil-weighted systems.*

Index